JOHN STOTT AT KESWICK

JOHN STOTT AT KESWICK

A LIFETIME OF PREACHING

John Stott

Keswick Classics

MILTON KEYNES ● COLORADO SPRINGS ● HYDERABAD

First published 2008 by Authentic Media
9 Holdom Avenue, Bletchley, Milton Keynes, Bucks, MK1 1QR, UK
1820 Jet Stream Drive, Colorado Springs, CO 80921, USA
OM Authentic Media, Medchal Road, Jeedimetla Village,
Secunderabad 500 055, A.P., India
www.authenticmedia.co.uk
Authentic Media is a division of IBS-STL U.K., limited by guarantee,
with its Registered Office at Kingstown Broadway, Carlisle,
Cumbria CA3 0HA. Registered in England & Wales No. 1216232.
Registered charity 270162

British Library Cataloguing in Publication Data
A catalogue record for this book is available from the
British Library
ISBN-13: 978-1-85078-808-9

Cover design David Smart
Print management by Adare
Printed and bound by J F Print Ltd., Sparkford

CONTENTS

Introduction

For more than one hundred years Keswick Ministries has known the blessing of excellent Bible teaching delivered at the annual Convention.

John Stott has been a key exponent of expository preaching during the latter half of the last century and Authentic Media have gone back into the archives to bring together his 'Keswick' talks in one collection, some of which are no longer in print.

Together they represent some of the best Bible teaching within living memory and give a new audience an opportunity to sample some of the great talks from the past. They are published at a time when John has stepped down from full-time public ministry but remind us of the tremendous contribution he has made to practical, wise, evangelical scholarship, enabling readers to be 'equipped for every good work' (2 Tim 3.17).

David Bradley
General Director of Keswick Ministries

1965

The Privileges of the Justified

1. Peace with God – Romans 5

Chapters 5 – 8 of the epistle to the Romans are without doubt among the greatest and most glorious of the whole New Testament. They portray in great fullness what I have called 'The Privileges of the Justified.' The earlier chapters of the Epistle are devoted to the need and the way of justification (how all men are sinners under the just judgement of God; and how only through the redemption that is in Christ Jesus can they be justified, by grace alone through faith alone). And now, having enforced the need, and unfolded the way, of justification, Paul describes its fruits, its results (especially a life of sonship and obedience here, and of glory hereafter).

This is important because too many of us think and behave as if the Gospel were only good news of justification, and not good news also of holiness and of heaven; as if (having come to God through Christ) we had arrived; as if we had come to a dead end, and there were no further road to travel. But this is not so! This section of the Epistle begins (5:1), 'Therefore, being justified by faith (having been brought into acceptance with God through trust in Christ) . . .' and the apostle goes on at once to indicate the consequences.

These chapters, then, depict the great privileges of justified believers, the rich inheritance (both now and in eternity) which is ours if we are Christ's. I have called these privileges, first, *Peace with God* (chapter 5); second, *Union with Christ* (chapter 6); third, *Freedom from the Law* (chapter 7); and fourth, *Life in the Spirit* (chapter 8).

1. Peace with God (chapter 5)

Romans 5 is actually in two clearly distinct paragraphs. The first eleven verses summarise the fruits of our justification, while verses 12–21 portray the mediator of our justification. He is Jesus Christ, the second Adam, the one man through whose one deed justification has been won for us.

(a) The Fruits of our Justification (vv. 1–11)

In verses 1 and 2 the fruits of justification are summed up in three sentences:

  (i) v1: We have peace with God through our Lord Jesus Christ.
 (ii) v2a: We have obtained access (through the same Christ by the same faith) into this grace in which we stand.
(iii) v2b: We rejoice in hope of God's glory.

Here are the major fruits of our justification – peace with God (which we have), grace (in which we stand), and glory (for which we hope).

On closer examination, these appear to relate to the three tenses or phases of our salvation.

'Peace with God' speaks of the immediate effect of justification. We were enemies (v10), but the old enmity has been put away by God's forgiveness, and we are now at peace with Him through our Lord Jesus Christ. That is the immediate effect of justification. 'This grace in which we stand' speaks of the *continuing* effect of justification. It is a state of grace, to which we have obtained access, and in which we continue to stand. 'We have been allowed to enter the sphere of God's grace' (NEB); now we are standing in it. 'The glory of God,' for which we hope, speaks of the *ultimate* effect of justification. 'The glory of God' means heaven, since in heaven God Himself will be fully revealed ('glory' is God revealed); we shall see His glory and share in it. 'Hope' is our sure and certain confidence or expectation of it. Indeed, so sure is this hope (this 'happy certainty' – J.B. Phillips) that we can rejoice in it now already. We give thanks for it in the General Thanksgiving in the words 'for the means of grace and for the hope of glory'.

These phrases constitute a beautifully balanced summary of the Christian life in relation to God (nothing is yet said about our duty to our neighbours) – 'peace,' 'grace' and 'glory'. These are the fruits of justification. In the word 'peace' we look back to the enmity which is now over. In the word 'grace' we look up to our reconciled Father in whose favour we now continue to stand. In the word 'glory' we look on to our final destiny, seeing and reflecting the glory of God, which is the object of our hope or expectation.

Not that, after justification, the narrow way is carpeted only with moss and primroses; No! Brambles grow on it, too – and brambles with sharp thorns. Verse 3, 'More than that' (RSV) 'we rejoice in our sufferings'. These sufferings are not, strictly speaking, sickness or pain, sorrow or bereavement, but tribulation, the pressures of a godless and hostile world.

Such suffering is always the pathway to glory. The risen Lord said so, namely that according to the Old

Testament, 'the Christ should suffer and so enter into his glory.' The apostle Peter, echoing these words, also said so several times in his first epistle. The apostle repeats that in 8:17, 'provided we suffer with Him, in order that we may also be glorified with Him.'

But please note what is to be the relation between our present sufferings and our future glory. It is not just that the one is the way to the other. Still less is it that we grin and bear the one in anticipation of the other. No, it is that we *rejoice* in both. If we rejoice in hope of the glory of God (v2), we rejoice in our sufferings also (v3). The verb is strong: it indicates that we 'exult' in them (NEB). Present suffering and future glory are both objects of a Christian's exultation.

How is this? How can we possibly rejoice in sufferings, and find joy in what causes us pain? Verses 3–5 explain the paradox. It is not the sufferings themselves which we rejoice in, so much as their beneficial results. We are not masochists, who enjoy being hurt. We are not even Stoics, who grit their teeth and endure. We are Christians, who see in our sufferings the working out of a gracious divine purpose. We rejoice, because of what suffering 'produces' (RSV). What does it produce? What are the outworkings of tribulation?

Three stages in the process may be discerned:

Stage 1: 'suffering produces endurance' (RSV). The very endurance which we need in suffering is produced by it, much as 'antibodies' are produced in the human body by infection. We could not learn endurance without suffering, because without suffering there would be nothing to endure.

Stage 2: 'Endurance produces character' (RSV). 'Character' (AV, 'experience') is the quality of something which, or someone who, has stood the test. It is the quality David's armour lacked, because he had not 'proved' it. Can we not usually recognise the ripe character of those who have gone through suffering and come out triumphant? 'Suffering produces endurance, and endurance character.'

Stage 3: 'Character produces hope.' That is, confidence of future glory. The character, which has a maturity born of past endurance of suffering, brings a hope of future glory. What Paul means is surely this, that our developing, ripening Christian character is evidence that God is at work upon and within us. And He who is maturing us through suffering will surely and safely bring us to glory. The apostle is back, you see, to the indissoluble link between sufferings and glory. The reason why, if we rejoice in hope of the glory of God, we rejoice in our sufferings also, is that our sufferings produce hope (through producing endurance and character). If the hope of glory is produced by sufferings, then we rejoice in the sufferings as well as the glory; we rejoice not only in the end, but in the means which bring us there.

But how can we know that this hope has substance to it, and is not wistful thinking? Paul asserts: 'Hope does not (that is, will not) disappoint us' (RSV) or 'such a hope is no mockery' (NEB). It is a true hope. But how can we be so sure? Paul's answer to this unspoken question is in the rest of verse 5: 'because God's love has been poured out (perfect tense) in our hearts through the Holy Spirit who was given to us' (literally). The solid foundation on which our hope of glory rests is the love of God. It is because God has set His love upon us that we know He is going to bring us safely to glory. We believe we are going to persevere to the end, and we have good grounds for this confidence. It is partly because of the character God is forming in us through suffering ('suffering–endurance–character–hope' is the order); and if He is thus sanctifying us now, He will surely glorify us then. But it is chiefly because of the love that will not let us go.

This is the argument: We have a Christian hope, that we are going to see and share in the glory of God. We believe this Christian hope is a sure hope. It is 'no mockery.' It will never disappoint us. We know this because we know that God loves us and will never let us down, never let us go.

But how do we know that God loves us? The answer is, because we have an inner experience of it: 'God's love has flooded our inmost heart through the Holy Spirit He has given us' (v5, NEB). The Holy Spirit has been given to every believer, and one of the works of the Spirit is to pour out God's love into our hearts, to flood our hearts with it, that is, to make us vividly and inwardly aware that God loves us. Or, as Paul expresses the same truth in chapter 8, to witness with our spirit that we are God's children and that He is our Father who loves us. The change of tense in the verbs of verse 5 is noteworthy. The Holy Spirit was given to us (*aorist*), a past event; God's love has been poured out into our hearts (*perfect*), a past event with abiding results. The Holy Spirit was given to us when we believed. At the same time He flooded our hearts with God's love. He still does. The flood remains; it continues. The once given Spirit caused a permanent flood of divine love in our hearts.

Let me sum up what we have learned so far. The fruits of justification are peace with God (the enmity over); grace as a state in which we stand; and a hope (a joyful confident expectation) of the glory of God. This is a hope produced by the character that God is working in us through the endurance of suffering, but a hope that is confirmed by the assurance of God's love which the Holy Spirit has given us. In other words, justification (which is itself a momentary act, a judicial decision of our righteous God who pronounces us righteous in Christ) yet leads to a permanent relationship to God summed up in the words 'grace' now, and 'glory' at the end – a state of grace now in which we stand, and glory at the end for which we hope, a hope grounded upon God's love which through the Spirit has flooded our hearts.

We turn now to verses 6–11, in which the fruits of justification are further revealed. In verses 1–5, Paul has joined peace and hope, justification and glorification, making *our* sufferings the link. In verses 6–11 he does it again, but this time makes *Christ's* sufferings and death the link.

Let us see what he tells us here about the death of Jesus. He reminds us that Christ died for the utterly undeserving. This is the emphasis of verses 6–11. We may begin by seeing the unflattering terms with which we are described. Four terms are used. We are called 'helpless' (v6), because we are unable to save ourselves. We are 'ungodly' (v6), because we are in revolt against the authority of God. We are 'sinners' (v8), because we have missed the mark of righteousness, however hard we may have tried to aim at it. And we are 'enemies' (v10), because of the hostility which exists between us and God. What a fearful, devastating description of man in sin! We are failures, rebels, enemies and helpless to save ourselves. Yet it is for *such* people that Jesus Christ died!

We would hardly die for a *righteous* man (one who is coldly upright in his conduct), although perhaps for a *good* man (warm and attractive in his goodness) some people would even dare to die (v7). But God shows *His* love (the word is emphatic, His own love, His unique love) in giving Christ to die for *sinners*. Not for the coldly upright, not even for the attractively good, but for sinners – unattractive, unworthy, undeserving.

This is the setting for his argument, which follows in verses 9–11. It is an *a fortiori*, a 'much more' argument, an argument from the lesser to the greater, which reaches up to a new truth by standing on the shoulders of an old one. Paul contrasts the two main stages of salvation, justification and glorification, and shows how the first is the guarantee of the second. Let us try to grasp the details of his contrast between these two salvations, present and future.

First, he contrasts what they are. Verse 9, 'Since we are now justified by His blood, much more shall we be saved through Him from the wrath of God.' Here the contrast is plain, between our present justification and our future salvation from the wrath of God on the day of judgment. If we are already saved from God's *condemnation* (because we are justified), much more shall we be saved from His *wrath*.

Secondly he contrasts how they are achieved. Verse 10, 'For if while we were enemies we were reconciled to God by the *death* of His Son, much more, now that we are reconciled, shall we be saved by His *life*.' Here the emphatic contrast is between the *death* of God's Son and His *life*. That is, the risen life of Christ in heaven will complete what the death of Christ began on earth. The best commentary on this truth is probably 8:34, 'Who can condemn? It is Christ – Christ who died, and more than that, was raised from the dead – who is at God's right hand and indeed pleads our cause,' completing by His life what He accomplished by His death.

Thirdly, he contrasts the people who receive them. This again is in verse 10. It was while we were *enemies* that we were *reconciled* to God by the death of his Son. Much more shall we be saved by his life now that we are *reconciled* to him. If God reconciled his *enemies* he will surely save his *friends*!

There is, in other words, a strong argument or presumption that we are going to inherit a full and final salvation; that we shall not be allowed to fall by the way, but shall be preserved unto the end, and glorified. This argument is not a sentimental optimism; it is grounded upon irresistible logic. If when we were enemies God reconciled us through giving His Son to die for us, how much more, now we are His friends, will he finally save us from wrath through His Son's life? If God performed the more costly service (involving His Son's death) for His enemies, he will surely do the easier and less costly service now that His erstwhile enemies have become His friends.

More than that (v11); the Christian life is not just looking back to justification and on to glorification. The Christian is not preoccupied always with the past and the future. He has a present Christian life to live. So 'we rejoice in God through Jesus Christ.' We rejoice in hope. We rejoice in our sufferings also. But above all, we rejoice in God Himself. And we do it through Jesus Christ. It is through Jesus Christ that we have peace with God (v1). It is through Jesus Christ we have obtained access into the grace in which we stand (v2). It is through the blood of Christ that we have been reconciled, and through the life of Christ that we are going to be saved (v9). It is through Jesus Christ that we have received (*aorist*) the reconciliation. It is a present possession which we enjoy. So we rejoice in God through the Christ who has achieved these priceless blessings for us.

It is time now for us to look back over the first paragraph of chapter 5 (vv1–11).

In both parts of it (vv1–5, and 6–11) the apostle's thought moves from justification to glorification, from what God has already done for us, to what He is still going to do for us in the consummation. Thus (vv1,2) having been justified by faith, we rejoice in hope of the glory of God; and in verses 9 and 10, being justified by His blood, we shall be saved from wrath. So both parts argue from our present salvation to our final salvation, from our justification to our glorification.

Further, both parts speak of the love of God, and build our assurance of final salvation upon it. See verses 5 and 8. If we Christians dare to say that we are going to heaven when we die, and that we are sure we shall be finally saved, it is not because we are self-righteous or self-confident. It is because we believe in the steadfast love of God; the love that will not let us go.

Moreover, both parts provide some ground for believing that God loves us. These grounds are two – objective and subjective. The objective ground for believing that God loves us is *historical*; it concerns the death of His Son (v8). The subjective ground for believing that God loves us is *experimental*; it concerns the gift of His Spirit (v5). God proves His love at the cross (notice in verse 8 that though a past event, the tense is present); and according to verse 5, God has poured His love into our hearts. So we know that God loves us. We know it rationally as we contemplate the cross (God gave His best for the worst). We know it intuitively as the Holy Spirit floods our hearts with a sense of it.

In each case the apostle links to this knowledge our assurance of final salvation. 'Hope does not disappoint us' (v5). That is, we know that our expectation of final salvation will be fulfilled. It is well grounded. It will not deceive or disappoint us. How do we know? 'Because the love of God has been shed abroad in our hearts.' Again, in verses 8–10, how do we know that we shall be saved from wrath? Answer, because God proves His love for us by having given His Son to die for us while we were sinners.

Is there a Christian here who is full of doubts about his eternal salvation; who knows that he has been justified but has no assurance that all will be well at the end? Let me emphasise again that final glorification is the fruit of justification – 'whom he justified, them, he also glorified' (8:30). Trust in the God who loves you! Look at the cross, and accept it as God's own proof of His love for you! Then ask him to flood your heart with His love by his Spirit! Then away with gloomy doubts and fears! Let them be swallowed up in the steadfast love of God.

We turn now from (a) the fruits of our justification (vv1–11) to (b) the *mediator of our justification* (vv12–21). In the first paragraph Paul has traced our reconciliation and final salvation to the death of God's Son. His exposition immediately prompts the question: but how can one person's sacrifice have brought such blessings to so many? It is not (in Sir Winston Churchill's famous expression) that so many owe so much to *so few*; it is that so many owe so much to *one person*! How can that be? The apostle answers this anticipated question by drawing an analogy between Adam and Jesus Christ. (And incidentally, the strongest argument for the historicity of Adam is not scientific, but theological. The Christian believes in the historicity of Adam, not even just because of the Old Testament story, but because New Testament theology requires him to do so). Both Adam and Jesus Christ demonstrate the principle that *many* can be affected (for good or ill) by *one* person's deed.

Verses 12–14 concentrate on Adam: 'As sin came into the world through one man and death through sin, and so death spread to all men because all men sinned.' This verse sums up in three stages the history of man before Christ. (i) Sin entered into the world through one man. (ii) Death entered into the world through sin, because death is the penalty for sin. (iii) Death spread to all men, because all men sinned (this is explained later). These are the three stages: sin – death – universal death. That is, the present situation of universal death is due to the original transgression of one man.

In verses 13–14, this progression (from one man sinning to all men dying) is further explained. Death is visited upon all men today, not because all men have sinned *like* Adam, but because all men sinned *in* Adam. This is plain, Paul argues, because of what happened during the time between Adam and Moses, between the Fall and the giving of the Law. During that period people certainly sinned, but their sins were not reckoned against them because sin is not reckoned when there is no law. Yet they still died. Indeed (v14) 'death reigned from Adam to Moses, even over those whose sins were not like the transgression of Adam.' So, Paul argues, logically, the reason they died is not that they deliberately transgressed like Adam, and died for their transgression, but that they and the whole of humanity were involved and included in Adam, the head of the human race. It is because we sinned in Adam, that we die today.

At the end of verse 14, however, the apostle calls Adam 'a type of the coming one,' and with verse 15 the analogy between Adam and Christ begins; an enthralling analogy containing both *similarity* and *dissimilarity*. What is the same is the pattern: that many are affected by one man's deed. What is different is the motive, and the nature, and the effect of the one man's deed (Adam's and Christ's), that is, the *motive* for the deed, or why he did it; the *nature* of the deed, or what he did; and the *effect* of the deed, or what happened as a result.

(a) *The motive* (v15a). This is seen in the contrast of verse 15, between 'the offence' and 'the free gift' ('the free gift is not like the trespass,' RSV), for 'the offence' was a deed of sin, a deviation from the path, while 'the free gift' was a deed of grace. Adam's deed was one of *self assertion*, going his own way; Christ's deed was one of *self sacrifice*, of free, unmerited favour (stressed in the following words).

(b) *The effect* of the deed (vv. 15b–17). Reference to the opposite effects of the work of Adam and Christ is already anticipated at the end of verse 15, where the sin of one man brought to many the grim penalty of *death*, whereas the grace of God and of one man, Jesus Christ, abounded to many in bestowing a free *gift*, which according to 6:23 is *eternal life*. So death and life are contrasted; and the next two verses (16, 17) elaborate the opposite effects of the deeds of Adam and of Christ. 'The judgment following one trespass brought condemnation, but the free gift following many trespasses brings justification' (v16b, RSV). 'If, because of one man's trespass death reigned through that one man, much more will those who receive the abundance of grace and the free gift of righteousness reign in life through the one man Jesus Christ' (v17, RSV).

These, then, are the contrasting effects of the deeds of Adam and of Christ. The sin of Adam brought condemnation; the work of Christ brings justification. The reign of death is due to Adam's sin; a reign of life is made possible through Christ's work. The contrast could not be more complete; it is in fact absolute, between condemnation and justification, and between death and life.

It is noteworthy, however, exactly how the apostle contrasts life and death. It is not just that the reign of death is superseded by a reign of life, for (v17) it is not life which reigns but we who are said to reign in life.

Formerly death was our king and we were its subjects,
slaves, under its totalitarian tyranny. We do not now
exchange that kingdom for another, so that we are in
another sense slaves, or subjects. No. Delivered from the
rule of death, we begin to rule over it and over all the
enemies of God. We cease to be subjects, and ourselves
become kings, sharing the kingship of Christ.

(c) *The nature* of the two deeds (verses 18, 19). We have
    seen that Adam's deed and Christ's deed were differ-
    ent in their motive (what prompted them) and in their
    effect (what resulted from them). Now the apostle
    contrasts the two deeds themselves, in their nature.
    The parallel drawn is similar to what has gone before,
    but the emphasis in verses 18 and 19 is now on what
    Adam and Christ did. According to verse 18, what led
    to condemnation for all was one man's *offence*, and
    what led to justification and life for all (in Christ) was
    one man's *righteousness*. Adam's 'offence' was a failure
    to keep the law; Christ's 'righteousness' (RSV, 'act of
    righteousness') was a fulfilment of the law.

According to verse 19, it is by one man's *disobedience* that
many were made sinners, and by one man's *obedience*
that many will be made righteous. Adam disobeyed the
will of God and so fell from righteousness; Christ obeyed
the will of God and so fulfilled all righteousness (cf.
Matt. 3:15; Phil. 2:8). Looking back over the paragraph,
we see a striking and significant contrast between Adam
and Christ. As to the *motive* for their deeds: Adam asserted himself; Christ sacrificed Himself. As to the *nature* of
their deeds: Adam disobeyed the law; Christ obeyed it.
As to the *effect* of their deeds: Adam's deed of sin
brought condemnation and death; Christ's deed of righteousness brought justification and life.

So, then, whether we are condemned or justified, alive or dead, depends on which humanity we belong to – the old humanity initiated by Adam, or the new humanity initiated by Christ. And this in its turn depends on our relation to Adam and to Christ. All men are in Adam, since we are in Adam by *birth*. But not all men are in Christ, since we are in Christ by *faith*. In Adam by birth we are condemned and die; but if we are in Christ by faith, we are justified and live.

This brings us back to the privileges of the justified with which we began, because these are only ours in and through Jesus Christ. Verse 1, 'we have peace with God *through our Lord Jesus Christ.*' Verse 2, '*through Him* we have obtained access to this grace in which we stand, and we rejoice in our hope of sharing the glory of God.' 'Peace,' 'grace' and 'glory' (the privileges of the justified) are given not to those who are in Adam, but only to those who are in Christ.

2. Union with Christ (Romans 6)

We are studying together in Romans 5–8 the privileges of the justified; the great immeasurable privileges which are ours if we are in Christ. The first privilege, which we considered yesterday from Romans 5, is that of peace with God – a continuing relationship, now of grace; and in the world to come, of glory. The second privilege that we consider today, from Romans 6, is *Union with Christ*.

The great theme of Romans 6, at least in the first part of it (vv1–11), is that the death and resurrection of Jesus are not only historical facts, nor only significant doctrines, but personal experiences of the Christian believer; events in which we have come to share. All Christians have been united to Christ in His death and resurrection; and if we have died with Christ, and risen with Him, it is inconceivable that we should go on living in sin.

Romans 6 consists of two parallel sections, verses 1–14, and 15–23; and the same general theme is elaborated in each section, namely, *the inadmissibility of sin in the Christian*. But although the same theme is elaborated, a somewhat different argument is used. In verses 1–14 it is our *union with Christ* which is elaborated; in verses 15–23, it is our slavery to God.

This is our position as Christians: we are one with Christ, and we are slaves of God. The argument for holiness is grounded upon this double fact: united to Christ, enslaved to God.

Let us take the first section first, *Union with Christ* (vv1–14). Paul asks in verse 1, 'What shall we say then? Are we to continue in sin that grace may abound?' The

fact that in the past increased sin brought increased grace
– the theme of the last two verses of chapter 5 – prompts
the question whether the same is not still true today.
Could I not argue something like this: I have been justified freely by the grace of God. If I sin again, I shall be
forgiven again by grace; and the more I sin the more
opportunity grace will have to express and exhibit itself
in my forgiveness. So, shall I continue in sin that grace
may abound?

Now the apostle was giving expression to one of the
objections raised by his contemporaries against the
Gospel of justification by grace alone through faith
alone; namely, that the doctrine of free grace leads to
antinomianism, to lawlessness; and that the doctrine of
justification by grace actually encourages people in their
sins. Critics objected to the Gospel on that ground in
Paul's day, and the same ignorant argument is frequently heard today.

Now, Paul's answer is one of outraged indignation.
'Shall we continue in sin that grace may abound? *God*
forbid!' That is, 'By *no* means.' And after his emphatic
negative, he counters the critics' question with another
question: 'How can we, who died to sin, live in it any
longer?' (v2). In other words, There is in our critics'
objection to justification by faith, a fundamental misunderstanding of it, and so of what it means to be a
Christian. The Christian life begins with a death unto sin.
And in view of this, it is ridiculous to ask if we are at liberty to continue in sin. How can we go on living in what
we have died to?

The Revised Standard Version and the New English
Bible are perhaps a little misleading in their phrase, '*How
can we* continue in sin,' as if Paul were arguing the
impossibility of it. In the Greek, the verb is just in the
simple future tense: literally translated it would be, 'We

died to sin (past): how shall we live in it (in the future)?' It is not the literal impossibility of sin, but the moral incongruity of it, which the apostle is emphasising. J.B. Phillips catches this rather well in his translation: 'We who have died to sin, how could we live in it a moment longer?'

But the question which I hope is in everybody's mind at the moment is this: How, and in what sense, have we died to sin? Clearly we cannot go on living in what we have died to. But what does it mean, that we have died to sin; and how and when did it happen? Well, the apostle Paul takes the rest of this paragraph to elaborate what he means, and I am going to suggest that we take it in five easy stages, as step by step his mighty, unanswerable argument is unfolded.

Here are these five steps. Step 1, Christian baptism is baptism into Christ. That is what he says in verse 3, 'Don't you know that all of us who were baptised into Christ . . .' Let's stop there. Christian baptism is baptism into Christ. That people can even think of asking whether Christians are free to sin, betrays a complete lack of understanding of what a Christian is, and of what Christian baptism is. The Christian is not just a justified believer: he is someone who has entered into a vital, personal union with Jesus Christ; and baptism signifies this union with Christ.

Of course, baptism has other meanings. It means a washing from sin, and it means the gift of the Holy Spirit; but essentially it signifies union with Christ; and again and again the preposition employed with the verb 'to baptise' is the preposition 'into.' In the great commission the Lord said that we were to baptise *into* the Name of the Father, the Son and the Holy Spirit.

In Acts, believers in Samaria and Ephesus were baptised *into* the Name of the Lord Jesus. In Galatians 3:27, 'As many of you as were baptised *into* Christ . . .' And it is just the same here: 'Baptised *into* Christ Jesus.'

Baptism in the New Testament is a dramatic sacrament, or ordinance. It indicates not just that God washes away our sins, not just that He gives us the Holy Spirit, but that He places us *into* Christ Jesus; so the essence of the Christian life as it is visibly signified in baptism, is that God by His sheer grace puts us, places us, grafts us *into* Christ Jesus. Not, of course, that the outward rite of baptism itself procures our union with Christ. No, no, no; it is inconceivable that the apostle, after three chapters arguing that justification is by faith alone, could shift his ground, contradict himself, and make baptism the means of salvation. We must give the apostle Paul credit for a little consistency of thought! No; when he writes that we are baptised into Christ Jesus, he means, of course, that this union with Christ that is invisibly effected by faith, is visibly signified by baptism.

Nevertheless, the first point he assumes is that being a Christian involves a personal, vital union or identification with Christ; and that this union with the Lord Jesus is dramatically signified in baptism. Well, that is stage 1. An easy step, is it not? Baptism is baptism into Christ.

Step 2: Baptism into Christ is baptism into His death and resurrection. Let me read you verses 3–5 in the Revised Standard Version: 'Do you not know that all of us who have been baptised into Christ were baptised into His death? We were buried therefore with Him by baptism into death, so that as Christ was raised from the dead by the glory of the Father – that is, the glorious demonstration of the Father's power – we, too, might walk in newness of life. For if we have been united with Him in a death like His, we shall certainly be united with Him in a resurrection like His.' And I have summed all that up in saying that baptism into Christ is baptism into His death and resurrection.

These verses probably refer to the pictorial symbolism of baptism. When baptisms took place in the open air, in some stream, the candidate would go down into the water and – if I may add in a whisper and in a parenthesis, whether he was only partially or totally immersed, really does not matter a bit! The point is that, as he went down into the water, whether partially or totally, he would seem to be buried and then to rise again. His baptism would dramatise his death, his burial, and his resurrection to a new life.

'In other words,' writes C.J. Vaughan in his commentary, 'our baptism is a sort of funeral.' Have you ever thought of your baptism like that? A sort of funeral; yes, and a resurrection from the grave as well.

This, then, is the second stage in the apostle's argument. It is that a Christian by faith inwardly, and by baptism outwardly, has been united to Christ in His death and resurrection. We are not to think of ourselves as just united to Christ in a vague and general sense. We must be more particular than that. The only Jesus Christ with whom we have been identified and made one, is the Christ who died and rose again. So you and I, if we are Christians by faith and baptism, willy-nilly have actually shared in the death and resurrection of Jesus. That is step 2: baptism into Christ is baptism into His death and resurrection.

Step 3: Christ's death was a *death unto sin*, and His resurrection was a *resurrection unto God*. 'We know that our old self was crucified with Him so that the sinful body might be destroyed, and we might no longer be enslaved to sin. For he who has died is freed from sin' – literally, has been justified from his sin. 'But if we have died with Christ, we believe that we shall also live with Him. For we know that Christ being raised from the dead will never die again; death no longer has dominion over

Him. The death He died' – mark this – 'He died unto sin *once*; and the life He lives He lives unto God. So you must consider yourselves dead to sin and alive to God' (vv6–10, RSV).

Let me read you verse 10 again: 'The death He died He died unto *sin* . . . and the life He lives He lives unto God.' This explains how we are to think of the death and resurrection of Christ with which we have been united. We are to think of His death as a death unto sin; and we are to think of His resurrection as a resurrection unto God.

Now, what is a death unto sin? What is this death that He died (v10), and the death that therefore we have died with Him? Verse 2, 'We died unto sin'; verse 11, 'We are to reckon ourselves dead unto sin.' What is this death unto sin? Now I am going to spend a while telling you what it is *not*. Frankly, I do not like to be negative, but I fear that it is necessary to be negative here; to demolish before one can construct, because there is abroad in Evangelical circles a popular view of the death unto sin, described in Romans 6, which I submit to you cannot stand up to a careful examination, and leads people rather to disillusion, to deception, or even to despair.

Now the popular interpretation, if I may call it this, is as follows: When you die physically your five senses cease to operate. You can no longer touch, see, smell, etc. You lose all power to feel or to respond to stimuli. Therefore by analogy, the popular view goes, to die to sin is to become insensitive to it; it is to be as unresponsive to sin as a corpse to physical stimuli. Now this view is often illustrated like this. One of the signs of life is ability to respond to a stimulus. Passing down a street, you see a dog or a cat lying prostrate in the gutter. As you look at it you do not know whether it is alive or dead. But touch it with your foot, and you will know. If it is alive, instantly it reacts; it jumps up, vibrant with life and energy and movement. But if it is dead it makes no response; it lies there unresponsive.

So, according to this popular view, we died to sin means that we became unresponsive to it. We became like a dead man – like a dead dog or a dead cat; and when the stimulus of temptation comes, we neither feel it nor react to it. We are dead. And this is so, in the popular interpretation of verse 6, because our old nature in some mysterious and mystical way, was actually crucified; that Christ bore not only our guilt, but our flesh. It was nailed to the cross and killed. So we are told in this popular view. And our task – note this – however much evidence we may have to the contrary, our task is to reckon it dead.

I want to give you some examples of this view. I fear J.B. Phillips has it. He says that we are to be 'dead to the appeal and power of sin,' unresponsive to it. C.J. Vaughan: 'A dead man cannot sin, and you are dead. Be in relation to sin as impassive, as insensible, as immovable, as he who has already died.' H.P. Liddon writes, 'This death has presumably made the Christian as insensible to sin as a dead man is to the objects of the world of sense.' Now I must say to you, brethren, that there are serious objections – indeed, I would say fatal objections – to this view. Indeed, if we consider the matter carefully, we know that this is not the sense in which Christ died to sin; and we equally well know that it is not the sense in which we have died to sin either.

Let us think very carefully. This phrase, 'died to sin,' comes three times in this paragraph; twice it refers to Christians (vv2,11), and once it refers to Christ (v10). 'He died to sin.' Now it is a fundamental principle of Biblical interpretation that the same phrase bears the same meaning in the same context; therefore we have to find an explanation of this death unto sin which is true of Christ and of the Christian – that He died to sin, and that we have died to sin. Whatever this death to sin is, it has to be true of the Lord Jesus, and it has to be true of us.

Now, take Christ and His death. What does it mean that He died to sin (v10)? It cannot possibly mean that He became unresponsive to it, because this would imply that He was formerly responsive to it. Was our Lord Jesus Christ at one time so alive to sin that He needed subsequently to die to it? Indeed, was He so continuously alive to sin that He had to die to it decisively, once for all? No, no, no, this is intolerable. It would never do.

Now move from the death of Christ to ourselves and our death to sin. Tell me, have we died to sin in the sense that our old nature has become unresponsive to it? The answer also to that question is, No. Another vital principle of Biblical interpretation is that you must explain the text in the light of the context; the part in the light of the whole, and each in the light of all, and the special in the light of the general. Now, what is the general teaching of the rest of Scripture about the old nature? It teaches that the old nature is still alive and active in regenerate believers. Indeed, the very context in which the text comes, teaches the same truth. In verses 12 and 13 the apostle says, 'Let not sin reign in your mortal bodies,' and 'Do not yield your members to sin' – commands which would be entirely gratuitous if we had so died to sin that we were now unresponsive to it.

The rest of Romans confirms this. Chapter 8 urges us not to set our minds on things of the flesh, and not to walk according to the flesh; and in 13:14, Paul says that we are not to make any provision for the flesh, to gratify its desires. Now these would be absurd injunctions if the flesh were dead, and had no desires. Besides this, my brethren, Christian experience proves that this is not the correct interpretation.

It is important to notice that the apostle is not referring to a few exceptionally holy Christians. He is describing all Christians who have believed and been baptised into Christ. He says, in verses 2–3, 'How can you who have died to sin still live in it? Don't you know that *all of us* . . .' He is not talking about some; he is talking about all Christians. So this death to sin, whatever it is, is common to every Christian.

But tell me, are all baptised believers dead to sin, in the sense of being inwardly unresponsive to it? Do they find that they have become insensible to it; that it lies quiescent within them, and that they can reckon it so? No; on the contrary, Scriptural and historical biographies, and our own experience, combine to deny these ideas. Far from being dead in the sense of being quiescent, our fallen and corrupt nature is alive and kicking – so much so that we are exhorted not to obey its lust; and so much so that we are given the Holy Spirit for the precise purpose of subduing and controlling it. And what would be the purpose of that if it were already dead?

Let me add this: one of the real dangers of this popular view – as I know in my own experience, because I held it once – is that when people have tried to reckon themselves dead in that sense, and know they are not dead, they are torn between their Scripture-interpretation and their empirical experience. As a result, some of them begin to doubt the truth of God's Word; while others, in order to maintain their interpretation, I am afraid resort to dishonesty about their experience.

I sum up the objections, then, to the popular view. Christ did not die to sin in the sense of becoming insensitive to it, because He never was thus alive to it that He needed to die to it. And Christians have not died to sin in this sense either, because we are still alive to it; so much so that we are told to mortify it, to put it to death. Why should we be told to put to death something that is already dead?

Now, after this demolition – and may I say, beloved, that if I have hurt anybody, because this is a cherished view of yours, I am sorry; but I believe that if you will absorb this, it will lead you into a new dimension of Christian living, and a new liberty. What, then, is the meaning of this death unto sin which Christ died, and which we have died in Him? How can we interpret this expression so that it is true of Christ and of Christians, all Christians? And the answer is not far to seek, if we look at the Biblical teaching of death rather than at the properties of a dead man. Then we shall immediately find help; for although I cannot elaborate this, the whole misunderstanding illustrates the great danger of arguing from an analogy.

Now death is thought of and spoken of in Scripture, not in physical terms so much as in moral and legal terms. Death is spoken of in Scripture not as a state of lying motionless like a corpse, but as the grim but just penalty for sin. Whenever sin and death are spoken of together in the Scripture, the essential relation to them is that death is sin's penalty. And this is true all through the Bible, from the second chapter in Genesis, when God says, 'In the day that you eat and therefore sin, you shall die,' to the last chapters of the Revelation, when we are told about that awful destiny of sinners which is called the second death.

Sin and death are linked in Scripture as an offence and its just reward. And that is certainly true in the epistle to the Romans. In 1:32 we are told of God's decree that those who sin deserve to die. And this is what we are told in the last verse of this chapter which is open before us: 'The wages of sin is death' (6:23).

This, then, is how dying and death are to be understood: not as a state of insensibility, but as the just reward
of sin. And this is the meaning of death which is true of
both Christ and the Christian. Of Christ the apostle says,
'The death He died He died unto sin, once for all' (v10).
That can only mean one thing: it means that Christ died
unto sin in the sense that He bore sin's penalty. He died
for our sins, bearing them in His own innocent and
sacred Person. He took upon Him our sins and their just
reward. The death that Jesus died was the wages of sin –
our sin. He met its claim; He paid its penalty; He accepted its reward: and He did it once and for all. So that sin
has no more claim on Him, no more demand upon Him;
and so He was raised from the dead to prove the satis-
factoriness of His sin-bearing, and He now lives for ever
unto God. That is the sense in which Christ died unto
sin.

And this is the sense in which you and I, by union
with Christ, have also died unto sin. We have died unto
sin in the sense that by union with Christ we have borne
its penalty. Consequently our old life is finished, and a
new life has begun.

Now let us come back to verse 6. Notice that it is in three
parts: 'We know that our old self *was* crucified with Him
(part 1), in order that the sinful body might be destroyed
(part 2), in order that we might no longer be enslaved to
sin (part 3).' Do you see that? Something happened in
order that something else might happen, in order that
something else might happen. Three clear stages.

Now the ultimate stage is clear; it is that we should no
longer be enslaved to sin. And that is our heart's desire,
is it not, that we should be delivered from the slavery
and bondage of sin. That is the ultimate thing in verse 6.
How does it happen? Well, look at the previous expression; the stage before being delivered from the bondage

of sin, is that the body of sin might be destroyed. Now the body of sin is not the human body: this body is not sinful in itself. It surely is the sinful nature which belongs to the body. The New English Bible is helpful: it renders it, 'the sinful self.' And it is God's purpose that this sinful self might be destroyed, so that we should no longer serve sin.

Now, careful! The verb 'to be destroyed' here is the same word that is used in Hebrews 2:14 of the devil. It means, not to become extinct, but to be defeated. Not to be annihilated, but to be deprived of power. Our old nature is no more extinct than the devil; but God's will is that the dominion of both should be broken – and it has been.

Now, have you grasped these second two stages? The ultimate is that we may no longer be enslaved to sin. To that end, God's will is that the sinful nature might be deprived of power. How does that happen? Well, look at the first phrase. It is only possible because of the crucifixion of the old man. We know that our old man was crucified with Christ in order that the sinful nature might be deprived of power, in order that we might no longer be enslaved to sin.

Now what is the old man? It is not the old nature. It cannot be the old nature, if the body of sin means the old nature. The two expressions cannot mean the same thing, or the verse makes nonsense. No, the old man denotes, not our old unregenerate nature, but our old unregenerate life, what the New English Bible calls 'the man we once were.' Not my lower self, but my former self. The Revised Standard Version: 'my old self.'

So what was crucified with Christ was not a part of me called my old nature, but the whole of me as I was before I was converted. My old man is my pre-conversion life, my unregenerate self. And this should be plain because

in this whole chapter the phrase 'our old man was crucified' is equivalent to 'we died to sin' in verse 1.

Now let us come back to verse 6, and the three stages
which we are now able to take in their right order. Our
old man was crucified with Christ; that is, *we* were crucified with Christ: we were identified with Him by faith-
baptism, and so we shared in His death to sin. We were
crucified with Christ in order that our sinful nature
might be deprived of its power, in order that we might
no longer be enslaved to sin.

Now if you are following me carefully, somebody will
be asking, How is it that to have been crucified with
Christ, and so to have died to sin in the sense of bearing
its penalty, how is it that this leads to an overcoming of
the old nature, and so to a deliverance from the bondage
of sin? And verse 7 gives you the answer: Because 'he
who has died has been justified from his sin.' Now the AV
and the RSV have taken an unwarranted liberty in translating the Greek word *dikaioo*, 'freed.' It occurs fifteen
times in Romans and twenty-five times in the New
Testament, and it always means 'justified.' He who has
died has been *justified* from his sin.

I hope we can understand this. The only way to be justified from sin is to receive the wages of sin. There is no
other escape from sin but that its penalty should be
borne. I think we shall understand this if I illustrate it
from the administration of justice in our country. How
can a man who has been convicted of a crime, and sentenced to a term of imprisonment, be justified? Well,
there is only one way; that is, that he must go to prison
and pay the penalty of his crime: and once he has served
his sentence he can leave the prison justified. He need
not any longer fear the police, or the law, or the magistrate. The law no longer has anything against him,
because he has paid the penalty of breaking it. He has

served his term. He has paid the penalty. He is now justified from his sin.

The same principle holds good if the penalty is death. There is no way of escape or justification except to pay the penalty. Now you might say that to pay the penalty in this case is no way of escape; and you would be right if we were talking about capital punishment on earth, for once a murderer had died – when capital punishment was still obtaining – his life on earth was finished. He cannot live again on earth justified as a man can who has served a prison sentence. Ah, but the wonderful thing about our Christian justification is that our death is followed by a resurrection in which we can live the life of a justified person, having paid the death penalty for our sin.

For us, then, it is like this. We deserve to die for our sins, and by union with Jesus Christ we did die – not in our own person: that would have meant eternal death – but in the person of Christ our substitute, with whom we have been made one in faith and baptism. And so by union with the same Christ we have risen again to live the life of a justified believer. And this life is altogether new: the old life is finished. I have died to it. The penalty is borne, and I can emerge from this death justified, and the law cannot touch me because the penalty of sin is paid.

With this in mind let us read verses 7–10: 'He who has died has been justified from his sin. If we died with Christ, we believe we shall live with Him. For we know that Christ being raised from the dead will never die again; death no longer has dominion over Him. The death He died He died to sin once, and the life He lives He lives to God. So you must realise that you are dead to sin, and alive to God.'

Let me try to bring it home to us a little more in this way. Suppose that an elderly Christian believer, John

Jones, is looking back over his long life. His career is divided by his conversion into two parts – the old man, which is John Jones before his conversion; and the new man, which is John Jones after his conversion. The old man and the new man are not John Jones's two natures; they are the two halves of his life, separated by new birth. At conversion, signified in baptism, John Jones the old man died in union with Christ, the penalty of his sin borne. At the same time John Jones rose again from death, a new man, to live a new life unto God.

Now John Jones is every believer. You are John Jones, and so am I. If we are in Christ, then the way in which our old man died is that we were crucified with Christ. By faith and baptism we have been united to Christ in His death. The death He died unto sin has become our death, and its benefits have been transferred to us. So having died with Christ to sin, we have been justified from our sin; and having risen with Christ, we are alive, justified unto God. Our old life finished with the death it deserved. But having risen with Christ, we are alive to God with this new life. And we have got to realise it.

That was a very long third step, was it not? It is time I had a little recapitulation. Step 1 is, Christian baptism is baptism into Christ. Step 2 is, Baptism into Christ is baptism into His death and resurrection. Step 3 is, His death is a death unto sin, and His resurrection is a resurrection unto God. Which brings me to Step 4, which is, *That we must reckon it so*.

'*We* have died unto sin, and we live to God.' We have been united to Christ, through faith and baptism, in His death and resurrection; and if *His* death was a death unto sin, we have died unto sin. Since His resurrection is a resurrection unto God, we have risen unto God, and we must reckon it so. Now this is not make-believe. Reckoning is not make-believe. It is not screwing up our faith to believe something we do not believe. It is not pretending that our old nature has died, when we jolly well know it has not. It is to realise that our old man – that is, our former self – did die, paying the penalty of its sin, putting an end to its old career. And we are to reckon ourselves, or, RSV, 'consider ourselves,' or better still, NEB, 'regard ourselves' as being what in fact we are, dead to sin and alive to God.

Once we realise that our old life is ended, the score settled, the debt paid, the law satisfied, we shall want to have nothing more to do with it. It is finished. Now I find it helpful to think in these terms: our biography is written in two volumes. Volume 1 is the story of the old man, the old self; of me before my conversion. Volume 2 is the story of the new man, the new self, me after I was made a new creation in Christ. Volume 1 of my biography ended with my judicial death – the judicial death of the old man. I was a sinner; I deserved to die; I did die; I received my deserts in my substitute, with whom I have become one. Volume 2 of my biography opened with my resurrection. My old life is finished, and a new life unto God has begun.

We are simply called to reckon this, to realise this – not to pretend it, but to realise it. It is a fact, and we have to lay hold of it; we have to let our mind play upon these truths; we have to meditate upon them until we grasp them firmly; we have to say to ourselves, 'Look here, volume 1 has closed. You are now living in volume 2. It is inconceivable that you should re-open volume 1.' Oh, it's not impossible, but it's inconceivable. Can a married woman still live as though she were a single girl? Yes, I suppose she can. It is not impossible. But let her feel that ring on the fourth finger of her left hand, the symbol of her new life, the symbol of her identification with her husband; let her remember who she is, and let her live accordingly.

Can a born-again Christian live as though he were still in his sins? Well, yes, I suppose he can. It is not impossible. But let him remember his baptism – the symbol of his identification with Christ in His death and resurrection, and let him live accordingly. We need to keep reminding ourselves who we are, and what we are. And when Satan whispers in our ear, 'Go on, go on! You sin. God will forgive you!' When he whispers in our ear like that; when we are tempted to presume on the grace of God, we are to say to him in the words of verse 2, 'God forbid! I died to sin. I cannot live in it any longer. Volume 1 is closed. I am in volume 2. I can't re-open volume 1.'

In other words, the apostle does not state the impossibility of sin in a Christian; he states the utter incongruity of it. He asks the astonished, the indignant question, 'How can we continue in sin? How *can* we live in it when we have died to it?' To have died to sin and to live in it are logically irreconcilable.

And so the secret of holy living is in the mind. It is in *knowing* that 'our old man was crucified with Christ' (v6). It is in *knowing* (v3) that baptism into Christ is baptism into His death and resurrection. It is in reckoning, intellectually realising (v11) that in Christ we have died to sin and we live in God. *Know* these things; *meditate on* these things; *reckon* upon these things. We are so to grasp intellectually in our minds the fact and the significance of our death and resurrection with Christ that a return to the old life is unthinkable.

A born-again Christian should no more think of going back to the old life than an adult to his childhood, a married man to his bachelorhood, or a freed prisoner to his prison cell. By union with Jesus Christ his whole status has changed. Our faith and baptism have severed us from the old life, cut us off irrevocably from the old life, and committed us to the new. Our baptism stands between us and the old life as a door between two rooms. It has closed upon one room, and has opened upon another. We have died; we have risen. How can we live again in what we died to? That is Step 4.

Now Step 5. Step 1, Baptism is a Baptism into Christ. Step 2, Baptism into Christ is baptism into His death and resurrection. Step 3, His death was a death unto sin, and His resurrection a resurrection unto God. Step 4, I am to realise, therefore, that my death, united with Christ, was a death to sin; and my resurrection, united to Christ, is a resurrection unto God. Step 5, As those who are alive from the dead, we must *not let sin reign in our mortal bodies, but yield ourselves to God*.

'As those who are alive from the dead.' That is the important phrase. This is verses 12–14, where we have the negative and the positive set over against one another. *Negative*: 'Let not sin reign' (v12) – do not let it be your king. 'Do not yield – or, do not go on yielding – your members as instruments of unrighteousness' (v13). Do not let sin rule you; do not let sin use you, your members, in furthering its unrighteous purposes. Do not let sin be your king; do not let sin be your lord. That is negative.

Positive: Instead, 'yield yourselves to God' (v13), as those who are alive from the dead – which is precisely what you are. You have died to sin, bearing its penalty; you have risen again, alive from the dead; now yield yourselves unto God, and your members as instruments of righteousness. In other words, do not let sin be your king; let God be your king, to rule over you. Do not let sin be your lord, to use you in its service; let God be your Lord, to use you in His service.

Now why? What is the ground of this exhortation? What is the basic reason for yielding ourselves to God, and not to sin? The answer is that we died to sin, and we have risen to God. So we cannot yield ourselves to sin;

we yield ourselves to God. You see the irresistible logic of it, step by step. We are those who are alive from the dead. And because we are alive from the dead, we are no longer under law, but under grace. God in grace has justified you in Christ; in Christ sin's penalty is paid, and the law's demands are met. Neither sin nor the law has any more claim upon you. You have been rescued from their tyranny. You have changed sides. Your status is new. You are no longer a prisoner of the law. You are a child of God, and you are under His grace.

Now, to know ourselves under grace and not under law, far from encouraging us to sin in order that grace may abound, actually weans us away from the world, the flesh, and the devil, because by grace we have opened a new volume in our autobiography. We cannot go back to the old. By grace we are alive from the dead. We cannot possibly go back to the old life we have died to.

Well, that is the first part of a chapter; and I am only going to take a few minutes on the second. We have been concentrating on this because it is the more difficult of the two, and it is the one which gives so much perplexity and confusion to many Christians.

The second section is not about union with Christ, but about *Slavery to God* (vv15–23). Notice that the second part begins in exactly the same way as the first. First comes a question: 'What then? Are we to sin because we are not under law but under grace?' just as he said in verse 1, 'What shall we say then? Shall we continue in sin that grace may abound?' The same question. This question is followed by the same answer – an emphatic negative, 'God forbid!' – 'By no means' (RSV); 'No, no' (NEB); or, 'Of course not!' Then comes another question, explaining this negative, and beginning, 'Don't you know . . .' 'Don't you know that all of us who were baptised into Christ were baptised into His death?' (v3). 'Don't you know that if you yielded yourselves – or if you yield yourselves to anyone – as obedient slaves, you are slaves of the one whom you obey' (v16).

Let us try to get the parallel clear in our minds. It is so beautifully symmetrical. In verses 1–14, what we are to know is that, through faith and baptism, we are united to Christ, and so have died to sin, and live to God. In verses 15–23, what we are to know is that through self-surrender, through yielding ourselves, we are slaves to God, and therefore committed to obedience. Verse 16, once you have chosen your master, you have no more choice but to obey. That spells a principle: that either you yield to sin which ends in death, or else you yield to obedience ending in righteousness.

In the next verses these two slaveries are contrasted: the slavery to sin, and the slavery of God. They are contrasted as to their beginning, as to their development, and as to their end.

Their *beginning* (vv17,18): 'You were slaves of sin' – it is an imperfect tense, and it suggests that this is what we are by nature, and what we have always been. But 'you obeyed' – that is the aorist tense, '. . . from the heart, the form – or standard – of doctrine which was delivered to you – that is, the Gospel – and when the Gospel was delivered to you, you obeyed it from your hearts.' Thank God!

So how did the two slaveries begin? Well, our slavery to sin began at our birth. It is our natural condition. But our slavery to God began when by grace we obeyed the Gospel. That is how the two slaveries began.

We turn now from their beginning to their *development*, or what in these verses he calls 'their fruit.' 'I am speaking in human terms, because of your natural limitations. For just as you once yielded your members to impurity and to greater and greater iniquity, so now yield your members to righteousness *for sanctification*' (v19).

In other words, the slavery of sin has as its result the grim process of a moral deterioration; but the slavery of God has as its result the glorious process of a moral sanctification. Each slavery develops; neither slavery stands still. In one we get better and better; and in the other we get worse and worse.

Their beginning, their development, and their *end* (vv20–22). 'When you were slaves to sin . . . the end was death. But now that you are the slaves of God, the end is eternal life.' And verse 23 sums it up: that sin pays the wage we deserve, which is death; but God gives us a gift which we do not deserve, which is life.

Here, then, are two totally different lives, lives totally opposed to one another: the life of the old man, and the life of the new man. And they are two slaveries: by birth we were slaves of sin; by grace we have become the slaves of God. The slavery of sin yields no return except a steady moral deterioration, and finally death. The slavery of God yields the precious return of sanctification, and finally eternal life.

So you see the argument of this section is that our conversion, this act of yielding or surrender to God, leads to a status of slavery, and slavery involves obedience.

To conclude. Both sections began with virtually the same question, 'Shall we continue in sin?' – a question posed by Paul's critics, who intended thereby to discredit the Gospel; a question that has been asked ever since by the enemies of the Gospel; a question that is often whispered in your ears and mine by the greatest enemy of the Gospel, Satan himself, who seeks to entice us into sin by whispering, 'Why not continue in sin that grace may abound? God will forgive you. You are under grace. Go on. Do it again. God will forgive you.'

The great enemy of the Gospel puts this same question to us every day. How do you answer the devil? I hope you begin with an outraged negative: '*God forbid!*' But I hope that you go further than that, and that you confirm your negative with a reason. Because there is a reason, a solid, logical, irrefutable reason why the subtle insinuations of the devil must be repudiated.

What is the reason that we can give for answering the subtle insinuation of the devil? Well, it is based on what we are. It is that we are one with Christ (vv1–14), and that we are the slaves of God (vv15–23). We became united to Christ by baptism – at least outwardly and visibly; and we became enslaved to God by the self-surrender of faith. But whether we emphasise the outward baptism or the inward faith, the point is the same. It is that our Christian conversion has had this result: it has united us to Christ, and it has enslaved us to God. And that is what we are. Every one of us is one with Christ, and the slave of God.

Now, what we are has these inescapable implications. If we are one with Christ – and we are – then with Christ we died to sin, and we live to God. If we are enslaved to God – which we are – then *ipso facto* we are committed to obedience. It is inconceivable that we should wilfully persist in sin, presuming on the grace of God. The very thought is intolerable. And we need constantly to be talking to ourselves about these truths. I remember saying three years ago at Keswick that to talk to yourself is not the first sign of madness; it is the first sign of maturity in the Christian life! It depends what you are talking to yourself about!

You and I need to be talking to ourselves, and saying, 'But don't you know that you are one with Christ; that you have died to sin, and risen to God. Don't you know that you are a slave to God, and committed therefore to obedience? Don't you know these things?' And go on asking yourself that question until you reply to yourself, 'Yes, I do know. And by the grace of God I shall live accordingly.'

3. Freedom from the Law – Romans 7

We are considering Romans 5–8, under the general title 'The Privileges of the Justified.' The first privilege that we considered, in chapter 5, we called 'Peace with God'; the second, in chapter 6, 'Union with Christ'; and now the third privilege, in chapter 7, is 'Freedom from the Law.'

But how on earth, somebody may immediately object, can freedom from the law be regarded as a Christian privilege? Surely, you may say, the law is the law of God, and it was one of the Jews' most treasured possessions? In 9:4 of this epistle the giving of the law is included among the special favours conferred upon Israel. To speak of the law in a derogatory fashion, or to hail deliverance from the law as a Christian privilege, would seem to Jewish ears akin to blasphemy. The Pharisees were incensed against Jesus because they regarded Him as a law-breaker. And as for Paul, the Jewish mob in the temple nearly lynched him because they believed that he was 'teaching men everywhere against the people and the law and this place'.

Then what is Paul's view of the law? Twice in Romans 6 he has written, 'You are not under the law, but under grace' (vv14,15). And such a statement, that you are not under the law, must have sounded revolutionary to Paul's readers. What did Paul mean? Was God's holy law now abrogated? Could Christians afford to disregard the law of God, or has it some continuing place in the Christian life? Now such questions as these were no doubt commonplace in the apostle's day. And, mark you, they are by no means of antiquarian interest today, because the law of Moses was, and is, the law of God. And if we are thoughtful Christians we need to know the place which God's law should occupy in our Christian lives today.

Besides, in recent days the whole subject has come to the fore again in the debate over 'the new morality,' because the new moralist is a kind of twentieth-century antinominan, and an antinomian – which is a word we all ought to know and understand – is somebody who sets himself against the law. The new moralist is the twentieth-century antinomian. He declares that the category of law is altogether abolished in the Christian life: that the Christian has nothing to do with the law, and the law has nothing to do with the Christian. That is what the new moralist says.

We shall therefore find that the somewhat intricate arguments of the apostle in Romans 7 speak with relevance to our contemporary situation.

By way of introduction, it may help us to find our way through this difficult chapter, if I suggest to you that there are three possible attitudes to the law. These three possible attitudes are represented, first by the legalist, second by the antinomian, and thirdly by the law-abiding believer.

Now the legalist, first, is in bondage to the law. He imagines that his relationship with God depends on his obedience to the law. And as he seeks to be justified by the works of the law, he finds that the law is a harsh and inflexible taskmaster. In Paul's language, he is 'under the law.' That is the legalist.

Second, the antinomian, or sometimes we can call him the libertine, goes to the other extreme. He rejects the law altogether, and he even blames the law for most of man's moral and spiritual problems.

Thirdly, the law-abiding believer preserves the balance – and I hope we may find that we are among the balanced! The law-abiding believer recognises that the weakness of the law – that is a phrase which comes in Romans 8:3, that 'God has done what the law, *weakened* by the flesh, could not do' – is that it can neither justify nor sanctify us, because we are not capable of obeying it. But the law-abiding believer delights in the law; he loves the law as an expression of the will of God, and he seeks by the power of the indwelling Spirit to obey it.

Let us sum up these three. The legalist fears the law, and is in bondage to it. The antinomian hates the law, and repudiates it. But the law-abiding believer loves the law, and seeks to obey it.

Let me now suggest to you that the apostle Paul, directly or indirectly, portrays these three characters in Romans 7. I do not say that he deliberately visualises and addresses each of them in turn, but I think we can see the shadowy forms of each of these three people in this chapter, as he overthrows the arguments of the legalist and the antinomian, and as he describes the conflict and the victory of the law-abiding believer.

Thus, if I may attempt a bird's-eye view of this whole chapter, in 7:1–6 Paul asserts that the law no longer exercises lordship over us. We have been delivered from its tyranny by the death of Christ. Our Christian bondage is not to the law, or to the letter of the law; it is a bondage to Jesus Christ, in the power of the Spirit. That is his message to the legalist.

In verses 7–13 he defends the law against unjust criticisms of it, the unjust criticisms of those who want to be rid of the law altogether; those who say that the law is responsible for our sin, and for our death. They blame the law for man's sorry state of sin and death. But, Paul argues in this paragraph, the cause of our sin and death is not God's law: it is our flesh; our sinful nature is to blame. The law itself, he says, is good (vv12, 13). It is in our flesh that there dwells nothing good (v18). Notice, incidentally, those references to 'good.' The law is *good*: it is in my flesh that there is nothing *good*. So the problem cannot be laid at the door of the law: you cannot blame God's law. The problem is our sinful nature, the flesh. That is his message to the antinomian who wants to be rid of the law, and blames it.

Then in 7:14–8:4 he describes the inner conflict, and the victory secret, of the believer. The conflict is between the mind and the flesh; and it is summed up in the last verse of chapter 7, where 'I myself' am said to be the servant of two masters: 'With my mind I serve the law of God' – I love the law of God, I want to keep the law of God with my mind, as a Christian . . . I serve the law of God; but with my flesh – my old nature – I serve the law of sin. So that if I am left to myself even as a Christian, I am a helpless captive, the slave of sin, and unable to keep the law. Why? 'The just requirement (the righteousness) of the law *is* fulfilled in us, if we walk not according to the flesh but according to the Spirit' (8:4). In other words, the Holy Spirit enables me to do what I cannot do by myself, even as a Christian; and that is Paul's message to the law-abiding believer.

I think it is important to notice what is the burden of the apostle's message to each of these three types of person. To the legalist, who is in bondage to the law, Paul emphasises the death of Christ as the means by which we have been delivered from that bondage. To the antinomian, who blames the law, he emphasises the flesh as being the prime cause of the law's failure, and of our consequent sin and death. To the law-abiding believer, who loves the law and seeks to obey it, Paul emphasises the power of the indwelling Spirit as the God-appointed means by which alone the righteousness of the law can be fulfilled in us.

I am going to entitle these three sections as follows. Verses 1–6, The *hardness* of the law, because this is what the legalist fears, regarding the law as his lord, and not realising that he has been emancipated from it. Verses 7–13, The *weakness* of the law, because this is what the antinomian does not understand. He imagines that the weakness of the law is inherent in the law itself, whereas the weakness of the law is not in the law itself, but in the flesh – in our sinful nature. Then 7:14–8:4, The *righteousness* of the law, because this is what is fulfilled in the Spirit-led and law-abiding believer.

First, *The Hardness of the Law* (7:1–6). 'Do you not know, brethren – for I am speaking to those who know the law – that the law is binding on a person only during his life?' (v1). The word 'is binding' – that is the RSV translation – is rendered in Mark 10:42, 'lord it over.' This verb speaks of the imperious authority or lordship of the law over those who are subject to it. And the principle that Paul states in verse 1 is that the law is intended for the benefit of men on earth; it only binds a person during his lifetime.

Of this general principle the apostle now gives a particular example, namely, marriage, which is contracted between two persons 'until death us do part.' Paul says marriage is a splendid particular example of the principle that law only binds you while you are alive. Marriage is binding, he says, till death parts you; but when death supervenes, then the person who survives is free to marry again: 'A married woman is bound by law to her husband as long as he lives; but if her husband dies she is discharged from the law concerning her husband. Accordingly, she will be called an adulteress if she lives with another man while her husband is alive, but if her husband dies she is free from the law, and if she marries another man she is not an adulteress' (vv2,3).

In this example, in one case a married woman lives with another man, and 'incurs the stigma of adultery' (J.B. Phillips) while in the other case, she marries another man and she is not an adulteress. And Paul says, What is the difference? Why does one remarriage make her an adulteress, and the other not? The answer is simple. It is that the second marriage is legitimate only if death has terminated the first. Death has set her free from the law governing her former relationship, and set her free to marry again.

After the principle that the law is only binding upon the living (v1), and the particular illustration in verses 2–3 about marriage, he comes on in verses 4–6 to the application. The application is this, that just as death terminates a marriage, so death has terminated our bondage to the law. 'Likewise, my brethren, you have died to the law through the body of Christ, so that you may belong to another, to Him who has been raised from the dead (namely, Jesus Christ), in order to bear fruit to God' (v4). Now, of course, it was the body of Christ that died on the cross, and we have only died through the body of Christ. That is, having been united to Jesus Christ by faith – as we were thinking yesterday – it is as if we have died through the body of Christ that died; and since we have died, death has removed us altogether out of that sphere, in which the law exercises lordship. The dread penalty for sin, prescribed by the law, was borne by Christ in our place, or by us in Christ. And since the demands of the law have been met in the death of Christ, I am no longer under the law, but under grace.

Now in the husband-wife relationship, it is the death of one which renders the other free to marry again. In the Christian life it is our own death in Christ which sets us free to marry again. We were married in a bondage-yoke to the law, but we have died now in the body of Christ, and we are free to marry another: we are married to Christ now. Joined to Christ.

What is plain in these verses is that becoming a Christian involves a complete change of relationship and allegiance. At the end of chapter 6, two slaveries were contrasted; and here, two marriages, the first being dissolved by death, and so permitting the second to take place. We were, so to speak, married to the law. Our obligation to obey the law was as binding as a marriage contract. But now we have been set free to marry Christ. It is a very remarkable illustration of the intimacy of our union with Jesus Christ, that we are married to Him.

That brings us to verses 5,6. Having contrasted the two marriages and their results, Paul now contrasts the place of the law in each. Look at them carefully. In the old life – 'While we were living in the flesh' (the old life), the law was the means of arousing our sinful passions. 'Our sinful passions, aroused by the law,' led to our death. But now (v6), 'we are discharged from the law, dead to that which held us captive.' All right. If we are discharged from the law, what next? I ask you very carefully to notice this, that emancipation from the law does not mean that we are now free to do as we please. No, no. Freedom from the law spells, not licence, but another kind of bondage. 'So that having been discharged from the law we are free to . . .' to do what? Not to sin, but 'to serve . . .' And our new Christian slavery is (literally) 'not in oldness of letter, but in newness of Spirit.'

Now, if you know Galatians, or 2 Corinthians 3, you know that metaphor is Paul's distinction between the old covenant and the new covenant; between the law and the Gospel. The old was 'the letter,' it was the external code written upon stone tablets, outside us. But the new covenant, the Gospel, is 'Spirit': it is the Holy Spirit writing the law, not on tablets outside, but in our hearts. And that is our new bondage.

Now we return, before we leave this section, to the question, Is the law still binding upon the Christian? It would be very interesting to know how you would answer that question! The answer is, No, and Yes. The law is not binding on the Christian in the sense that our acceptance before God depends on it. Our acceptance does not depend on our obedience to the law, for Christ in His death has met the demands of the law. We are delivered from it. It no longer has any claims on us, as it is no longer our lord.

But is the law still binding on the Christian? Yes; in the sense that our new life is still a bondage. We still serve; we are still slaves, although discharged from the law. But the motive and the means of our service have altered. The motive: why do we serve? Let us get this. Why are we in bondage to the law, in that sense? Not because the law is our master and we *have* to, but Christ is our husband, and we want to. Not because obedience to the law leads to salvation, but because salvation leads to obedience to the law.

The law says, 'Do this, and you will live.' The Gospel says, 'You live, so do this.' The motive has changed.

And how do we serve? 'Not in oldness of letter, but in newness of Spirit.' Not by obedience to an external code, but by surrender to an indwelling Spirit. So that, to sum up this argument, we are still slaves: the Christian life is still a bondage of a kind, but the Master we serve is Christ not the law; and the power by which we serve is the Spirit, and not the letter. The Christian life is serving the risen Christ by the power of the indwelling Spirit. So much for our first section, the hardness of the law.

Now, *The Weakness of the Law* (vv7–13). Verse 5 *seems* to make the law responsible for our sins and our death.

'When we were living in the flesh, our sinful passions, aroused by the law, were at work in our members to produce death' – so that sin and death appeared in verse 5 to be due to the law. The apostle now defends the law against such an unjust criticism, to which he may have seemed to lay himself open. Please notice in verse 7 he asks the question, 'What shall we say? Is the law sin?' that is, is it responsible for our sin? And in verse 13 he asks, 'Did that which is good' – meaning the law – 'bring death to me?' Is God's law responsible for my sin and for my death?

Let us look at those two questions, and his answers. First, *Is the law sin?* (vv7–12). Is it responsible for sin? Paul's answer is a categorical 'God forbid!' And he proceeds in the next verses to show what the relation is between the law and sin. He says, The law does not create sin. If you are a sinner, it is not the law's fault. The relation between sin and the law is these three things –

(a) *The law reveals sin* (v7): 'If it had not been for the law, I should not have known sin. I should not have known what it is to covet, if the law had not said, "Thou shalt not covet".' The law reveals sin.

(b) *The law provokes sin* – not only exposing it, but actually stimulating and arousing it, as has already been said in verse 5. Verse 8, 'Sin, finding opportunity' – which is a military word for a springboard for offensive operations – 'finding opportunity, or a foothold within us, by means of the commandment which provokes us . . .' And this is what the law does: it provokes us to sin.

The way in which the law does this is a matter of everyday experience. Coming to Keswick a few days ago, if any of you drove along the M1, or the M6, when you saw the peremptory traffic sign which says, 'Reduce speed now,' if I am not greatly mistaken, the instinctive reaction of many of us was, 'Why should I?' Now that is the reaction the law provokes in us. Or again, when we read a prohibition on a door, 'Do not enter. Private,' we immediately want to do what is forbidden us, because the commands and prohibitions of the law provoke us to the opposite. And that is what St. Paul found: 'Finding opportunity in the commandment, sin wrought in me all kinds of covetousness . . .' (v8).

So the law exposes sin; the law provokes sin. And:

(c) *The law condemns sin*: 'Apart from the law sin lies dead. I was once alive apart from law, but when the commandment came, sin revived, and I died' (vv8–9) – that is, under the judgment of the law. 'The very commandment which promised life proved to be death to me. For sin, finding opportunity in the commandment, deceived me and by it killed me.'

Here the apostle may well be relating his own early experiences: how in childhood he was ignorant of the law's demands, and 'in the absence of law' (NEB), he was spiritually alive. But how then, maybe as a boy of thirteen, when a Jewish boy took on the obligations of the law, and became what is called 'a son of the commandment,' in his own graphic words of verse 9, 'when the commandment came,' when I became a son of the commandment, and took upon me its obligations, 'sin sprang to life, and I died under the law's judgment.' At all events, the very law that promised life, that said, 'Do this and you shall live,' brought spiritual death to Paul.

Now these are the three devastating results of the law. The law reveals sin; the law provokes sin; the law condemns sin. But the law is not in itself sinful. The law in itself does not cause men to sin. What causes men to sin is – sin, that is our sinful nature, which uses the law, as it were, to make men sin and so bring them to ruin. But 'the law itself is holy, and the commandment is holy and just and good' (v12). So, the answer to the question, Is the law sin? is, No. I sin, not because of the law, but because of my sinful nature.

Now this second question: Does the law then bring death? (v13), 'Did that which is good (the good commandment of the law), did it bring death?' 'Are we to say, that this good thing was the death of me?' (NEB). Did the law actually offer life with one hand, and inflict death with the other? Is it the law's fault that I died? And again the apostle's answer is, By no means! The reason why death, under the judgment of the law, comes to me, is not the law's fault; it is due to my sin. 'It was sin working death in me through that which is good . . .' (v13).

Now let me illustrate this. A man is caught red-handed, perpetrating some crime, some breach of the law. What happens? Well, he is arrested; he is brought to trial; he is found guilty; and he is sentenced to imprisonment. As he languishes in his prison cell he is tempted to blame the law for his imprisonment. It is quite true that the law has convicted him, and the law has sentenced him. But when you come to think of it, he has nobody to blame but himself for his criminal offence. The reason why he is in prison is that he has committed a crime. Of course the law condemns him for doing it, but he cannot blame it on the law; he has only himself to blame. And so Paul exonerates the law. The law exposes sin; the law provokes sin; the law condemns sin: but it cannot be held responsible for our sins or for our death.

Says Professor F.F. Bruce, 'The villain of the piece is sin' – that is, indwelling sin. The villain of the piece is not the law. These antinomians who say that our whole problem is the law are quite wrong. Our real problem, the villain of the piece, is sin, not the law. And it is thus that indwelling sin, our flesh, or fallen nature, explains the weakness of the law to save us. The law cannot save us for the simple reason that we cannot keep it: and we cannot keep it because of indwelling sin – the flesh. That is the weakness of the law.

The third section 7:14–8:4, *The Righteousness of the Law*. We have considered the hardness of the law, its unbending demands from which we have been delivered by the death of Christ, so that we are not under the law any longer. We have considered the weakness of the law, which is not in itself but in us, the flesh. Now the righteousness of the law – because now we are going to see how the Christian believer delights in the law in his mind, and how he fulfils the law by the power of the indwelling Spirit.

Before we consider the text in any detail, however, there is an important question which must occupy our attention. Let me approach it in this way. As the reader enters the section beginning with verse 14, there are two changes which will immediately strike him. The first is a change of tense in the verbs. In the previous paragraph (vv7–13) the verbs are predominantly in the past tense: they are aorists, and they thus appear to refer to Paul's past experience. 'I was alive, but sin sprang to life, and I died' (v9). 'Sin killed me' (v11). 'Did that which is good bring death to me? By no means. It was sin' (v13). And so on – all in the past tense.

But from verse 14 onwards the verbs are in the present tense, and they seem to refer to Paul's present experience: 'I am carnal' (v14). 'I do not do what I want to do. I do do what I don't want to do' (v15) – present tenses. There is a change of tense from the aorist to the present.

The second difference is this: there is a change of situation. In the previous paragraph Paul describes how sin sprang to life through the commandment, and killed him – finished him off. But in this paragraph he describes his fierce, continuing conflict with sin, in which he ref-uses to admit defeat, but is an active combatant.

Now these two changes seem at once to suggest that what Paul is portraying is in verses 7–13 his pre-Christian life, and in verse 14 onwards his life as a Christian. Now some commentators, from the Greek fathers onwards, have rejected this view. They cannot conceive how a believer, let alone a mature believer like Paul, could describe his experience in terms of such a fierce conflict, and indeed a conflict that he cannot win. They argue, therefore, that this paragraph must describe Paul's pre-Christian conflict. Now I want to suggest to you that there are two traits in the apostle's self-portrait in this paragraph, verse 14 onwards, which led the reformers – and have led most reformed commentators since – to be sure that these verses are actually the self-portrait of Paul the Christian.

The first is the opinion that he has of himself in this paragraph; and the second is the opinion he has of the law. Let us think of these. First, the opinion he has of himself. What is that? 'I know that nothing good dwells in me, that is in my flesh' (v18). 'Oh, wretched man that I am . . .' and he cries out for deliverance (v23). Now I say to you, who but a mature Christian believer thinks and talks of himself like that? The unbeliever is characterised by self-righteousness. He would never acknowledge himself a 'miserable creature,' which is the New English Bible's version of, 'Oh, wretched man . . .' The immature believer is characterised by self-confidence, and he does not ask, Who is going to deliver him?

It is the mature believer only who reaches a position of self-disgust and self-despair. It is the mature believer who recognises with limpid clarity that in his flesh 'dwells no good thing.' It is again the mature believer who acknowledges his wretchedness, and appeals for deliverance. That is his opinion of himself.

Now his opinion of the law. He calls God's law 'good' (v16): 'I agree that the law is good.' He calls it good in verse 19: 'I do not do the *good* that I want to . . .' That is the law. He acknowledges that the law is good in itself, and he longs with all his being to do it. Again (v22) he says, 'I delight in the law of God in my inmost self.' Now, friends, this is certainly not the language of the unbeliever. The unbeliever's attitude to the law is given us in 8:7, where we are told that the flesh, our unredeemed human nature, is hostile to the law of God; it neither does submit to the law nor even can submit to the law. However, here, far from being hostile to the law of God, Paul says that he actually loves it. That is not the language of an unbeliever. The hostility of this person speaking here is not to the law: it is to what is evil. It is this, he says, that he hates; but the good, he loves and delights in.

Now from these two points we deduce that the speaker in the last part of chapter 7 is a mature believing Christian; a believer who has been given a clear and a proper view, both of his own sinful flesh and of God's holy law. His position is that in his flesh dwells no good, whereas in God's law is the good that he desires. And this is summed up in verse 14: 'I am carnal; but the law is spiritual.'

Please notice the phrase, 'The law is spiritual.' We must never set the law and the Spirit in opposition to one another. The law and the Spirit are not contradictory, for the Holy Spirit writes the law in our hearts. What Paul contrasts with the indwelling Spirit is not the law itself, but the letter – that is, the law viewed as an external code. And I want to say to you that anybody who acknowledges the spirituality of God's law and his own natural carnality, is a Christian of some maturity.

Now, so far so good. But you will say to me, But why does Paul describe his experience in terms not only of conflict, but of defeat? Why does he say not only that he wants to do good, but that he does not, and even cannot, do it? I suggest to you that the simple answer surely is this: That in the previous paragraph, verses 7–13, Paul has shown that as an unbeliever he could not keep the law. In this paragraph, verse 14 onwards, he shows that even as a Christian believer, by himself he still cannot keep the law – by himself. He recognises the goodness of the law in a way that he did not as an unbeliever, and he delights in the law, and he longs to keep the law in a way that he did not as an unbeliever; but the flesh, his fallen human nature which was his undoing before his conversion, leading him to sin and death, is still his undoing after his conversion – unless the power of the Holy Spirit subdues it. Which is what he comes to in chapter 8. Indeed, an honest and humble acknowledgment of the hopeless evil of our flesh, even after the new birth, is the first step to holiness.

Let me talk to you quite plainly, my brethren. There are some of us who are not leading holy lives for the simple reason that we have too high an opinion of ourselves. We have never come to a position of self-despair. We have never cried, 'Oh, miserable creature that I am, who shall deliver me?' In other words, the only way to come to faith in the power of the Holy Spirit is through self-despair. You will never come to put your trust in the Holy Spirit till you despair of yourself. And that is what Paul is doing here.

So both paragraphs, 7–13 and 14 onwards, emphasise that whether we are believers or unbelievers, whether we are regenerate or unregenerate, it is indwelling sin, the flesh, that is our big problem, and that it is responsible for the weakness of the law to help us.

Now let us come to verses 14–20. It is helpful, I think, to see in this paragraph that Paul says precisely the same thing twice over, no doubt for emphasis. First in verses 14–17, and then in verses 18–20. And these two sections are almost exactly parallel, so it may be best to look at them together.

(i) Each section begins with *a frank acknowledgment of our condition*, of what we are in ourselves, and what we know ourselves to be. 'We know that although the law is spiritual, I am carnal' (v14). That is what I am in myself. The flesh is still in me, and I am 'sold under sin' – 'the purchased slave of sin' (NEB). That is what I am, even as a Christian, in myself. The flesh dwells in me; the flesh assaults me, and I am no match for it. Rather, in myself I am its slave; its reluctant, resistant slave. And that is what I know about myself – 'in myself.'

Now glance on to v. 18: 'I know . . .' You see the parallel beginning: '*We know* that I am carnal' (v14); '*I know* that nothing good dwells in me, that is, in my flesh' (v18). Now I want to ask you, brethren, if that is what *you* know about yourself. And is it because you do not know this about yourself that you are not leading a holy life? Has the Holy Spirit shown you these things about yourself? Can you say, This is what I know, that the flesh still dwells in me, and no good dwells in it; that even as a Christian, if I am left to myself, it brings me into captivity and bondage. That is the first thing. Each of these sections begins in the same way, with a frank acknowledgment of our condition.

(ii) Each section continues with *a vivid description of the resulting conflict*. 'I do not even acknowledge my own actions as mine' (v15, NEB): that is, I do things against my will; things to which as a Christian I do not give my consent. So the NEB goes on, 'What I do is not what I want to do.' As a Christian I don't want to do it: the things I do are the things that I detest, when I fall into sin. And again, 'I can will what is right.' I *do* will what is right, 'but (in myself) I cannot do it. So that the good I want to do I don't do, and the evil I don't want to do is what I do' (vv18,19, RSV).

Brethren, I want to urge you again: This is the conflict of the Christian man. This is the conflict of a man who knows the will of God, who loves the will of God, who longs to do the will of God: but – at least when he is not walking according to the Spirit – he cannot do it. He finds that because of his flesh he cannot do what he wants to do. His whole being, his mind and his will, is set upon the will of God, and the law of God: He longs to do what is good; he hates what is evil with a holy hatred. And if he does sin, and when he sins, it is against his mind, and against his will, and against his consent; it is against the whole tenor of his life. The resulting conflict in a Christian.

Each section begins with a frank acknowledgment of what I am. It continues with the resulting conflict. And (iii) each section *ends with a conclusion*. And the conclusion is couched in identical words about the cause of the Christian's personal inability apart from the Holy Spirit: 'If I do what I do not want . . .' (vv16,17), if my situation can be summed up in the words, 'I want, but I can't,' then clearly it is not the law's fault if I misbehave, because I agree that the law is good. It is not I even that do it, because I do not do it voluntarily, but only against my will. 'It is sin that dwelleth in me.' And again precisely the same words in verse 20: 'If I do what I do not want it is no longer I that do it, but sin that dwelleth in me.'

So I recapitulate the teaching of these two parallel sections, verses 14–17 and verses 18–20. First comes our condition, what I know myself to be, indwelt by the flesh, which contains no good, and – if I am left to myself – brings me to captivity. Next, the resulting conflict: I cannot do what I want to do, but I do what I detest. And then the conclusion: that if my actions are thus against my will as a Christian, the cause is sin that dwelleth in me.

All along, you see, what Paul is doing is exposing the no-goodness of my flesh, the evil of my flesh, so that only the Holy Spirit can deliver me.

In verses 21–25 the apostle takes the argument a stage further. He has been giving a plain description of his condition and conflict, and he now expresses it in terms of a philosophy, in terms of laws, or principles at work in his situation. The general principle is set forth in verse 21: 'I find – this is my sort of philosophical conclusion from my experience – I find it to be a law' (RSV), or 'I discover this principle' (NEB), 'that when I want to do right, evil lies close at hand.'

This general principle is broken up into two principles, or forces in opposition to each other, which are named in verse 23. One is the law of my mind; the other is the law of sin. The law of my mind is that I delight in the law of God in my inmost self. The law of sin (v23) is this law in my members that makes me captive to itself: the law of sin in my members. You see, the law of my mind is a force in my inmost self, my mind and my will, that simply loves the law of God: that is the law of my mind. But the law of sin is a force in my members, in my flesh, and it hates the law of God. And this is the conflict; this is the philosophy of Christian experience. It is that the good I want I do not do, and the evil I hate I do; and the philosophy behind this is two laws in conflict – the law of my mind, and the law of sin; or more simply, my mind and my flesh. My mind – what I want to do; and my flesh – the old nature.

This conflict is a real, bitter, unremitting conflict in every Christian's experience. His mind is simply delighting in the law of God, and longing to do it; but his flesh is hostile to it, and refuses to submit.

Now this conflict is one that leads us repeatedly to utter two apparently contradictory cries: 'Wretched man that I am! Who will deliver me?' (v24), and 'Thanks be to God through Jesus Christ our Lord' (v25). The first is a cry of despair, and the second is a cry of triumph. Both of them are ejaculations of a mature believer. I tell you that I cry every day, 'Oh, wretched man that I am, who will deliver me?' because as a Christian I bemoan this inner corruption of my nature, and I long for deliverance. And that deliverance, mark you, is not just self-control now. What I long for is deliverance out of the body of death – that is, when I get the redemption of the body on the last day.

Do you not long to be rid of this flesh? Do you not long to be rid of indwelling sin and corruption as a Christian? Then if you do, my brother or sister, this is the cry for you to cry: 'Oh, miserable creature! who will deliver me?' But then you will add the cry of triumph, 'Thanks be to God!' because you know that He is the one and only Deliverer. He is the one who can give you deliverance now through the Holy Spirit, and He is the one who on the last day, at the resurrection, will give us a new body; and we shall have no longer any indwelling sin and corruption.

I do not myself believe that the Christian ever passes for good and all out of the one cry into the other; out of Romans 7 into Romans 8; out of despair into victory. He is always crying for deliverance, and he is always exulting in his Deliverer. Whenever we are made conscious of the power of indwelling sin it is the same.

In the last verse, Paul sums up with beautiful lucidity this double servitude: that 'with my mind – with all my heart and soul, we might say – with my mind I serve the law of God, but with my flesh – unless it is subdued by the Spirit – I serve the law of sin' (v25).

Now whether I serve the law of God or the law of sin, depends on whether my mind or my flesh is in control;

and the question now is, How can the mind gain ascendancy over the flesh? And that question brings us to chapter 8, the first four verses, to the gracious ministry of the Holy Spirit, who in the latter section of chapter 7 – although He has never been far away in the background – has not once been named.

Now brethren, please notice this. There is in fact a progression of thought from Romans 7 to 8 in this way: the conflict at the end of Romans 7 is in my mind and my flesh; between what I want to do and what in myself I cannot do. But the conflict at the beginning of Romans 8 is between the Holy Spirit and the flesh – not between my mind and the flesh, but between the Spirit and the flesh; the Holy Spirit coming to my rescue, allying Himself with my mind, the renewed mind He has given me, and subduing the flesh.

It is the same conflict, but it is differently viewed; and it has a different outcome, because according to 7:22 the believer delights in the law of God but cannot do it in himself because of indwelling sin, but according to 8:4 he not only delights in it, but he actually fulfils the law of God, because of the indwelling Spirit.

In 8:1–2, the apostle steps back and surveys the whole Christian landscape, portraying together the two great blessings of salvation that we have in Christ Jesus. 'In Christ Jesus' are the words common to verses 1–2. '*In Christ Jesus* there is no condemnation' (v1). '*In Christ Jesus* the law of the Spirit of life – the life-giving Spirit – has set me free from the law of death' (v2); so that salvation, which belongs to those who are in Christ Jesus, includes both deliverance from condemnation and deliverance from the law of sin and its bondage.

But how is this twofold salvation made available to us? Verses 3 and 4 tell us. In verses 1 and 2, it is the scope of salvation that is stated: no condemnation, no bondage. In verses 3 and 4, it is the way of salvation that is unfolded. We are told here *how* God effects it. Notice verse 3: '*God* has done what the law, weakened by the flesh, could not do.' We have seen all along that the law is weak, weak because of the flesh. The law cannot sanctify, and law cannot justify, because we cannot obey it. But God has done – praise His Name! – God has done what the law cannot do. And how has He done it? He has done it through His Son (v3), and through His Spirit (v4). Through the death of His incarnate Son He justifies us; and through the power of His indwelling Spirit He sanctifies us. God sent His Son, in the likeness of sinful flesh – that is, real flesh, but sinless flesh – and for sin – probably, 'as a sin offering' – He condemned sin in the flesh.' Just think of that for a moment: In the sinless flesh of Jesus, made sin with our sins God condemned sin. The reason why there is no condemnation for us who are in Christ Jesus, is that God has already condemned our sins in the sinless but sin-contaminated flesh of Jesus Christ His Son. That is how, through His Son, He has delivered us from condemnation.

Now (v4), He delivers us from bondage by the Spirit, in order that 'the righteousness of the law might be fulfilled in us, who walk not according to the flesh, but . . . the Spirit.' This verse teaches some major truths about holiness. One, that holiness is the purpose of the incarnation and death of Christ. 'God sent His Son' – not only that we might be justified, but in order that the righteousness of the law might be fulfilled in us; in other words, that we might obey the law. Two, holiness is the righteousness of the law – a verse that is a very uncomfortable one for antinomians and new moralists. Far from the law being abolished in the Christian life, it is God's purpose that its righteous requirement might be fulfilled in us. And, three; holiness is the work of the

Holy Spirit. The righteousness of the law is only fulfilled in us if we walk according to the Spirit.

We have seen that the whole of Romans 7 is devoted to the theme that we cannot keep the law because of the flesh. But 8:4 says that we *can* fulfil the law if we walk, not according to the flesh, but according to the Spirit who can subdue it. These, then, are vital Christian truths about holiness: The reason for holiness is the death of Christ. The nature of holiness is the righteousness of the law. The means of holiness is the power of the Holy Spirit.

Could we look back over this whole long, involved, and intricate passage, 7:1–8:4? I have entitled it 'Freedom from the law': I might equally have entitled it 'The Fulfilment of the law,' because the passage teaches both. It began with a statement of the Christian's discharge from the law; it ends in 8:4 with a statement of the Christian's obligation to keep it, 'that the righteousness of the law *might be fulfilled*.' Moreover, both our discharge and our obligation are attributed to the death of Christ.

But somebody says, 'But this is an intolerable contradiction. How may I at the same time be free from the law, and obliged to keep it?' I hope you know the answer! The paradox is easy to resolve. We are set free from the law as a way of acceptance before God; but obliged to keep it as a way of holiness. It is as a ground of justification that the law no longer binds us; but as a standard of conduct the law is still binding, and we seek to fulfil it – but in the power of the Spirit. That is our subject tomorrow.

4. Life in the Spirit (Romans 8)

We come now to chapter 8 of the Epistle to the Romans, from verse 5 to the end. Under our general title, 'The Privileges of the Justified,' we have seen so far that the great and glorious privileges of the justified include peace with God (ch5), union with Christ in His death and resurrection (ch6), freedom from the law (ch7), and now our fourth privilege is, *Life in the Spirit*.

The Holy Spirit has not figured prominently in these chapters so far. He is not named at all in chapter 6; He is mentioned only once in chapter 5, as the One through whom God's love has flooded our hearts (v5); and once only in chapter 7, where it is written that our Christian bondage is not to an external code but to an indwelling Spirit (v6). However, in chapter 8 the Holy Spirit comes to the fore; and the Christian life, the life of a justified believer, is seen as being essentially life in the Spirit, life that is animated by, sustained by, directed by, and enriched by the Holy Spirit.

The ministry of the Spirit in these chapters is portrayed particularly in four areas. First, in relation to our flesh, our fallen human nature. Second, in relation to our sonship, our adoption to be the sons of God. Third, in relation to our final inheritance, including the redemption of our bodies on the last day. And fourth, in relation to our prayers, in which we have to acknowledge our weakness. The Holy Spirit's gracious activity in these four areas may be summed up as follows – which are my four sub-headings. One, the Spirit subdues our flesh (vv5–13). Two, the Spirit witnesses to our conscience (vv14–17). Three, the Spirit guarantees our inheritance (vv18–25). Four, the Spirit helps our weakness in prayer (vv26,27). The chapter ends with an affirmation unsurpassed in grandeur, that the purposes of God are invincible, and that the people of God are therefore absolutely and eternally secure (vv28–39).

Firstly, then, *the Holy Spirit subdues our flesh* (vv5–13). Verse 4, with which we ended yesterday, says that the righteousness of the law – 'the just requirement of the law' (RSV) – can be fulfilled in us believers only if we walk, not according to the flesh, but according to the Spirit, following His promptings, and yielding to His control. Now the apostle Paul explains why this is so. And a good deal of it, as Mr Motyer was mentioning last night, has to do with our mind. Our walk depends on our mind; our conduct depends on our outlook. 'As a man thinks in his heart, or mind, so is he' – and so he behaves. It is ultimately our thoughts which govern our behaviour. That is what the apostle says in verse 5. 'For,' he says – and this is the reason why we can only fulfil the law if we walk according to the Spirit – '*For* those who *are* according to the flesh, set their *mind* (RSV) on the things of the flesh. While those who *are* according to the Spirit set their *mind* upon the things of the Spirit.'

Now to set the mind upon the flesh, or upon the Spirit, means to occupy ourselves with the things of the flesh or of the Spirit. It is a question of our preoccupations, the ambitions which compel us and the interests which engross us; how we spend our time, and our money, and our energies; what we give ourselves up to. That is what you set your mind on. And verse 6 describes the results of these two outlooks. To set the mind on the flesh, he says, is death. Not, it *will* be: it is, now, death, because it leads to sin, and therefore to separation from God, which is death.

But to set the mind on the Spirit, and on the things of the Spirit, is *life* – now. This is life, to set the mind on the things of the Spirit, because it leads to holiness, and so to continuing fellowship with God, which is life. Further, it brings not only life, but peace: peace with God, which is life; and peace within ourselves – integration, harmony. Brethren, I believe that many of us would pursue holiness with far greater zeal and energy and eagerness and ambition, if we were convinced that the way of holiness is the way of life and peace. And that is precisely what it is. To set the mind on the things of the Spirit is life and peace; and there is life and peace no other way.

By contrast, to set the mind on the flesh brings death and war (vv7,8). The mind that is set on the flesh is hostile to God. 'It does not submit to the law of God, indeed it cannot; and those who are in the flesh cannot please God.' They cannot please God because the only way to please Him is to submit to His law and to obey it. Thus the mind of the flesh is hostile to God's law, and will not submit to it; while the mind of the Spirit is friendly to God's law, and delights in it.

Here, then, are two categories of people: those who are according to – or in – the flesh, and those who are in the Spirit; who have two mentalities or outlooks, called 'the mind of the flesh' and 'the mind of the Spirit.' These lead to two patterns of conduct, called 'walking according to the flesh,' and 'walking according to the Spirit.' These lead to two spiritual states: death and life. If we are in the flesh we set our mind on the things of the flesh, so we walk according to the flesh, and so we die. But if we are in the Spirit, we set our mind upon the things of the Spirit, and so we walk according to the Spirit, and so we live. What we *are* governs how we think: how we think governs how we *behave*; and how we behave governs our relation to God, death or life.

Once more, then, we see how much depends on our mind: where we set it, how we occupy it, and on what we focus and concentrate its energies. That brings us to verse 9, in which the apostle applies personally to his readers the truths which he has so far expounded in general terms. He has just written in verse 8, 'Those who are in the flesh cannot please God,' and now in verse 9, he says, that '*You* are not in the flesh, but in the Spirit, if so be that the Spirit of God dwells in you. Now if any man have not the Spirit of Christ, he does not belong to Christ.'

Notice, in passing, that certain expressions in verse 9 are synonyms: The Spirit of God and the Spirit of Christ – synonyms; do not believe the people who tell you that they are different – they are not. The Spirit of God and the Spirit of Christ are the same person. The second synonym is that to be in the Spirit, and to have the Spirit dwelling in us, are the same thing – two ways of looking at the same thing. And thirdly, to have the Spirit dwelling in us (v9), and to have Christ dwelling in us (beginning of verse 10): 'If Christ is in you,' are the same thing.

This verse 9, quite apart from these interesting and instructive synonyms, is a verse of great importance. It tells us plainly that the distinguishing mark of the true Christian, that which sets him apart from all unbelievers, is that the Holy Spirit dwells within him. Twice in chapter 7 (vv17 and 20), the apostle writes of 'sin which dwells in me.' Ah, but now he writes of 'the Spirit who dwells in me.' Indwelling sin is the lot of all children of Adam; but the great privilege of the children of God is the indwelling Spirit, who subdues and controls indwelling sin. And if anybody does not have the Spirit of Christ, he does not belong to Christ.

Now verses 10, 11, which indicate the great consequence of having the Spirit dwelling in us. Notice that both verses begin similarly, with an 'if' clause. '*If* Christ is in you . . .' (v10). '*If* the Spirit of Him who raised up Christ lives in you . . .' (v11). Here are the results, the consequence, of having the Spirit indwelling us. What is the consequence of having Christ by His Spirit indwelling us? Well, the answer is, life: life for our spirits now, and life for our bodies at the end. Because the Holy Spirit is the Spirit of life; He is the Lord the life-giver. Thus verse 10, 'If Christ is in you, although indeed your bodies are dead because of sin, your spirits are alive because of righteousness' (RSV). That is, although our bodies are still – not yet dead, but prone to death, and mortal, yet our spirits are alive. The Holy Spirit has given them life. Because of Adam's sin we die physically; but because of Christ's righteousness we live spiritually. Our spirits are alive because Christ by His Spirit dwells in us, and has given us life. Further, although at present it is only our spirits which live – our bodies are mortal, and are going to die – yet on the last day our bodies are going to live as well, incorruptibly (v11).

Verse 11 says, 'If the Spirit of Him who raised Jesus from the dead dwells in you, He who raised Jesus from the dead will give life to your *bodies* through His Spirit who dwells in you.' He is going to raise our bodies. Why? Because of the Spirit who dwells in us, and hallows our bodies. How is He going to raise us? Answer, by the same Spirit who dwells in us. It is the Holy Spirit who is going to quicken our body, as He has already quickened our spirit.

'So then' (v12) 'we are debtors, not to the flesh to live according to the flesh, but . . .' and the apostle breaks off before completing the sentence; but if he had completed the sentence, it seems certain that he would have said, 'we are debtors not to the flesh to live according to the flesh, but to the Spirit to live according to the Spirit.' This

idea of being debtors to the Holy Spirit is an interesting
and compelling one. It indicates that we have a debt, an
obligation to holiness. It is an obligation to be what we
are; to live up to our Christian status and privilege, and
do nothing that contradicts it. And in particular, if we
live in the Spirit, we have an obligation to walk according to the Spirit; to be what we are.

I am anxious that you should grasp this argument. Let
me put it like this: If the Holy Spirit is our life-giver, and
if He dwells within us, we cannot possibly walk according to the flesh, because that way lies death. And such an
inconsistency between what we are and how we behave,
between possessing life and courting death, is unthinkable. We are alive; our spirits are alive! The Holy Spirit
has given us life, and therefore we are debtors to this life-
giving Spirit; and by the power of the Spirit we must put
to death anything that is inconsistent with His life. We
must put to death the deeds of the body that threaten our
spiritual life, because it is only by the death of the deeds
of the body that we shall live, that we shall continue to
enjoy this life that the Holy Spirit has given us.

You see then in verse 13, the solemn alternative. If you
let the flesh live, if you let your old nature live and flour-
ish, you – that is the real you – will die. But if you kill the
deeds of the body, if you mortify the deeds of the body,
and put them to death, then you – the real you – will live.
And each of us has to choose between the way of life and
the way of death. But Paul's point is that our choice is
not really in doubt, because we are debtors, we are under
obligation to make the right choice. If the Spirit has given
life to our spirits, then we *must* put to death the deeds of
the body so that we may continue to live the life that the
Spirit has given us.

Now, let us look back over this paragraph, and grasp
the apostle's progression of thought. The essential

background to all that he has said is, that there are two categories of people: those who are in the flesh – the unregenerate; and those who are in the Spirit – the regenerate, in whom the Spirit dwells. Now you, he writes to the Romans – and I have no doubt if he were in the tent today he would say this to *you*: he would say, 'Now *you* are not in the flesh; you are in the Spirit, if, as I believe, the Spirit of God dwells in you.' Further, 'because Christ dwells in you by His Spirit, you are alive' (v10).

These are the two facts, the incontrovertible, inescapable, irrefutable facts about every Christian. One, we have the Holy Spirit dwelling in us. Two, as a result, our spirits are alive: this indwelling Spirit has quickened us. *Therefore* we are debtors. Because of what we are, we are debtors, not to the flesh, but to the Spirit. We are under a most solemn obligation to be what we are, to conform our conduct to our character, to do nothing inconsistent with the life of the Spirit that is in us, but rather to nourish this life and to foster it.

Now more specifically: if we are going to be honourable and to discharge our debt, then we shall be involved in two processes whose theological names are *mortification* and – I think I may use the word – *aspiration*; words that express the proper attitude that we should adopt toward the flesh on the one hand, and the Spirit on the other. We must put to death the deeds of the flesh, or body – that is mortification. And we must set our minds on the things of the Spirit – that is aspiration. Mortification, putting to death the deeds of the body, means a ruthless rejection of all practices we know to be wrong; a daily repentance, turning from every known sin or habit or practice or association or thought. That is mortification – cutting out the eye, cutting off the hand, cutting off the foot, if temptation comes to us through what we see, or do, or where we go. That is mortification – the only attitude to adopt to the flesh: to kill it.

Aspiration, setting the mind on the things of the Spirit, is a whole-hearted giving of ourselves in thought and energy and ambition, to whatsoever things are true and honest, just and pure, lovely and of good report. And in order to give our mind to the things of the Spirit, it will include a disciplined use of the means of grace – that is, prayer, the reading and meditation of the Scripture, fellowship, worship, the Lord's Supper, and so on. All this is involved in setting our mind upon the things of the Spirit.

Now, in both cases, mortification and aspiration, the verbs are in the present tense, because they are attitudes to be adopted, which are then constantly and unremittingly maintained. We are to keep putting to death the deeds of the body, or, as Jesus said, 'take up your cross daily, and follow me': it is the same thing. And we are to keep setting our minds on the things of the Spirit, daily. Not only so, but they are both the secrets of life in the fullest sense. There is no true life without the death called mortification; and there is no true life without the discipline called aspiration. It is when we put to death the deeds of the body that we shall live (v13); and it is while we set our minds upon the things of the Spirit that we find life and peace (v6).

So the Holy Spirit subdues the flesh as we mortify it in His power, and as we set our minds upon the things of the Spirit. That is the first thing.

The second gracious work of the Holy Spirit is that *He witnesses to our sonship* (vv14–17). The emphasis on the work of the Spirit continues in this paragraph, but our Christian status is now described, not in terms of life, but in terms of sonship. What the apostle has just said is, that if by the Spirit you mortify the deeds of the body, you

will live; what He now says is, that if you are led by the
Spirit you are the sons of God. The two sentences are
closely parallel. Both refer to the activity of the Spirit, but
the first in terms of life, and the second in terms of sonship.

Sonship – what visions of intimacy with God the word
conveys! Access to God, fellowship with God our Father
– these are the privileges of His children. Oh, not all
human beings are God's children. Verse 14 definitely and
deliberately limits this status to those who are being led
by the Spirit, who are being enabled by the Spirit to walk
along the narrow road of righteousness. To be led by the
Spirit, and to be a child of God, are synonymous. All
who are led by the Spirit of God are the children of God;
and all the children of God are being led by the Spirit of
God.

That is made even clearer in the next verse, verse 15,
which refers to the kind of Spirit we received – an aorist
tense – when we were converted. We *received* the Spirit
when we were converted; and the Spirit we received was
not a Spirit of slavery, but a Spirit of sonship or adoption.
The Holy Spirit who is given to us when we believe,
makes us sons, not slaves. He does not recall us to the
old slavery, spoiled by fear. He gives us a new sonship,
in which we approach God as our Father; and more than
that, He assures us of the status that He brings us. 'When
we cry Abba, Father (the very words that the Lord Jesus
Himself used in intimate prayer to God) it is the Holy
Spirit bearing witness with our spirit, that we are the
children of God' (end of verses. 15, and 16, RSV). I believe
that the RSV way of rendering the verse is right, and it
shows that the inner witness of the Spirit is given us
while we pray. It is in our access to God in prayer that we
sense our filial relationship to God, and we know ourselves the children of God.

Is not that true? When we pray, when our spirit is in communion with God, is it not then that the Holy Spirit bears witness with our spirit, so that there are two concurrent testimonies that we are indeed God's children? 'If children, then heirs, heirs of God and joint heirs with Christ, if we suffer with Him that we may be glorified with Him' (v17).

Once more, as in chapter 5, suffering is the pathway to glory. Notice that it is 'with Christ.' The whole Christian life is identification with Christ. If we share His sonship, we shall share His inheritance in glory; but if we share His glory, we must first share His sufferings. We share His sufferings, we share His sonship, we share His glory: we are identified with Christ.

So (i) the Spirit subdues our flesh; (ii) the Spirit witnesses to our sonship; and (iii) *the Spirit guarantees our inheritance* (vv18–25). The theme of this paragraph is the contrast between present sufferings and future glory, which the apostle has just mentioned at the end of verse 17. And in verse 18 he says that the two are not to be compared – they are to be contrasted, because future glory will far outweigh all present suffering. This he proceeds to elaborate in a magnificent cosmic setting. He goes on to show in the rest of the paragraph how in present suffering and future glory, the whole creation and the new creation, the church, are together involved. The two creations suffer together now, and are going to be glorified together in the end. As nature has shared man's curse (Genesis 3), so nature now shares man's tribulation, and is going to share in man's glory. 'The creation waits with eager longing – as if standing on tiptoe with expectation – for the revealing of the sons of God' (v19). And the creation is waiting for this because that is the time when it – nature – too will be redeemed.

Now let us look at the *creation* (vv19–22), mentioned four times, once in each verse. The AV, 'creature' is the creation: NEB, 'the created universe.' And notice how its present sufferings are described. It was subjected to futility, or frustration (v20), not by its own will, but by the will of God who thus subjected it. It is held in the bondage of decay (v21); and it is groaning and travailing in pain (v22).

Let us look at these for a moment. *Futility*, frustration (v20). It is the same word that is translated 'vanity' in the Greek version of the Book of Ecclesiastes, and C.J. Vaughan says, 'The whole Book of Ecclesiastes is a commentary on this verse. "Vanity of vanities, saith the preacher, all is vanity".' The whole creation has been subjected to vanity; and this frustration to which God has subjected nature, is explained in the next verse (v21) as *a bondage to decay* – a continuous process of deterioration in a universe that appears to be running down. And further this process is, whether literally or metaphorically, accompanied by pain.

Futility, decay, pain. These are the words that the apostle uses to depict the present suffering of nature, of the creation. But it is only temporary, for the present sufferings of nature are going to give way to a future glory. 'If the creation was subjected to vanity, it was subjected in hope' (v20) – *hope* of coming glory. 'The creation will be set free from bondage to decay, into the liberty of the glory of the children of God' (v21) – from bondage to liberty, from decay to glory incorruptible.

So that if we are to share Christ's glory, the creation is going to share ours. The groans and pains of the creation are likened to 'the pangs of childbirth' (verse 22, NEB). In other words, they are not meaningless or purposeless pains; they are pains necessarily experienced in the bringing to birth of a new order. Now that is the present suffering and the future glory of the created universe.

We move from the creation to *the church*, the new creation of God (vv23–25). 'The whole created universe groans in all its parts as if in the pangs of childbirth' (v22, NEB). 'And not only the creation, but we ourselves . . . groan inwardly' – not outwardly; at least I cannot hear any outward groans from the congregation – but we groan inwardly (v23, RSV). Now what is this inward groaning which we share with the creation? What is the present suffering of the church to which the apostle is here referring? Oh, not persecution here, but the simple fact that we are only half-saved.

Did you know that? There is not a single man or woman in the tent this morning who is wholly saved. You are only half-saved! Oh, your souls are wholly saved, but your bodies are not saved yet, and so we are only half-saved, and it is our unredeemed bodies which cause us to groan. For one thing, these bodies are weak and fragile and mortal, subject to fatigue and sickness and pain and death; and it is this the apostle has in mind in 2 Corinthians 5, when he says, 'In this body we groan,' because of our physical mortality. But it is also that the flesh – our fallen, sinful human nature – is in our mortal bodies, indwelling sin that leads us to cry out, 'Oh, wretched man that I am, who will deliver me out of this body of death?'

Now that is exactly the kind of groaning that Paul is talking about; only there the inward groan is ejaculated out of the mouth. But that is the groaning, that is the travail; what makes us groan inwardly is our physical frailty on the one hand, and our fallen nature on the other. And so we long ardently for the future glory. And this is called 'the redemption of our body,' because we are going to be given new bodies on the last day, delivered from the two burdens of the body, which are their frailty, and their flesh, or indwelling sin. Our resurrection bodies are going to have new undreamed-of powers, and they are going to have no indwelling sin.

Now the future glory is not only called the redemption of our bodies, but it is called the adoption. The Greek word is the same as in verse 15. In one sense we have already received our adoption; but in another sense we are still awaiting it, because our present sonship, although glorious, is imperfect. We are not yet conformed in either body or character to the image of God's Son, nor has our sonship been publicly recognised and revealed. But the last day is going to witness what in verse 19 is called a 'manifestation of the sons of God.'

You see, we are not yet recognised by the world as the sons and daughters of God: but on the last day is going to come the manifestation of the sons of God, publicly revealed and recognised; and then we shall obtain what is called 'the glorious liberty of the children of God.' And the creation is going to obtain it with us.

Of this future and glorious inheritance we are sure. We have no doubt in our minds. Why? Well, because we already have the first-fruits of the Spirit (v23). Oh, we have not yet received the adoption; we have not yet received the redemption of our bodies. But we have received the Holy Spirit, the indwelling Spirit Himself, who is the God-given guarantee of our full inheritance to come. Indeed, He is more than the guarantee of it; He is the foretaste of it. He Is the Spirit of glory.

Sometimes Paul uses a commercial metaphor, and calls the Holy Spirit the 'earnest,' the first instalment, the down-payment, which certifies that the remainder is going to be paid later. But here the metaphor is agricultural, the first-fruits of the harvest being a pledge of the full crop to come. So the Holy Spirit not only makes us the children of God as the Spirit of adoption; He not only witnesses with our spirit that we are the children of God; but He is Himself the pledge of our complete adoption to be the sons of God when our bodies are redeemed. And verses 24 and 25 enforce this further, asserting that it is (literally) in this hope that we were saved. Oh, we were saved; but we were only half-saved. We were saved in hope of a full salvation, including our bodies. The object of that hope is invisible. We do not yet see it. But we wait for it with patient fortitude.

So (i) the Spirit subdues our flesh; (ii) the Spirit witnesses to our sonship; (iii) the Spirit guarantees our inheritance; and (iv) *the Holy Spirit helps our weakness in prayer* (vv26,27). 'Likewise . . .' There is yet another ministry that the Holy Spirit fulfils, and He is mentioned four times in the brief compass of these two verses. He helps us in our weakness, and the particular weakness which the apostle has in mind here is our ignorance in prayer. We do not know precisely what to pray for as we ought; but the Spirit helps us in our weakness.

Now the general ministry of the Holy Spirit in prayer is much neglected, yet we are clearly taught in Scripture that our access to the Father is not only through the Son, but by the Spirit; that the Holy Spirit's inspiration is as necessary as the Son's mediation, in our access to God in prayer. But here the Holy Spirit's ministry in our prayer-life is more specific, and it seems to be this. Sometimes when believers do not know how to pray in words, they groan without words. Sometimes, to quote Dr E.F. Kevan, 'we find ourselves brought to silence by the very intensity of our longings.' Or again, sometimes we feel so burdened by our mortality, or by our indwelling sin, that we can only *groan*.

Notice these groanings – We can only groan . . . 'with sighs too deep for words' (RSV). Now these unutterable sighs, or groans – what J.B. Phillips calls 'those agonising longings which never find words' – are not to be despised, as if we ought to be able to put them into language. On the contrary, when we thus sigh with inarticulate desires, it is the Holy Spirit Himself interceding on our behalf, prompting these groans. We do not need to be ashamed of these wordless prayers. God the Father understands prayers which are sighed rather than said, because God the Father searches our hearts, and He can read our hearts and our thoughts, and He knows what is the mind of the Spirit, because the Holy Spirit always prays in accordance with the will of God. And so the Father in heaven answers the prayers prompted by the Spirit in our hearts.

> *Prayer is the soul's sincere desire,*
> *Uttered or unexpressed;*
> *The motion of a hidden fire*
> *That trembles in the breast.*

> *Prayer is the burden of a sigh,*
> *The falling of a tear;*
> *The upward glancing of an eye*
> *When none but God is near.*

Here, then, are the four gracious activities of the Holy Spirit. He subdues our flesh; He witnesses to our sonship; He guarantees our inheritance; and He helps our weakness in prayer. That brings us to the conclusion and the climax. For in the last twelve verses of the chapter (vv28–39) the apostle rises to sublime heights unequalled anywhere in the New Testament.

He does not now mention the Holy Spirit specifically. Instead, having described some of the privileges of the justified – peace with God, union with Christ, freedom from the law, life in the Spirit – having described these privileges, the apostle's great, Spirit-directed mind now sweeps over the whole counsel of God, from an eternity that is past to an eternity that is yet to come; from the divine foreknowledge and predestination, to the divine love from which absolutely nothing whatsoever is able to separate us. And the burden of the apostle's climax is the unchangeable, irresistible, invincible purpose of God; and by this purpose, and in it, the eternal security of God's people.

Now these simply tremendous truths, far too great for our puny minds to absorb, these stupendous truths the apostle expresses, first, in a series of five undeniable affirmations; and then in a series of five unanswerable questions, in which he challenges *anybody* to contradict the affirmations which he has just made.

Take the affirmations first. He introduces them in verse 28, with a promise on which you and I have often stayed our troubled hearts and minds: that 'all things work together for good to them who love God.' Now the subject of the verb is probably not 'all things,' but He, God – because all things do not work themselves into a pattern for good: it is God who works all things together for good, including the pains and the groans of the previous paragraphs. And He works all things for good in the case of those who love Him, and are 'called according to His purpose.'

Now come the five undeniable affirmations (vv29,30), which explain what is meant by the divine calling, and in what sense God works all things together for good. This working together for good, this purpose in the salvation of sinners, is traced from its beginnings in the mind of God to its culmination in the eternal glory. The five stages are foreknowledge, predestination, calling, justification, and glorification.

First He foreknew, and second He predestined. Now the difference between foreknowledge and predestination is, perhaps, that God's electing choice was formed in His mind before He willed it. His decision preceded His decree. Now this is not the occasion on which to delve into the mysteries of predestination, but I should like to quote some wise and true words of the commentator, C.J. Vaughan. Listen to them carefully: 'Everyone who is eventually saved can only ascribe his salvation, from the first step to the last, to God's favour and act. Human merit must be excluded; and this can only be by tracing back the work far beyond the obedience which evidences, or even the faith which appropriates, salvation; even to an act of spontaneous favour on the part of that God who foresees and foreordains from eternity, all His works.'

Notice that the purpose of the divine predestination is not favouritism. The purpose of the divine predestination is holiness, Christlikeness. He predestined us that we should be conformed to the image of His Son. So the next, the third of the five undeniable affirmations, is that He called; and the fourth is that He justified. The call of God is the historical outworking of His eternal predestination, and those whom God thus calls respond in faith to the call. And those who thus believe, God justifies, accepting them in Christ as His own.

Fifth, He glorified, bringing them to resurrection and to heaven, with new bodies in a new world. The process of sanctification is omitted, but as Professor Bruce has pointed out, it is involved in glorification. Professor Bruce neatly expresses it: 'Sanctification is glory begun: glory is sanctification completed.' So certain is this final stage of glorification that it is even expressed by an aorist tense, as if it were past, like the other four stages that *are* past. It is a so-called prophetic past.

Here, then, is the apostle's series of five undeniable affirmations. It is like a chain with five unbreakable links: Whom He did foreknow He also did predestine; whom He did predestine He also called; whom He called He also justified; and whom He justified He also glorified. God is pictured as moving on steadily from stage to stage, from an eternal foreknowledge and predestination, through an historical call and justification, to a final glorification of His people in heaven. Five undeniable affirmations.

Now from the affirmations to the questions (vv31–39). 'What shall we then say to these things?' This is a little formula which the apostle has already used three times in the chapters we have been studying. It is a formula which he uses to introduce some conclusion. He says, in effect, 'In the light of what I have just said, what are we now going to say? In the light of the foregoing, in the light of the five great affirmations of verses 29 and 30, how shall we conclude? What shall we then say?'

Paul's answer to this question is to ask five more questions which have no answer: five unanswerable questions. 'If God be for us, who can be against us?' (v31). 'He who spared not His own Son, but delivered Him up for us all, how shall He not with Him also freely give us all things?' (v32). No answer to that one. 'Who shall bring any charge against God's elect?' (v33). 'Who is to condemn?' (same verse). 'Who shall separate us from the love of Christ?' (v35). The apostle hurls out these questions into space, as it were, defiantly, triumphantly, challenging any creature in heaven or earth or hell, to answer them or to deny the truth that is contained in them. But there is no answer, for nobody and nothing can harm the redeemed people of God.

Now, it is very important to observe – if you want to understand these unanswerable questions – the reason why each question remains unanswered. And the reason is this: it is because the assertion applied in the question is grounded upon some immovable truth. Thus each question, either explicitly or implicitly, is attached to an 'if' clause. I think you will understand what I mean, because the clearest is the first: '*If* God be for us, who can be against us?' (v31).

Now you see, if Paul had simply asked the question, 'Who can be against us?' without the introductory 'if' clause, there would have been many replies – certainly from hell! Many, many replies could have been given. Who is against us? Well, there are many people against us; we have formidable enemies arrayed against us. Unbelievers are in opposition to us; indwelling sin is a powerful force assaulting us; death is an enemy, so is he who has the power of death, the devil. In fact, the world, the flesh, and the devil, are all too strong for us. Ah, but Paul, you see, does not ask this simple question, 'Who is against us'? His question is, *If God be for us*, if the God who foreknew and pre-destined and called and justified and glorified – if that God is for us, who can be against us? To that question there is no answer. The world, the flesh and the devil may still set themselves in array against us, but they can never prevail against us *if God is on our side*.

Question 2: 'He that spared not His own Son, but delivered Him up for us all, how shall He not with Him also freely give us all things?' (v32). Now again, if the apostle had merely asked, 'Will God not freely give us all things?' we might very well have hummed and hawed and given an equivocal answer, because we need so many things, great things, difficult things. How could we be certain that God would supply all our need? Ah, but the way Paul expresses the question banishes all our lingering doubts. The God of whom we ask our question, whether He will give us all things, is the God who has already given us His Son. 'With this gift, how can He fail to lavish upon us all He has to give?' (NEB). If God has given us this indescribable gift, how will He not give us lesser gifts which we can easily describe? The cross proves the generosity of God.

Then, thirdly, 'Who can bring any charge against God's elect?' (v33). Now commentators point out that the next two questions about accusing and condemning us, seem to bring us as it were, into a court of law. The argument is that no prosecution can be of any avail if Jesus Christ is our advocate who pleads for us, and if God the judge has already justified us who will accuse us? Now again, brethren, if that question stood alone it would not have been at all difficult to answer. My conscience accuses me: does not yours? The devil accuses us: why, the devil's very name means 'Slanderer' or 'Calumniator'; the devil is called 'the accuser of the brethren.' Ah, but the point is this: the devil's accusations fall to the ground; they do not hurt us; they are like arrows off a shield. Why? Well, the answer is because we are God's elect whom He has justified. And if God has Himself justified us, no accusation can stand against us.

'Who can condemn us?' (v34). Once again, many seek to. Sometimes our heart condemns us. According to 1 John 3:20–21, it tries to. So do our critics and our enemies, yes, and all the demons in hell are trying to condemn us. But all their condemnations are idle nonsense. Why? Because Christ has died: He died for the very sins for which otherwise we should indeed be condemned; and He has been raised from the dead to prove the efficacy of His death; and now He sits exalted at the Father's right hand, where He is our heavenly advocate, pleading our cause.

Beloved, with such a Christ as our Saviour, crucified, risen, exalted, our advocate interceding on our behalf:

with such a Christ as our Saviour we can confidently say,
'There is now therefore no condemnation to them that
are in Christ Jesus,' and we can hurl out even to the
demons in hell: 'Which of you is going to condemn me?'
and there will be no answer.

Question 5 – and the last one: 'Who shall separate us
from the love of Christ' (v35). With this last question
Paul himself does what we have been trying to do with
his other four questions. That is, he looks around for a
possible answer. He brings forward all the adversities
that he can think of, which might be thought to separate
us from the love of Christ: tribulation, distress, persecution – that is, the pressures of an ungodly world; famine
and nakedness – that is the lack of adequate food and
clothing, which, since Jesus promised that our heavenly
Father would feed and clothe us, might seem to be an
evidence that God does not care if we have inadequate
food and clothing; peril, and the sword – that is the danger of death, and actual death by the malice of men, martyrdom, the ultimate test of our faith, and a very real test,
too, in those days and in our days, because the Scripture
warns us in Psalm 44:22 that God's people are for His
sake 'being killed all the day long' (v36), that is, they are
continuously being exposed to the risk of death, like
sheep to the slaughter.

Well, these are some adversities indeed. What about
these things? They are real sufferings all right, painful
and perilous. Ah, but can they separate us from the love
of Christ? No. Far from separating us from Christ's love,
in these very sufferings, in the experience and the
endurance of them, 'we are more than conquerors' (v37).
Those five words represent only one in the Greek,
'hyper-conquerors,' 'super-conquerors,' in these things.
And we are 'super-conquerors through Him that loved
us.' That is, they cannot separate us from His love today,

because we conquer in them through Him who has proved His love at the cross. Did you ever notice that little phrase? It seems to say this to me: 'Christ has proved His love by His sufferings, so our sufferings cannot separate us from His love.'

And so Paul reaches his climax: 'I am persuaded – this is my fixed, unshakeable conviction – that neither the crisis of death nor the calamities of life; nor superhuman agencies, good or evil, angels, principalities and powers; nor time, whether present or future; nor space, whether height or depth; nor anything else in all creation, will be able, however hard it tries, to separate us from the love of God which is in Christ Jesus our Lord' (vv38,39).

The love of God historically displayed in the death of Christ, the love of God poured into our hearts by the Spirit of Christ! And, brethren, in that conviction of the love of God, through all the pains and perplexities of human experience, may we, too, both live and die!

1969

God's Gospel in a Time of Crisis

Introduction to 2 Timothy

Bishop Handley Moule confessed in his commentary on 2 Timothy that he found it difficult to read the letter 'without finding something like a mist gathering in the eyes.' And understandably so. It is a most moving document.

We are to imagine the apostle, 'Paul the aged,' languishing in some dark, dank, underground Roman dungeon, from which there is to be no escape but death. His apostolic labours are now over. 'I have fought the good fight,' he can say; 'I have finished the race, I have kept the faith' (4:7).

Yes, but what will happen to the faith when he has gone? That's the question which dominates his mind throughout this letter. He must make some arrangement for its transmission (uncontaminated, unalloyed) to future generations. So he now solemnly charges Timothy both to preserve what he has received, at whatever cost, and to hand it on to faithful men who in their turn will be able to teach others also.

The church of our day urgently needs to hear the message of this letter. All around us we see the church losing its grasp of the Gospel, fumbling it, in danger of letting it drop from its hands altogether. A new generation of young Timothys is needed, who will guard the sacred deposit of the gospel, who are determined to proclaim it and are prepared to suffer for it, and who will pass it on pure and uncorrupted to the generation that will rise up in due course to follow them.

1. The Charge to Guard the Gospel (2 Timothy 1)

There are four introductory points which I think it is necessary to make before we begin our study of 2 Timothy.

First, this is *a genuine letter of Paul to Timothy*. I do not think that this is a proper occasion on which to debate or argue the matter; but I venture to suggest that the arguments which have been advanced against the Pauline authorship of 2 Timothy – historical, ecclesiastical, doctrinal, and linguistic arguments – are not sufficient to overthrow the evidence, both internal and external, which authenticates it as a genuine Pauline epistle. That is the first thing: this is a genuine letter of Paul to Timothy.

Secondly, *the Paul who wrote this letter was a prisoner in Rome* – not now in the comparative freedom and comfort in his own hired house, in which the book of Acts took leave of him, and from which he seems to have been set free, as he himself expected. But rather, to quote Hendriksen in his commentary, 'in some dismal, underground dungeon, with a hole in the ceiling for light and air,' perhaps in the Mamertine prison, as tradition says, to which a second arrest and imprisonment brought him, and from which he was to escape only by death.

So Paul wrote this letter under the imminent shadow of execution; and although it is a personal letter from Paul to Timothy, it is also – unconsciously so – his last will and testament to the church.

My third introductory point is this, *that the Timothy to whom the letter was addressed was being thrust into a position of Christian leadership far beyond his natural capacity*. For over fifteen years Timothy had been Paul's missionary companion and trusted apostolic delegate. He was now the accepted leader of the church in Ephesus; but still heavier responsibilities were about to fall on him when the apostle's anticipated martyrdom took place. Yet humanly speaking Timothy was totally unfit for these responsibilities.

(a) He was still *comparatively young*. We do not know his precise age: he may have been in his mid-thirties. But he was a comparatively young man. Paul addressed him in the first letter to Timothy: 'Let no one despise your youth,' and in this letter, written a year or two later, he urges him to 'shun *youthful* passions' (2:22). So he was still comparatively young.

(b) He was *prone to sickness*. In the first letter the apostle Paul refers to Timothy's frequent ailments, and advises him for the sake of his poor stomach to exchange water for a little wine.

(c) He was *timid by temperament*. If he had lived in our day, I think we should probably describe him as an introvert. He shrank from difficult tasks, so that Paul had to write to the Corinthians, 'When Timothy comes, see that you put him at ease among you,' and 'let no one despise him.'

This, then, was Timothy, young in years, frail in physique, and retiring in disposition, who nevertheless was called to exacting responsibilities in the service of Jesus Christ. I wonder if there is somebody like that at Keswick this year – young and weak and shy, whom God is calling nevertheless to important responsibilities in Christian service. This second letter to Timothy brings a special message to all timid Timothys, of whom there are very many in the Christian church.

That brings me to the fourth introductory point, which is that *Paul's preoccupation in writing to Timothy was with the Gospel*, the deposit of truth which had been revealed and committed to him by God. You see, the apostle Paul's Gospel work was now over. A prisoner now, he would become a martyr soon. And the question was, what would happen to the Gospel when Paul was dead. This was the question that preoccupied his mind as he languished in his underground dungeon. It is to this vital question that he addressed himself in this letter. He reminded Timothy that the Gospel was now committed to him: it was now Timothy's turn to assume responsibility for it. And in each of these four chapters he emphasises a different aspect of this responsibility.

So I have called Chapter 1, *The Charge to Guard the Gospel*. Chapter 2, *The Charge to Suffer for the Gospel*. Chapter 3, *The Charge to Continue in the Gospel*. And Chapter 4, *The Charge to Preach the Gospel*.

So we come to the opening paragraph, which in a vivid way introduces to us both Paul and Timothy, the writer and the recipient of the letter. In particular these verses tell us something of how each man, Paul and Timothy, had come to be what he was. These opening verses throw a great deal of light on the providence of God, and how God fashions men and women into what He wants them to be.

Let us take Paul first. 'Paul, an apostle of Christ Jesus by the will of God according to the promise of the life which is in Christ Jesus.' I do not think there is any need to remind you that Jesus Himself chose twelve men out of the wider company of His disciples, and how He Himself named the apostles. Nor how He appointed them to be with Him; and how He deliberately gave them unrivalled opportunities to *see His works, to hear His words*, in order that they might be witnesses to Him of what they had seen and heard. Nor, I think, is there any need for me to remind you that He promised them a special, extraordinary inspiration of the Holy Spirit, to remind them of His teaching, to teach them more, and to lead them into all the truth which God purposed to reveal to them.

Now, to this select company of apostles Paul was later added, when Jesus first apprehended him upon the Damascus road, and commissioned him as an apostle. And Paul describes his apostleship in two ways, telling us both its *origin* and its *object*:

(a) *Its origin* was the will of God: 'Paul an apostle of Jesus Christ by the will of God.' Paul has used almost identical words at the beginning of both Corinthian epistles, and the two great prison epistles to the Ephesians and the Colossians. Indeed, I wonder if you know that in nine out of the thirteen Pauline epistles he refers either to the will of God, or to the call of God, or to the command of God, by which he had been made an apostle. It was Paul's sustained conviction, from the beginning to the end of his apostolic career, that he had been appointed an apostle of Jesus Christ neither by the church, nor by any man or men, nor was he self-appointed; but that his apostleship originated in the eternal will and historical call of almighty God through Jesus Christ. 'Paul, an apostle of Jesus Christ by the will of God.' That is its origin.

(b) *Its object*. 'According to the promise of the life which is in Christ Jesus.' In other words, the great object of Paul's apostleship was that he should first *formulate* and then *communicate* the Gospel. The Gospel is the good news to dying sinners, that God has promised them life in Christ Jesus. The Gospel offers life, true life, abundant life, eternal life – both here and hereafter. The Gospel declares that this new life is in Jesus Christ, who 'abolished death and brought life and immortality to light through the Gospel' (vv10–11). Moreover, the Gospel promises life to anybody who is in Christ Jesus.

Such, then, was Paul: an apostle of Jesus Christ, and his apostleship originated in the will of God and issued in the proclamation of the Gospel of God, which is 'the promise of the life which is in Christ Jesus.'

So much for Paul: now Timothy. 'My beloved child,' Paul calls him, and calls him thus because Paul had led him to Christ, and so become his father through the Gospel. To him Paul sends his customary greeting of 'grace and peace,' but in the two letters to Timothy adds 'mercy' as well. Grace to the worthless; mercy to the helpless; and peace to the restless. And 'God our Father and Christ Jesus our Lord' together constituting the one source from which flows this threefold stream – of grace, and mercy, and peace.

Then follows a very personal paragraph, in which the apostle expresses his deep thanksgiving for Timothy, and says, 'Whenever I remember you, Timothy, I thank God.' Now when you come to think of it, that is a remarkable statement. 'Whenever I remember you, I thanked God.' Why? Why, because Paul recognised that Timothy was what he was because God had made him what he was. And because God had made Timothy what he was, whenever Paul remembered Timothy he thank God.

Now we are going to see the various factors which had made Timothy what he was. Directly or indirectly in this paragraph Paul mentions the four major influences which had contributed to the shaping and the making of Timothy.

(a) His Parental Upbringing

In verse 5 Paul refers to his grandmother Lois and his mother Eunice, and then goes on to say, 'I am sure their faith dwells also in you.' Now this was right, because every man is to a great extent the product of his inheritance. The most formative influence on every one of us is our parentage and our home. That is why good biographies never begin with their subject, but with his parents, and probably his grandparents as well.

Now Timothy had a godly home. We know from Acts 16: 1 that his father was a Greek, and presumably an unbeliever. But his mother Eunice was a believing Jewess who became a Christian; and before her, his grandmother Lois had been converted – although we do not know how. These women, even before Timothy's conversion, had instructed him out of the Scriptures, so that 'from childhood you have known the holy Scriptures . . .' (3:15).

This, then, was the first influence on Timothy: his parental upbringing, a mother and a grandmother who were sincere believers, and who had taught him out of the Scriptures since he was a child. Do I need to say to you, that anybody who has been born and bred in a Christian home has received from God a blessing without price?

(b) Spiritual Friendship

The second influence on Timothy was a spiritual friendship. For after our parents, it is our friends who influence us most, especially if they are also teachers. And Timothy had in Paul an outstanding teacher-friend. Paul was Timothy's spiritual father. But having led him to Christ, he did not abandon him, as many of us abandon our converts. No, he constantly 'remembered' him, as he repeats here in verses 3–5. 'I remember you constantly in my prayers' (v3). 'I remember your tears' (v5). 'I am reminded of your sincere faith' (v5). Not only did he remember him: Paul took Timothy with him on his missionary journeys, and had done so for more than ten years. When they parted Timothy could not restrain his tears, and, mindful of his tears, Paul *longed* – the Greek word meaning, in Bishop Moule's phrase, 'a homesick yearning' – he longed night and day to see him. Meanwhile he prayed for him unceasingly, and from time to time he wrote letters to him, letters of encouragement and counsel, like this one we are studying together. Now such a Christian friendship, including the companionship, the letters and the prayers through which it is expressed, did not fail to have a powerful moulding and shaping influence upon Timothy, strengthening and sustaining him in his Christian life.

The third influence on Timothy was –

(c) A Special Endowment

Paul turns from indirect means that God had employed to shape Timothy's character, namely his parents and his friends, to a direct gift that God had given him. 'I remind you to rekindle the gift of God that is within you through the laying on of my hands' (v6). Now what this divine gift, this *charisma* was, we simply do not know for certain – for the very good reason that we are not told. Nevertheless it is possible for us to make tentative guesses. It is clear from this verse, and also from 1 Timothy 4:14, that it had been given to Timothy when Paul and the elders had laid their hands upon him. That is, to say, it was given him at his ordination. It was, therefore, what we might call an ordination gift; a gift related to his ministry. Paul may, indeed, be referring to the ministry itself, through which by the laying on of hands Timothy had been commissioned – for the ministry undoubtedly is a charisma, a gift of God.

Or it may be the gift of an evangelist, which Paul later urges Timothy to do, and so fulfil his ministry (4:5). Or, since the apostle proceeds at once to refer to the Holy Spirit, the gift may be a special anointing or enduement of the Spirit at his ordination, to equip him for his work. Perhaps we can best sum it up in the words of Alfred Plummer, that this gift is 'the authority and power to be a minister of Christ.' At all events, we learn that a man is not only what he owes to his parents and his friends and his teachers, but he is what God has made him by calling him to some particular ministry and by endowing him with appropriate natural and spiritual gifts.

That brings me to the fourth influence on Timothy –

(d) Personal Discipline

All God's gifts, whether natural or spiritual, need to be developed and used. Indeed they carry with them that responsibility. So Paul tells Timothy not to neglect his gift (1 Tim. 4:14), but rather to kindle it, as we have it here in verse 6. 'I remind you to rekindle the gift that is in you.' The gift here is likened to a fire, and the Greek verb, *anazopureo*, which is unique in the New Testament, does not necessarily imply that Timothy has let the fire die down, and that he must now fan the dying embers into flame again. No; it could equally well be exhortation that he should continue to fan the fire. 'Stir up that inner fire' (Phillips). 'Keep it in full flame' (Abbott Smith, in his Lexicon), presumably by exercising it faithfully, and by waiting upon God in prayer for its constant renewal. Because the Spirit that God has given us is not 'a spirit of timidity' – so that you do not need to be shy of exercising your gift – 'but . . . of power and love and self-control' (v7). Of power, so that we may be bold and effective in the exercise of our ministry; of love, so that we may use God's authority and power in serving other people, and not in self-assertion and in vain-glory; and of self-control, that we may use God's gift with seemly reverence and restraint.

Now, what have we learned from this first paragraph? I think what we have learned is this: the most striking thing about these four influences on Timothy is their combination of divine sovereignty and human responsibility. Let me put it to you like this: Timothy's mother and grandmother could teach him out of the Scriptures, and lead him toward conversion. Paul could bring him to Christ, befriend him, pray for him, write to him, exhort him. And God could give him a special gift at his ordination. But still Timothy himself must 'Stir up the gift of God that is within him.' And we must do the same. However much or little we may have received from God, either directly in natural and spiritual endowment, or indirectly through our parents and friends and teachers, we must still apply ourselves in active self-discipline to co-operate with the grace of God, and to fan the inner fire into flame. Otherwise we shall never be the men and women God wants us to be, and we shall never be able to fulfil the ministry to which He may be calling us.

That brings us to verse 8. Paul now turns from the complex factors that have contributed to the making of Timothy, to *the truth of the Gospel*, and to Timothy's responsibility in relation to it. 'Do not be ashamed . . . but take your share of suffering' for the Gospel of Christ (v8). So, not shame, but suffering, is to characterise Timothy's ministry. In other words, 'You may be young, you may be frail, you may be sick, you may be timid, you may shrink from the tasks to which God is calling you; but, listen Timothy, God has gifted you, God has moulded you into the person you are; and He has equipped you for your ministry. Now, don't be ashamed, and don't be afraid to exercise it.'

(a) 'Don't be ashamed of bearing witness to Christ' (v8). Every Christian is called to be a witness to Christ, and must be ready to be a fool for Christ's sake.

(b) 'Don't be ashamed of me, His prisoner.' Because you know, it is possible to be proud of Christ but ashamed of the people of Christ, and embarrassed to associate with them – especially if, like Paul, they are in prison.

(c) 'Take your share of suffering for the Gospel in the power of God.' The Gospel of Christ crucified is still a stumbling block and folly.

Now these are still the three main ways in which Christian people, like Timothy, are tempted to feel ashamed. We are tempted to feel ashamed of the Name of Christ, to which we are called to bear witness. We are tempted to be ashamed of the people of Christ, to whom we also belong if we belong to Christ. And we are tempted to be ashamed of the Gospel of Christ which is entrusted to us to spread. This temptation is real and strong; and we have to resist it.

Now Paul enlarges on this Gospel, the Gospel of which Timothy is not to be ashamed, and for which he must be willing to suffer. It is mentioned, you notice, in verses 8, 10, and 11. First Paul describes its main features in verses 9 and 10, what the Gospel is. Then in verses 11–14 he outlines our responsibility *vis-à-vis* the Gospel. First, God's Gospel, and then our duty.

First, *God's Gospel*. Look on to the end of verse 8: 'Take your share of suffering for the gospel in the power of God, who saved us.' Now it is impossible to speak of the Gospel without speaking of salvation in the same breath, because the Gospel is 'the power of God unto salvation.' Now some people are telling us that it is time the church stopped talking about sin and salvation. I tell you that if we have to stop talking about sin and salvation, then the church might just as well shut up shop and go into liquidation altogether, because there is no Gospel without salvation. It is the good news of salvation. 'I bring you glad tidings of great joy . . . that unto you is born this day a *Saviour* . . .' This is the Gospel. On his first missionary journey Paul called it 'the message of this salvation,' and to the Ephesians he called it 'the Gospel of your salvation.'

Well, what does Paul tell us here about salvation? He tells us three things – Its character (what salvation is); Its source (where salvation comes from); and Its ground (on what salvation rests).

(a) *Its character* – what it is. I hope all of us are clear in our minds that salvation is more than the forgiveness of sins. Salvation and forgiveness are not convertible or interchangeable terms. Salvation is bigger than forgiveness. It includes, for example, holiness. So that in verse 9 we are told that 'God, who saved us' also, and simultaneously 'called us with a holy calling.' So the 'holy calling' is an integral part of the plan of salvation. So is the immortality which Paul comes to in the next verse: 'Christ Jesus brought life and immortality to light through the Gospel.' So we may say that forgiveness and holiness and immortality are all aspects of our salvation.

Salvation is a good word; it denotes that comprehensive purpose of God by which He justifies, sanctifies, and glorifies His people: first pardoning their offences and accepting them as righteous in His sight; then progressively transforming them by His Spirit into the image of Christ, until finally they become like Christ in heaven, when they see Him as He is, and their bodies are raised incorruptible like Christ's body of glory. I long to rescue salvation from the narrow concepts to which even

Evangelical Christians sometimes reduce it. Let us not minimise the greatness of so great a salvation. Its character: what it is.

(b) *Its source* – where it comes from. If we would trace the river of salvation to its source, we have to go right back beyond conversion, beyond time, into a past eternity. Because there is a reference here, in verse 9, to God's 'own purpose and the grace which He gave us in Christ Jesus ages ago' – literally, according to the Greek, 'before eternal times.' 'Before the world began' (AV); 'Before time began' (J.B. Phillips); 'From all eternity' (NEB). It is plain, therefore, that our salvation is not due to any merit or any good works of our own, because God gave us His purpose of grace in Christ before we did any good works; before we were born and could do any good works; indeed, before history, before time, and in eternity.

Now, of course, we have to confess that this doctrine of election is difficult to finite minds; but it is incontrovertibly a Biblical doctrine, and it emphasises that salvation is due wholly to the grace of God, and not in the tiniest bit to the merit of man. Not to our works performed in time, but to God's grace in eternity. It therefore engenders humility and great gratitude, because it excludes all boasting. And nothing can bring us assurance and a sense of security like the knowledge that our salvation rests in God's own purpose of grace.

Its character: what it is. Its source: where it comes from. And –

(c) *Its ground* – on what it rests. It rests on the historical work of Christ at His appearing (v10). This purpose of grace that God gave us in Christ in eternity, He has manifested in time through the appearing of our Saviour Jesus Christ. And what did Christ do when He appeared and manifested God's eternal purpose of grace? Well, He 'abolished death,' and He 'brought life and immortality to light through the Gospel.'

First, He 'abolished death.' How glorious that is! I hope we all believe it. Death summarises our human predicament as a result of sin, for death is the wages of sin (Rom. 6: 23), the grim penalty that sin has deserved. This is true of every form that death takes. It is true of *physical death*, the separation of the soul from the body. It is true of *spiritual death*, the separation of the soul from God. And it is true of *eternal death*, the separation of the soul and body from God for ever in hell. All three, physical, spiritual, eternal death, are due to sin: they are sin's just reward. But Jesus Christ, who dealt with sin on the cross, has therefore abolished death.

Now the Greek verb does not mean that He has *eliminated* it. As we know very well from our everyday experience, sinners are still spiritually dead through their trespasses and sins. Until God quickens them, all human beings die physically, except those who will be alive when Christ comes again. And some, alas, are going to die the second death in hell. So that death is still a reality: it has not been eliminated. But what is triumphantly asserted here is that Christ has defeated it: He has overthrown it. The Greek verb, *katargeo* means that He has rendered it ineffective, or nullified it. In 1 Corinthians 15 death is likened to a scorpion whose sting has been drawn; oh, the scorpion is still alive and active, but it has been rendered harmless, stingless. So the NEB translates this phrase here, that 'He has broken the power of death.' And the same Greek verb *katargeo* is used of the devil in Hebrews 2, and of our fallen nature in Romans 6. But neither the devil, nor our fallen nature, nor death, has been annihilated. Rather, what has happened is that by the power of Christ the tyranny of each has been broken, and in Christ we can be set free.

Physical death is no longer for the Christian believer an ogre, holding us in the bondage of fear. To die, for the Christian, is gain. It is falling asleep in Jesus, and it has been rendered so innocuous that Jesus could say of the believer, 'He shall never die.' Spiritual death has been overcome, because for believers it has given place to eternal life – communion with God here, now, and hereafter. All those in Christ will not be hurt by the second death, because they have passed out of death into life. In these ways Jesus Christ has abolished death.

Then He has brought 'life and immortality to light through the Gospel.' This is the positive counterpart. It is by His death and resurrection that He abolished death; and it is through the Gospel today that He makes it now known. He brings it to life. He reveals it. He spreads the good news.

Let me pause a moment. Let us remember who it is who is writing these words about life and death, about the abolition of death and the revelation of life. Who is it? It is one who is himself facing the imminent prospect of death. Any day now Paul will receive the sentence of death. Already the final summons to the executioner's block rings in his ears. Already he can see with his mind's eye the flash of the executioner's steel. Yet in the very face of death Paul can shout defiantly, 'Jesus Christ has abolished death!' I tell you, this is Christian faith triumphant; this is magnificent! How one longs for the Christian church to recover this lost certainty of the victory of Jesus Christ! How I long for the church to declare this good news to a world for whom death is the great unmentionable! How I long for the church to write as an epitaph for Christian believers, not a dismal 'R.I.P.' – 'May he rest in peace' – or its Latin equivalent; but a glorious 'C.A.D.' – 'Christ abolished death' – or its Latin equivalent.

Now such is the salvation of Jesus Christ offered us in the Gospel: its character is man's re-creation and transformation into the image of Christ; its source, God's eternal purpose of grace; its ground, Christ's historical appearing and abolition of death. And the *sweep* of God's purpose of grace is majestic indeed, from the past eternity through an historical outworking in Christ, to a future destiny when we are with Christ and like Christ in a future eternity. Is it not truly wonderful that the apostle Paul, whose body is confined within the narrow compass of a little underground cell, with its stench and its darkness, and this little hole in the ceiling for light and air – although his body is here confined, his mind and his heart can soar into eternity. And this is what the Gospel does to you if only you lay hold of it. So much for God's Gospel.

Now *our duty in relation to it*, in verse 11 to the end. There is a threefold duty that Paul here mentions.

(a) We are to *communicate* it. If the life and immortality that Christ won are revealed through the Gospel (v10), then we had better preach it. Is not that the logic? So verse 11: 'For this Gospel I was appointed a preacher and apostle and teacher.' The apostles formulated the Gospel; preachers proclaim it like heralds; teachers instruct people in it systematically. Now there are no apostles of Christ today. The Gospel was formulated by the apostles, and it has now been bequeathed by them to the church in the New Testament. The Gospel is found in its definitive form in the New Testament, and this apostolic New Testament faith is regulative for the church of every age and every place. There is no other Gospel but the New Testament Gospel, and there can be no other Christianity but New Testament Christianity. This is the apostolic faith. The apostles formulated the Gospel; they bequeathed it to the church.

But although there are no apostles of Christ today, there are preachers and teachers, men and women who are called to devote themselves to preaching – and, indeed, every Christian is a witness. So that is the first duty: to communicate the Gospel; to lift up our voices and not be afraid to make it known.

(b) Our second duty is to *suffer for the* Gospel. 'And therefore I suffer as I do. But I am not ashamed' (v12). Now why do you have to suffer for the Gospel? What is there about the Gospel that men hate and oppose, and on account of which those who preach it have to suffer? Surely the answer is this, that God saves sinners in virtue of His own purpose and grace, and not in virtue of any merit and goodness of their own. And it is the undeserved freeness of the Gospel which offends. Natural man hates to have to admit the gravity of his sin and guilt, his helplessness to save himself, the indispensable necessity of God's grace and of Christ's sin-bearing death to save him; and therefore his inescapable indebtedness to the cross. The natural man hates it. This is the stumbling-block of the cross; and there are many preachers who succumb to the temptation to mute it. They preach man and his merit, instead of Christ and His cross. And why? They do it in order to escape persecution for the cross of Christ.

No man can preach Christ crucified faithfully, and escape opposition and persecution. When I was a student at Cambridge University God taught me the hatred of the human heart for the Gospel in a very dramatic way. I was speaking in my rooms to a young man, a fellow-student, and I was trying to explain the Gospel of the free gift of God in Christ. I shall never forget how he shouted at the top of his voice, three times: 'Horrible, horrible, horrible!' God gave me at that moment a little insight into the human heart. The human heart hates the

Gospel because it is free, and it cannot be deserved. That is why we are called to suffer for it.

We are called to communicate it. We are called to suffer for it. And –

(c) We are called to *guard* it. 'Follow the pattern of the sound words which you have heard from me, in the faith and love . . . in Christ Jesus; guard the truth that has been entrusted to you by the Holy Spirit who dwells within us' (vv13–14). You see, a double command to guard the Gospel. The Gospel is called in verse 13, 'the pattern of sound words.' Sound words are healthy words; they have been given to Timothy by Paul in a certain pattern, in a certain outline or prototype; and this Timothy was to follow. He was to hold it fast. 'Follow the pattern of the sound words that you have heard from me.'

Then the Gospel is called the 'good deposit' (v14). The AV phrase, 'that good thing which was committed unto thee,' translates the Greek expression 'the good deposit.' And the RSV explains that it is the truth that has been entrusted to you; the Gospel has been deposited with Timothy. So the Gospel, the pattern of sound words, is a treasure; a good, noble, beautiful, precious treasure, first deposited by God with Paul, and now deposited by Paul with Timothy. And Timothy must guard it. It is a military verb. He must guard it as the police would guard a palace, or some treasure, to stop it from being lost, stolen, or damaged. And Timothy is the guard to the Gospel: it is a precious treasure; lest he lets it drop from his hands and loses it.

It is to be guarded all the more tenaciously (v15), because everybody in the Roman province of Asia has, Paul says, 'turned away from me.' Probably at Paul's arrest his former followers in Asia had defected. They had rejected his apostolic authority, and Timothy was left alone – except for Onesiphorus, who is the one exception in the final verses.

Now this was Timothy's heavy responsibility – to follow the pattern of the sound words that he had heard from Paul; and to guard the good deposit that he had received from Paul. And he was to do it because everybody else had defected. He must stand alone, guarding the Gospel. And so Paul goes on to reassure him. He cannot hope to guard the Gospel treasure by himself. He can only do it 'by the Holy Spirit who dwells within us' (v14). That is where verse 12 comes in. We are all familiar with the King James version: 'I know whom I have believed, and am persuaded that He is able to keep that which I have committed unto *Him* against that day.' And it is true; the Greek words could be translated like that. But literally the words mean this: 'I am persuaded that He is able to keep my *deposit* until that day,' in which the verb 'keep' and the noun 'deposit' are the same as in v14. The context therefore strongly suggests that 'my deposit' which Christ is able to keep, is not what I have committed to Him – my soul, myself – but what He has committed to me – the Gospel. In that case the sense is this: The deposit is mine because entrusted to me; but I am persuaded that although it is mine, He is able to keep it safe.

My brethren, there is tremendous comfort here. Ultimately it is God Himself who is the Guarantor of the Gospel, and will keep it safe. We look out from our Evangelical fellowship here to the wider church and world; and everywhere the Evangelical faith is spoken against, the apostolic faith of the New Testament is ridiculed; there is increasing apostasy in the church as our generation abandons the faith of its fathers. But I say to you, Do not be afraid. God will never allow the light of the Gospel to be finally extinguished. Oh, it is true He has committed it to us, frail, fallible creatures. This treasure of the Gospel is in very earthenware vessels: and we must play our part in guarding and in protecting it. Nevertheless God Himself is its final Guardian. God is going to preserve the truth He has committed to the church. We know this because we know Him in whom we have believed. And we are persuaded that He is able to keep that which He has committed to us – the Gospel.

So I conclude. The Gospel is good news of salvation, promised from eternity, secured by the historical Christ, offered today to faith. First we must communicate it, spread it abroad. Second, if we do so faithfully, we shall suffer for it. And when we suffer for it we shall be tempted to trim it, to eliminate those elements which give offence and provoke opposition. Thirdly, above all, we must guard it, keep it pure whatever the cost, and preserving it against every corruption. Guard it faithfully, spread it actively, suffer for it bravely – that is our three-fold duty *vis-à-vis* the Gospel.

2. The Charge to Suffer for the Gospel (2 Timothy 2)

At the end of 2 Timothy 1, in verse 15, the apostle reminded Timothy that all who were in the Roman province of Asia, in which Timothy was working and leading, had turned away from Paul: they had defected from his apostolic authority and message, with the one bright exception of the household of Onesiphorus. And it is in the light of this widespread defection that he begins the second chapter, 'You then, my son . . .' 'You Timothy,' in contrast to the majority, 'You are to be strong in the grace that is in Christ Jesus.'

It is a splendid exhortation. To begin with, it is a call to *be strong*. Timothy was weak and timid, and yet called to leadership in the church in the very area where Paul's authority was being repudiated. It is as if the apostle said to him, 'Now listen, Timothy. Never mind what other people think. Never mind what other people say. Never mind what other people do. Never mind how shy or weak or feeble you may feel. Be strong.'

Then he goes on, 'Be strong in *the grace* that is in Christ Jesus.' If he had simply said to Timothy, 'Be strong,' it would have been absurd indeed. You might as well tell a snail to be quick, or a horse to fly, as a weak man to be strong, or a shy man to be brave. Paul's call to fortitude is Christian, not stoical. It is not a call to Timothy to be strong in himself; to grit his teeth, to clench his fists, to set his jaw. Literally in the Greek it is a call to 'be strengthened,' and to be strengthened in the grace that is in Christ Jesus; to find his resources for service, not in his own nature, but in the grace of Jesus Christ.

Then it is a call to be strong in the grace of Christ *for the ministry to which he had been called.* 'What you have heard from me among many witnesses entrust to faithful men who will be able to teach others also' (v2). I remind you that Paul was writing this in prison for the second time, awaiting his final trial, and expecting to be condemned to death and executed. It is therefore essential for him to arrange for the preservation of the truth, and for its accurate transmission to succeeding generations.

I ask you to notice the four stages that Paul envisages here. The first stage he has already mentioned in calling the truth 'my deposit' (1:12), in the sense that it had been entrusted, or deposited with him by the Lord. Stage two is in 1:14 in which Paul, having received the truth from the Lord, now deposits it with Timothy and tells Timothy to 'guard the good deposit.' In stage three (2:2), Timothy is now to deposit it – it is the same Greek word – or entrust it to faithful men, who in the context are probably ministers of the Word, whose chief function is to teach the Word; Christian elders whose responsibility – like the Jewish elders in Old Testament days – was to preserve the tradition. Then stage four was that the men with whom Timothy was to deposit the Word, were to be competent to teach others also. Competent, because of their teaching gift and because of their integrity and faithfulness.

Now this, my brethren, is the only kind of apostolic succession which the apostles themselves envisaged. It is a succession of apostolic tradition; it is a transmission of apostolic doctrine, handed down from the apostles unchanged to each successive generation: from God to Paul, from Paul to Timothy, from Timothy to 'faithful men,' from 'faithful men' to 'others also.' This was to be the succession; and the succession was a transmission, not of authority or orders – like the laying on of hands – but a transmission of the Gospel, of the good deposit, of the apostolic faith of Scripture passed down from hand to hand like the Olympic torch.

Now that is the introduction to chapter 2. The rest of the chapter contains six metaphors illustrating various aspects of this ministry of handing down the truth to others. The first three are old favourites with those who know the Pauline epistles: the soldier, the athlete, and the farmer. They occur in various contexts, and Paul gives them a fresh turn in this chapter.

First, then, *A Dedicated Soldier* (vv3–4). 'Take your share of suffering as a good soldier of Jesus Christ. No soldier on service gets entangled in civilian pursuits, since his aim is to satisfy the one who enlisted him.' Now there are several references to the Christian soldier in the New Testament. We read about the warfare in which he is engaged; about the armour with which he is to be clothed; and about the weapons with which he is to fight. But here the good soldier of Jesus Christ is so called because he is a dedicated man, and he shows his dedication first in a willingness to suffer, and second in a willingness to concentrate.

(a) *A willingness to suffer.* 'Take your share of suffering as a good soldier of Jesus Christ.' Soldiers on active service do not expect a safe or easy time. They take hardship, risk and suffering as a matter of course, for these things are part and parcel of a soldier's calling. So, too, the Christian, if he is loyal to the Gospel, and is faithfully handing on the apostolic deposit, must expect opposition and persecution and ridicule. He must take his share of these things with his many comrades in arms, as we saw yesterday.

(b) Then he must be not only willing to suffer, but *willing to concentrate.* 'No soldier on service gets *entangled* in civilian pursuits,' or 'gets himself entangled in business,' as J.B. Phillips puts it. On the contrary, he frees himself from civilian affairs in order to give himself to his soldiering, and to satisfy his superior officer. Or, 'He must be wholly at his commanding officer's disposal' (NEB). Those of you who are old enough to remember World War II will recall that people frequently said to one another with a wry and understanding smile, 'There's a war on!' which was a watchword entirely sufficient to justify any austerity, self-denial, or abstention from innocent activities because of the current emergency. So, too, the Christian.

Now of course, living in the world, the Christian cannot possibly avoid the ordinary duties of home, at work, and in the community. Indeed, as a Christian he should be outstandingly conscientious in the fulfilment of these duties. What is forbidden to the good soldier of Jesus Christ is not all secular activities, but entanglements which, although perfectly innocent in themselves, distract him from fighting Christ's battles. So every Christian is a soldier, even timid Timothy, who, I have no doubt, shrank from the conflict. But whatever our temperament may be, we cannot escape from Christian warfare. And if we are to be good soldiers of Jesus Christ we must be dedicated men and women, committing ourselves to a life of hardship and suffering, and renouncing the entanglements of the world.

Secondly, the active Christian witness is *A Law-Abiding Athlete* (v5). Paul turns from the Roman soldier to the competitor in the Greek games. 'An athlete is not crowned unless he competes according to the rules.' That is, in no athletic contest whatever is the competitor giving a random display of strength or skill. No; every sport has its rules. Every event had its prize as well: in the Greek games they were evergreen wreaths rather than silver trophies. But no athlete, however brilliant he might be, was ever crowned – that is, ever received the evergreen wreath placed upon his head – unless he had competed according to the rules. 'No rules, no wreath,' was the order of the day. Now the Christian life is like a race, not in the sense that we are competing with one another, but in other ways: partly in the strenuous discipline of our training, partly that we lay aside every hindrance – as is mentioned in other passages of the New Testament – but here, in keeping the rules.

We are to run the Christian race, we are to live the Christian life – and the Greek adverb there is *nomimos*, according to the law, 'lawfully.' And in spite of the fashionable teaching of the new morality, in which it is said that the category of law has been altogether abolished in the Christian life, I have to say from this and many other passages of the New Testament, that the Christian is under obligation to live lawfully, to keep the rules, to obey the laws of God. He is not 'under the law' as a way of salvation; but he is 'under the law' as a guide to conduct. And there is no crown otherwise. No rules, no wreath.

That brings me to the third metaphor, which is *A Hard-Working Farmer*. 'It is the hard-working farmer who ought to have the first share of the crops' (v6). If the athlete must play fair, the farmer must work hard: he *toils*, this word means, at his farming. For hard work is indispensable to good farming, especially in developing countries before mechanisation arrives, when successful farming depends as much on sweat as on skill. However poor the soil, however inclement the weather, however disinclined the farmer may feel, he cannot afford to stay at home and be a sluggard. He must keep at his work, and having put his hand to the plough, he must not look back. But, Paul says, the first share of the harvest goes to the hard-working farmer: he deserves it. And only if he has worked hard, and perseveres in his work, can he expect a good crop.

What is the harvest that Paul is thinking about, in which we are to be hard-working farmers? There are several possible applications, and I shall only mention two.

(a) *Holiness* is a harvest. It is the harvest of the Spirit, the fruit of the Spirit; which means that the Holy Spirit is the chief Farmer. But we also have our part to play. We have to walk by the Spirit; we have to sow to the Spirit, if we would ever reap the harvest of holiness. Sowing to the Spirit refers to the discipline of the Christian life, the habits we develop, the thoughts we think, the aspirations we have, and so on. All this is sowing to the Spirit.

I find, not least in Keswick, that there are many Christians who are surprised that they are not gaining the victory over temptation, or growing in holiness of life. So let me ask you, Is it because you are a sluggard? Is it because you are not a hard-working farmer? Is it because you are neglecting to cultivate the field of your character? As Bishop Ryle says again and again in his great book called *Holiness*, 'No gains without pains.' 'It is the hard-working farmer who has the first share in the crops.'

(b) *The winning of converts* is a harvest also. 'The harvest is plenteous,' Jesus said. Now of course it is God who gives the growth, but once again we have no liberty to be idle. For both the sowing of the good seed of God's Word, and the reaping of converts, are hard work, especially when the labourers are few. I tell you that souls are hardly won; not by the slick, automatic application of a formula, but by tears and sweat and blood and toil – especially in prayer and in sacrificial Christian friendship. 'It is the hard-working farmer who has the first share in the crop.'

Here, then, are three qualities of a wholehearted Christian worker, who seeks to pass on to others the good news that has come to him; and each of these three is essential: the dedication of the soldier, the law-abiding obedience of the good athlete, and the painstaking labour of a good farmer. Without these he cannot expect results. Why should he? There is no victory for the soldier unless he gives himself to his soldiering. There is no wreath for the athlete unless he competes according to the rules. And there is no harvest for the farmer unless he toils at his farming.

Now verse 7. 'Think over what I say, for the Lord will grant you understanding in everything.' That is, if you do not understand these metaphors, meditate on them, and the Lord will help you to understand them. If Timothy was to know and understand the truth, two processes were necessary. He was to think over what Paul had written; and then the Lord would give him understanding. And both processes are necessary. I want to ask you to consider the very important implications of this combination of thinking, and the Lord giving understanding. For one thing, what Paul says is this, 'The Lord will give you understanding, Timothy, if you consider what *I* say.' What astonishing arrogance in the apostle Paul! It is a good example of Paul's self-conscious apostolic inspiration and authority. He commands Timothy to study his teaching diligently, and he promises Timothy that if he does so the Lord will grant him understanding. Paul sees nothing anomalous in claiming that his apostolic teaching both merited careful study, on the one hand, and could be interpreted only by the Lord, on the other. It is clear evidence that Paul believed his teaching to be not his own, but God's.

The second implication of this combination is this: 'That the Lord will grant you understanding if, and only

if, you consider what I say' – that is, you've got to use
your nut! For that is what so many Christians don't do!
Some Christians never get down to any serious Bible
study. All they do is to skim, in a half-hearted and desul-
tory way, through a few verses, like a butterfly, flitting
from verse to verse; instead of like a bee, sucking the nec-
tar from each flower. And they hope against hope that
perhaps the Lord will give them a bit of understanding.
I say, Why should He? It is only if you *consider* what is
written that the Lord will give you understanding.

There are other people who are very good at their
study: they are hard-working farmers, as it were. They
use their minds; they grapple with the text; they compare the versions; they study the commentaries and the
concordances; their libraries are high up to the ceiling
with ancient tomes . . . but they forget that it is only the
Lord ultimately who grants (and notice that it is a gift)
understanding in all things. So, brethren, do not let us
divorce what God has joined together. For an understanding of Scripture, a balanced combination is essential of thought and prayer; of giving our minds to the
study of God's Word, and of looking to the Lord to give
us understanding.

Now verses 8–13. So far we have really been considering a single theme. I could put it to you like this, that
nothing that is easy is ever worth while. Or I think I
ought to reverse it and say, Nothing that is worthwhile is
ever easy. No soldier, or athlete, or farmer, expects
results without labour and suffering. And now Paul continues the same theme of suffering and labouring, as a
condition of blessing. And having illustrated it from
metaphor – the soldier, the farmer, the athlete – he further enforces it from experience: the experience of Christ
(v8); the experience of himself, the apostle (vv9–10); and
the experience of all Christian believers (vv11–13).

(a) *The Experience of Christ* (v8). 'Remember Jesus Christ.' Now that was a funny thing for Paul to tell Timothy to do. How on earth could Timothy ever forget Jesus Christ? Why was it necessary for Paul to urge Timothy to remember Him? Well, I think essentially because Jesus Christ is the Gospel. 'Remember Jesus Christ according to my Gospel.' Jesus Christ is the heart and soul of the Gospel, of the good deposit which Timothy was to commit to faithful men, and faithful men to others also. So if Timothy was to guard the deposit and the communicate it to others, he must remember Jesus Christ.

But as we meditate on these two expressions, it is remarkable how full an account of the Gospel they give. 'Remember Jesus Christ, risen from the dead, and of the seed of David.' Strange expressions: but when you meditate on them you will find that there are references here to the birth, death, resurrection, and ascension of Christ. The four great saving acts of Jesus are all brought together in the compass of these two little expressions.

'Of the seed of David . . .' How was He descended from David? By His birth. 'Risen from the dead . . .' He could not rise if He had not died; so He died, and rose again. And what is the point of saying that He was 'the seed of David'? Because He had ascended David's throne. When did He ascend David's throne? When He ascended into Heaven, and sat down upon His throne. So here in these little phrases we have an implied reference to the birth, death, resurrection, and ascension of Jesus. You also have references to His humanity: 'Of the seed of David,' and to His Divinity: because He was demonstrated 'the Son of God with power by the resurrection from the dead.' His humanity and divinity are in these two little phrases: and so in His saving work. He is a Saviour because He died and rose again. And He is our

Lord and King because He is seated upon David's throne. How much there is compressed within these little phrases: 'Remember Jesus Christ, risen from the dead, and of the seed of David.'

There is another reason why Timothy must 'remember Jesus Christ, risen from the dead, and of the seed of David,' and that is that Christ's own experience illustrates the principle that death is the gateway to life, and suffering the pathway to glory. For who is it who rose again? He who died. Who is it who is reigning upon David's throne? He who was born in lowliness, of David's seed. So both phrases emphasise the truth, whichever way you interpret the couplet, that humiliation is the way to exaltation. 'He who humbles himself shall be exalted'; and that is a great truth. 'So, Timothy, when you are tempted to avoid pain and humiliation and suffering in your ministry, remember Jesus Christ; and think again.' So that is the experience of Christ.

(b) *The Experience of Paul* (vv9–10). 'The Gospel for which I am suffering and wearing fetters, like a criminal. But the Word of God is not fettered. Therefore I endure everything for the sake of the elect, that they also may obtain the salvation which in Christ Jesus goes with eternal glory.' Paul was suffering for the Gospel. He was having to endure the painful humiliation of wearing fetters in prison, like a common criminal. But though he was chained, the Word of God was not chained. He could still write letters, and he could still preach to anybody who visited him in prison. But the relation between Paul's sufferings and the effectiveness of the Gospel is not just the contrast: 'I am chained; the Gospel isn't!' I want you to notice this very carefully: it is actually a relation of cause and effect. 'Therefore I endure in order that the elect may obtain salvation' (v10).

Now this is an amazing truth, that in some sense the salvation of others was being secured by Paul's sufferings. 'I endure suffering in order that *they* may be saved.' Not, of course, that our suffering in any sense has any redemptive efficacy, like the sin-bearing suffering of Christ. But rather, that the elect are saved through the Gospel; and you cannot preach the Gospel without suffering for it. Therefore there is a very real sense in which suffering, if we are suffering for the Gospel, is contributing to the salvation of others who are saved through the Gospel for which we suffer.

So there is the experience of Christ, and the experience of Paul. And –

(c) *The Common Christian Experience*. 'The saying is sure . . .' He quotes a common current Christian proverb of some kind:

> If we have died with Him, we shall also live with Him;
> if we endure, we shall also reign with Him;
> if we deny Him, He will also deny us;
> if we are faithless, He remains faithful –
> for He cannot deny Himself.

Now here are two pairs of epigrams. The first pair concerns those who remain true and endure. The second pair is about those who are false, or faithless. Now the first pair tell us that the Christian life is a life of dying and enduring; and if we share Christ's death – and only then – we shall share His life. And if we share Christ's sufferings and endure – and only then – we shall share His reign, because the road to life is death, and the road to glory is suffering. And this is the experience, not only of Christ, but of every Christian, Paul says.

Then at the end of verse 12 and verse 13, he comes to the dreadful possibility of our denying Christ and proving faithless. 'If we deny Him, He will deny us' – as He said He would in Matthew 10:33. 'And if we are faithless, He remains faithful' – and in the context I believe, with a number of commentators, that this means that He will be faithful, not only to His promises, but also to His threats. That if we deny Him, He will deny us: and if He did not deny us in His faithfulness, He would deny Himself; but He *cannot* deny Himself.

Now let us conclude the first part of the chapter. We have really only learned one main lesson. From secular analogy (soldiers, farmers, and athletes), and from spiritual experience (Christ's, Paul's, and every Christian's), we have learned this lesson: Blessing comes through pain; fruit through toil; life through death; and glory through suffering. And so, why should we *expect* our Christian life and service to be easy? The Bible never gives us any such expectation. Rather the reverse: the Bible says again and again, No cross, no crown; no rules, no wreath; no pains, no gains. It is this principle which took Christ through lowly birth and suffering death, to His resurrection and His reign in heaven. It is this principle that brought Paul his chains, and his prison cell, in order that the elect might obtain salvation in Jesus Christ. It is this principle which makes the soldier willing to endure hardship, the athlete discipline, the farmer toil. I beg you, Do not expect Christian service to be easy.

Now we come to the second part of the chapter, and to three more metaphors about the Christian worker. Verse 15, A workman who does not need to be ashamed; verse 21, A vessel for noble use; verse 24, The Lord's servant. The active Christian is the Lord's workman, the Lord's vessel, and the Lord's servant. And what characteristic is expected of each? Well, the fourth metaphor is – *The Unashamed Workman* (vv14–19). We will leave aside verse 14 for the moment, and come on to verse 15. 'Do your best to present yourself to God as one approved, a workman who has no need to be ashamed, rightly handling the Word of truth.' Now it is evident from this verse that the kind of work that the Christian workman does is teaching; 'handling the Word of truth.' It is also clear that there are two kinds of teacher: those who are approved – who having been tested, pass the test; and those who are not approved. There are those who ought to be ashamed of themselves, and there are those who have no need to be ashamed of themselves. It is also clear that the difference between these two types of workmen concerns their handling, or their treatment, of the Word of truth.

So Paul sets the two in contrast with one another. Timothy, in verse 15, is to be a good workman, approved and not ashamed. But Hymenaeus and Philetus, in verse 17, on the other hand, are bad workmen who have forfeited the approval of God, and have every reason to be ashamed of themselves. And the work of these workmen in relation to the truth – the good workmen and the bad workmen – is summed up in two pregnant verbs. The good workman 'cuts the Word of truth straight' (v15). But the bad workman 'Swerves, or deviates from it' (v18). Let us look at these two.

The good workman 'cuts straight the Word of truth' (v15). The Greek word *orthotomeo* does not mean 'to divide rightly,' which is the AV translation. It means literally, 'to cut it straight.' It is a very unusual word: it occurs only three times in Biblical Greek, twice in the Greek Old Testament, in the book of Proverbs, and here. For example, it comes in the Greek version of Proverbs 3:6, 'He will *make straight* your paths.' Or Proverbs 11:5, 'The righteousness of the blameless *keeps his way straight.*' So the Word of truth, the Scripture, is likened to a road, or a path, which is to be cut straight – straight as a motorway – across the countryside. The Arndt-Gringrich *Lexicon* puts it like this: 'It is to cut a path in a straight direction, or to cut a road across country that is forested or otherwise difficult to pass through, and to cut it in a straight direction, so that the traveller may go directly to his destination.' No hairpin bends; no corners that you have to negotiate, but a straight path.

Or possibly the metaphor might be taken from ploughing, rather than from road-making; so that the NEB translates it, 'driving a straight furrow, in your proclamation of the truth.' What does it mean? Surely it is obvious what it means. The Word of truth is Scripture, the apostolic faith which God had given to Paul, and Paul had passed to Timothy. Now Timothy was to 'cut it straight,' to make it a straight path; he was to be accurate on the one hand, and plain and simple on the other, in his exposition. The good workman is true to Scripture: he does not falsify it; and he handles Scripture with such care that he stays on the path himself, keeping to the highway and avoiding the byways; and he makes it easy for people to follow. It is not a tortuous exposition, which leads people astray; it is a straight path which even a fool can follow.

Now the second metaphor describes the bad workman. It is taken not from civil engineering – road-making; nor from agriculture – ploughing; but from archery – shooting arrows. And here the truth is likened, not to a road that is being built, or a furrow that is being ploughed, but to a target that is being shot at. So the verb in verse 18, people who 'swerve' from the truth, is the verb *astocheo*, which means to miss the mark, from *stochos*, a target. When you miss the mark you deviate from the target. It comes three times in the pastoral epistles. This, then, is the alternative put before every Christian minister, every missionary, every parent instructing his or her children, every Bible class teacher, Sunday-school teacher, handling the Word of truth. The alternative is this, That as you shoot at the target you either hit it or miss it; and as you cut the road you either make it straight or crooked. As a result, other people will be affected for better or for worse. If you cut the road straight, then other people will be able to follow; but if, when you are shooting at the target, you miss the mark and the arrow goes off . . . You know what happens if ever you have been to an archery contest: the eyes of everybody else go off the target, following the arrow. And that is what happens when there are false teachers in the church. The rest of the church is misled, swerving and deviating from the truth.

Now of this danger Paul warns Timothy here, because there were people in Asia teaching serious error; and instead of preaching Jesus Christ risen from the dead (v8), the pledge of His own people's resurrection, they said (v18), 'the resurrection is past already.' They were probably denying the resurrection because they were gnostics; they believed that matter was evil, and they could not contemplate a resurrection of the body. So they were spiritualising the resurrection as a kind of release from the flesh, through *gnosis*, knowledge, as other people in the church today are de-mythologising the resurrection. They substituted for the Word of truth what Paul calls in verse 14 'word strife,' and in verse 16, 'godless chatter.' And there is much 'godless chatter,' I can tell you, in the church today. There are a great many godless chatterboxes! And Paul urges Timothy, and through him the Ephesian church, to avoid them both, and to concentrate on teaching the truth and cutting like a straight road.

The fifth metaphor is the Christian worker as *The Clean Vessel* (vv20–22). The picture here is fairly clear, that in every house there are vessels or utensils; and that in a large house these are many and varied. Some, perhaps made of gold and silver, are for noble use, the personal use of the master or mistress of the house. Then there are wooden and earthenware and cheap vessels, for menial use in the kitchen and scullery. So in God's house, the church, there are true and false members. There are Timothys on the one hand, and Hymenaeuses and Philetuses on the other. And it is only the true, who prove their reality by their purity, who are fit for the Master's use. This surely is the Christian's greatest desire: to be a vessel for noble use, set apart, ready for any good work, and fit for the Master's use.

Paul now applies this to Timothy, and every Christian. 'The essential condition on which Jesus Christ will make use of you,' he says, is 'if anyone purifies himself from what is ignoble' (v21, RSV). Now the AV is 'from these' – and that literally translates the Greek expression. And 'these' must mean 'vessels for ignoble use,' but I want humbly to urge you to be cautious in your interpretation. I know that this verse is used by some Christians as a justification for separating from all those in the visible church with whom they do not agree. I want to suggest to you that the context indicates a different application. For these verses are introduced by the phrase in verse 19, 'Let everyone who names the Name of Christ depart from evil,' and it is followed in verse 22 by, 'shun youthful passions.' In other words, Timothy is to purify himself from all evil, in himself, and from all evil associations insofar as they exercise a corrupting influence on him. It is moral rather than doctrinal purity which is here in view. At all events, the essential condition of usefulness is *to be clean*.

So he goes on. I want you to notice the negative and the positive counterparts in v22: 'Shun youthful passions, and aim at righteousness, love, and peace . . .'

These are very important: 'Shun youthful passions: aim at these moral qualities.' Now these two verbs, to shun and to aim at, are placed in striking contrast. To shun (*pheugo*, the Greek word) means literally 'to seek safety in flight,' to escape, or to run away. It is sometimes used literally of flight from physical danger, like Moses fleeing from Pharaoh in the Midian desert; of the holy family fleeing from Herod's wrath; of the hireling who sees the wolf coming and takes to his heels and runs. So figuratively it is used of flight from spiritual danger. Sinners are urged to flee from the wrath to come; and Christians are urged to flee from idolatry, from immorality, from the spirit of materialism and the love of money – and here, 'from youthful lusts.' We are to resist the devil, that he will flee from us: but we are also to flee from anything we know to be wrong. We are to recognise sin as something dangerous to the soul. We are not to negotiate with it, not to come to terms with it; we are not even to dilly-dally, or linger in its presence. We are to get as far away from it, as quickly as possible. Like Joseph when Potiphar's wife attempted to seduce him, we are to take to our heels and *run*.

And, by the way, youthful passions are not just sexual lust. There are many other youthful passions, like self-will, and sinful ambition, and so on; and from all these things we are to run. Then the opposite is to aim at – and if the Greek word *pheugo* means 'to run away from,' the Greek word *dioko* means 'to run after, to pursue, to chase'; it is used of chasing people in warfare and in hunting – and we are to chase these moral qualities.

Now let us get it clear, as we put these two together, that the Christian is urged to run away from spiritual danger, and to run after spiritual good; to flee from the one in order to escape it, and to pursue the other in order to attain it. And this is the consistent, reiterated teaching of Scripture, that we are to deny ourselves and follow Christ; that we are to put off everything that belongs to the old life, and put on what belongs to the new; that we are to mortify our members on the earth, and to set our minds on things in heaven; that we are to crucify the flesh and walk by the Spirit. There is no other way to become holy. This is the only way to become a fit vessel for noble use, so that the Master is able to make use of us. Indeed, there is a plain promise here: 'If anyone purifies himself from what is ignoble, he shall be a vessel unto honour, fit for the Master's use.' Lay hold of that promise, *if* you fulfil the condition.

That brings us to the sixth and the last metaphor: *The Lord's Servant* (vv23–26). Now in verse 23 the apostle reverts to the wordy debates of verse 14, and the godless chatter of verse 16, and this time he calls them 'stupid, senseless controversies.' Now do not misunderstand this: this is not a command to avoid all controversy. When the truth of the Gospel is at stake, Paul himself was an ardent controversialist; and he urges Timothy and Titus to be the same. Jesus Christ was a controversialist as well. He engaged in debate with the religious leaders of the day. Sometimes we are obliged, however much we may shrink from it, to come forth and do battle in controversy, for the sake of the truth.

What is to be avoided is controversy for controversy's sake: hair-splitting; an argumentative preoccupation with trivialities; these wordy debates – this is what we are to avoid, because they breed quarrels. And 'the Lord's servant must not be quarrelsome but kindly . . . an apt teacher, forbearing (or tolerant)' (v24); and 'correcting – or instructing – his opponents with gentleness' (v25). So that the only demeanour that is fitting in the Lord's servant is gentleness. The servant of the Lord portrayed in Isaiah 42:3 is so gentle that 'a bruised reed He will not break, and a dimly burning wick He will not quench.' And the Lord Jesus – the Lord's Servant *par excellence* – described Himself as gentle and lowly in heart. So the Lord's servant, even when engaged in controversy, is kindly and forebearing and gentle. Then, and only then, if he adorns his Christian teaching with a Christian character, it may be that God will 'grant' – notice that it is a gift – that his opponents will 'repent and come to know the truth' (v25), and so 'escape from the snare of the devil, after being captured by him to do his will' (v26).

There are different interpretations here: I have not time to go into the alternatives. I take the *AV* and the *ASV* that the 'escaping from him' and 'to do his will' both refer to the devil. If so, then this verse allows us to peep behind the scenes of every Christian evangelistic and teaching ministry. Behind the scenes, invisible to men on the stage, and invisible to the audience, a spiritual conflict is in progress; and the devil's grim activity is graphically described. He is likened to a hunter who captures his quarry alive in some clever snare: 'That they may escape from the snare of the devil, after being captured by him.' You see, he is a hunter, capturing his quarry in a snare. But he also drugs or inebriates them; because the Greek verb for 'to escape from the snare of the devil' literally means 'to be restored to sobriety' after a period of diabolical intoxication. And from the captivity of the devil, in which men are both snared and doped, only God can rescue them, by giving them repentance and the knowledge of the truth. And God does it, not only when the Lord's servants instruct their opponents, but when they avoid as much quarrelling as they can, and instruct their opponents with *gentleness*.

So we conclude. Here is a clarion call to Christian workers, to all those who have received the commission, as it were, not only to receive the deposit of the Gospel from Scripture, but to spread it into the lives of others. We are to be good soldiers, good athletes, good farmers, utterly dedicated in our work. We are to be unashamed workmen, accurate and clear in our exposition. We are to be vessels for noble use, righteous in our character and conduct. And we are to be the Lord's servants, gentle in our demeanour. Or, if you like alliteration: We are to be committed in our labouring, clear in our teaching, clean in our living, and courteous in our speaking.

Only so can we be of use. Only if we give ourselves without reserve to soldiering, farming, running, can we expect results. Only if we cut the truth straight and do not swerve from it, can we be approved unto God and have no need to be ashamed. Only if we purify ourselves from everything that is ignoble, shall we be vessels for noble use, useful to the Master of the house. And only if we are gentle and not quarrelsome, may God grant to our opponents repentance and a knowledge of the truth. Such is our Christian responsibility, to suffer and labour for the Gospel.

Brethren, if I may bring you back to where we started: no wonder Paul begins his chapter: 'My son; be strong in the grace that is in Christ Jesus.'

3. The Charge to Continue in the Gospel
(2 Timothy 3)

We called the first chapter of 2 Timothy, The Charge to Guard the Gospel; the second chapter, The Charge to Suffer for the Gospel, and we call the third chapter, *The Charge to Continue in the Gospel*.

2 Timothy 3:1, 'Understand this, that in the last days there will come times of stress.' That is the verse that introduces this chapter, and the theme of our Bible Reading. Three introductory points need to be made, and the first concerns the phrase 'in the last days.' It may seem natural at first sight to apply this expression to some future epoch, to the days immediately preceding the end. But Biblical usage will not allow us to do this. It is the conviction of the New Testament writers that the new age, promised by the Old Testament, arrived with Jesus Christ; and that with His Coming, therefore, the old age had begun to pass away, and the last days had come.

Thus Peter on the day of Pentecost could quote Joel's prophecy that 'in the last days' God would pour out His Spirit; and Peter declared that this prophecy relating to the last days had been fulfilled. This, he said, on the day of Pentecost, is what the prophet Joel is referring to. So the last days to which the prophecy referred, had come. Or again, if you look at Hebrews 1:1, we are told that 'God, who in many ways and parts, and at many times, in time past spoke through the prophets to the fathers, has in *these last days* spoken unto us by His Son.'

So we are living in the last days, and what follows in 2 Timothy 3 is a description of the present, not of the future. It is a description of the whole period that elaps-es between the first and second advents of Christ. It is a description of what is sometimes called 'the inter-adven-tual period' in which you and I are living. So that is the first thing: the last days are these days.

Secondly, in these last days there will be perilous times. What we are to know about these last days in which we live, is not that they will be uniformly and con-sistently perilous; but that they will include perilous sea-sons, or, as the RSV has it, 'times of stress.' And church his-tory has amply confirmed the truth of this. The Greek word for 'perilous,' or as it is translated, 'stress,' is the adjective *chalepos*, which literally means 'difficult' or 'hard,' either hard to bear, of any kind of pain, physical or mental; or hard to deal with, because dangerous or men-acing. The word is used of a raging sea, and of wild ani-mals; and the only other New Testament occurrence of the word is of the Gadarene demoniac, who was so fierce – it is the same word – that nobody could pass that way.

So the Christian church in these last days between the two advents of Christ, is to expect periods both painful and perilous. That is the second thing. Thirdly, the rea-son for these painful and perilous times is because 'men will be . . .' this, that and the other (v2). It is important, then, to grasp that it is *men* who are responsible for the menacing seasons which the church has to endure; fallen men, evil men, whose nature is perverted, who are self-centred, whose mind is hostile to God and His law, and who spread evil, heresy, and dead religion in the church.

The rest of the opening paragraph (vv2–9) is devoted to a portrayal of these bad men who are responsible for the perilous seasons through which the church has to pass. The paragraph tells us: something about their con-duct; something about their religion; and something about their proselytising zeal.

(a) *Their Moral Conduct* – or perhaps I should say, their immoral conduct. For in the next verses (vv2–4) nineteen expressions are used with which to describe them. It would, I think, be a little tedious if we were to examine each of these words separately and in detail. But I want to ask you to notice the first and the last. The first says that they will be 'lovers of self,' and the last, at the end of verse 4 says they are not what they should be: 'lovers of God.' It is very interesting that four of the nineteen words are compounded with love, suggesting that what is fundamentally wrong with these people is that their love is misdirected. They are lovers of self, lovers of money, lovers of pleasure, instead of – first and foremost – lovers of God. And in between these four expressions, these four love-words, come fifteen others which are almost entirely descriptive of a breakdown of men's relations with one another.

The first three enlarge on self-love. 'Men will be proud, arrogant, abusive,' so full of themselves in their arrogance that they are scornful and abusive of other people. The next five, from the middle of verse 2, seem to refer to family life, and especially the attitude of young people to their parents. In the Greek form these five words are all negative, seeming to stress the tragic absence of qualities which nature alone would lead you to expect. Thus they are disobedient to their parents, when Scripture says that children – at least during their minority – are to honour and obey their parents. Next they are ungrateful, devoid of elementary gratitude. Next they are unholy, and the word is used in classical Greek sometimes to denote a lack of filial respect, the respect that boys and girls, young people, should have toward their parents.

Next inhuman, which J.B. Phillips translates, 'utterly lacking in normal human affections.' And then fifthly, implacable – or, as the Greek word means, 'irreconcil-able,' that is, that these young people are so completely in revolt that they are not even willing to come to the conference table to negotiate. Now the relationship of children to their parents should, according to Scripture, be marked by obedience, gratitude, respect, affection, and reasonableness; but in perilous seasons all five are lacking.

The remaining seven words are wider than the family. 'Slanderers' – that means backbiters, or scandalmongers (NEB), the sin of speaking behind other people's backs; profligates, which describes the lack of self-control; fierce, that is untamed, more like savage beasts than human beings; haters of good, or 'strangers to all good-ness' (NEB); treacherous, a word that is used in Luke of the traitor Judas; reckless, whether in word or deed; and swollen with conceit – that is, bumptious! And so we return, at the end of the list, with the basic evil with which it began, namely pride.

Now all this unsocial and anti-social behaviour, this disobedient, ungrateful, disrespectful, inhuman behav-iour toward our parents; this backbiting, this absence of restraint and gentleness and loyalty and prudence – mark you, all this is the inevitable consequence of a god-less self-centredness. God's order throughout Scripture is that we love the Lord our God first, with all our heart and soul and mind and strength; then we love our neigh-bour as ourself. So God's order is that we put Him first, neighbour next, and self last. But if you reverse the order of the first and third, putting self where God ought to be, and God where self ought to be, being a lover of self instead of a lover of God, your neighbour in the middle is bound to suffer.

That is what all these nineteen words tell us. The root of the trouble in perilous seasons is that we are lovers of

self instead of lovers of God: 'utterly self-centred' (J.B.
Phillips). And only the Gospel offers a radical solution to
this problem, because the Gospel offers a new birth, a
new creation, involving being turned inside-out and
upside-down. Conversion is a change from self to un-
self; it is a real reorientation of heart and mind and life.
Conversion makes us fundamentally God-centred,
instead of fundamentally self-centred. And when conversion has reversed the first and the last, putting self
where it ought to be, at the end, and God where He
ought to be, at the beginning, then we begin to love our
neighbour as ourself. We begin to love the world that
God loves, and we seek to give and to serve like God. So
much, then, for their moral conduct.

(b) *Their Religious Observance.* It may come as a shock
to us to discover that people like this, lacking the common decencies of civilised society, let alone of God's
laws, could also be religious. But it is true: look at verse
5. These people he has been describing, 'hold the form of
religion but deny its power.' And I fear that in the long
history of mankind religion and morality have been
more often divorced than married. Like the inhabitants
of Judah and Israel in the seventh and eighth centuries
BC whom the prophets castigated; and like the Pharisees
in our Lord's day, whom He condemned, these men in
the apostle Paul's day and in our day, preserve an outward form of religion, but are strangers to its reality and
moral power. That is, they put on their Sunday best to go
to church; they sing the hymns, say Amen to the prayers,
and put their money in the offering plate; they look and
sound egregiously pious. But it is form without power; it
is outward show without inward reality; piety without
sincerity; religion without morals; faith without works.
No wonder the apostle says to Timothy, 'Avoid such
people.'

Not that we are to avoid all contact with sinners, for Jesus Himself was the Friend of publicans and sinners; and if we were to avoid contact with sinners, as Paul says in I Corinthians 5?, we should have to go out of the world altogether. But rather, that in the church – for this is a description of religious sinners – what the Book of Common Prayer calls 'open and notorious evil livers' are to be disciplined and rebuked, and if they remain unrepentant, to be excommunicated.

(c) *Their Proselytising Zeal.* It is surely astonishing to discover that the kind of people Paul is describing, 'filled with godless self-love and malice' includes not only those who profess religion, but some who actively propagate it. Yet this also is true, 'for among them are those who make their way into households and capture weak women burdened with sins and swayed by various impulses, who will listen to anybody and can never arrive at a knowledge of the truth' (vv6–7). Their proselytising zeal is likened to, and portrayed as, a military operation, for the word 'to capture' means to take captive in warfare; but the method of these people was not direct and open, but furtive, secretive and cunning. They were sneaks, using, no doubt, the back door rather than the front. These tradesmen of heresy insinuated themselves into private homes; choosing a time when the menfolk were out – presumably at work – they concentrated their attention on weak women. And as Bishop Ellicott says, 'This expedient is as old as the fall of man,' because it was Eve, you remember, that the devil tempted first, rather than Adam.

The weakness of these so-called weak women here was double. They were morally weak, 'burdened with sins and swayed by various impulses,' and they were intellectually weak, unstable, credulous and gullible, so that they would listen to anybody, and were unable, mark you, to arrive at settled convictions. Now I do not want the ladies to be up in arms: the apostle Paul is not describing *all* women, you understand! He is describing certain weak women, who are weak in character and weak in mind; and it is upon them that these religious salesmen concentrate. Weak in character, weak in intellect, they are an easy prey to door-to-door religious tradesmen.

As an example of this kind of thing Paul mentions Jannes and Jambres (v8), the names – according to Jewish tradition; they do not come in Scripture but appear in one of the Jewish Targuns in Exodus 7:11 – the names of the two chief magicians in Pharaoh's court. Notice what Paul says about them. It is very interesting and important. He says, 'As Jannes and Jambres opposed Moses, so these men . . .' the heretics he is talking about, the false teachers '. . . oppose the truth' (v8).

What is remarkable about this analogy is not just that the false Asian teachers are likened to the Egyptian magicians, but that Paul likens himself to Moses. For Moses was the greatest figure of the Old Testament. No prophet arose like Moses in Israel either before or since, in his knowledge of God; for the Lord knew him face to face, and spoke to him as a man speaks unto his friend. Nonetheless, despite this uniqueness of Moses, Paul does not hesitate to put himself on a level with Moses, as one who spoke and taught God's truth. For Jannes and Jambres opposed the law of Moses, and the false teachers in Asia were opposing the Gospel of Paul. But whether it was the law or the Gospel, whether it was the teaching of Moses or the teaching of Paul, it was God's truth which these men were rejecting.

And so Paul rejects them: he says they are 'men of corrupt mind' (v8); despite their claim to *gnosis*, knowledge, they are corrupt in their mind and counterfeit – tried and found wanting – as to their faith, or as to *the* Faith, the truth (v8). Paul is confident that such men 'will not get very far' (v9). True, false teaching will spread like gangrene (2:17) for a while; but its success will be limited and temporary, because 'their folly will be plain to all' (v9) 'as the folly of Jannes and Jambres came to be evident also'.

Let us sum up what we have learned so far. I think it is plain that these dangerous seasons, through which the church has to pass, arise because in that part of God's field, the world, in which God has sown wheat, the devil has also sown tares. That is to say, the devil has his fifth column actually in the church. Now because I happen to be a member and minister in the Church of England, I quote to you from Article 26 of the Thirty-nine Articles: 'In the visible church the evil is ever mingled with the good, and sometimes the evil has chief authority in the ministration of the Word and sacraments.'

Yes, in the church, within the visible society of professing believers, are men of immoral character and conduct, of purely external religiosity, of corrupt mind and counterfeit faith. They are lovers of self, of money and pleasure, rather than lovers of God and their fellows. They retain a false form of godliness, but deny its power. They oppose the truth, and seek to win weak women to their pernicious views. That is, morally, intellectually, and religiously, they are perverse. Would you not agree with me that this is a remarkably apt portrayal of the permissive society in which we live, which genially tolerates every conceivable deviation from Christian standards of righteousness and truth?

Now, what was Timothy to do in a situation like that? Let me begin my answer by saying that I am reading from the RSV – and I thank God for the RSV: I have used almost nothing else in my own study since it was first published. And very, very seldom do I want to disagree with the RSV: but I do now – and in particular with the next word, in verse 10, which is so feeble in the RSV: 'Now you . . .' It should be, 'But you . . .' Well, it is not a very big difference, you may say; but it is an important one. And if you look on to verse 14 you will see that the RSV is right there, and says, 'But as for you . . .' Now in the Greek they are the same word; and twice, you see, in verses 10 and 14, Paul says to Timothy, 'But you, Timothy, are to be different.' In other words, Timothy was not to catch the prevailing infection. He was not to be carried away by the tide. In contrast to these men who had been described in the early part of the chapter, Timothy was to be totally different.

Now, my friends, every Christian is called to be different from the world. Indeed, if you do not like the word 'holy' because it sounds too pious to you, try the word 'different.' It is exactly what the word 'holy' means. Somebody who is holy is somebody who is different. He is set apart from the world unto God: his standards are not worldly but godly. He is different. The Christian is called, not to be like a reed shaken with the wind, feebly bowing down before it, from whatever direction it may blow. There are hundreds, even thousands, of people in the church like that today; when the wind blows from the north they bow down to the south; and when the wind veers round to the south they bow down to the north. Whatever the prevailing theological or moral fashion is, they succumb to it. They are reeds shaken with the wind. I do not deny that the pressures to conform put upon us in our generation are colossal; and I have every sympathy, particularly with young people who are carried away with the prevailing stream, because the current is so strong.

The pressures that come – we heard about them last night from Canon Cragg as he expounded what the apostle John means by the world; physical pressure, intellectual pressure, moral pressure, just exactly the same, not only from the direct challenge today to traditional views and standards of Christianity, but the pressure from this insidious, pervasive atmosphere of secularism that comes into our homes through television and the mass media of communication that infiltrates the church. And there are many people who give in to it, sometimes not realising what they are doing. But again and again the Word of God tells us not to be moved: as Christians we ought not to be like a reed shaken with the wind, but like a rock in a mountain torrent, that stands immoveable against the pressure. As J.B. Phillips translates Romans 12:2, 'Don't let the world squeeze you into its own mould.'

Now let us come to the details. What is Paul's challenge to Timothy? In what sense is he to be different? Well, look again at verses 10 and 14, and then at the details surrounding these verses. In verse 10 Paul reminds Timothy what Timothy has been doing thus far. 'But you' – in contrast to these evil men and false teachers – 'you have been observing my teaching.' That is what Timothy has been doing in the past. Then verse 14: 'But as for you, continue' – in the future – 'in what you have learned,' and been persuaded about in the past. So ver-ses 10–13 describe Timothy's past loyalty to the apostle Paul, while verses 14–17 urge him to remain loyal in the future. And the two main verbs sum up the gist of the section: '*you have followed*' faithfully thus far (v10); now '*continue* in what you have learned' (v14). The charge to continue in the Gospel.

Let us look first at the past (vv10–13). Verse 10, 'You have observed . . .' The Greek is, 'you have *followed* my teaching, my conduct, my aim in life, my faith, my patience, my love, my steadfastness, my persecutions,

my sufferings.' Timothy's position is explained in terms
of a certain 'following.' The Greek verb literally is used
of following a person as he goes somewhere. A friend
walks out of the tent, and you follow him. It is used in
that way: just simply following somebody who walks
ahead of you. Figuratively it is used, if I may quote from
a Greek lexicon, of 'to follow faithfully, or to follow as a
rule'; and it is used in this sense in 1 Timothy 4: 6, 'The
good doctrine which you have followed.'

So what this means is that Timothy has been a loyal
disciple of Paul. Timothy has taken the pains to grasp the
apostle Paul's teaching, and he had made it his own. He
had also observed the apostle's manner of life, and had
sought to imitate it. So in his mind, in what he believed;
and in his conduct, in how he behaved, Timothy had
been and was Paul's faithful follower: 'You have followed, step by step' (NEB). The contrast, therefore,
between Timothy and the false teachers of the first paragraph, is pretty obvious and glaring. For those evil men
were portrayed as following their own inclinations. They
were lovers of self, lovers of money, lovers of pleasure,
following their own evil inclinations. But Timothy has
followed an altogether different standard. He has not followed himself: he has followed the teaching and the
example of Christ's apostle, Paul.

And so Paul lists the characteristics of his life, in contrast to the self-lovers in verses 2–5. Notice, then, the
emphatic pronouns. These evil men he has been describing, *they* are this, they are that, they are the other. But *you*,
in contrast to *them*, have followed *my* teaching, *my* conduct, *my* this, *my* that. You see, 'let them do what they
want to do, but you, Timothy, are to follow me.' That is the
contrast in these paragraphs, and surely it is very striking.

Somebody may say, 'But why this list of Paul's virtues,
and Paul's sufferings? Is it not more than a little conceited?

It is all right, perhaps, for Paul to mention his teaching that Timothy followed: but why go on to blow his own trumpet about his virtues and his sufferings? Isn't it a little unseemly for the apostle Paul to boast like this?' No, it is not. What Paul is doing is to supply two objective evidences for the genuineness of his teaching, namely the life he lived and the sufferings he endured. When you come to think of it, these are good tests of the sincerity, and indeed the truth of a person's teaching: that is, whether what he believes and teaches sanctifies his behaviour on the one hand, and whether he is prepared to suffer for it on the other. And Paul did both. Thus verse 10: 'You have followed my teaching; and not only my teaching, but my manner of life and my aim in life . . .' No cult of meaninglessness for the apostle: he had an aim in life: '. . . my faith, my patience, my love . . .' note, my love – my love for God and man, not for myself and for pleasure and money: '. . . and my steadfastness.' That is my conduct.

Then his sufferings: verse 11, where he says, 'You have seen … my persecutions, my sufferings, what befell me at Antioch, at Iconium, and at Lystra' – Galatian cities – 'what persecutions I endured.' Timothy himself had been a citizen of Lystra, and had no doubt witnessed with his own eyes that dramatic occasion when Paul had been stoned by an infuriated mob, had been dragged out of the city and left in the gutter for dead. 'But even from this,' Paul says, 'the Lord rescued me.' He goes on in verses 12–13 to show that his experience of persecution was not unique. Everybody who through union with Christ aims at godliness, will be persecuted by the world. The godly always arouse the antagonism of the worldly. It has always been so, and it always will be so. Why? Well, because 'evil men and imposters will go on from bad to worse . . .' (v13).

So let us recapitulate this paragraph. Timothy is seen here to stand out like a rock in a mountain torrent; to stand out in contrast to the prevailing fashions in the church and in the world of evil-doers and false teachers. Why? Well, because he has taken Paul as his guide. He has followed the teaching of the apostle Paul; and he has been right to do so, because Paul's teaching has been confirmed and guaranteed by his godly life and his many persecutions.

Now we turn from the past (vv10–13) to the future (vv14–17). Once again Paul begins the paragraph, 'But as for you' . . . distinguishing Timothy from the evil men and the imposters of verse 13. 'They go on . . .' (v13), notice that, they go on, but it is a strange kind of progress, because their advance is 'from bad to worse.' Timothy is to abide. He is not to go *on*; he is not to advance: he is to abide in what he has learned and what he has believed. Now this kind of summons – to continue, or to abide, or to stay put, and to hold fast to the teaching of the apostles – this kind of summons is not infrequently heard in the New Testament. It is specially relevant in these days when innovators arise in the church, who claim to be advanced and progressive thinkers, radicals who reject everything that is traditional in the church.

This kind of exhortation and summons was never more needed than it is today, when men actually boast of inventing a so-called 'new' Christianity, with a 'new' theology and a 'new' morality, and even boast that they are inaugurating a new reformation. We may perhaps be forgiven if, borrowing some words of Jesus, we say to them that 'No one, after tasting old wine, desires new, for he says, The old is better.' And so here in verse 14, Timothy abides: that is, Timothy has learned certain things from Paul; he has come firmly to believe them. Now he must abide, he must continue in what he has learned and come firmly to believe; and he must let no one shift him from his ground.

Having issued that summons to abide in what he has learned and come to believe, Paul goes on to give two reasons. The first is, 'knowing from whom you learnt them,' and the second is, 'From a child you have known the holy Scriptures.' Let us look at these two reasons for Christian stability – abiding in what we have learned and come to believe.

First, 'knowing from whom you have learnt them.' That is, 'Timothy, you must abide in what you have learned because you know from whom you learnt it.' Who is that 'whom'? Well, there are alternative readings here in the Greek manuscripts; some manuscripts have the singular 'from whom,' as if the 'whom' is one person; and some have a plural 'whom' as if it is several people. Now if it is singular, which is a well-attested reading – though perhaps not quite so strong as the other – the reference will be to Paul only: 'Knowing from whom you have learned it, namely from me.' If it is plural, then probably it refers to his grandmother and his mother, as well as Paul.

But I suggest to you that the context seems to place the emphasis on what Timothy has learned from Paul. That is why I believe that the singular is the correct reading. That is what he stressed, you remember, in 1:13, 'Follow the pattern of the sound word that you heard *from me.*' This is what he said in 2:2, 'What you have heard from *me* among many witnesses, entrust to faithful men.' This is what he has just said in verse 10, 'Now, Timothy, you have followed *my* teaching.' So surely, in the context of the epistle it is reasonable to accept the singular reading. That is 'Timothy, you are to abide in what you have learned and come firmly to believe, knowing that you have learned it from me.'

And who is 'me'? Well, 'an apostle of Jesus Christ by the will of God' (1:1). That is the 'me'; it is 'an apostle of

Christ Jesus by the will of God,' who has dared, a verse or two previously, to liken himself to Moses; and who claims to be teaching the truth of God; and who not only taught it, but confirmed the truth of his teaching by his godly life and his constant persecution.

It is the same today. Paul's Gospel is still authenticated to us by his apostolic authority, by who he was, uniquely commissioned by Jesus Christ and inspired by the Holy Spirit. By his apostolic authority, his consistent godliness; and his many sufferings bravely borne.

So that is the first reason. And the second reason: 'And that from a child you have known the holy Scriptures' (v15). Timothy had been taught the holy Scriptures – the Old Testament Scriptures, that is – from his childhood, doubtless by his mother and his grandmother. He was therefore extremely familiar with them, and he believed them to be inspired by God, as Paul is about to say. And so Timothy must abide in what he has learned, not only because he knows he has learned it from Paul, but also because it was consistent with the Old Testament Scriptures.

The same two grounds apply today. The Gospel in which we are to continue is the Biblical Gospel: it is the Gospel of the Old Testament, and of the New Testament. It is vouched for by the prophets of God and by the apostles of Christ. And we intend, by the grace of God, to abide in it, for these two very good reasons; because of this double authentication.

Now notice what we may learn from these verses about *Scripture*. (The end of verse 15 on to verse 17.) And two absolutely fundamental truths about Scripture are taught in these verses: Its origin – where it comes from; and its purpose – what it is meant for.

(a) *Its Origin*. 'All Scripture is given by inspiration of God' (v16). Probably most of us know that those five words, 'given by inspiration of God,' translate one word in the Greek, the word *theopneustos*, which literally translated is 'God-breathed.' 'All Scripture is God-breathed.' That does not mean that Scripture, or its human authors, were breathed *into* by God, but that Scripture was breathed *out* by God. 'God-breathed' – issuing out of His mouth: the Word of God.

So although 'inspiration' is a convenient term to use, *expiration*, or spiration would convey the meaning of the Greek word more accurately. It is breathed by God: God-breathed. That is why we call it the Word of God. It originated in the mind of God, and was communicated from the mouth of God, although it was spoken through human authors without destroying either their human individuality or its divine authority. But it is the Word of God, spoken from the mouth of God, conveyed by the breath of God.

This is the consistent teaching of the Bible about the Bible. And so we have the prophetic formulae: 'The Word of the Lord came unto so-and-so'; 'Hear the Word of the Lord, ye people'; 'The mouth of the Lord has spoken it.' This is absolutely reasonable, because as it is written in Isaiah 55, God says, 'My thoughts – the thoughts of my mind – are not your thoughts, neither are your ways my ways, saith the Lord. For as the heavens are higher than the earth, so are my ways higher than your ways and my thoughts than your thoughts.'

There is, in other words, a great gulf fixed between the thoughts in the mind of God, and the thoughts in the mind of men. How, then, can my little mind ever climb up into the mind of God? Why, I cannot even read your thoughts, and you certainly cannot read mine. If I stood here on the platform dumb and mum and said nothing, you would have no idea whatever of what I was thinking. I could have a poker face; I could be thinking about anything under the sun, and you could not read my thoughts. But as a matter of fact you can read my thoughts at the moment: you know exactly what I am thinking because I am conveying the thoughts of my mind by the words of my mouth. And the words of my mouth are communicating to you at this moment the thoughts in my mind.

So that if communication between a human mind and another human mind is by speech, how much more must this be true between the divine mind and human minds. I can never read what is in the mind of God unless He speaks. And thank God He has spoken in a succession of prophets and apostles, and supremely in Jesus Christ, the Word made flesh. God has spoken, and we know His mind and His thoughts because He has spoken them in His Word. 'All Scripture is God-breathed': the thoughts of His mind expressed in the words of His mouth, and conveyed by the breath of His mouth through human authors, without destroying their individuality or its, the Scripture's, divine authority.

So much for its origin: it is God-breathed.

(b) *Its Purpose*: it is profitable. 'All Scripture is given by inspiration of God, and is profitable . . .' And it is profitable for men only because it has been breathed by God. Only its divine inspiration secures and explains its human value and profit. And what is its profit? Well, go back to verse 15 for a moment: 'It is able to make us wise unto salvation.' The Bible is a book of salvation, and not primarily a book of science. Its purpose in the providence of God is not to teach scientific facts which men can discover by their own empirical investigation, such as the precise nature of moon rock, or moon dust! It is to teach moral and spiritual truths, which space exploration or any other kind of scientific exploration could never discover; but which can only be known by divine revelation.

For example, that although he is a noble creature made in the image of God, man is a guilty sinner under the judgment of God; and that God loves him despite his rebellion, and has from eternity planned his salvation; and that Christ died, bearing his sin, guilt, curse, and judgment in His own body, and rose again; and that the sinner can be saved if he trusts in Jesus Christ. I tell you, the astronauts are not going to discover that on the moon! These things cannot be discovered by scientific investigation; these are moral and spiritual truths that can only be discovered in Scripture, where God in His grace has revealed them.

Now, since the Bible is a guide book to salvation, it focuses on Jesus Christ the Saviour. The Bible is full of Christ. It makes us wise unto salvation through faith in Christ Jesus. So the Old Testament foretells and fore-shadows Him. The Gospels tell the story of His birth, life, death, and resurrection. The Acts describe how through His apostles the good news of His salvation spread, and His church began to be established. The epistles display the full glory of Jesus in His divine-human person and work. And the Revelation portrays Jesus Christ sharing the throne of God, and promises His final victory. The Bible is full of Christ. Wherever you go you see Christ. As the ancient writers used to say, Just as in England every motorway – except that there weren't in the ancient writers' day – every motorway and road and highway and country lane and footpath, linking on to other roads and country lanes and roads, ultimately leads you to London: so in the Bible every verse, every paragraph, every chapter, every book, linking on to others, will ultimately lead you to Christ.

The Bible is a book of salvation. So Evangelicals are not Bibliolators: that is, we do not worship the Bible. We worship the Christ of the Bible. But just as lovers treasure the letters and photographs of their sweet-hearts, not for themselves – although when nobody is looking he might kiss her photograph, but it is a poor substitute for kissing her: but he loves her photographs because they speak to him of her – so the Christian loves the Bible, not for itself, but because it speaks to us of Christ.

The Scriptures are 'able to make you wise unto salvation.' Then they are profitable in the Christian life. They are profitable for 'teaching the truth and refuting error, or for reformation of manners and discipline in right living' (v16, NEB). That is, if you want to overcome error and grow in the truth; if you want to overcome evil and grow in holiness, it is to the Bible that you must supremely turn. Because the Bible is profitable for these things, in order that – and this is God's ultimate purpose in Scripture – 'the man of God may be complete, thorougly equipped for good works.'

So this chapter is a message for our lax, pluralist, permissive society. These times in which we are living are very distressing. Sometimes I wonder if both the church and the world have gone mad, so strange are their views and so low their standards; and some people are being swept from their moorings by the floodtide of sin and error. Others go into hiding into their little Christian ghettos, as offering the only hope of survival, the only alternative to surrender. Yet neither of these is the Christian way. Paul says, 'Let these evil men live in self-indulgence and propagate their lies: but as for you, Timothy – the difference! – never mind if you are young and timid and sensitive and shy, never mind what other people think and say and do, never mind if everybody else turns away, never mind if you find yourself alone in your Biblical witness. You have followed my teaching thus far: now, Timothy, continue: abide: don't fall away:

don't advance beyond it. The Scripture is God-breathed and profitable; it can make you wise unto salvation; and above all, even in the midst of these grievous times, it can make you complete. The Word of God makes a man of God, so abide in it; continue in it, and it will lead you on to Christian maturity'.

4. The Charge to Proclaim the Gospel (2 Timothy 4)

The words we are to study together in 2 Timothy 4, The Charge to Preach the Gospel, are some of the very last words which the apostle Paul wrote: they are certainly the last words which have survived. He is writing within weeks, perhaps even within days, of his martyrdom; and according to tradition he was beheaded on the Ossian way.

For thirty years without intermission, Paul had laboured as an itinerant evangelist or missionary, and an apostle of Jesus Christ. As he tells us in this chapter, he has fought a good fight; he has finished his course; he has kept the Faith. And now he awaits his reward, the crown of righteousness that is laid up for him in heaven. These words therefore are Paul's legacy to the church: they breathe an atmosphere of great solemnity, and it is, I think, impossible to read them without being profoundly stirred. They take the form of a solemn charge to Timothy – a charge which, in a secondary way, is equally applicable to us today. 'I charge you . . .' (v1). And although it is addressed in the first instance to Timothy, Paul's delegate, it is applicable to every man called to the ministry – and in a further sense to every Christian who is a witness to Jesus Christ. I bring you three aspects of this charge.

First, *The Nature of the Apostolic Charge*. 'I charge you . . . preach the Word' (vv1,2). Notice that the message we are called upon to proclaim is a word – *the* Word, God's Word, which God has spoken. It is equivalent to '*the* sound teaching' in verse 3, or '*the* truth' in verse 4, or '*the* faith' in verse 7. And it is the same as *'the* deposit' of chapter 1, that we considered on Monday morning.

This word, this truth, this sound teaching, consists of the Old Testament Scriptures, God-breathed and profitable, which Timothy had known since his childhood. It consists also of the teaching of the apostles, now enshrined in the New Testament, which Timothy had heard and learned, and come firmly to believe; and which Paul had entrusted to him to guard and to teach. So the message that we are to preach is not our own invention. It is a word, a message that God has spoken, and that He has now committed to the church as a sacred trust or treasure. And our calling is to preach it – to speak to others what God has spoken to us: or rather, what He spoke to the prophets and to the apostles, and which they have bequeathed to us, their successors, as it were, in the church.

So our responsibility is not just to hear the Word, to believe it and to obey it; not just to guard it, preserving it from every false implication; nor even just to suffer for it and to continue in it – but to *preach* it, because it is the good news of salvation to sinners. We are to proclaim it, the Greek word implies, like a herald in the market place. We are to lift up our voices without fear or favour, and boldly to make it known.

What are the details of this preaching to which we are called? Notice that Paul goes on to tell Timothy how he is to preach the Word; and he gives four characteristics for preaching –

(a) It is to be *urgent*: 'Preach the Word, be urgent in season and out of season . . .' J.B. Phillips, 'Never lose your sense of urgency.' In other words, it is no use preaching in a listless and lackadaisical way. All true preaching, whether it is from a pulpit or a platform, or even Christian witness from one person to another, has a

note of urgency about it. For the Christian herald knows
that he is handling matters of life and death: the sinner's
plight under the judgment of God; the love of God who
gave His Son to die for us; and the summons to repent
and believe.

Do you know this quotation from Richard Baxter's
book, *The Reformed Pastor?* He says, 'How few preachers
preach with all their might. Some ministers preach so
softly that weeping sinners cannot hear. The blow falls so
lightly that the hard-hearted cannot feel it. Sirs, you cannot break men's hearts by jesting with them, or patching
up a gaudy oration. Men will not cast away their dearest
pleasures upon the drowsy request of one who seemeth
not to mean as he speaks, or to care much whether he be
heard. Let us therefore rouse up ourselves to the work of
the Lord, and preach as for life and death, seeking to
save sinners, pulling them out of the fire.' The RSV, 'Be
urgent in season and out of season.' NEB, 'Press it home
on all occasions, convenient or inconvenient.'

Let us interpret that cautiously. This phrase, 'in season
and out of season,' is not to be taken as an excuse for that
insensitive rashness which has often characterized our
evangelism and brought it into disrepute. We have no
liberty to barge unceremoniously into other people's privacy, or to tread clumsily on to other people's corns. No;
the occasions 'convenient or inconvenient' are convenient or inconvenient *for the speaker*, rather than for the
hearers. So that the margin of the NEB puts it, 'Be on duty
at all times, convenient or inconvenient.' So what we are
given here is not a Biblical warrant for rudeness, but a
Biblical appeal against laziness, which is a very different
thing. So there is the first characteristic of our preaching:
urgent.

(b) *Relevant*. 'Convince, rebuke, and exhort.' These are
three different ways of preaching the Word. God's Word

speaks to men in different conditions, and it can be applied to them in different ways. As the NEB puts it, 'Use argument, reproof, and appeal.' There are some people who are full of doubts, and they need to be convinced by argument. There are some people who are full of sin, and they need to be rebuked for their sin. There are others who are full of fear, and they need to be exhorted and encouraged. God's Word does all this, and more. We need to preach it relevantly, according to the people's need.

(c) Our preaching is to be *patient*. Paul goes on, 'Be unfailing in patience.' So that although we are to be urgent, longing for the people's ready response to the Word, we are to be patient in waiting for that response. We are never to use human pressure techniques, or to attempt to force or contrive a decision. Our responsibility is to be faithful; the results are the responsibility of the Holy Spirit, and we can afford to wait patiently for them. And we are to be patient in manner as well, because as we have seen, the servant of the Lord must not be quarrelsome, but kindly and forbearing and gentle. So however solemn our commission and however urgent our message, we have no excuse for a brusque or an impatient manner. Patient, and –

(d) The fourth characteristic of our preaching is *intelligence*. That is, we are to be unfailing in patience and *teaching*, or 'with all doctrine' (AV). So we are not only to preach the Word: we are to teach the Word; or rather, we are to preach it with all teaching. The proclamation of the Word, whether we are seeking to convince, to rebuke, or exhort, must be a doctrinal proclamation.

Now let me say a word to my brother ministers here. The Christian ministry, according to the News Testament, is fundamentally a teaching ministry. Candidates for the ministry are, according to Paul's letter to Titus, to be those who 'hold firm the sure Word as taught' – and they must be *didaktikos*, that is 'apt to teach.' And I want to suggest to you that in these days of universal secondary education, when tertiary education in college or university is becoming increasingly common, there is urgent need for an educated ministry; men who can preach the Word with all teaching. It is a great need in every country especially as the process of urbanization continues and standards of education rise. We ought to have a bigger burden for the intelligentsia of the world, in the universities and in the capital cities of the world. Now do not misunderstand me: I am not for one moment denigrating the heroic work of missionaries in villages and simple rural communities. I thank God for them. But have we not sometimes neglected the towns and the universities and colleges, and the intelligentsia? Paul said he was in debt and under obligation to teach 'both to the Greeks and to the barbarians, both to the wise and to the foolish.' And in our concentration on simple people, we have often neglected those among the intelligentsia. But this kind of preaching 'with all teaching' is an exacting ministry, because it involves us in serious study.

Here is Paul's charge: to preach the Word, and in the proclamation of our God-given message to be urgent, to be relevant, to be patient, and to be intelligent. In our whole ministry, urgent; in our application, relevant; in our bearing and manner, patient, and in our presentation, intelligent. That is the nature of this apostolic charge: 'Preach the Word.'

Secondly, *The Basis of the Charge*. We have already seen that Timothy was young in years, weak in physique, and timid by disposition; and we have seen that the times in which he lived were both difficult and dangerous. Now just picture him as he read this letter: do you not think he would have quailed as he read the apostle's solemn charge? Do you not think his knees would have trembled, and he would have been tempted to shrink from thus preaching the Word? I think so. And we too, in our own generation are called to a responsibility far beyond our natural capacity. So let us notice that Paul does more than issue a charge: he adds incentives, he adds arguments, upon which the charge is based. And he bids Timothy look in three directions.

(a) Timothy is to look at *the coming Christ*. 'I charge you in the presence of God and of Jesus Christ who is to judge the living and the dead, and by His appearing and His kingdom: preach the Word . . .' (v1). You notice Paul is not issuing this charge in his own name or on his own authority, but in the conscious presence of God and of His Christ. And the main thrust of verse 1 is based not so much on the presence of God, but on the coming of Christ.

Notice that the apostle at the end of his ministry still believes in the Second Coming: he has not given up his belief in the Second Coming, as some foolish commentators imagine. No, he still believes in the epiphany of Christ, the visible and personal and glorious Coming. He wrote of it in his earlier epistles, in 2 Thessalonians; and although now he knows he is going to die before it takes place, he still lives in the light of it, and he describes Christians as 'those who love Christ's appearing' (v8). He knows that Christ is going to appear. I hope we all know and believe that. And that Christ when He appears, is going to judge the world and consummate His Kingdom, or His reign.

These things – the appearing, and the judgment, and the kingdom, all of which are mentioned in verse 1 – although they are future, should be as clear and certain realities to us as they were to the apostle Paul. We should live our lives, and do our work, and maintain our witness in the light of Christ's appearing and judgment and kingdom. And in particular we should never forget that those who preach, and those who listen, will have to give an account to Christ when He appears. So that is the first argument: that anybody called to witness in a difficult situation should look at Jesus Christ who is going to appear, and judge, and consummate His kingdom. He is to look at the coming Christ.

(b) He is to look at *the contemporary scene*. 'For' – that is, you are to preach the word urgently, fervently, relevantly, because 'The time is coming when people will not endure sound teaching' (v3). Now, as at the beginning of chapter 3, so in these verses the times described are present rather than future. Timothy was to frame his ministry in relation to them; and so must we. Well, what are these times like? Paul singles out a single characteristic. He states it negatively and positively, and he says it twice. In a word it is this, that men cannot bear the truth. 'They will not endure sound teaching . . . but . . . accumulate for themselves teachers to suit their own likings.' They 'turn away from listening to the truth, and wander into myths' (vv3–4). That is, they cannot bear the truth, and they will not listen to it: instead they 'wander into myths,' and 'accumulate teachers' to suit their own fancy. And it is all to do with their ears.

Their ears are mentioned twice, in verses 3 and 4: for these people suffer from a strange pathological condition called 'itching ears.' As Bishop Ellicott says, 'it is an itch for novelty.' So they stop their ears against the truth, and they open their ears to any teacher who will relieve the itch by scratching it! And you notice that what they reject is '*the* sound teaching,' or '*the* truth.' That is what Paul calls it in these verses. What they prefer instead is 'their own likings,' or 'their own fancy' (NEB). They substitute their personal preference for God's revelation. The criterion by which they judge their teachers is not God's Word, as it ought to be, but their own subjective taste.

Now what is Timothy's reaction to this to be? You might think that this desperate situation should silence him. Surely, if men cannot bear the truth, and if they will not listen to the truth, surely the prudent thing to do is to shut-up, and to hold your peace. Paul reaches the opposite conclusion. 'As for you . . .' and for the third time he tells Timothy to be different. He said it twice, you remember, in 3:10, 14, 'But as for you . . .' and he uses exactly the same expression here again: 'But as for you, always be steady, endure suffering, do the work of an evangelist, fulfil your ministry' (v5). That is, because other people are unstable, unable to reach settled conviction, having itching ears, listening to any teacher; because everybody else is unstable, Timothy must be stable. He must be steady – 'calm and sane' (NEB). The Greek word really means 'sober' – it is the opposite of being drunk – because other people seem to have become intoxicated with heretical novelties. And in contrast with this kind of intoxication, Timothy is to be sober, stable and steady in his convictions.

Next, because people will not endure sound teaching, Timothy must be willing to endure suffering by continuing to teach it. Then because people are ignorant of the evangel, Timothy is to do the work of an evangelist. And then because people accumulate teachers to suit their own likings, Timothy is to be all the more conscientious in fulfilling his own ministry. In other words, these difficult times in which it was very hard to gain a hearing for the Gospel, were not to discourage Timothy. They were not to deter him from his ministry: still less were they to induce him to trim his message to suit his hearers, or to stop speaking. They were rather to spur him to preach the more.

And it is precisely the same for us. The harder the times, the deafer the people, the louder and clearer must be our proclamation. That is the second argument, from the contemporary scene.

And (c) Timothy is to look at *the aged apostle*, 'Paul the aged.' 'For . . . here is another reason for Timothy's faithfulness. Because I am already on the point of being sacrificed. 'The time of my departure has come . . .' (v6). Now verses 5–6 belong closely to each other. He says in verse 5, 'But you, Timothy, are to be faithful, Because I . . .' (v6) '. . . have come to the end of my ministry.' In other words, it is all the more vital for Timothy to fulfil his ministry because the apostle's was about to close. As Joshua succeeded Moses, as Solomon succeeded David, so Timothy was to succeed Paul. 'I am already on the point of being sacrificed' (v6): 'My life is being poured out on the altar' (NEB). He likens his life to a libation, a drink offering; and so imminent is his martyrdom that he speaks of the sacrifice as having already begun. Indeed, he says, 'The time of my departure is at hand,' and the Greek word for 'departure' is used of loosing a boat's mooring. It is therefore as if Paul thinks of his death, not only as the end of one life when he is sacrificing himself, but it is the beginning of a new life, for already the anchor is weighed, the ropes are slipped, and his little boat is about to set sail for another shore.

In verse 7 he looks back over the ministry of thirty years, and he describes it in three terse expressions. 'I have fought the good fight; I have finished the race; and I have kept the faith', as a faithful guardian of the Gospel, the sacred deposit, the treasure committed to my trust. So the work of preaching the Gospel is described as fighting a fight, running a race, guarding a treasure. Each involves labour, danger, and sacrifice; and Paul has been faithful in them all. Now nothing is left for him but the prize (v8), 'the garland of righteousness' given to all those who love Christ's appearing – and it is waiting for Paul just now.

Notice, before I pass on, that it is called 'a garland of righteousness.' Now *dikaiosune*, righteousness, from the pen of Paul usually means 'justification,' and it may very well mean that here, in the sense of vindication. It may be that what Paul is really saying is this: 'The Emperor Nero may in a few days' or weeks' time declare me guilty: he may condemn me to death and have me executed. But immediately the righteous Judge, Jesus, will reverse the verdict and declare me righteous.'

This, then, was Paul the aged. He has fought the fight, he has finished the race, he has kept the faith; his life is on the point of being offered, his little boat about to set sail; he is waiting for his crown. Do you not think these things will have spurred Timothy? I think so. These facts are to be Timothy's third spur to faithfulness. Our God is a God of history: 'God is working His purposes out as year succeeds to year.' He buries His workmen, but He carries on His work. The torch of the Gospel is handed down from generation to generation, and as the leaders of the former generation go, it is all the more urgent for the next generation to step forward bravely, and to take their place. Timothy's heart will have been moved by this exhortation from Paul the aged, who had led him to Christ.

Who led you to Christ? Is he growing old? The man who led me to Christ is in retirement now. We cannot for ever rest upon the leadership of the preceding generation. The day comes when we must step into their shoes, and ourselves take the lead. That day had come for Timothy. It comes to all of us in time.

And so, therefore, in view (a) of the coming of Christ to judgment; (b) of the temporary world distaste for the

Gospel; and (c) of the imminent death of the aged apostle, Paul's charge to Timothy had a note of solemn
urgency: 'Preach the Word.'

So far, then, we have considered the nature of the
charge, and the basis of the charge; and thirdly we come
to – *An Illustration from the Example of the Apostle Paul*
(vv9–22). For the apostle Paul preached the same Word
that he urged Timothy to preach; and he preached it in
court when he was on trial for his life before imperial
Rome. But before we consider this illustration of preaching the Word, let us look at the circumstances in which it
took place. From a majestic sweep and survey of the
past: 'I have fought a good fight . . .' and a confident
anticipation of the future, 'Henceforth a crown of righteousness is laid up for me,' Paul returns in thought to his
present predicament. The apostle Paul was flesh and
blood: he was a man of like passions with ours. And
although he has finished his course, and is awaiting his
trial, he is still a frail human being with ordinary human
needs. He describes his plight in prison, and in particular he expresses his loneliness.

Notice, then, these three things. (a) *He was deserted by
his friends*. It is quite true that he has friends overseas to
whom he sends greetings (v19), like Prisca and Aquila,
and the household of Onesiphorus in Ephesus. It is true
also that he sends Timothy bits of news about two other
friends, Erastus, who had stayed at Corinth, and
Trophimus, whom he had left ill at Miletus (v20). It is
true, again, that there were Christian brethren in Rome;
three men, Eubulus, Pudens, and Linus are mentioned,
and one woman, Claudia, who probably visited him
sometimes (v21). Nevertheless despite these friends at
home and overseas, Paul felt himself cut off and aban-
doned, separated from the churches he had founded,
and from the people in them, whom he knew and loved.

Further, a number of his travelling companions had for different reasons left him. Demas had 'deserted him,' the Greek word means, and gone to Thessalonica, because, instead of setting his love on Christ's future appearing, 'he is in love with this present age' (v10). Also Crescens had gone to Galatia; and Titus, who had evidently finished his job in Crete, had gone to Dalmatia; while Tychicus, 'I have sent to Ephesus' (v12) – probably carrying this letter with him, and probably going to replace Timothy during Timothy's absence. Luke alone – the beloved physician – 'is with me' (v11).

So you see, for reasons good and bad, Paul is alone at present, except for Luke, his doctor and his companion for many years. How does he react in this situation of abandonment? Well, he wants three things. First, *he wants people to keep him company*. 'Do your best, Timothy, to come soon' (v9). 'Soon, because I shan't be alive much longer.' 'Do your best to come before winter, because when the winter storms begin, navigation will be impossible, and you won't be able to come. So come soon. Come before winter!' Now, my friends, notice this: Paul, who has set his love and his hope on the coming of Christ, nevertheless desires the coming of Timothy. I sometimes meet super-spiritual people who tell me that they never feel lonely, and that the presence of Jesus is quite satisfying for them, and they do not need any human companions. I am tempted to be rather ruder to them than I usually am! I want to say to you that human friendship is part of the provision of God for human beings. It is God Himself who said, 'It is not good for man to be alone.' And it was Calvin who saw that this at least applies to more than marriage. Wonderful as is the presence of Jesus – satisfactory if you are alone, marooned on a desert island; and wonderful as is the prospect of the coming of Jesus, these are no substitutes for human friendship. 'Come soon,' Paul says, 'and bring Mark with you when you come' (v11). He wanted people to keep him company.

Next, he wanted *a cloak to keep him warm* (v13). He anticipating winter; he wanted Timothy to come before winter; he knew that when winter came in that dank, dark underground dungeon, he was going to shiver with cold if he did not have a further cloak to keep him warm. And next he wanted *books and parchments to keep him occupied* (v13); the books made of papyrus, and the parchment documents. Now we do not know what they were. Some commentators think they would have included official documents, like his certificate of Roman citizenship. Other people think they were notebooks upon which he could write – writing material. But I have no doubt that they included his Greek version of the Old Testament, his copy of the Scriptures, which he missed.

Now although later he tells us that the Lord stood by him and strengthened him; and although the Lord can stand by and strengthen us, we are not to despise the use of means. When our spirit is lonely, we need friends; when our body is cold, we need clothing; when our mind is bored, we need books. This is not unspiritual; this is human. It is the natural needs of frail and mortal men; and I like Bishop Handley Moule's phrase – and nobody could blame him for unspirituality! Bishop Handley Moule said, 'Man is never for one moment de-naturalized by grace.'

Grace does not de-naturalise you. It still leaves you a human being. So do not let us deny our humanity, or our frailty; do not let us pretend that we are greater than the apostle Paul, or that we are made of other stuff than dust. There is a rather lovely, more modern illustration of this, in William Tyndale, which several commentators mention. Let me quote from Bishop Moule: 'In 1535, immured by the persecutor of Villevord in Belgium, Tyndale wrote, not long before his fiery martyrdom, a Latin letter to the Marquis of Bergen, governor of the castle, in these terms: "I entreat your Lordship, and that by the Lord Jesus, that if I must remain here through the winter, you will bid the commissary to be so kind as to send me from the things of mine which he has, a warmer cap. I feel the cold painfully in my head. Also a warmer cloak, for the cloak which I have is very thin. He has a woollen shirt of mine, if he will send it. But most of all my Hebrew Bible, grammar, and vocabulary, that I may spend my time in that pursuit." '

So there, then is the first condition of Paul: he was deserted by his friends; and in that condition he wanted friends to keep him company, a cloak to keep him warm, and books to keep him occupied.

(b) *He was opposed by Alexander the coppersmith* (vv14–15). We do not know who this Alexander was; there is no certainty, even probability, that he was the heretic of that name mentioned in 1 Timothy 1:20, or the orator of Acts 19:33. It is more likely that he was another unknown Alexander, for the name was quite common. But he did Paul great harm, possibly because he was the informer who was responsible for Paul's second arrest and imprisonment. Paul adds that Timothy should beware of him, and that the Lord 'would requite him for his deeds.'

So he was deserted by his friends, and opposed by his enemies; and (c) *Paul was unsupported at his first trial* (vv16–18). 'At my first defence no one took my part; all deserted me.' Now this defence is probably not a reference to the first imprisonment from which he had been delivered – as a result of which he was able to go on with more preaching. The context seems to require reference to some recent event; and it must have been the first

hearing, what the Romans called the *prima actio*, the preliminary investigation before the trial proper. Now
Roman law would have permitted Paul to employ an
advocate, a barrister, and to call witnesses. But, if I may
quote Alfred Plummer's commentary, 'Of all the
Christians in Rome there was not one who would stand
at his side in court, either to speak on his behalf, or to
advise him on the conduct of his case, or to support him
by a demonstration of sympathy.'

But if ever an accused man needed help, it was now.
We are not told what the charges were that were brought
against him, but we know from Tacitus and Pliny and
other contemporary writers the kind of allegations that
were being made against Christians at that time. They
were said to be guilty of horrid crimes: of atheism,
because they eschewed the idolatry of the Roman gods
and emperor worship. They were accused of cannibal-
ism, because they talked of eating Christ's flesh and
blood. They were accused of a hatred of the human race,
because they were supposed to be disloyal to Caesar,
and partly because of their denunciation of the popular
pleasures of sin. These, perhaps, were some of the allegations made against Paul; and Paul had no one to take
his part. He stood there all alone. This, one might
humbly say, was Paul's Gethsemane, for like his Master
he was alone in his ordeal, and in his greatest hour of
need his friends forsook him and fled. 'All deserted me'
(v16). But like his Master before him, he too prayed that
it might not be charged against them. Nevertheless there
is a sense in which he was not alone. Just as Jesus, when
He was deserted, could say, 'The hour is coming, indeed
it has come, when you will be scattered, every man to his
home, and will leave me alone and yet I am not alone; for
the Father is with me,' so Paul could say that although all
deserted him, 'But the Lord stood by me and gave me

strength' (v17). And Christ's presence at his side, and inward strength, fortified him to preach the Gospel to all the Gentiles present, and led to his rescue, at least temporarily, from 'the mouth of the lion.'

There is much speculation as to the identity of 'the lion.' It could not have been the lions of the amphitheatre, for no Roman citizen was ever thrown to the lions. The early Greek commentators thought 'the lion' was a word-symbol for Nero, which is possible. Or it may be simply a figure of speech for any great peril, like death. But anyway, Paul emerges as a New Testament Daniel, for whose protection the lion's mouth was shut. Moreover, he goes on confidently, 'The Lord will rescue me . . .' not indeed from death, but '. . . from every evil (outside God's will) and save me for His heavenly kingdom (v18), because through Nero's sentence I am about to leave the earthly kingdom.'

Now let us look at this superb illustration of preaching the Word. Picture the scene, if you can. Paul is on trial for his life, deserted by his friends, opposed by his enemies, and unsupported at his first trial by any barrister or witness – all alone. Surely now he will think of himself for a change; surely now we shall see some trace of self-pity. Surely now he will defend himself and plead his own cause. But no. Still now, in grave personal danger, facing the probability of a death sentence, Paul's overmastering concern is not himself, but Christ; not to be a witness in his own defence, but a witness to Jesus Christ; not to plead his own cause, but the cause of Jesus Christ. At one of the highest tribunals of the empire, before his judges, and possibly before the Emperor Nero himself, and possibly with a large crowd of the general public present – because the trial will have been held, either in a large basilica or in the forum itself – he preached the Word. 'The Lord stood by me and gave me

strength to proclaim the Word fully, that all the Gentiles
. . .' cramming into the basilica, crowding into the forum
to listen to his trial '. . . that all the Gentiles might hear it'
(v17).

If ever there was a sermon preached 'out of season' it
was this. We do not know what he said, except that he
preached the *kerygma*, the Gospel, fully. He took the
opportunity to expound the Gospel in its fullness; the
good news of Jesus Christ incarnate, crucified, risen, triumphant, and coming again. And only because he
preached the Word fully to all the Gentiles in Rome
could he say, 'I have finished the course.'

This, then, was to be Timothy's model. In issuing a
solemn charge to Timothy to preach the Word, and to do
it urgently, in season and out of season, Paul had not
evaded the challenge himself.

So now let me conclude with a brief summary of the
message of the whole epistle, and then just a final word.
Underlying this whole letter is Paul's sustained conviction that God had spoken; that through the prophets of
the Old Testament and the apostles of the New, God had
revealed Himself and His purposes and His will; and
this unique revelation He had committed to the churches as a deposit. His Word, the truth, the faith, the sound
teaching, the pattern of sound words, the Gospel, this
was a deposit, a revealed truth committed to the church.
But now the apostle, who for thirty years has faithfully
delivered to others what he himself has received, is on
his deathbed, his active ministry over, on the point of
being sacrificed, catching this glimpse of the gleaming
steel of the executioner's sword. And so he burns with a
passion of longing that Timothy, his young but trusted
lieutenant, shall step into his shoes and carry on where
he has had to stop; and then in his own time pass on the
torch to others.

But Paul knows the problems Timothy will have to face, not only because Timothy is young and frail and shy, but because the devil hates the Gospel; and because of the contemporary opposition. And so Paul issues Timothy with this fourfold charge: to guard the Gospel, because it is a precious treasure worth guarding; to suffer for the Gospel, because it is an offence to the unbeliever; to continue in the Gospel, because it is the truth, and there is no other truth; and to proclaim the Gospel, because it is the good news of God, of salvation.

Timothy was called to be faithful in his generation. Where are the men and women who will be faithful in ours?

That brings me to the last word. Somebody might say, 'Who is sufficient for these things? The responsibility is too heavy.' May I bring you to two tiny phrases, that I have so far left out. The last verse: 'The Lord be with your spirit' (v22). 'The Lord stood by *me* and strengthened *me*. The Lord was with *me*.' Paul says, 'May the Lord be with you, Timothy, as he has been with me.' And 'grace be with you,' for without being strengthened with the grace that is in Christ Jesus, you cannot fulfil this responsibility. 'Grace be with you.'

Then the end of verse 18: 'To Him be the glory for ever and ever.' There is no better summary of Paul's life and ambition: first receiving grace from Christ, and then returning glory to Christ. From Him grace, to Him glory. In all our life and service we have no other Christian philosophy than this. May God keep us faithful.

Christ's Easy Yoke

I bring you, for our final message, some wonderfully familiar words of Jesus, in Matthew 11:28–30. There is always a danger in venturing to speak on a familiar message, lest people say, 'Well, I know all this; I have heard it all before,' and stop listening. Well, don't listen to me, but listen to this word of Christ, and perhaps there are depths to this word that we have not yet heard. Hear the word of Jesus, then: 'Come to me, all who labour and are heavy-laden, and I will give you rest. Take my yoke upon you, and learn from me; for I am gentle and lowly in heart, and you will find rest for your souls. For my yoke is easy, and my burden is light.'

Because the text is so familiar as a Gospel text, we often lose its significance for the life of Christian obedience and the life of Christian holiness. I wonder if all of us are clear that here are two invitations of Jesus, and not one only. It is, I fear, a mark of our tendency to unbalance in the Christian life that we probably know verse 28 by heart, but are not so familiar with verses 29 and 30.

The first invitation is, 'Come to me, if you are labouring and heavy laden, and I will give you rest.' The second invitation is, 'Take my yoke upon you, and learn from me.' The first is an invitation to come to Christ in order to lose our heavy burden; the second is an invitation to come to Him and to take upon us His burden and His yoke. Indeed, I hope it is plain to us that what Jesus Christ offers is a kind of exchange. He offers to take off our yoke and our burden, in order to give us His burden and His yoke instead. Further, the yoke that we lose when we come to Christ is a misfit yoke which chafes upon our back; and the burden that we lose is heavy, because we were heavy-laden. But the yoke that we gain is easy, and the burden that we gain is light.

Now there are too many Christian people who want the rest that Jesus offers, but not the yoke. They want to lose their burden, but they don't want to gain His. I invite you to notice this striking thing, that although there are two invitations of Jesus, the promise that is attached to both if you accept the invitation is precisely the same.

'Come to me, all who labour and are heavy laden, and *I will give you rest.*'

'Take my yoke upon you, and learn from me . . . *and you will find rest* for your souls.'

In other words, the rest and the refreshment that Jesus offers are due not only to the freedom that we have when we lose our burden, but to the bondage that we gain when we take His. Let us look into this: it is very important, very wonderful.

First, I ask you to notice more plainly – *The Invitation that Jesus Gives.* 'Take my yoke upon you, and learn from me.' The yoke was, and still is in developing countries, a transverse horizontal wooden bar that is laid upon the necks of oxen when they are harnessed to the plough or to a wagon. Now the thought is not that Christ and the Christian be yoked together like a couple of oxen. The thought here is that Christ is the farmer who lowers His harness and His yoke upon our necks. 'Take my yoke upon you.' Christ therefore portrays Himself here not as our yoke-fellow, as if we are simply walking together in partnership, but He portrays Himself as a teacher, and as we have just been hearing, as our Lord, who expects us to submit to His discipline. That is absolutely plain from the words that follow, 'Take my yoke upon you, and learn from me.' To take upon us the yoke of Christ is to learn from Christ. It is to accept a position of voluntary subordination to Jesus. It is to submit to Jesus as our teacher and our Lord.

Let me drive this home a little further. Jesus said on another occasion, to a group of His apostles gathered round Him, 'You call me a teacher and Lord. These are the polite courtesy titles that you give to me. You call me teacher and Lord.' And He went on, 'You are quite right; that is what I am.' In other words, these are not just courtesy titles. These bear witness to a reality. If Jesus is our teacher, then we have to submit our minds to His mind; and if Jesus Christ is our Lord, we have to submit our wills to His will. And that is precisely what it means to take upon us the yoke of Christ. Jesus Christ places His yoke upon our minds, because He instructs us what to believe. But He also places His yoke upon our will, because He commands us how to behave. And when a Christian man or woman has truly submitted himself to the yoke of Christ, then he never again presumes either to disagree with Jesus, or to disobey Jesus.

Show me a person who wanders selectively through the Gospels picking what he likes out of the teaching of Jesus, and rejecting what he doesn't like – like a gardener walking through a herbaceous border, picking a flower here and a flower there, and leaving the rest – and you show me a Christian who has never submitted to the yoke of Christ. Indeed, I would even venture to say that he is not properly converted. Nobody is truly converted who is not both intellectually and morally converted. And nobody is intellectually converted until he has brought his mind under the yoke of the mind of Christ. And nobody is morally converted who has not brought his will under the yoke of the will of Christ. This is what it means to be converted. It is to take His yoke upon us and learn from Him.

Now I ask you, Is your mind submitted to the mind of Christ, or do you disagree with some of His teaching? Is your will submitted to the will of Christ, or do you disobey some of His commands? If so, you have not come under the yoke of Christ, and the voice of Christ comes to you tonight, 'Take my yoke upon you, and learn from me.' That is the invitation Christ gives.

Secondly, I ask you to notice – *The Promise that Christ Makes*, that if you accept this invitation, 'take my yoke upon you and learn from me,' you will find rest unto your souls. Aren't they sweet and refreshing words? Why, they positively make the mouth water! This is one of the most refreshing promises of all God's exceeding great and precious promises. There are multitudes of people seeking rest for their souls. There are many who have come to Keswick for this precise purpose. You are looking for rest of soul. Where is this rest to be found? Well, partly at the cross, of course, where our burdens are lifted. The Christian takes three leaps for joy as his burden looses from off his shoulders and falls from off his back, and begins to tumble, as Bunyan described it in *Pilgrim's Progress*. That is where rest begins: at the cross, in the rest of faith, as we learn to put our whole confidence in Christ crucified and risen, and stay our minds upon God, and experience His perfect peace.

But also, when we take Christ's yoke upon us, and submit our minds to His mind and our wills to His will, and begin to learn from Him as our teacher and our Lord, in that very submission and bondage, 'you will find rest unto your souls.' This is one of the glorious paradoxes of the Christian life that so many men and women do not discover. Their true rest, the deep rest of heart and mind and soul and spirit, is not to be found in seeking escape from the yoke of Christ, but in humbly submitting to it. Here is how Dietrich Bonhoeffer expressed it in his book, *The Cost of Discipleship* – 'Only the man who follows the command of Jesus without reserve, and submits unresistingly to His yoke, finds His burden easy, and under its gentle pressure receives the power to persevere in the right way.' The command of Jesus is hard, unutterably hard, for those who try to resist it. But for those who willingly submit, the yoke is easy, and the burden is light.

Again and again Jesus Christ reverts to this paradox, in different words. He says, 'If you want to find yourself, if you want to discover your true identity, the way to find yourself is to lose yourself; for he who saves himself, holds on to himself, will not let himself go, loses himself, but whoever loses himself for my sake and the Gospel's finds himself.' It is the same paradox. Because the only way to learn to live is to die. Or again, the only way to find rest of soul is to take Christ's yoke upon you. The only way to find liberty is in bondage to Jesus Christ.

I have a burden for young people. I think I understand a little bit the widespread revolt against authority, which there is throughout the world today; all forms of authority are being challenged today – political authority, social, intellectual and moral. Anything that savours of the establishment, of ancient and unchallengeable authority, in the view of many people, must go. That is what people are saying today; this hatred of authority and of lordship. In very much modern talk, authority and freedom are set over against each other as irreconcilable opposites. It is commonly thought and said that where authority rules there is no freedom; whereas where freedom is gained, there is no longer any authority.

The Christian is obliged to say that this is a dangerously false antithesis. Christian conviction is the true freedom. Far from being incompatible with authority, freedom is actually impossible without it. The proper function of authority is not to remove or to stifle freedom, but to guarantee a true expression of it. That is certainly the teaching of the New Testament, where authority or lordship and freedom belong together. On the other hand we have the great statement we have been considering, 'Jesus Christ is Lord,' and on the other, 'Stand fast in the freedom with which Christ has made you free.' There is no other freedom, except in bondage to Jesus Christ.

I want to pursue this a little. What is freedom? Well, you know perhaps that when the soap box orator, the communist, was saying, 'When we get freedom, you will all be able to smoke cigars like that' – as a prosperous looking gentleman walked by – 'I prefer my fag,' said a heckler in the crowd! 'When we get freedom,' went on the orator, rising to his theme, 'you will all be able to drive in cars like that' – seeing some handsome Cadillac drive by. 'I prefer my bike,' said the heckler in the crowd. And the orator turned on his tormentor and said, 'When we get freedom, you will do what you are told!'

Now I want to talk to you about freedom, Christian freedom in the service of Christ. Let me bring you two statements. First, it is *in submission to the authority of Christ as teacher* that the mind finds its true freedom. For the true freedom of the mind, exercising itself as God intended, is not to disagree with God's self-revelation, but to study it and to elucidate it and to apply it and to obey it. The Christian believes in freedom of thought in the sense that no government or institution can tell a person what he must believe. But free thought which denies the facts of God's revelation, either in nature or in

Scripture, asserting, for example that the earth is flat or that Jesus Christ was only a man, is an abuse of the freedom of the mind. The glorious freedom which Christ gives to the mind when it has taken Christ's yoke upon it, and submits to His teaching, is freedom from the despair that says that life has no meaning; freedom from the shifting sands of subjectivity, in which there are no objective criteria by which to test people's opinions; and freedom from shifting theological fashion. I tell you that when the mind submits to the teaching of Christ, it is truly free.

Secondly, it is in *submission to the authority of Christ as Lord* that the *will* find its true freedom. The will is free, not when it disobeys Christ, but when it obeys Him.

A girl came to see me in London only three weeks ago, a professing Christian girl, and told me that she had just got engaged to a non-Christian man. I felt it was my duty to ask her if she knew the teaching of Christ, through his apostle Paul, that a believer is not at liberty to be unequally yoked together with an unbeliever. She said she did know that teaching. How, then, I continued, did she feel able to disregard it. 'Because I must be free to choose,' she said. 'If Jesus Christ tells me what I have got to do; if the issue is settled before I begin, I am no longer free.' I said to her, 'My dear, you have not yet learned the meaning of Christian freedom. Christian freedom, the true freedom of the Christian man and woman, is not freedom to disobey. It is freedom to obey.'

Let me give you another example from free love, so loudly proclaimed today. Free love, so called, is freedom to indulge my sexual desires when I please, where I please, and with whom I please. Well, it is a type of freedom. It is freedom from conventional morality. It is freedom from the responsible choice of one life partner, and freedom from any restriction upon my sexual desires, but promiscuity, this freedom from all sexual restraint, is actually bondage to the very passions which men claim freedom to indulge. It is not freedom at all: it is bondage. Jesus said that anybody who commits sin is a slave to sin. The freedom that Christ gives is a freedom from animal passions. True freedom is never absolute freedom to do anything that I like. It is the freedom of a person to be his true self. It is a freedom to live and behave as God meant him to live and to behave.

May I give you another example or two.

Take a train. Trains were invented, and are still constructed, to run on rails. That is their nature. And trains express themselves in fullest freedom only when they accept the restriction which their nature imposes upon them. Now if a train should develop illusions of grandeur, and if it should make a bid for freedom, saying to itself, 'I find this track so constricting. Why cannot I go off the rails? Why cannot I wander in freedom over the meadows and the valleys?' such freedom is disaster. Why? Because it is a denial of a train's true nature that has been imposed upon it by its maker.

Let me give you another example. The keyboard of a piano is made according to an accepted tonal system, with so many tones and semitones in the octave. And a pianist who wants to express himself freely, must accept the discipline which the piano keyboard imposes upon him. The greatest flights of freedom which a pianist ever experiences are not in defiance of the rules of music and the piano, but in strict submission to them. In other words, a person and a thing only expresses its full freedom when it lives according to its nature. Man is only free when he is under the yoke of Christ. That is his nature. That is how God has made him.

That brings me, in my last moments, to – *The Reasons that Christ Adds*. The invitation He gives. The promise He makes: 'If you take my yoke, you will find rest unto your soul.' The reasons He adds: 'For my yoke is easy and my burden is light,' and 'I am gentle and lowly in heart.'

First, *'My yoke is easy.'* I know that one of the major reasons why men and women resist the yoke of Christ, is that they believe it will be hard. They are afraid of it. They think it will be a misfit yoke. They think it will chafe them, and be heavy and be a burden. And Jesus says, 'Listen, my yoke is easy. It fits.' It fits for the reason I have been giving you, that it is adapted to the nature of man. God's law is not an alien thing. It is not an arbitrary thing. It is an expression of His nature adapted to our nature, because He made us in His own image. And we only learn a fully human existence when we take upon us the yoke of Christ.

I do not hesitate to say that if you submit to the yoke of Christ, you not only become Christian, you become human. This is a truly human existence. If you resist the yoke of Christ, and if you live your own freedom in disobedience, you are beginning to behave like an animal, and not like a human being. For God created human beings to live in obedience to His laws, and He has written His law upon our heart. There is a sense in which, even before we are Christians and born again, God's law is on our heart. You can read about it in Romans 2.

Not only is His yoke easy, but *Christ's character is gentle.* You know that, don't you? Jesus laid His hand in tender blessing upon little children. Jesus healed the sick. He comforted the sad. He made friends with publicans and sinners. He dealt gently with the woman taken in adultery. He died in agony for sin upon a cross because of His mercy and compassion. Can you not trust Him?

I sometimes wonder, who is this Jesus you believe in? You people who are resisting His yoke, don't you see that every time you disobey Christ, you are casting an aspersion on His character? You are saying either that His yoke is not easy, or that His character is not gentle. Is the Christ you believe in some cruel tyrant, some oppressor, some ogre? If you believe that, you are simply believing the lies of the devil; that is what the devil has been trying to make people believe from the beginning of time. He has been leading us to doubt the wisdom and the benevolence of God. But the Christ God sent is the one who said, 'I am gentle and lowly in heart. My yoke is easy.' It is the easy yoke of a gentle, gentle master. Then can you not trust Him? What are you afraid of? That is what I cannot understand.

So I conclude: the voice of Jesus echoes down the centuries, right up to tonight. Have you heard it? Listen again: 'Take my yoke upon you, and learn from me; because my yoke is easy, and my burden is light; and I am gentle and lowly in heart, and you will find rest unto your souls.'

Will you hear His voice tonight? Mind you, it is not something that you can settle for good. It is something that you have to do every day. You have to take up the cross every day. You have to take His yoke upon you every day. But you have to start somewhere. Will you start tonight? Have you a quarrel with Jesus Christ you need to settle? Is there revolt and rebellion in your heart you have to confess? Is there a resistance that has to cease? Let me say again, His yoke is easy; His burden is light. You will find rest. Let Him place His yoke upon you. Don't resist. Don't struggle. Don't be afraid. Submit. Take His yoke, and you will find rest unto your soul. His service is perfect freedom.

1972

Christ's Portrait of a Christian

A Study of the Sermon on the Mount

1. A Christian's Character (Matthew 5: 1–16)

The Sermon on the Mount is certainly the best known, although I think possibly the least heeded, part of the teaching of Jesus Christ. In this sermon He set forth His ideals for Christian discipleship. He listed the chief characteristics which are to mark the citizens of the kingdom of God. And so the Sermon on the Mount remains still today Christ's own description of Christians; or, to use more popular phraseology, it is Jesus' portrait of Jesus' people.

I do not think this is the occasion on which to discuss the authenticity of the sermon – that is, if it is a true sermon of Jesus Christ. Personally I like the suggestion made by A.B. Bruce, at the end of the last century, namely that the material in these chapters represents instruction, not of a single hour or day, but of a period of retirement. Bruce thought that Jesus may have had the disciples with Him in the hills, for what he called a 'holiday summer school': the first Palestinian Keswick Convention!

There He delivered what Augustine was the first to call our Lord's Sermon on the Mount; what A.B. Bruce calls 'The teaching on the hill.' We, too, have found a way and a path into the hills for a period of retirement, in order to be with Jesus. And I beg you, at the beginning of this first Bible Reading, to come each morning to listen to Jesus Christ; to sit at His feet like Mary in order to listen to His word, and to try to put yourself into the place of those first disciples, and imagine yourself there on the mount of beatitudes, actually hearing the Sermon on the Mount as it was first delivered.

This morning, then, our text is the first sixteen verses of chapter five, and I have entitled it 'A Christian's Character.' We shall look at the eight beatitudes which describe what a Christian ought to be like, followed by the metaphors of salt and light, which indicate the influence in the community which a Christian like that will have.

First the beatitudes: and I have three introductory points to make about them. First, *the people described*. These are not eight separate and distinct groups of Christian disciples, some meek and others merciful; some poor in spirit and others pure in heart. No, they are eight qualities of the same group, who at one and the same time are to be meek and merciful, poor in spirit and pure in heart, mourners and hungry, and so on. All these eight together form Christ's specification of what a Christian ought to be.

Second, *the qualities commended*. These are spiritual qualities. The poverty, for example, and the hunger, here mentioned in the beatitudes, do not refer to the undernourished proletariat in the world. No; they are the poor in spirit, the spiritually poor; and those who hunger and thirst after righteousness; and all the others are spiritual qualities as well.

Thirdly, *the blessings promised*. Each quality is commended, and each person who exhibits it is pronounced blessed. The Greek word *makarios* can, and does, mean 'happy'; yet that would be, I think, an unfortunate rendering, because happiness is a subjective state, whereas Jesus is making an objective judgment about these people. He is declaring what God thinks of these people, and therefore what they are: they are blessed.

The second half of each beatitude elucidates what this blessing is: they possess the kingdom of heaven; they inherit the earth; the mourners are comforted; the hungry are satisfied; they receive mercy; they receive God; they are called the sons of God; and their heavenly reward will be great. These eight blessings also belong together; just as the eight qualities describe every Christian, at least in the ideal, so the eight blessings are given to every Christian. The eight qualities together constitute the responsibilities; and the eight blessings, the privileges of being a citizen of God's kingdom. This is what the enjoyment of God's rule means, beginning now in this life, and perfected in the life to come.

These are my three introductory points. The people described are all Christian disciples – at least in the ideal. The qualities commended are spiritual qualities. And the blessing promised is an unearned, free gift. It is the gloriously comprehensive blessing of the kingdom of God, tasted now, consummated later.

So we turn to the beatitudes in great detail. Although they have been classified in various ways, I want to suggest to you that the first four describe *the Christian's relation to God*; and the second four, his *relations and duties to men*. The first, in verse 3, is 'Blessed are the poor in spirit, for theirs is the kingdom of heaven.' There is an Old Testament background to this, and from it we may easily deduce that to be poor in spirit is to acknowledge spiritual poverty, our spiritual bankruptcy in ourselves, before God. To be poor in spirit is to acknowledge that we are sinners, under the wrath of God, and deserving the judgment of God. It is to acknowledge that we have nothing to offer, nothing to plead, nothing with which to buy the favour of heaven. 'Nothing in my hand I bring,' is the language of the poor in spirit. As Calvin puts it in his commentary: 'He only who is reduced to nothing in himself, and relies on the mercy of God, is poor in spirit. To such, and only to such, the kingdom of God is given as a free gift.' It is a gift – absolutely free, and utterly undeserved; to be received humbly, like a little child.

Thus at the very beginning of the Sermon on the Mount Jesus contradicted all human judgments and all nationalistic expectations with regard to the kingdom of God. The kingdom is given to the poor, not the rich. It is given to the feeble, not the mighty. It is given to little children, humble enough to accept it, not to soldiers who want to obtain it by their own prowess. It was not the Pharisees who entered the kingdom of God, who thought that they were rich, and thanked God that they were such wonderful people. It was rather the publicans, who knew they were poor in spirit, with nothing to offer, and cried, 'God be merciful to me, a sinner.' They were poor in spirit, and to them was given the kingdom of God. The indispensable condition of receiving the kingdom is spiritual bankruptcy. Spurgeon wrote, 'The way to rise in the Kingdom is to sink in ourselves.'

Secondly, 'Blessed are those who mourn, for they shall be comforted' (v4). The mourners here are surely not those who mourn the loss of a loved one, but those who have reason to mourn the loss of their innocence and righteousness and self-respect. It is not the sorrow of bereavement, but the sorrow of repentance, to which Jesus is referring. This is the second stage of spiritual blessing. For it is one thing to be spiritually poor, and acknowledge it; it is another thing to bewail it, and to mourn over it. Confession is one thing; contrition is another.

We need, then, to observe, not least in our own day, that the Christian life is not all joy and laughter. There are some Christians today who seem to imagine that Christians have always got to be boisterous and bubbly. I don't find that in Scripture. No, there are such things as Christian tears; and too few of us ever weep them. Jesus wept over the sins of others, and over Jerusalem, and over the bitter consequence of human sin in judgment. We, too, should weep over the evil and the sorrows of the world; but we have our own sins to weep over as well. Have our sins never caused us any grief? Are we wrong in the Church of England confession in Holy Communion to say, 'We acknowledge and bewail our manifold sins and wickedness'? Was Ezra mistaken to pray and make confession, weeping and casting himself down before the house of God? I fear that we Evangelicals, by making much of grace, sometimes make light of sin. There is not enough sorrow for sin among us. There should be more godly grief of Christian penitence. Such mourners, Jesus promised, bewailing their sinfulness, will be comforted by the forgiveness of God, until that glorious day when in the final state of glory, sin is no more, and God wipes all tears from our eyes.

That brings us, thirdly, to 'Blessed are the meek, for they shall inherit the earth' (v5). What sort of gentleness is it that Jesus pronounces blessed? It is important, I think, to note that the meek come between those who mourn over their sin and those who hunger and thirst after righteousness. So surely in that context the meekness that Jesus declares blessed will have something to do with this secret. I believe Dr Lloyd-Jones is right in his classic studies in the Sermon on the Mount, that this meekness indicates our attitude to others as determined by a true estimate of ourselves. He points out with great perceptiveness that it is comparatively easy to be honest with ourselves when we are alone before God, and acknowledge that we are poor in spirit. But, he observes, 'How much more difficult it is to allow other people to say things like that about me. I instinctively resent it.' And he goes on, 'We all of us prefer to condemn ourselves, than to allow somebody else to condemn us.' Let me put it in my own words a bit more familiarly. I don't find it difficult when I go to church to call myself a miserable sinner: I can take it in my stride in the General Confession. But if I go out of church and somebody comes up to me and says, 'You're a miserable sinner!' I want to punch him on the nose. In other words, I am not prepared for other people to think of me what I have just said I am before God.

But meekness is being willing for other people to think of me what I know I am. 'Meekness', Dr. Lloyd-Jones says, 'is essentially a true view of one's self, expressing itself in attitude and conduct with respect to others.' And the meek inherit the earth.

You might have expected the opposite. You would think that meek and gentle people won't get anywhere in this hard world; everybody ignores them and tramples on them. Why, it is the tough and the overbearing who succeed in the struggle for existence! But no; the condition of our entering our spiritual inheritance in Christ is not might, it is meekness. It is the meek who inherit the earth. They don't need to boast and throw their weight about, for in Christ, the apostle Paul says, everything is yours, including the world and life and death, and the present and the future: all are yours if you are Christ's.

Fourthly, 'Blessed are those who hunger and thirst after righteousness, for they shall be satisfied.' Such spiritual hunger is a characteristic of all the citizens of the kingdom of God. Our supreme ambition as citizens of the kingdom is, not material, but spiritual. Christians are not like pagans, engrossed in the pursuit of possessions; we seek first God's rule and God's righteousness. Now this righteousness for which we hunger and thirst is both moral and social. Moral righteousness for which we hunger and thirst is the righteousness of character and conduct that pleases God. It is the righteousness that exceeds the righteousness of the scribes and Pharisees, because it is more than an external conformity to rules and regulations; it is an inner righteousness of heart and mind, and motive and character. That's moral righteousness.

But righteousness in the Bible is more than a private and personal thing. It includes social righteousness as well, seeking men's deliverance from oppression and discrimination in the community; seeking the promotion of justice in the law courts, integrity in our business dealings, and honour in our homes and family relationships. This, too – righteousness in the human community – is pleasing to our righteous God; and Christians are committed to hunger and thirst after it, because it is pleasing to God.

There is perhaps no greater secret of progress in the Christian life than a hearty and healthy appetite. Again and again Scripture addresses its promises to the hungry. God 'satisfies him who is thirsty, and the hungry He fills with good things' (Ps. 107:9).

Tell me, is jaded appetite the reason for our slow spiritual progress? Hopefully our presence at Keswick this year is a token of our spiritual hunger. And if you hunger and thirst after righteousness, Jesus says you will be satisfied. Claim that promise for yourself, until you inherit it. It is not enough to mourn over past sin, longing for forgiveness; we have to hunger for future improvement, longing for righteousness. Yet in this life our hunger will never be fully satisfied, nor our thirst fully quenched.

True, we are satisfied, as the beatitude promises; but we are satisfied only to hunger and thirst again. Beware of those Christians who claim they have attained, and who look all the time to past experiences, rather than to future developments. Hunger and thirst are perpetual characteristics of the disciples of Jesus. Not until heaven shall we 'hunger no more, neither thirst any more,' for only then will Christ our Shepherd lead us to springs of water where we shall slake our thirst.

Now we turn, in the next four beatitudes, from our attitude to God to our attitude to our fellow human beings (vv5–8). The fifth beatitude is, 'Blessed are the merciful; they shall obtain mercy' (v7). The New English Bible rendering is, 'How blessed are those who show mercy; mercy shall be shown to them.' Now Jesus does not specify what categories of people He is thinking of, to whom mercy should be shown. He gives no indication whether He is thinking of those overcome by disaster, or whether He is thinking of the hungry, the sick, and the outcast, on whom He Himself had compassion; or whether He is thinking of those who do wrong to others, in whose case justice cries for punishment, while mercy cries for forgiveness. But there was no need for Jesus to specify. Our God is a merciful God. He shows mercy to all, and the citizens of His kingdom must be merciful likewise.

Those who show mercy – and we need more mercy and compassion in the Christian church. We are sometimes very critical, very judgmental; we are sometimes more like the Pharisees in gathering up our skirts round us, and shrinking away from contact with sinful people. We don't show too much mercy for the sinful and the drop-out and the outcast. But those who show mercy, find mercy; just as those who forgive are themselves forgiven. Don't misunderstand that; this is not because we can merit mercy by mercy, or merit forgiveness by forgiveness. No, no. What Jesus means is that we can't receive the mercy and forgiveness of God unless we repent; and we cannot claim to have repented of *our* sins if we are unmerciful toward the sins of others.

Next, the sixth beatitude, 'Blessed are the pure in heart, for they shall see God' (v6). Now who do you think the pure in heart are? The popular interpretation is to regard purity of heart as an expression for inward purity, as opposed to ceremonial purity – washing hands and cups and pots, as the Pharisees did: that what Jesus wanted was not ceremonial cleanness, but purity of heart, something inward. And that is perfectly true. Yet in the context, purity of heart seems to refer in some sense to our relationships to other people. I suggest to you that the reference is primarily to sincerity. The pure in heart, in J.B. Phillips's translation, are 'the utterly sincere.' Their whole life is transparent before God and men. Their very heart – their inward being, thoughts, motives – is pure; it is unmixed with anything devious or ulterior or base. Hypocrisy and deceit are abhorrent to them. The pure in heart are without guile; yet how few of us there are who live one life, and live it in the open. Most of us wear different masks, and play different parts, according to the occasion. There are some people who weave round themselves such a tissue of lies, that they simply don't know what is real and what is make-believe.

But Jesus was pure in heart, utterly sincere, without any guile; and He calls His followers to be pure in heart as well. Only the pure in heart will see God, for only the utterly sincere can bear the dazzling vision before which all shams are burnt up.

The seventh beatitude is, 'Blessed are the peacemakers, for they shall be called sons of God' (v9). The sequence from purity of heart to peacemaking is a natural one, because openness and sincerity are an essential condition of peacemaking. Every Christian should be a peacemaker in the community. And we urgently need more peacemakers today, not least in Northern Ireland. Now peacemaking is a divine work, because peace is reconciliation, and our God is a God of peace and reconciliation. His purpose was, we are told, to 'reconcile to Himself all things . . . making peace by the blood of His cross' (Col. 1:20); 'that He might create in Himself one new man in place of the two, so making peace (Eph. 2:15).

It is not surprising, therefore, that peacemakers are called the sons of God, because they are seeking to do what their Father has done. God is the supreme peacemaker, and we who are the sons of God should follow His example, and seek to make peace ourselves. It is the devil who is a troublemaker: it is God who loves reconciliation and peace. And the fact that peacemaking is a divine institution will remind us that the words 'peace' and 'appeasement' are not synonymous: they are not the same thing. The peace which God makes is not peace at any price. To proclaim 'Peace, peace' when there is no peace is the work of the false prophet, not a Christian witness. For when God made peace, He did it at tremendous cost, at the price of the life-blood of His only Son. And we, too, may find peacemaking costly, although in lesser ways.

There is, for example, the pain of apologising to somebody we have injured, in order to make peace. Or there is the pain of rebuking somebody who has sinned against God, and waiting until he has repented before we forgive him. That, too, is painful. Then there is the pain of struggling to reconcile to each other those who are estranged and at enmity with each other. There is the pain of insisting on the necessity of repentance toward God, as we proclaim the Gospel of peace. In these and other ways peacemaking is a costly enterprise. But the sons of God are prepared to engage in it.

The eighth and last beatitude concerns the persecuted. 'Blessed are those who are persecuted for righteousness' sake, for theirs is the kingdom of heaven. Blessed are you when men revile you and persecute you and utter all kinds of evil against you falsely on my account. Rejoice and be glad, for your reward is great in heaven, for so men persecuted the prophets before you' (vv10–12). It may seem strange to pass from peacemaking to persecution; from the way of reconciliation to the experience of conflict. But the truth is that however hard we try to make peace, there are some people who refuse to live at peace with us. Not all attempts at reconciliation succeed. Indeed, there are some people who take the initiative to oppose us, to revile us, to slander us, and to persecute us.

But notice that Christ is referring to persecution 'for righteousness' sake' (v10), and 'on my account' (v11); that is, because we are followers of Christ.

Now, how are Christians to react under persecution? Answer: 'Rejoice and be glad! ' (v12). That is, we are not to retaliate, to hit back, as the non-Christian would; we are not to sulk like a child, or to lick our wounds like a dog. We are not to grin and bear it, like a stoic; still less to pretend we enjoy it, like a masochist. We are to rejoice as a Christian should rejoice, and even, according to Luke 6: 23, 'leap for joy.' So if you have never danced in your life, wait till you are persecuted!

Why should we rejoice? Well, partly because our reward will be great in heaven. We may lose everything on earth, and gain everything in heaven. Partly because our persecution will be a token of our genuineness, a certificate of authenticity, because 'so men persecuted the prophets who were before you' – we shall be in a good succession if we are persecuted; and partly because we are enduring it, Jesus said, 'on my account,' because of our loyalty to Christ, and Christ's standards of truth and righteousness, and it is a privilege to suffer for Jesus.

Now notice that this is a beatitude like the others, so that the state of being slandered and persecuted is as much a normal mark of Christian discipleship as being pure in heart or merciful. Christ said so; the apostles Peter and John said so; and Paul as well. So let's be ready. Let us not be surprised if persecution increases; let us rather be surprised if it doesn't. Let us remember the corresponding 'Woe' in Luke's version of this teaching: 'Woe to you when all men speak well of you.' For this was the treatment which the false prophets received.

Now let us look back at the eight beatitudes. Here is a comprehensive portrait of the Christian; Jesus' portrait of Jesus' people. Can we see ourselves in this portrait? We see the Christian first alone on his knees before God, acknowledging his spiritual poverty: he is a bankrupt, with nothing to offer; mourning and bewailing his sin. Meek as well, because he is willing for other people to think he is what he says to God he is. And then hungering and thirsting after righteousness; longing to improve, to grow in grace and in goodness. And in the next four beatitudes we see the Christian with others, out in the human community. He is not insulated from the world's sorrows; he is not harsh in himself; he is merciful, compassionate toward others. He is pure in heart: open, transparent, sincere. He plays a constructive role in the community as a peacemaker, even when he is not thanked for his pains, and is opposed, slandered, insulted, persecuted, by those who reject Christ.

Such is the man who is truly blessed. He has the approval of God, and he finds self-fulfilment, the blessing of God upon his life. Yet in all this the values and the standards of Jesus are totally at variance with the values and standards of the world. Why, the world judges the rich blessed, not the poor, both spiritually and materially. The world judges blessed the happy-go-lucky and the carefree, not those who take evil seriously, and mourn over it. The world judges the strong and the brash to be blessed, not the meek; the full, not the hungry; those who mind their own business, not those who meddle in other men's matters and occupy their time in do-goodery. The world counts blessed those who attain their ends, even if necessary by devious means, not the pure in heart, who refuse ever to compromise their integrity. The world judges blessed those who are secure and popular, and live at ease; not those who have to endure persecution. But Jesus challenges the standards of the world, and He requires different standards from the citizens of His kingdom. In a word, Jesus congratulates those whom the world most pities. He calls the world's rejects blessed.

Now we turn from the beatitudes to the two metaphors of salt and the light (vv13–16). If the beatitudes describe the essential character of the citizens of the kingdom of God, the salt and light metaphors indicate their influence for good in the community. Now, just saying that ought to bring us up sharp. Influence, did you say? What possible influence could the people described in the beatitudes exert in this tough, harsh world? What lasting good can the poor and meek and mourners do, and those who try to make peace and not war? Wouldn't they be simply overwhelmed by the floodtide of evil? What can they accomplish whose only pattern is an appetite for righteousness, and whose only weapons are mercy and purity of heart? Aren't they too feeble to accomplish anything, especially if they are a small minority in the world?

Now if anybody is tempted to think like that, that is worldliness; that is adopting the standards and the outlook of the world, for evidently Jesus was of an entirely different opinion. He said that although the world may persecute the church, the church is called to serve the world; and, incredible as it may sound, Jesus called this little handful of Palestinian peasants who had gathered round Him – these illiterate peasants – the 'salt of the earth' and 'the light of the world.' Why, it's tremendous, isn't it? How can such feeble people accomplish anything in the world? But Jesus believed they could, and He said so. And I want just now to look at these two domestic metaphors.

Every home, our own included, however poor, uses both salt and light. The boy Jesus in His Nazareth home must often have watched His mother use salt in the kitchen, and light the lamps when the sun went down. Salt and light are essential household commodities: light to dispel the darkness of the night; and salt – especially in the days before refrigerators – for preservative purposes, to keep the meat wholesome, and to prevent decay.

Now let us notice that what is common to both metaphors is that there is an essential distinction between two communities: the church and the world; that on the one hand there is what Jesus calls 'the earth,' and on the other there is 'you who are the earth's salt.' On the one hand there is what He calls 'the world,' and on the other there is a community He calls 'you who are the light of the world.' Here are two distinct communities; and the metaphors tell us something about both communities. They tell us that the world is a dark place, with little or no light of its own; and it manifests a constant tendency to deteriorate or putrefy. The world cannot stop itself from going bad. The church, on the other hand, Jesus' people, the followers of Christ, are set in the world with a double role to fulfil: as salt they are to arrest, or at least to hinder the process of, social decay; and as light they are to illumine the darkness.

Let us look in greater detail at these metaphors. They are deliberately worded in order to be parallel to each other. In each case Jesus first makes an affirmation: 'You are the salt of the earth'; 'you are the light of the world.' Then He adds a rider, or a condition upon which the affirmation depends. That is, 'You are the salt of the earth – but the salt must retain its saltness, if you are to be the salt of the earth.' Or again, 'You are the light of the world – but the light must not be concealed. You must let the light shine if you are to be the light of the world.' Salt is good for nothing if its saltness is lost; and light is good for nothing if its light is concealed. So in each case, you see, there is an affirmation, and then a condition upon which the affirmation depends.

Now let us take the salt of the earth (v13). 'You are the salt of the earth,' is the affirmation; and I hope all of us are clear what that means. It means that when each community is true to itself, the world decays – like rotten fish or rotten meat – but the church can hinder the decay. Now of course God has set other restraining influences in the secular community. God has Himself established certain institutions in His common grace to all mankind: the state, the judiciary, the whole process of law and order, marriage, the home, the family – these are divine institutions that God has put in the human community to restrain evil. All of them have a wholesome influence in the community.

Nevertheless God intends the most powerful of all restraints in the community to be His own redeemed and righteous people. As Professor Tasker puts it in his Commentary, the disciples have to be 'a moral disinfectant in a world where moral standards are low, constantly changing, or non-existent.' So that is what the affirmation means, 'You are the salt of the earth.' But the condition? 'You must retain your saltness.' Sodium chloride, I understand, itself cannot ever be changed: but what we commonly call salt can lose its sodium chloride, and then it cannot be restored. De-salted salt is useless, even for manure. So, too, a Christian. Christian saltiness is Christian character as portrayed in the beatitudes; committed Christian discipleship. For effectiveness in the community the Christian has got to retain his Christlikeness, as the salt must retain its saltness. But if Christians get assimilated to non-Christians, if they lose their Christlikeness, then they lose their influence. The influence of Christians in our society depends on our being distinct from the world, not on our being identical with the world. If we lose our saltiness we are useless. We might just as well be discarded, like saltless salt, thrown out and trodden underfoot. As A.B. Bruce comments, 'But what a come down, from being saviours to society to supplying material for footpaths! "Men tread it underfoot"!'

Now we come to the second metaphor – the light of the world (vv14–16). First the affirmation, 'You are the light of the world.' Now it is quite true that Jesus later in His ministry said, '*I* am the light of the world' (Jn. 8:12). But by derivation we are the light of the world, too, if we shine with the light of Christ, shining in the world like stars in a night sky. I wish they would come to us and say –

Twinkle, twinkle, little star,
How I wonder what you are . . .

What this light of the Christian is, Jesus clarifies. It is our good works (v16): when men see our good works, then the light is shining. And in addition to our good works, no doubt – because light always means, as well, the truth of the Gospel – it is our spoken testimony too. 'You are the light of the world': that is the affirmation. The condition: 'Let your light shine.' For as salt can lose its saltness, the light in us can become darkness. But we are to let our light shine before men, like a city set on a hill, that cannot be hid (v14); like a lamp set upon a lampstand to give light to the house, and not stuck under a bed, or under a bucket, where it can do no good.

That is, the disciples of Jesus are not to be ashamed of who and what they are. We are not to conceal the truth about ourselves. We are not to pretend to be other than we are. We are to be ourselves, our true Christian selves, filled with the Spirit of Jesus Christ, doing good works in the community, and letting our light shine. Then men will see *us*, and glorify *God*, because they will recognise that it is by the grace of God that we are what we are; that our light is His light, and our works are His works, done in us and through us.

Malcolm Muggeridge tells us that when asked sometimes on television, or when he is interviewed, what he most wants to do in the little that remains of his life, he says, 'I always nowadays truthfully answer, I should like my life to shine, even if only very fitfully, like a match struck in a dark, cavernous night, and then flickering out.' 'Let your light *shine*,' Jesus says.

Now as we conclude, three vital lessons from the salt and the light metaphors. One, there is a fundamental distinction between the Christian and the non-Christian. True, some non-Christians adopt the deceptive veneer of Christianity, while some professing Christians seem indistinguishable from non-Christians. Nevertheless the essential distinction remains. We might say they are as different as chalk from cheese: but Jesus says they are as different as light from darkness, and as salt from decay and disease. There is an essential difference.

Secondly, we must accept the responsibility which this distinction puts upon us. 'You are the salt of the earth' – all right, then retain your saltness, and don't lose your Christian tang. 'You are the light of the world' – all right, let your light shine, and don't conceal it.

I want to say a word to young people. Is there somebody here, I wonder, who feels frustrated because the problems of the world are so colossal? You long to do something with your life, but you feel so feeble and ineffective and small. 'Alienated' is the word used nowadays to describe this condition. In the inaugural address of Jimmy Reid when he was installed as Rector of Glasgow University in May this year – Jimmy Reid, the chief spokesman, you know, of the Upper Clyde shipyard workers, and a Communist councillor – he spoke about alienation; and some of his words could very well have been uttered by a Christian. 'Alienation,' he said, 'is the cry of men who feel themselves to be the victims of blind economic forces beyond their control. It is the frustration of ordinary people who are excluded from the processes of decision-making.' That's Jimmy Reid. Make no mistake about it, alienation is increasing in the western world. There are multitudes of young people who are frustrated like that.

Now if you feel yourself overwhelmed by political, social, economic forces over which you have no control; if you feel yourself, in the language of the young, 'strangled by the system,' or 'crushed by the machine of modern bureaucracy and technocracy,' and you say, What can you do?, you know as well as I do that it is from this soil of frustration that revolutionaries are being bred all over the world, dedicated to the violent overthrow of the system, because of their frustration. Now, listen, it is out of the same soil of frustration that dedicated revolutionaries of Jesus can arise to spread His revolution of love, joy, and peace in the community.

This peaceful revolution of Jesus is far more radical than any violent revolution, because it changes people. 'With this single word of Jesus,' said Luther in his commentary, 'with the Gospel of Jesus alone, I am more defiant and more boastful than they, with all their power and swords and guns.' That's Luther in the sixteenth century. Just with the word and with the Gospel of Jesus, I am more powerful than all the revolutionaries in the world! So, you see, you are not powerless, after all! If we have Jesus Christ, and Jesus Christ is all the salt and light this dark and rotten world needs, we've got to have salt in ourselves, and let our light shine, and accept the responsibilities which these metaphors place upon us. That's the second truth.

Now, thirdly, we must see this responsibility as twofold, for the effects of salt and light are beautifully complementary. Salt is negative: it prevents decay. Light is positive: it illumines the house. So Christians are to have a double influence on the secular community. Negatively, they are to arrest social decay; positively, they are to bring light into the darkness of the world. Because it is one thing to stop the spread of evil; it is another to promote the spread of truth and beauty and goodness through the Gospel.

Now putting these two metaphors together, it is, I think, legitimate to discern in them the proper relation between evangelism and social action in the total mission of Christ in the world; a subject which vexes many Christian people today. What is our Christian duty in the secular society?

We are given at the end of Romans 1 a grim picture of what happens when society rejects what it knows, and extinguishes whatever light it has by nature. Society deteriorates, its values and standards steadily decline till it becomes utterly corrupt, and God gives men over to their own lusts and evil passions, until society stinks in the nostrils both of God and of all good men and women. Now, Christians are set in stinking secular society – set there by God – not to recoil and withdraw into little Evangelical monastic ghettos and establishments, but to penetrate the stinking society for Christ. We are intended to hinder this process.

God intends us to penetrate the world, to be rubbed into the putrefying secular community like salt in meat. And we Christian people should be more outspoken in condemning evil, and in standing boldly for decency in our neighbourhood and our job; in seeking not only to help the casualties of a sick society, but to concern ourselves with moral preventive medicine, and moral public health, and moral hygiene. We Christians should play our part, however small, in seeking to create better social structures, and foster higher ideals of justice, and legislation, and civil rights, and industry, and race relations. Don't despise those things, don't avoid them. They are part of the purpose of God for His people, and whenever Christians are conscientious citizens they are acting as the salt of the earth.

Ah, yes, but fallen human beings need more than barricades to stop them from becoming as bad as they could be. They need regeneration. They need to be born again. They need new life through the Gospel. And the truth of the Gospel is the light that we are to shine with in the world: contained, it is true, in very fragile earthenware vessels, but shining through our very openness with a more conspicuous brightness.

Here, then, to sum up these complementary effects of salt and light: do not put salt and light – our Christian social and evangelistic responsibilities – over against each other, exaggerating one, discouraging the other. The world needs both. It is bad: it needs salt. It is dark: it needs light. Our Christian vocation is to be both. Jesus Christ said so, and that should be enough.

So my conclusion. We have listened to Jesus, the supreme Legislator in the kingdom of God, describe in the beatitudes the character expected of citizens of the kingdom. Does somebody say, 'The standards are too high. Why should I live like that? Why should I give myself to these high standards of purity of heart, meekness, mercy, being a peacemaker, etc.?' Jesus gives His reasons. Listen: because this is the way that we ourselves are blessed. 'Blessed' are these people; these people please God, and they find themselves. This is the way of self-fulfilment. This is the way to be truly blessed. True blessedness is found in goodness; it is not found anywhere else. The first reason: it is the way to be blessed ourselves.

Second reason: it is the way that the world may best be served. Jesus offers us the immense privilege of being the world's salt and light. You can't be the salt of the earth, you can't be the light of the world, if you don't live by the beatitudes. You want to bless the world, you've got to live this way.

Thirdly, because God will be glorified thereby. They will 'see your good works'; they will 'glorify your Father in heaven.' So this is the desirability of goodness. It brings blessing to ourselves; it brings blessing to the world; and ultimately it even brings blessing to God Himself.

2. A Christian's Righteousness (Matthew 5:17–48)

Yesterday morning we saw how Jesus began the Sermon on the Mount by describing the Christian's character, in the eight beatitudes. And we went on to see how He spoke of the Christian's influence in the community if he exhibits this character, like salt, and light. But now a Christian's character is further defined in terms of *righteousness*, the righteousness for which we hunger and thirst (v6); the righteousness on account of which Christians are persecuted (v10); the righteousness that consists in conformity to the law of God, and which exceeds the righteousness of the scribes and Pharisees (v20).

This is an extremely important passage for all of us to seek to understand, not least because it throws light on the relation between the New Testament and the Old Testament; between the Christian and the law. It is in two sections. The first is quite short (vv17–20), which concerns *Jesus Christ and the law*. The second is the longer section (vv. 21-48), which concerns *the Christian and the law*.

Firstly then –

Jesus Christ and the Law. 'Do not think that I have come to abolish the law and the prophets; I have not come to abolish them, but to fulfil them' (v17). The way in which Jesus phrases His statement, 'Do not think that I have come . . .' indicates that there must have been some people who were thinking the very thought which He goes on to contradict. These must have been people who were deeply disturbed already by His teaching, and by His attitude to the law. Because from the beginning of His ministry Jesus had spoken with great authority, and men had been struck by His authority. They said, 'What is this new teaching with authority, which He teaches?'

It was very natural, therefore, that people were asking what the relation was between the authority of Jesus, and the authority of Moses and of the prophets. It was quite clear to them that the scribes and the Pharisees were submissive to the law. The scribes never spoke without quoting their authorities; but it wasn't so with Jesus. Jesus spoke with His own authority. Jesus said, 'Verily, verily I say unto you . . .' and the people were saying, 'But who is this . . .?' and, was Jesus setting Himself up as an authority over against the sacred law of Moses, and the teaching of the prophets?

That was the question in people's minds; and people are still asking the same kind of thing today in different ways: What is the relation between the New Testament and the Old, between Jesus Christ and the law of Moses?

So Jesus grasped the nettle, and He declared Himself on this issue in no uncertain terms. Verse 17: 'Do not think that I have come to abolish the law. If that's what you are thinking, you are mistaken. I have not come to abolish the law and the prophets; I have come to fulfil. I have not come to abolish, to set aside, to abrogate. I have not even come merely to endorse the law in a dead and literalistic way. I have come actually to fulfil it.'

Now let us try to understand that. The law and the prophets, that is the Old Testament, contain a variety of teaching; and the relation of Jesus to that teaching differs according to the kind of teaching it is. But the word 'fulfilment' covers it all. For example, the Old Testament contains *doctrinal teaching*, teaching about God and man and so on. But it was a partial revelation, and Jesus fulfilled it in the sense that He brought it to completion.

Again, the Old Testament contains *predictive prophecy*, but it was only an anticipation of what was to come; and Jesus Christ fulfilled it in the sense that what was predicted then has come to pass, and will come to pass, in Jesus Christ. Again, the Old Testament contains *moral precepts*: do this, don't do that. But these precepts were often misunderstood, and Jesus Christ came to fulfil these precepts in the sense that He gave them their true interpretation.

So, then, the attitude of Jesus Christ to the Old Testament was not one of destruction, or discontinuity; it was one of a constructive, organic continuity. Not abolition, but fulfilment. And he gives His reason in the next verse. 'Because,' He goes on, 'not an iota . . .' that is the smallest letter in the Hebrew alphabet, '. . . not a dot . . .', which is either a little tiny projection on a Hebrew letter, or one of the accents which was written above the letters, '. . . not an iota or dot, not the tiniest part of the law, will pass away until all has been fulfilled.'

Now, certainly the ceremonial laws have passed away – the sacrifices and the food regulations; and the civil laws of the Old Testament are not necessarily binding on states today. But the moral law has a permanent authority, and Jesus could not have emphasised it more strongly than He did. And the consequence He states in verses 19 and 20.

'Therefore . . .' He goes on. That is, because Jesus came not to abolish, but to fulfil; and because He said that not an iota or dot would pass from the law, 'therefore whoever relaxes one of the least of these commandments, and teaches men so, shall be called least in the kingdom; and whoever does the commandments and teaches them, will be great in the kingdom.' Indeed, 'unless your righteousness – your obedience to the moral law – exceeds the righteousness of the scribes and Pharisees, you'll not even enter the kingdom at all' (v20). Amazing teaching!

Greatness in the kingdom of God is measured in terms of obedience. As Spurgeon put it, 'The peerage of Christ's kingdom is ordered according to obedience.' Entry into the kingdom is impossible without a righteousness that exceeds the righteousness of the Pharisees and the scribes. 'But,' you say, 'surely the Pharisees were extremely righteous. How can Jesus expect Christian righteousness to exceed Pharisaic righteousness?' Well, His answer, as illustrated by the rest of the chapter, is that Christian righteousness is greater because it is deeper. It is a righteousness, not of external deeds, but of the heart; a righteousness of the mind and of the motive; an inner righteousness that is impossible without a new birth. That is why you cannot enter the kingdom unless you have been born again and become capable of such a righteousness. So much, then, for Jesus Christ and the law (vv17–20).

Now we come to much the longer section, verses 21–48:

The Christian and the Law. I want to introduce this at some length, because we must try to understand it. It is terribly important. Here are six parallel paragraphs, and they illustrate the principle which has been stated in verses 17–20, namely that Christ did not come to abolish, but to fulfil. Each of these paragraphs contains a contrast, or, as it is usually called, an antithesis; and each is introduced by the expression, 'You have heard that it was said to the men of old, but I say unto you . . .' something different.

What is this antithesis? Jesus says, '*I* say unto you . . .' and it is clear He is referring to Himself. But what does He mean when He says, 'You have heard that it was said to the men of old . . .'? What is 'that' with whom He is contrasting Himself? It is frequently maintained today that Jesus was setting Himself up against Moses; that He was inaugurating a new morality, and was contradicting and repudiating the old. There are people who say that in each of these six paragraphs Jesus was saying, 'You have heard what Moses said, but I say to you something different.' There are many in the church today who say that Jesus contradicted Moses. This is not so. What Jesus Christ is contradicting is not the law itself, but certain perversions of the law, certain distortions of the law of Moses, of which the scribes and the Pharisees were guilty. Far from contradicting the law of Moses, Jesus endorsed it, and insisted upon its abiding authority. So important is this that I want to give you four arguments to demonstrate this.

The first is in the antitheses themselves. At first sight, these six antitheses appear to be quotations from the law: and as a matter of fact all six of them do consist of, or include, echoes of the law – You shall not kill; you shall not commit adultery, etc. But it is not until you come to the last that you suddenly realise that something is amiss. Verse 43, 'You have heard that it was said, Love your neighbour and hate your enemy.' Where do you find that in the Old Testament? Answer: You don't! You can search the Old Testament from beginning to end, and you will never find that command. Oh, the first part is there, Love your neighbour – except that it is truncated, because the whole commandment is, Love your neighbour *as yourself*: little words that are omitted here. But, 'You shall hate your enemy'? That is nowhere in the Old Testament. And so it is that, in the other five antitheses, a similar distortion is implied. That is the first argument.

The second argument is from the introductory formula, 'You have heard that it was said to the men of old . . .' Now, that is not the formula that Jesus used when He was quoting the Old Testament. When Jesus quoted the Old Testament He said, 'It is written . . .' Not, 'You have heard that it is said . . .' but, 'You have read that it is written . . .' It is a different formula. So in the six antitheses what Jesus is contradicting is not Scripture, the written Word of God, but oral tradition – what was said and spoken; the traditional interpretation of the law, which the scribes continued to give in their synagogue instruction. These were not Scripture, the Word of God; these were traditions, the words of men.

The third argument is from the context. We have already seen how, in the introductory paragraph (vv17–20), Jesus affirmed in the strongest possible way the abiding authority of the law. He said His mission was not to abolish, but to fulfil; not an iota or dot would pass from the law till all was accomplished. Greatness in the kingdom is measured by obedience to the law. Now, are we to suppose that immediately afterwards Jesus contradicts Himself, and that He proceeds at once in His teaching to do what He said He had *not* come to do; that He now abolished the very thing that He said He had *not* come to abolish? Why, that is ludicrous!

The fourth argument is Christ's main attitude to the Old Testament. The reverent submission of Jesus to the authority of the Old Testament, in His teaching and in His personal obedience, is beyond question. To Him, what Moses said, God said.

So for those four reasons it is plain that these six antitheses are not between Christ and Moses, the New Testament and the Old Testament, the Gospel and the law; but between Christ on the one hand, and the scribal misinterpretations of Moses on the other – the 'tortuous methods,' as Calvin called them, 'by which the Pharisees debased the law.' In other words, the contrast is between Christian righteousness (what is expected of us today), and Pharisaic righteousness, which was a distortion.

Let me come on to ask the vital question, What were the Pharisees doing? If Jesus is contradicting their righteousness, what were they doing? In general, the Pharisees were trying to reduce the challenge of the law. They found the law very uncomfortable: don't all of us? So they tried to make it a little more comfortable, a little more easy. They were the Jesuits, the casuists, of their day. They tried to relax the commandments of God, and to make the law less exacting and more manageable. In particular they sought to restrict the commandments of the law, and to extend the permissions of the law. They made the commandments less commanding, and the permissions more permissive. They found the law a yoke that chafed upon them, and they tried to make this yoke easier for themselves.

Before coming to the details of these six antitheses, let me give you a summary of them. Four of them are commandments which they restricted. Thus, there were commands not to murder, and not to commit adultery; and they restricted these to the deed only. Jesus extended the command to include our thoughts and words and looks. They found a command about swearing – that is, taking oaths – and they restricted this to oaths involving the divine name. They said, 'As long as you don't use the divine name, you don't need to bother too much as to whether you keep your oaths.' They restricted it to the use of the divine name; Jesus said that all vows have to be paid, whatever formula you use. The true implication of the commandment, He said, is that swearing – using an oath – is unnecessary: a simple promise is enough.

Then they took the command about loving your neighbour, and restricted it to loving certain people – 'thy neighbour.' 'Well, that is a person of my own race; it is a person of my own religion – a fellow-Jew,' they said. 'I must love him. But it means I can hate everybody else.' Jesus said, 'On the contrary, you've got no business to restrict your 'neighbour.' 'Your neighbour' is an inclusive term; it includes your enemy, and you must love him as well.' You see, they were restricting the commandments, but Jesus extended them.

Then you turn to the other two, which are permissions, and they extended the Biblical permission of divorce. Divorce was permitted in the Old Testament in apparently only one situation. They extended it to include a husband's every whim. 'A husband can divorce his wife for any fancy, if he likes,' they said. But Jesus restricted this permission to refer to sexual immorality only, and He called divorce, for other reasons, adultery.

Then again they extended the Biblical permission of retribution, 'An eye for an eye, and a tooth for a tooth,' to include personal revenge. 'Get your own back on your enemy,' they said. 'The law says you can. 'An eye for an eye and a tooth for a tooth'!' Jesus restricted that permission to the law courts; and He said that in private relations with one another, 'You must not resist evil.'

I hope that this preliminary survey of the six antitheses has helped us to see that Jesus did not contradict the law of Moses. On the contrary, this is what the Pharisees were doing. What Jesus did was to explain the true meaning of the law, with all its uncomfortable implications. He extended the commands which the Pharisees were trying to restrict; and He restricted the permissions which the Pharisees were trying to extend. To Jesus Christ, Moses' law was God's law, and its full implications have got to be accepted and obeyed. And in the Sermon on the Mount we see Jesus, as Calvin says, 'not as a new legislator, but as the faithful expounder of a law which had been already given.' In this the Christian disciple must follow Christ, and not the Pharisees. We have no liberty to try to lower the standards of the law. We have no liberty to make the moral demands of God easier, because we find them difficult to attain. That is the casuistry of Pharisees, not of Christians. Christian righteousness must exceed the righteousness of the scribes and Pharisees.

And yet the advocates of the so-called 'new morality' are in principle trying to do exactly what the Pharisees were doing. True, they claim to take Christ's part against the Pharisees. Yet the 'new morality' people resemble the Pharisees in their dislike of the law. Like the Pharisees, they are attempting to relax the law's authority. They declare, in fact, that the category of law has been abolished for Christians, when Jesus said He had *not* come to abolish it. They set law and love at variance with each other in a way that Jesus never did. No; Jesus disagreed with the Pharisees' interpretation of the law, but He did not disagree with the Pharisees' acceptance of the law's authority. On the contrary, Jesus asserted its authority in the strongest possible terms, and gave His disciples its most true and most exacting interpretations.

Now I hope that will help us as we look at the details. And first, *Murder* (vv21–26). 'You have heard that it was said to the men of old, You shall not kill.' Notice that this sixth commandment is a prohibition, not of the taking of all human life in general and in every circumstance; but it is a prohibition of homicide or murder in particular. I say that because the same law of Moses which prohibits here, elsewhere enjoins it in the form of capital punishment: and I mention this only because the vexed questions of the death penalty and of war cannot be solved by a simple appeal to the commandment, 'You shall not kill.' 'You shall not kill' here means, 'You shall not commit murder.'

The scribes and Pharisees were seeking to restrict the prohibition to *the deed* of murder, the act of spilling human blood in homicide. Jesus maintained that the true · application was much wider than that: it included the thought and the word, as well as the deed; and it included anger and insult, as well as murder. Anger is mentioned in verse 22, although the words, 'If you are angry *without a cause*' are probably not original, yet that is undoubtedly what Jesus meant. There is such a thing as righteous anger, but He is speaking of unrighteous anger – the anger of hatred, the anger of pride and malice and revenge: that, too, is tantamount to murder.

Then insults are mentioned at the end of verse 22: *Raca* is probably an Aramaic word and *more*, 'You fool,' is certainly a Greek word. As A.B. Bruce puts in his commentary, 'Raca expresses contempt for a man's head: "You stupid",' or as Tasker says, 'You nitwit!', or as A.M. Hunter says, 'You blockhead!' – and commentators vie with one another for words to translate it. 'And *more* expresses contempt for his heart and character: "You scoundrel." But both of them are terms of abuse.'

Now these things, angry thoughts and insulting words, may never lead to the ultimate act of murder. But they are tantamount to murder, Jesus said, in the sight of God. They express a desire to get rid of somebody who is in my way, so I insult him, or am angry with him. I want to get my own back. In my heart and mind, even if it never issues in the act of murder, Jesus said it is tantamount to murder; and those who do these things are liable to the same penalties to which the murderer exposes himself – not in human courts, but before the God of gods.

'If, therefore . . .' Jesus goes on in verse 23, and He proceeds to give practical applications of the principle. That is, if anger and insult are so serious and dangerous, avoid them like the plague, and that speedily. And His illustrations are, first, from going to the temple to offer a sacrifice to God (vv23–24); and, second, going to court to answer charges of an enemy (vv25–26). Although the pictures are different – one, as we might say, from church-going, and the other from going to law – yet the teaching is the same. In both, somebody has a grievance against us, and there is an appeal for immediate, urgent action. It is like this: in the very act of worship, right in the middle of a church service, if you remember that your brother has something against you, leave church, and go and put it right. First go, and then come. 'First go and be reconciled to your brother, and then come and offer your gift,' because religion without righteousness is an abomination in God's sight. Again, in the very act of going to court, on your way to the law court, when your enemy is accusing you of something, come to terms with him speedily; settle the issue out of court before it is too late. Do it at once, Jesus said. Don't delay.

How little we obey these injunctions! We allow our broken relationships to remain. We allow the wounds to fester. We need to heed these solemn warnings. If murder is a horrible crime, malicious anger and insult are horrible also. We need to be more sensitive to them: we must not allow estrangements to remain. We must not let the sun go down upon our wrath. As soon as we are conscious of a broken relationship, we must take steps to mend it, and live in peace and love with all men.

Now we come to *adultery*. I want to spend a longer time on this, partly because Jesus Himself does, and partly because sexual sin is such a trouble, sexual temptation such a problem to all of us, and not least to young people. Now once again the Pharisees were attempting to limit the scope of the prohibition. Verse 27, 'You shall not commit adultery'; and they implied that as long as I do not actually go off with my neighbour's wife, then I do not commit adultery.

Jesus taught differently. He extended the implication of God's command, and affirmed that its true meaning was much wider than a prohibition of the act alone; and that as the prohibition of murder includes the angry thought and the insulting word, so the prohibition of adultery includes the lustful look. 'Whoever looks at a woman lustfully has . . . committed adultery . . . in his heart.' Note the phrase. We can commit murder with our words, and we can commit adultery with our hearts.

This statement leads Jesus to very practical instruction about sexual purity in verses 29–30: that if your eye 'causes you to sin, pluck it out – gouge it out – and throw it away'; and if your hand 'causes you to sin, cut it off – chop it off – and throw it away.' Now the argument seems to be this, that if to look lustfully at a woman is to commit adultery in your heart – that is, if heart-adultery is the result of eye-adultery, the eyes of the heart being stimulated and inflamed by the eyes of the flesh – then the only way to deal with the problem is at the beginning, namely with your eyes. Now Job had learnt that. 'I have made a covenant with my eyes – I have refused to look lustfully at any woman – so how can I look upon a virgin,' because, he said, 'I am a married man' (Job 31: 1). This teaching is right up to date, right up to modern psychology and everyday experience. Deeds of shame are preceded by phantasies of shame; and the inflaming of the imagination is preceded by the indiscipline of the eyes.

Now our vivid imagination, one of the many ways in which humans are distinct from animals, is a very precious gift of God. None of the world's art, little of man's noblest achievement, would ever have been possible without our vivid imagination. But all God's gifts need to be used responsibly; and they can be readily degraded and abused. I doubt if ever humans have fallen victim to immorality who have not first opened the sluice-gates of passion through their eyes. Similarly, whenever men and women have learned sexual self-control in deed, it is because they have first learned it in the eye – both of flesh and of phantasy.

So that brings us to verses 29–30, where Jesus speaks quite clearly about cutting off the hand, and in another passage the foot, and plucking out the eye. What did He mean by it? It is a dramatic command. A few Christians, whose zeal has been greater than their wisdom, have taken Jesus literally and actually mutilated themselves. Origen of Alexandria, at the beginning of the third century AD, went to extremes of asceticism in denying himself food and sleep and possessions; and in an over-literal interpretation of this, and of our Lord's words in Matthew 19, actually made himself a eunuch. But the Council of Nicaea, in 325, were wise to forbid this barbarous practice. Surely this is an example of our Lord's dramatic figures of speech. What He was advocating was not a literal physical self-maiming, but ruthless moral self-denial; not mutilation, but mortification, is the path of Christian holiness.

'Well,' you say, 'what do you mean? That's all theological terminology. What is it in practice?' Thank you for asking! It means this: that if your eye causes you to sin, because temptation comes to you through your eye – through what you see – pluck out your eye; that is, don't look. Behave as if you had plucked out your eyes, as if you had gouged them out and flung them away, and made yourself blind. Don't look.

If your hand or foot cause you to sin, because temptation comes through your hand through things you do, or through your feet, through places you visit – cut them off, chop them off; that is, Don't do it, with your hand. Don't go to those places, with your feet. Behave as if you had chopped them off; behave as if you were now crippled, and as if you had no hands and feet, as if you were unable to go to those places. That is the meaning of mortification.

I wonder if there has ever been a generation in which this teaching of Jesus was more needed, or in which it had more obvious indication, than our own – in which the river of filth, of pornographic literature and sex films, is now in spate. If our feet take us to those films, if our hands handle that literature, if our eyes feast upon the pictures they present to us, then we are asking for trouble. And in saying this Jesus is not laying down a law; maybe I should say I am not laying down a law, or making any man-made rules. I am not telling you what books and magazines a Christian may read, or what plays and films he may see live or on television, or what art exhibitions he may visit. We are not laying down man-made regulations, because we must recognise that men and women are made differently. Sexual desire is more easily aroused in some than in others, and sexual self-discipline and self-control come more naturally to some than to others. There are some Christians who can read books or see films and remain entirely unscathed; films and books which would be terribly corrupting to others. Our temperaments are different, and therefore our temptations are different. So don't let's stand in judgment on one another in what we allow ourselves and each other. All we have liberty to say is this, because Jesus said it: If, *if* your eye causes you to sin, pluck it out. *If* your hand and foot cause you to sin, cut them off. *If* these are temptations to you, then deal with them ruthlessly.

So, then, in all of us what is needed is discipline in guarding the approaches to sin. It is an essential part of military tactics; the posting of sentries is commonplace in warfare. And moral sentry duty is equally indispensable. Are we so foolish as to allow the enemy to overwhelm us because we have posted no sentries to warn us of his approach?

Now one other thing. To obey this command of Jesus will lead us to a certain maiming, a plucking out of eyes and a cutting off of feet and hands: that is, not looking, and not doing, and not going, in certain respects. It will lead us to eliminate from our lives certain things which, although they may be, and some of them are, innocent in themselves, are – or easily become – a source of temptation. We may find ourselves, in this metaphorical language, without eyes, feet, or hands. As a result we shall be regarded by certain of our contemporaries as culturally maimed, narrow-minded, and half-educated Philistines. 'What, you've never been to such-and-such an exhibition!' or, 'You've never seen *Oh Calcutta!*' or, 'You've never read that book! Why, you're not educated, man. You're not cultured!' You see? A certain maiming. And the question is whether we are prepared to pay the price, and bear that ridicule. Now Jesus is quite clear about it. He says it is better to lose one member and enter into life 'maimed' than to retain your whole body and go to hell. It is better to forgo some cultural experiences in this life, in order to enter into life that is life indeed. Better cultural amputation in this life, than final destruction in the next.

This teaching runs clean counter to modern strands of permissiveness. It rests on the principle that eternity is far more important than time; and that any sacrifice is worth while in this life, if it is necessary to ensure our entry into the next. And, my friends, you and I have got to decide whether ultimately we live for this life or the next, for Jesus Christ or the world.

Now thirdly, *divorce* (vv31–32); and of course this could take us the whole morning, it is such a complex subject. I can only deal with it summarily. We know now that at the time when Jesus lived, a certain controversy or debate about divorce was going on between rival rabbinical schools, the schools of Rabbi Hillel and Rabbi Shammai. Shammai was a rigorist, and he said that the sole ground for divorce was some grave offence; something which, in the language of Deuteronomy 24, was indecent, or 'unseemly,' in the partner. Hillel was lax, and he interpreted the word 'unseemly' in the widest possible way, saying that if a husband finds in his wife anything that he doesn't like – if she burns his porridge in the morning and is a bad cook; or if she's plain, and he ceases to be attracted to her, and finds another woman more attractive – if there is anything that is unattractive or unseemly, well, then, he can divorce her. That was the controversy going on; and the Pharisees came to Jesus and said, 'On whose side are you?' They were attracted by the laxity of Hillel, and they asked Jesus, according to Matthew 19: 3, 'Is it lawful to divorce one's wife for any cause?' And summing up the teaching of Jesus from the Sermon on the Mount in verses 31 and 32, and Matthew 19 – I haven't time to go into details – Jesus dissented from the Pharisees in these three respects:

One, the Pharisees said that Moses *commanded* divorce. They said, 'Why then did Moses command divorce?' Jesus said, 'He never commanded it. He allowed it, which is a very different thing: a concession is quite different from a command. He allowed it as a concession to the hardness of human hearts. But in the beginning it was not so. In principle, divorce is always inconsistent with the divine institution that God made man male and female, and said, "A man shall leave his parents and cleave to his wife, and they shall become one flesh," and this implies the exclusive, permanent part-nership of one man and one woman for ever. And what God has joined together, let no man put asunder.'

Secondly, the Pharisees were preoccupied with the grounds for divorce, and how widely they could be extended; whereas Jesus said the purpose of Moses' teaching in Deuteronomy was entirely different. If you look at Deuteronomy 24 in a modern version like the Revised Standard Version, you will see that it is in a hypothesis: that if a divorce takes place – if – if – if; not enjoined or commanded – that if a divorce takes place, then there must be a certain procedure, not least in order to protect the woman who is being divorced. So the pur-pose of the legislation in Deuteronomy was not to encourage divorce in any way.

Thirdly, the Pharisees wanted to extend the phrase in Deuteronomy about anything 'unseemly,' to cover virtu-ally any whim of a husband who lost interest in his wife. Jesus restricted it to grave sexual sin, and says if any-body divorces his wife except on the grounds of unchastity – and I do not think the word is necessarily adultery or fornication, but both, and any grave sexual sin – with that sole exception, He forbids divorce, it seems, for any other reason.

Now what can we learn for today? I am very hesitant to take this subject so briefly, because the subject of divorce is exceedingly difficult and complex. I can only say that my own careful study assures me that it is per-missible on the ground of sexual sin to divorce a partner; and perhaps in the so-called Pauline privilege, in the case of an unbeliever who deserts his believing partner. But, this is the point; this is the emphasis – it is never the place to begin a discussion. You must never begin by saying, 'What are the grounds of divorce? Would I be allowed to divorce my partner?' To be preoccupied with the grounds for divorce is to be guilty of Pharisaism. The whole emphasis of Jesus was positive. It was on God's original intention that marriage is a permanent and exclusive relationship: and, we may add, His emphasis was on forgiveness and reconciliation.

If I may say a word to my fellow-pastors here, speaking as a pastor: You have to counsel in this very difficult subject. I always refuse to speak to anybody about divorce until I have first spoken with them on two other subjects. The first is marriage, and the second is reconciliation. We must be positive, as Jesus was, on the permanence of marriage, and not get preoccupied with the grounds for divorce.

Now, fourthly, *swearing*; that is, taking oaths. 'You have heard that it was said to the men of old, You shall not swear falsely, but shall perform to the Lord what you have sworn' (v33). Now there are several prohibitions in the Old Testament about swearing falsely. 'You shall not take the name of the Lord your God in vain,' and so on. They prohibit false swearing, or perjury; that is, making a vow and breaking it. Now let us try to understand that the casuistical Pharisees got to work on these awkward prohibitions, and they tried to restrict them and make them easier to obey. So they shifted people's attention away from the vow itself, and the need to keep it, to the formula which was used in making a vow.

What the law was really prohibiting, the Pharisees argued, was not taking the *name* of the Lord *in vain*, but taking the name of the Lord in vain. 'The important thing,' they said, 'is whether you use the name of the Lord in your vow; if you do, it is binding; if you don't, it isn't.' So they said, false swearing means profanity, a profane use of the name of God – not perjury, a dishonest pledging of one's word. So the Pharisees developed elaborate rules for taking vows. They listed the formulae that were permitted, and they indicated that only those using the divine name were binding vows.

Now Jesus' answer is simple. First, He says, 'The question of what formula you use is totally irrelevant. All vows are binding, whatever formula you use. You cannot avoid reference to God. If you swear by heaven – well, heaven is God's throne. If you swear by earth – earth is God's footstool. If you swear by Jerusalem – Jerusalem is God's city. If you swear by your head – it is God's creation. You cannot use any formula without referring to God. It's irrelevant, your formula business.' And He adds that preoccupation with formulae is not the point at all. Indeed, since anyone making a vow must keep his vow, whatever formula of attestation he uses, strictly speaking, Jesus says, all formulae are superfluous.

The formula does not add to the solemnity of a vow. The vow is binding, whatever formula you use. Therefore, Jesus says, you don't really need to use any at all. Verse 34, 'Don't swear at all! There is no need to confirm your promises with an oath.' Verse 37, 'Let what you say be simply "Yes", not, "I swear by Almighty God I will do it." There is no need to say that: just say, "I will do it. Yes." Not, "I swear by Almighty God I'll never do it." Just say, "No." It is quite enough. No need to add an oath to your promises.'

Swearing – that is, oath-taking – is really a pathetic confession of our own dishonesty. We know perfectly well that our simple word is not going to be believed. I say 'yes,' and I am afraid people are not going to believe me and trust my word. So I have to add some tremendous formula to persuade them to believe me after all. As A.M. Hunter says, 'Oaths arise because men are so often liars!' Now that is true of all forms of exaggeration and hyperbole, and all superlatives. The more we resort to them, the more we devalue human language and human promises. Christians should say what they mean, and mean what they say. Yes! No! And it is quite enough.

Now the fifth is *retaliation* (vv38–42). 'You have heard that it was said, An eye for an eye and a tooth for a tooth.' Now it is true that comes from the Old Testament, and there are many ignorant people who imagine that the morality of the Old Testament is 'An eye for an eye, and a tooth for a tooth,' and that it encourages personal revenge. It does nothing of the kind. 'An eye for an eye and a tooth for a tooth' is a quotation from Exodus 21: 24, where it is an instruction for the magistrates of Israel. It taught the principle of retribution, of what the criminal deserves when he has committed a crime: and it limits it to an exact retribution, although very often it was commuted to another sentence, or remitted altogether.

But the Pharisees extended this principle from the law courts, where it belongs, to the realm of personal relationship, where it does not belong; and they used it to justify personal revenge. Now Jesus did not contradict the principle of retribution. Divine judgment rests upon the principle of retribution: it is a true principle. When we do wrong we deserve to be punished. But what Jesus said is that personal relationships with one another are not to be based on justice, but on love. Our duty to individuals is not to resist evil; when they wrong us, our duty is not retaliation nor revenge, but the acceptance of injustice without retaliation and without revenge.

There is a place for retribution still, in the law courts. God has appointed the state as His minister to execute *His* vengeance, and *His* wrath upon the evil-doer. That is what the law courts are for: it is divine justice through human beings, in a law court. But we are not allowed to take the law into our own hands. We must never repay injury, but suffer it, and so overcome evil with good.

Now the last one is *neighbour-love* (vv43–48). 'You have heard that it was said, You shall love your neighbour and hate your enemy. But I say to you, Love your enemies.' Here again the Pharisees seized upon the command to love your neighbour, and said, 'It's wonderful; I've only got to love my neighbour – that's the bloke next door, and my fellow-Jew, and the people I like. But I can hate everybody else as my enemy.' And Jesus said that in the vocabulary of God 'your neighbour' includes your enemy. That is the teaching of the parable of the Good Samaritan. The man may have nothing to do with you; he may belong to another race, another rank, another religion; he may have no connection with you whatever; he may not in human vocabulary be your neighbour at all. But if he is in need, and if you can meet his need, *he is your neighbour* – even if he is your enemy. 'Your neighbour' includes your enemy, and the command to love your neighbour includes the command to love your enemy.

'Now,' Jesus goes on. 'If you only love those who love you, you are no better than tax collectors. Sinners love those who love them. You've got to love those who don't love you – your enemies, after you with a knife. Then you will prove to be the children of your heavenly Father, for He sends His sun upon the just and upon the unjust, and sends His rain on the good and on the evil.' The love of God is indiscriminate: He loves His enemies; He gives His sun and rain and His common grace to those who hate Him and are unthankful to Him, and are evil men and women. And Jesus says, 'You must do the same. Don't follow the example of sinners who can only love those who love them. Follow your heavenly Father, and love those who don't love you.' One commentator, Alfred Plummer, has summed it up – listen to it carefully, it is beautifully phrased: 'To return evil for good is devilish; to return good for good is human; to return good for evil is divine.'

That is where we end this morning – just with these final sentences: that the Pharisees tried to dodge the law. Law-dodging is a Pharisaic hobby! But Christians hunger and thirst after righteousness. They want to know the full implications of the law, in order to obey them. And so the final thrust of the passage is our Christian calling, not to imitate the world, whether Jews or Gentiles, whether Pharisees or publicans: don't take them as your standard and love those who love you. We are called to imitate God, our heavenly Father, whose sons and daughters by grace we are.

3. A Christian's Ambition (Matthew 6:1–34)

Our text this morning is the whole of Matthew 6, the middle part of the Sermon on the Mount. So far we have thought together about the Christian's character as portrayed in the beatitudes; and the influence which he can exert in the community as salt and light, if he exhibits this character. Yesterday morning we turned to a Christian's righteousness, which is to exceed the righteousness of the scribes and Pharisees – a righteousness that accepts the full implications of the moral law of God, without dodging any of them; an inner righteousness of heart and mind and motive, as well as word and deed.

Now, thirdly we turn to *A Christian's Ambition*: what a Christian lives for. I want to ask you to look at verse 8, 'Do not be like them . . .' Maybe we ought to underline those words in our Bible, because they are five of the most important monsyllables in the whole of the Sermon on the Mount. God calls His people to be different. 'Be holy,' He says, 'because I am holy.' God's people are a holy people, which means that they are a distinct people, a separate people, a different people, called out from the world to belong to Him and to honour Him.

We are not to conform our lives to the people around us. We are not to ape contemporary fashion. If we are Christian people we have entirely different standards: the standards of God. This was already made clear to the people of God in the Old Testament. Listen to this: ''You shall not do as they do in the land of Egypt, where you dwelt, and you shall not do as they do in the land of

Canaan, to which I am bringing you. You shall not walk in *their* statutes. You shall do *my* ordinances and keep *my* statutes and walk in them. I am the Lord your God' (Lev. 18: 3–4).

Now the Christian church stands in direct continuity with the people of Israel, and has the same holy calling. 'You shall not do as they do,' God said to Israel through Moses. 'Do not be like them,' says Jesus to us in the Sermon on the Mount. Now all of us feel the great pressures upon us in the world, to conform to the standards of the world: in J.B. Phillips' well-known words, to 'let the world squeeze us into its mould.' But in the Sermon on the Mount Jesus issued this clarion call to us to be different. Already in Matthew 5 the call has sounded forth. According to 5:20, our righteousness is 'to exceed the righteousness of the scribes and Pharisees.' According to 5:47, if we 'salute only our brethren, what more are we doing than others'? Even Gentiles salute Gentiles. So Christ tells us that we are to have higher standards: higher standards of righteousness than the Pharisees, and higher standards of love than the pagans.

Now in Matthew 6 He enlarges on this Christian calling to be different, in both our religious life and in our secular life. For this is how Matthew 6 divides itself. The first eighteen verses concern our religious life; and verses 19–34 our secular life. Now I know that distinction is misleading in some ways, because Christians cannot separate the two into watertight compartments; everything we do if we are Christians is in a sense religious, that is, it is done in the presence of God, and for the glory of God, and according to the will of God. And the divorce of the sacred from the secular has been disastrous throughout history. Nevertheless I think you will understand what I mean. There is a distinction between these two realms. By our religious life I mean our distinctively religious practices – almsgiving, prayer, and fasting. By our secular life I mean earning our living in the world, seeing to material things like our food and clothing. Now in both these spheres the call of Jesus to His disciples is to be different from everybody else. 'Do not be like them,' especially in the matter of ambition. We are to be different from the hypocrisy of religious people like the Pharisees; and we are to be different from the materialism of irreligious people like the pagans.

Let me enlarge on that for a moment. In our religious life we are not to be like the hypocrites. Glance down at your Bible – When you give alms, don't be like the hypocrites (v2); But you, when you give alms – you are to be different (v3); When you pray, you are not to be like the hypocrites (v5); When you pray, you are to be different (v. 6). Again, glancing on to verse 16, When you fast, you are not to look dismal, like the hypocrites; and 17, When you fast you are to be different. In each case in our religious life, we are to be different from hypocrites. Our ambition is to glorify God, not to glorify ourselves. Similarly in prayer we are not to be like the pagans either, purely mechanical in our devotions. Verse 7, In praying do not heap up empty phrases as the Gentiles do; verse 8, Do not be like them; and verse 9, When you pray you are to be different.

So you see, in our religious life, Jesus said again and again, 'You are to be different.' The same is true at the end of the chapter. In our secular life we are not to be like non-Christian people. They are all the time fussed and bothered about what they are going to eat and drink and wear. It is material things that preoccupy and obsess them. But Christians are to be different (vv32–33). The Gentiles, the pagans, the non-Christians, are seeking food, clothing and drink. But as for you, you are to 'seek first' something quite different: God's kingdom, and God's righteousness.

So I pray that this simple message of Jesus may ring out through the tent this morning, and every one of us may lay hold of it. Matthew 6, in a few words, is the call of Jesus to be different.

So we come to the first eighteen verses, *our religious life*, or as it is called in the first verse, the practice of our piety. And Jesus gives us three examples – giving, praying, and fasting. He has got no quarrel with the practices themselves, but only with the way in which we do them. And He paints a very vivid contrast. First there are *alternative forms of piety*. One is ostentatious, and the other is secret.

The *ostentatious*: Jesus portrays with graphic and almost humorous detail the religious display of the Pharisees. Verse 2: When he is about to give alms, or make a donation to charity, he blows a trumpet in order to draw attention to what he is doing. As Spurgeon says, 'To stand with a penny in one hand, and a trumpet in the other, is the posture of hypocrisy.' When he prays, he chooses a conspicuous place, either in the synagogue or at the street corner, in order to be sure to be seen (v5). And when he fasts, he disfigures his face, making himself dirty and dishevelled, perhaps smearing himself with ashes, so as to look pale through his austerity, and very dismal and religious as well (v16).

Now it is easy to poke fun at the Pharisees. But our Christian Pharisaism is not so funny. We may not blow our own trumpet, but we like to see our names on subscription lists. We may not pray at street corners, but we like to be known for the prayer meetings we attend. We may not put on sackcloth and ashes, but if we ever do fast, we certainly want to make certain that people know about it. Ostentatious piety!

The opposite is *secret*. This is the emphasis of the whole section: the word 'secret' is repeated six times.

When you give alms, do it in secret. Not only are we not to tell other people about our Christian giving, but there is a sense in which we are not even to tell ourselves (v3). We are not to let our left hand know what our right hand is doing. We are not to be self-conscious about our giving, and give in a spirit of self-congratulation. Similarly, when we pray we are to go into our room and shut the door; shut it against interruption and distraction, and especially against human spectators (v6). Then in privacy and secrecy we are to pray to our Father who is in the secret place. Then, when we fast, we are to anoint our head and wash our face (vv17–18). That is not to do anything unusual! That is, this is not to put hypocrisy in reverse, and affect a grinning countenance instead of a dismal one! As J.B. Phillips translates it, 'Brush your hair and wash your face.' And Jesus assumed we do it every day! So don't do anything unusual when you are going to fast: brush your hair, wash your face, be quite ordinary, so that nobody will guess that there is anything extraordinary about what you are doing that day. Now these are the alternative forms of piety: the ostentatious and the secret. Ostentation, the stock-in-trade of the Pharisee. And the Christian form of piety: secret.

Then, secondly, we come from *alternative forms* to alternative motives in piety. The motive of the Pharisee in the parade of his piety is to catch the attention and win the admiration of men. The Pharisees were essentially men-pleasers. They did their piety before men; they prayed before men, in order to be seen by men; they gave alms that they might be praised by men; they fasted to be seen by men. These phrases are repeated in these verses. And the word Jesus gave to this religious show was 'hypocrisy.' Now the hypocrite – the Greek word means an actor on the stage – is a man who plays a part; he is not himself; he is acting a part, pretending to be somebody else. He is in disguise, wearing a mask, act-ing a fantasy. And the hypocrite in religion is exactly this. He is playing a game of religious make-believe, and he does it like an actor on a stage, in order to be seen by men. And the Greek word for 'to be seen' is *theaomai*, and you can recognise it as the word 'theatre.' He is giving a theatrical display before an audience. So it is not the real person we are seeing; it is the religious showman, and it is all done for applause. That is his motive. He gives, not to benefit others, but to benefit himself. He prays, not to seek the face of God, but to seek his own glory. He fasts, not to discipline himself, but to display himself. He actu-ally uses God and his fellow men – or rather, practices that are intended to glorify God and benefit his fellow men – in order to pander to his own conceit. He turns religion and charity into an exhibitionist parade, in order to boost his own ego: and it would be very hard to exag-gerate the perversity of that. Yet all of us are guilty of it, from time to time.

The alternative is the Christian motive. And if the motive of the Pharisee is selfish, the advancement of his own glory, then the motive of the Christian is godly, the advancement of God's glory. Because the secret place in which the Christian gives, and prays, and fasts, is the secret place that God sees, and where God is. And the beautiful thing is this: that whereas the practice of piety before men is certain to degrade it, to practise our piety before God is equally certain to ennoble it. Indeed, to do it in the conscious presence of God is the only way to make it real. If I know that God is watching me when I am praying and giving and fasting, then I've got to be real. It is the only thing that ensures reality, and prevents my piety from becoming a charade.

That leads us, thirdly, to the *alternative rewards* for piety. What reward does the Pharisee get for his vain, ostentatious display? Well, at first sight the answer would be, None. 'You will have no reward from your Father who is in heaven' (v1). But although they will get no reward from God, it does not mean they will get no reward at all. They will get a reward; the reward they are seeking, a reward from men – the reward that the actor wants when the play is over, namely applause. But that is all they'll get; and when the applause has died down there is no further reward to come. That is the thrust of the solemn words repeated three times, 'Truly, I say to you, they have their reward' – they have had it already. The reward they want is the reward they will get, and nothing more to come – except judgment. And indeed, the Greek scholars tell us that the word 'they have,' the Greek verb apecho, is used in the papyri in connection with receipts. So that when you have paid something you get a receipt, and the word indicates, Dr Tasker says in his commentary, that the payment has been made in full. There is nothing more to come but judgment.

But what reward will a Christian get? Well, since the Christian gives, prays, and fasts in secret, he neither expects nor receives a reward from men. But our heavenly Father sees him and rewards him; but not 'openly' – the adverb is not there in the Greek, and should be crossed out. Now, some Christians recoil from this. They say, 'But I don't want any reward.' They even dismiss that sentence. But Christians are not at liberty to treat the teaching of their Lord and Master in this high-handed way! If Jesus said it, He meant it; and we must not presume to contradict Him. The difficulty has arisen partly because of the gloss of the adverb 'openly,' which makes us think of prize day at school or college, with everybody clapping; and partly because the word 'reward' to us means a pat on the back, or a silver cup on the mantelpiece; and we cannot easily imagine any other kind of reward. But there are other kinds of reward.

There is nothing in the context to suggest that the reward is future, at some future prize-giving. After all, the hypocrite gets his reward then and there, in the applause of men; and I think the Christian gets his reward at once as well, an immediate and spiritual reward. And what rich rewards God does give to those who are real and sincere and godly in their piety! For example, we give secretly; nobody knows. But then we share with God the secret joy of seeing somebody's need relieved, or some work on the mission field extended, as a result of our giving; and we have earned the great reward, 'It is more blessed to give than to receive.' Or we pray in the secret place, and rewards are heaped upon us. Oh, there is no *man* to see or to know or to comment or to congratulate; but there is God, in the secret place, ready to receive us, ready to refresh us with His presence, ready to renew our strength, to show us His glory, to satisfy our hunger, to quench our thirst. Or again, we fast in secret, and are rewarded by gradually increasing self-control, and by the joy and the peace and the liberty which are the fruits of self-control.

So we have seen there are alternative forms of piety: the ostentatious and the secret. Alternative motives in piety: self-glorification or the glory of God. And alternative rewards for piety: the applause of men, or the blessing of God. Which is it to be? Are we Pharisees, or Christians?

Now so far I have left out the little paragraph (vv7–15), which is also about prayer, but contrasts the Christians' prayer – not now with the Pharisees' – but with the pagans'. For hypocrisy is not the only sin to avoid in prayer: what are called 'vain repetitions,' or meaningless and mechanical utterance, is another. The former, hypocrisy, is the folly of the Pharisees; the latter, mechanical utterance, is the folly of the pagan. And again Jesus paints the contrast. Let us look at the pagan way of prayer.

'When you pray, don't heap up empty phrases like the Gentiles' (v7). The Greek word is *battalogeo*, and it is a very interesting one because it is unique, not only in Biblical Greek, but anywhere else. There is no other contemporary use of the word anywhere, that is known. So nobody knows its meaning, and nobody knows the derivation of the word for sure. But it is commonly supposed to be an onomatopoeia, that is, a word whose sound carries its own meaning, like the word 'barbarian' that is supposed to be the noise that foreigners make, 'Ba-ba-ba-ba-ba,' when you cannot understand them! So this word, *battalogeo* – and Tyndale is the first one to translate it 'babbling' in prayer: and the New English Bible takes it up: 'Do not go babbling on like the heathen.' 'Vain repetitions,' the Authorised Version rendering, is a little misleading, unless the emphasis clearly is on 'vain,' rather than on 'repetitions': because repetitions are not forbidden in prayer. Jesus Himself used them in the Garden of Gethsemane, when we are told that three times He went away 'saying the same words.' Nor is it a condemnation of perseverance, or importunity: both are commended by Jesus and the apostles. It is a condemnation of verbosity, of speaking without thinking.

What is the application of this prohibition of Jesus'? Well, it is certainly applicable to the Bhuddist prayer wheel, or to the rosary – that is, saying prayers that are purely mechanical and not intelligible. The mind is miles away, and you are not thinking what you are saying. Is it applicable, you may ask, to liturgical forms of worship? Are all Anglicans guilty of *battalogia*? Well, I do not doubt that some of us are, because the use of set forms does permit an approach to God with the lips when the heart and the mind are far away. But it is equally possible to use empty phrases in extempore prayer, and to lapse into jargon while the mind wanders.

So what Jesus is condemning is prayer with the mouth, when the mind is not engaged. That is *battalogia*, babbling on like the heathen. And the folly of this practice, this heathen practice, is exposed at the end of verse 7, 'They think that they will be heard for their many words.' New English Bible, They 'imagine that the more they say the more likely they are to be heard.' Jesus goes on at once: 'Do not be like them' (v8), either in what you suppose or in what you do. Why not? Why are Christians to be different, and not guilty of this babbling, this *battalogia*? Well, the answer is very simple: because we don't believe in that kind of God. We don't do what pagans do, because we don't believe in the kind of gods they believe in. The gods of the heathen may be interested in mechanical utterance: our heavenly Father is not. He knows what we need before we ask Him. He is not ignorant, that we need to inform Him; and He is not reluctant to answer our prayers, that we have got to badger him, and cajole Him, and bully Him into doing something. Those are not the reasons for prayer. Our heavenly Father is knowledgeable and loving.

So Jesus goes on at once: 'When *you* pray say, Our heavenly Father.' Beautiful, isn't it? And 'our heavenly Father' is personal, not mechanical. He is not interested in rosaries and prayer wheels. He is personal, He is loving. He is our Father, He has adopted us into His family, He has made us His children, He loves us with a father's love. And He is powerful: He is our Father in heaven; He combines fatherly love with heavenly power – he is not only our Father, he is a great King. So, then, Jesus is saying, 'Whenever you pray, and before you pray, spend time recalling the nature of the God you are praying to. Then you will never babble in unintelligible speech, just babbling on when your mind is wandering. You'll use your mind; you'll think what you are saying; you'll concentrate on your heavenly, loving Father. You will turn your mind to Him, humble yourself before Him, and worship Him as a personal, living, and infinitely great Father in the heavens.

Then your prayer will be intelligent – like the Lord's Prayer, with its six petitions, which you know so well that I don't really need to expound them at any length – three expressing our concern for God's glory: God's name hallowed, God's kingdom established, God's will obeyed. And three concerning our dependence on the grace of God: for daily bread – our material dependence; for the forgiveness of our sins – our spiritual dependence; and for deliverance from evil – our moral dependence. A wonderfully comprehensive prayer!

So Jesus says, 'When you come to pray . . .' and this sums up the whole of the first part of chapter 6 – 'Don't come hypocritically, like play-actors. Don't come mechanically, like pagan babblers. Come humbly, thoughtfully, trustfully, like little children to their heavenly Father. Do not be like them.'

That's our religious life. Now we turn, in the second part (vv19–34), to what I am calling our *secular life*. Our religious life is our private life with God; our secular life is our public life in the world. And here, too, in each paragraph the alternative is set before us. Verses 19–21, there are two treasures: one on earth, the other in heaven. Verses 22–23, there are two bodily conditions: one is light and the other is darkness. Verse 24, there are two possible masters: God or mammon, that is, wealth. And verses 25–34, there are two possible preoccupations, or ambitions: one is material necessities and luxuries – food

and clothing and the rest; and the other is God's kingdom and God's righteousness.

So you see, all the way through there is this clarion call
to be different, not now from the nominal church, represented by the Pharisees; but from the secular world, represented by the materialists, the Gentiles, who seek
material things alone, and are engrossed in them. 'Ah,
but,' you may say, 'how can I make my choice? Worldly
ambition has a very strong fascination for me. The spell
of materialism is very hard to break.' So in this section,
in His wonderfully understanding and compassionate
way, Jesus helps His followers to choose. He points out
the folly of the wrong way, and the wisdom of the right
way. And as in the section on piety, so here He sets the
false and the true over against each other, as much as to
say to us, 'Now compare them, and see for yourself!'

So let us look at the alternatives. First, their *comparative durability*: how long they will last (vv19–21). This is
the point in the section about treasure. There are two
sorts of treasure: treasure on earth, treasure in heaven. So
it ought to be pretty easy to decide which to collect,
because if you are a collector, presumably you want to
collect something which is durable. If your object is to
lay up treasure, then you will concentrate on what will
last; on what can be stored without deterioration. 'But
don't you see,' Jesus says, 'that if you are a collector of
treasure on earth, it's corruptible.'

Now let us think carefully here. To 'lay up treasure on
earth' is not to be provident; that is, to make provision
for the future: it is to be covetous, to be a materialist or a
miser. Now let us get this absolutely clear. What is Jesus
prohibiting when He says, 'Don't lay up treasure on
earth'? He is not prohibiting all material possessions in
themselves. Scripture nowhere teaches that mere possession is evil. It is Marxist and not Christian philosophy to

attribute the ills of society to private ownership. He is not prohibiting the investment of capital. 'Usury' is a Biblical word for money-lending at exorbitant interest, which is a very different thing. He is not prohibiting saving for a rainy day: on the contrary, the Bible says that a man who does not provide for his own family has 'disowned the faith, and is worse than an unbeliever' (1 Tim. 5:8). You've got to interpret Scripture with Scripture. Jesus is not prohibiting the enjoyment of the good things our Creator has given us: He has given them 'richly to enjoy' (1 Tim. 6:17). What Jesus is prohibiting is the selfish accumulation of treasure. 'Lay not up *for ourselves* treasure on earth' – selfishness. He is prohibiting the foolish fantasy that a man's life *consists* in the abundance of what he possesses. He is prohibiting extravagance and luxurious living, the materialism that tethers our hearts to this earth, and the hard-heartedness that ignores the colossal need of the under-privileged world.

Now such earthly treasure 'grows rusty and moth-eaten, and thieves break in to steal it' (verse 19, NEB) – or as we moderns might say, who try to protect our treasure by insecticides, by rust-proof paint, and by burglar-alarms. Our treasure may diminish through inflation, or devaluation, or an economic slump. And it certainly cannot be taken with us into the next life. You know the story of what happened after the funeral, when somebody came up to the vicar and said, 'How much did she leave?' The vicar's answer: 'She left everything!' 'Naked I came out of my mother's womb, and naked I shall return.'

Now in contrast with treasure on earth there is treasure in heaven; and it is incorruptible. And to lay up treasure in heaven is to do anything on earth whose effect lasts for eternity. For example, the development of Christian character, being 'transformed into the image of

Christ'; increasing in faith and love and charity, all of which Paul said 'abide'; growth in the knowledge of Jesus, whom one day we shall see face to face; the active endeavour by prayer and witness to introduce others to Christ, for they too will inherit eternal life; the use of our money for Christian causes, the only investment whose dividends are eternal. All these – and other things beside – are temporal activities with eternal consequences: and this is what it means to lay up treasure in heaven. No vermin and no burglar can ever destroy *this*: there aren't any moths in heaven; there aren't any mice or marauders in heaven. Treasure laid up in heaven is eternally secure: it is indestructible. So if it is safe investments you are after, nothing could be safer than these. It is the only gilt-edged security whose gilt will never tarnish. Their comparative durability.

Second, their *comparative benefit*. Here in verses 22–23 the contrast is between a blind person and a sighted person, and between the light and the darkness in which respectively they live. The eye, Jesus says, is 'the lamp of the body.' That is to say everything, by and large, which the body does, depends on our ability to see. We need to see in order to run, and jump, and drive a car, and cross the road, and sew, and knit, and mend. The eye illumines what the body does through its hands and its feet. Now it is quite true that a blind person's other faculties are often wonderfully developed in such a way as to compensate for his lack of sight. And yet the principle holds good. A sighted person walks in the light: a blind person is in the darkness. And the great difference between the darkness and the light is due to this little organ called the eye. When the eye is sound, Jesus said, the whole body is 'full of light.' But when the eye is not sound, the whole body is 'full of darkness.'

What does He mean? What is the application? Surely this: the eye in Scripture is sometimes equivalent to the heart. To set your heart upon something, and to fix your eye upon something, are synonyms in the Bible. So Jesus here passes from the importance of our heart being in the right place ('Where your treasure is your heart will be also' – verse 21), to the importance of our eye being sound and healthy. So the argument is this: that just as our eye affects our whole body physically, so our ambition – where we fix our eyes, or our heart and mind – affects the whole of our life. Just as a seeing eye gives light to the body, while a blind eye gives darkness to the body, so a noble ambition to serve God and not mammon, is an uplifting thing: it adds meaning and purpose to your life; it throws light on everything you do, and your whole life is full of light, when you have a noble Christian ambition. But an ignoble, a selfish ambition, to be covetous and miserly, and lay up treasure for yourself on earth – why, it is degrading! It makes us intolerant, inhuman, ruthless, miserly; it deprives life of meaning, and it plunges us in darkness.

It is a question of vision. If you have physical vision, you can see what you are doing and where you are going. And if you have spiritual vision, if your spiritual perspective is accurately adjusted, your whole life is full of significance and drive. But if our vision is clouded by the false goals of materialism, our whole life is plunged in darkness. So, you see, Jesus not only speaks of the comparative durability of the ambitions that drive us, but the comparative benefit that we can enjoy now, if we make the right choice.

His third comparison is their *comparative worth*. The ultimate choice is between *two masters whom we serve*: God or mammon – that is materialism, money (v24). It is a choice between a living, personal Creator and a thing, a creature called money. And when the choice is seen to be what it is, between a creature and a Creator, between a personal God and a material thing – between God and money – it is really inconceivable that we should make the wrong choice. Having grasped the comparative durability of the two treasures – corruptible and incorruptible; the comparative benefit of the two eye conditions – light and darkness; the comparative worth of the two masters – the intrinsic worth of the One, God, and the intrinsic worthlessness of the other, money: and having made our choice to lay up treasure in heaven – to have a sound and single eye; to serve God and not mammon ... 'Therefore ...' Jesus goes on (v25) ... this is what we must do. Our basic choice of whom we shall serve will radically affect our attitude to both God and mammon. We are not to be anxious about the one, but we are to concentrate on the other; to 'seek first' something else. Our lack of anxiety and bother about the one, and our preoccupation with the other, you see, is a natural, logical consequence of the choice that we have made.

Then glance on to verses 31–33; 'Seek first the kingdom of God and His righteousness.' Jesus assumes that everybody is a seeker. The only difference between people is the object of our search or our ambition – what we are seeking; what we set before ourselves as the supreme good to which we devote our lives. That is the question. Well, Jesus says that ultimately there are only these two possibilities. One is food, drink, and clothing for ourselves – material things; and the other is God's kingdom and God's righteousness. The Gentiles seek the one, and Christians must seek the other. And we hear again Christ's call to be different.

Let us look first at the *wrong* ambition. Most of this paragraph is negative: 'Do not be anxious . . .' Three times He said it. Christians have no business to be worried about material things. Our preoccupation is not to be food, drink and clothing. Yet I think you will agree with me that this is the average person's preoccupation. You have only got to look at the glossy magazines on the bookstalls, or the advertisements on the bus or in the tube. It's food, drink, clothing. I was sent – for some reason I have yet to discover – some months ago, a complimentary copy of a fairly new glossy called *Accent on Good Living*. There were enticing advertisements for champagne, cigarettes, antiques and carpets. There was a description of an esoteric weekend's shopping in Rome. There were articles on how to have a computer in your kitchen, how to win a luxury cabin cruiser, or one hundred twelve-bottle cases of Scotch instead! And there was a fascinating article on how fifteen million women can't be wrong about their cosmetic choices. And we were promised in the following month's edition – which, I may say, I neither bought nor was sent – alluring articles on Caribbean holidays, staying in bed, high fashion warm underwear, and the delights of reindeer meat and snow-berries! Food, drink, clothing.

Now don't misunderstand this: Jesus Christ neither denies nor despises the needs of the body for food and clothing. But what He says is, that these things are unsuitable and unworthy as a Christian person's preoccupation. They are not the supreme good in life. 'A man's life does not consist in the abundance of what he possesses.' So, Jesus said, 'Don't be anxious about them!' What He is prohibiting is not thought or forethought, but anxious thought; not prudence, but worry – preoccupying, distracting, self-centred worry. That is what is forbidden.

He gives two arguments. First, anxiety is incompatible with Christian faith (vv25–30). He dubs those who get het up over food and clothing 'men of little faith' (v30). Then He uses what are called *a fortiori* arguments – 'how much more' arguments – from human experience and from sub-human experience. The human experience is quite simple. He says, 'God looks after your life. You don't keep yourself alive: God does. And if He looks after your life, don't you think you can trust Him for the food and the drink that nourish and sustain your life? He looks after the greater, can't you trust Him for the lesser? Again, He looks after your body; it is He who is pumping the heart all the time. And if He looks after your body, can't you trust Him to look after the clothes that cover the body? If he looks after the greater, can't you trust Him to look after the lesser?' Very logical, isn't it? An argument from human experience.

The second is from sub-human experience: the birds and the plants – the birds as an example of God's supply of food; and plants of His supply of clothing. In both cases Jesus says, 'Look at the birds; look at the plants – and learn a lesson from them.' Now some of you may know that I happen to be a fairly fanatical bird-watcher. Bird-watching is regarded by some with quizzical and rather paternalistic amusement; but I claim good Biblical warrant for it! For when Jesus said, 'Consider the fowls of the air,' in plain, basic English He said, 'Watch birds!' 'Now,' He says, 'If you do watch birds and flowers, you'll learn some lessons: that although birds don't sow or reap or garner, our heavenly Father feeds them. And flowers don't toil and spin, but our heavenly Father clothes them – more gorgeously even than Solomon. So how much more will He clothe you: you're of greater value than they.' See? It is the opposite argument: not now from the greater to the less, but from the less to the greater. The greater to the less is – If He looks after your life, trust Him for food and drink; if He looks after your body, trust Him for clothes. The argument from the less to the greater is – If He looks after birds and flowers, you are much more precious than they are, so trust Him to look after you. The logic of Jesus.

I want here to allow myself a little digression to comment on the problems which may have arisen in your minds. I can only touch on them lightly; but they all arise from Jesus' basic promise that our heavenly Father can be trusted to feed and clothe us.

The first is this: I'll put them in affirmations. One, this promise does not exempt us from earning our living. We cannot sit back in a deck chair, twiddle our thumbs and say, 'My heavenly Father has promised to feed and clothe me! Isn't it wonderful?' No, no. Jesus used the birds as an example of God's ability to feed us. Have you ever asked yourself, How does God feed birds? Answer: They feed themselves! Have you ever thought of that? Now Jesus was no fool, you know: He was an acute observer, and He knew perfectly well that some birds are berry-eaters, some are seed-eaters, some are carrion-eaters, some are insectivorous, some are predators, some are scavengers: but they all feed themselves. When Jesus says, 'Your heavenly Father feeds them,' He was not imagining a kind of invisible divine Hand full of food, that was stretched out, so that the birdies could come and eat! No, no. Our heavenly Father feeds birds by providing the wherewithal by which they can feed themselves. When He says He can feed us, it is the same thing. We are not exempt from the business of earning our living.

Secondly, it does not exempt us from responsibility for other people. Now if God promises to feed and clothe His children, a thoughtful person will ask: 'How is it that there are so many who are under-nourished and ill-clad in the world – yes, even Christian people?' Now this is a big subject, and again I can only touch on it. But the first answer I give is this, that the cause of their under-nourishment and lack of clothing is not an inadequate divine provision, but an inequitable human distribution. God has provided ample resources, but men hoard them, and squander them, and don't share them. Have you ever thought how significant it is that in the same Gospel of Matthew Jesus, who here says our heavenly Father feeds and clothes us, later says that on the last day we are going to be judged according to whether *we* have fed the hungry and clothed the naked? So if our heavenly Father feeds and clothes other people, it does not exempt us from the responsibility to do the same. We must always interpret Scripture with Scripture.

Thirdly, this promise does not exempt us from experiencing trouble. Jesus forbids us to worry: but to be free from worry is not the same as to be free from trouble. He commands us not to be anxious, but He does not promise us freedom from all misfortune. On the contrary, He says that although God clothes the grass, it is cut down and thrown into the oven and burned; and although God feeds the birds, some do die of cold and starvation in the winter; and although God protects the sparrows, Jesus specifically said they fall to the ground. He didn't say they don't fall to the ground: He said they don't fall to the ground 'without your heavenly Father,' that is, without His knowledge and permission. But they do fall to the ground, and are killed. And Jesus again says that although we are not to be anxious for tomorrow, the reason is not because tomorrow will bring no trouble, but because tomorrow's trouble is enough for tomorrow – so don't worry about it for today.

So God's children are promised freedom neither from work, nor from responsibility for others, nor from trouble and misfortune. But they are promised freedom from worry, because our heavenly Father can be trusted. It is worry that is forbidden us. Anxiety is incompatible with Christian faith.

Second, very briefly, it is incompatible with common sense. Verse 34, 'Don't be anxious for tomorrow.

Tomorrow's troubles are enough for tomorrow.' Notice the references are to today and tomorrow. All worry is about tomorrow, the future. But all worry is experienced today, in the present. Our fears are about tomorrow, but we feel our fears today. Now these fears may never be fulfilled. 'Don't worry: it may never happen!' is perfectly true. People worry about this and that and the other in the future; but it is all fantasy. Fears may be liars: they often are. Many of our worries never materialise, so all worry is a waste – waste of time, waste of thought, waste of nervous energy: and Jesus said, 'Live a day at a time. Each day has troubles enough of its own.' If you worry, you double your trouble, because if your fear does not materialise, then you have worried once for nothing; if it does materialise, then you have worried twice instead of once! So in both cases it is plain stupid! Worry doubles trouble. Worry is a waste. That is what Jesus said. It is incompatible with Christian faith, and it is incompatible with common sense.

So it is a false ambition to be preoccupied with material things. The right ambition is to seek first God's rule and God's righteousness, and to be preoccupied with that – that is, to be concerned that God's rule in my own life will increase, until He dominates and reigns in every aspect of my life; and that God's rule will spread in the world as I preach the Gospel, and people are born again and enter the kingdom of God; and that God's righteousness, moral and social, will spread in the community. This is what we are to give our lives to, and seek this first.

So, we conclude. We look back over the chapter, and in every paragraph He has set His disciples an alternative. Two forms of piety: ostentatious and secret. Two ways of prayer, mechanical and real. Two treasures to store: earthly, heavenly. Two realms to inhabit: darkness or light. Two masters to serve: God or mammon. Two goals to seek: material security or God's rule and righteousness. My friends, in each case we have got to choose. We are called to be different: we are not to be like the hypocrites, the pagans, the materialists. 'Do not be like them,' Jesus said. In the end, the choice boils down to the question of ambition. In our private religious life, is it God's glory, or ours? In our public secular life, is it God's rule or our security? The choice is absolutely clear-cut. It concerns the direction and the driving force of our whole life; and fundamentally, between being self-centred, obsessed with myself, my glory, my interest, my treasure, my things, my security; or being God-centred, obsessed with God's glory, God's kingdom, God's name, God's will, God's righteousness. What is the supreme good of our lives? What are we seeking? Is our magnificent obsession God Himself and His glory? Really, it is not only the right, it is the only choice.

4. A Christian's Relationship (Matthew 7: 1–29)

Matthew 7 consists of several apparently self-contained paragraphs. Their links with each other are not obvious, and there is no very clear connecting theme. Yet I think it is fair to say that each paragraph treats the Christian's relationship to some personal group, and maybe we could look over the chapter in advance in this way. There are seven of them.

First, in verses 1–5: Our relationship to *our brother*, in whose eye we may detect a speck of sawdust. Secondly, to a group startlingly designated *dogs and pigs* – though they are people all right, but such is their animal nature that we are not to share God's Gospel with them (v6). Thirdly, there is our relation to *our heavenly Father*, to whom we pray like little children (vv7–11). Fourthly, our relation to all men in general: 'Whatever you would that men should do to you, do to them' (v12). Fifthly, our relation to our *fellow-pilgrims* on the narrow way that leads to life (vv13–14). Sixthly, *false prophets*, of whom we are to beware (vv15–20). Seventh and last, there is our relation to *Jesus Christ our Lord*, whose teaching we are not only to hear, but to obey (vv21–27). Now as we make that survey we see that a Christian is involved in a very complex network of relationships to all these different kinds of people. His behaviour is to be sensitive and discriminating, according to the character of each group or person.

We begin with –

Our Relation to Our Brother – which may include, indeed, in this context, our fellow-man, as well as our fellow Christian (vv1–5).

'Judge not that you be not judged' (v1) – a well-known command, much misunderstood. We begin negatively by seeing what Jesus was *not* meaning. He was not forbidding all criticism. The very word 'critic,' of course, has come to be misunderstood. A critic, you know, is not necessarily a fault-finder; for example a literary critic reviews books, an art critic or a drama critic assesses the merits of art and drama. The critic's task is to evaluate, not to condemn. In that sense Jesus is not condemning criticism. 'Judge not' cannot possibly be understood as a command to suspend our critical faculties in relation to other people; to turn a blind eye to their faults, and to pretend not to notice them. It cannot be a command to eschew all criticism, refusing to discern between truth and error, between good and evil.

How can I be so sure in saying that? Well, for many reasons, partly because it would not be honest to behave thus. We could only do it by pretence, and by becoming the very hypocrites whom Jesus condemns. Partly because such behaviour would encourage evil and error; partly because we should then be contradicting our nature as men and women whom God has created as capable of making value-judgments; but specially because Christ's teaching so far in the Sermon on the Mount assumes that we shall use our critical powers, and assess people for what they are. For example, take the call to be different, in Matthew 6. How can our righteousness exceed the righteousness of the scribes and Pharisees, unless we have clearly discerned the way in which their righteousness is inadequate? How can our love be more than the love of the Gentiles, unless we have first discerned how the love of the Gentiles is inadequate? The whole teaching of chapter 6, contrasting the piety of Pharisees with the piety of Christians, the ambition of pagans with the ambition of Christians, implies our responsibility to be critical. We have got to assess both forms in order to reject the one in favour of the other.

Similarly in chapter 7 this very command not to judge other people is followed almost at once by two further commands: to avoid giving what is holy to dogs, or pearls to pigs (v7); and to beware of false prophets, and discern them by their fruits (v15). Now both commands would be impossible to obey unless we use our critical judgment; unless we discern who are the dogs and the pigs and the false prophets; unless we are able to tell good fruit from evil, and go on to modify our behaviour accordingly. So Jesus is not forbidding us to use our critical faculties.

What is He doing? Well, He is telling us *not to be a judge*. The follower of Jesus is to be a critic in the sense of using his critical faculties and evaluating moral and intellectual matters; but he is not to be a judge in the sense of being censorious. Censoriousness is a compound sin, consisting of a number of very unpleasant ingredients. It does not mean to assess people critically, but to judge them harshly. The censorious critic is the fault-finder who positively enjoys seeking out other people's sins; he is negative and destructive in his attitude to other people; he pours cold water on every scheme; and he assumes the worst possible motive in everybody's actions.

Worse than that, to be censorious is to set oneself up as a censor; that is, to claim a competence and an authority to sit in judgment upon our fellow-men. But this is to cast both myself and my fellows in the wrong role. Since when have they been my servants, and been responsible to me, that I can pass judgments upon them? Since when have I become their judge? Paul says to the Corinthians, it is the Lord who judges. Man is not God. Man is not qualified to be a judge, because he cannot read the hearts of men, he cannot know the thoughts and motives of men; and to be censorious is to dare arrogantly to anticipate the day of judgment, and to assume myself the role of a divine judge. It is to try to behave like God. And Jesus says you are not to be a judge.

Not only so, but man is himself among the judged. 'Don't judge yourself, and you will not be judged' (vv1–2). Jesus warns us of the danger to which we expose ourselves if we stand in judgment on others. But if we do this, we are giving clear evidence of our highly developed powers of critical judgment; and if we pose as judges, we cannot claim ignorance of the law which we presume to administer. So the command, 'Judge not' is not a requirement to be blind, but a requirement to be generous; not that we should cease to be men, and suspend the critical faculties that God has given us, and which distinguish us from the animals, but that we should renounce the sinful ambition to be like God. We are not to be a judge.

Second, *we are not to be a hypocrite*. In verse 3 Jesus goes on to tell His little parable about foreign bodies in people's eyes – the specks of dust on the one hand, the logs and beams on the other. This is a prohibition of hypocrisy. At the beginning of chapter 6, Jesus exposes our hypocrisy in our duty to God, in giving, praying, fasting. Here He exposes our hypocrisy in relation to one another: meddling with their faults, while failing to deal with our own.

This is another reason why we are unfit to be judges. It is not only because we are human and fallible and not God; but it is also because we are fallen human beings ourselves. The fall has not only made us sinners, but it has warped our judgment. As a result, we have a fatal tendency – and don't we all know it in our own experience?

– to exaggerate the faults of others, and minimise the gravity of our own. As fallen human beings we find it almost impossible, in comparing ourselves with others, to be strictly objective and impartial. On the contrary, we have a wonderfully rosy view of ourselves, and a jaundiced view of other people. So, in verse 5, 'You hypocrite,' is an expression of the paragraph. What we should do is to apply to ourselves at least as strict and critical a standard as we do to others.

We are not to be a judge; we are not to be a hypocrite: What are we to be? Answer: a brother, which is a very different thing. In the parable of foreign bodies, if I may call it that, some people imagine that Jesus is forbidding any attempt to become a moral and spiritual oculist, and meddle with other people's eyes; and instead, that He is telling us to mind our own business. Now, Jesus is telling us nothing of the kind. The fact that censoriousness and hypocrisy are forbidden us does not relieve us of a brotherly responsibility to other people. The fact that I am forbidden to play the judge or the hypocrite is no excuse for refusing to be a brother. Oh, to be sure, in certain circumstances Jesus is forbidding us to interfere with other people's eyes; but the only circumstance in which we are to leave other people's eyes alone, is when we have got considerable eye trouble ourselves. But as soon as we have got rid of the log and the beam out of our own eye, then we have a responsibility to remove the speck of dust from other people's eyes.

This, then is our duty: not just to see the speck in the brother's eye (v3), still less to say to him, 'Brother, let me take this speck out of your eye' while there is a log in ours; but having taken the log out of ours, we are actually to take the speck out of his. Now this is a command that is greatly neglected in the Christian church. We have a responsibility to our brethren.

Secondly:

Dogs and Pigs (v6). At first sight and hearing, it is startling language from the lips of Jesus. But Jesus always called a spade a spade: He was extremely outspoken in His references to Herod, whom He called a fox; and to the Pharisees, whom He called 'a brood of vipers' and 'white-washed tombs.' There are people, evidently, who can be justly and truly designated dogs and pigs, because they are human beings with an animal nature, who express their nature in bestial behaviour. Who are these people? Now clearly, in referring to dogs and pigs, Jesus is asserting that they are more animals then men, and that they are animals with dirty habits as well. For the dogs He is talking about, we may be sure, are not the little lap-dogs of an elegant drawing-room; they are the wild pariah dogs who scavenged in the city streets. And the pigs, of course, were unclean to the Jews; and they loved to roll in the mud. Peter refers to them, too, in the proverb, 'The dog turns back to his own vomit, and the sow is washed only to wallow in the mire' (2 Pet. 2: 22). The reference clearly is to unbelievers whose nature has never been renewed, who possess a physical animal life, but not a spiritual or eternal life.

But it is more than that. We are not to give to dogs what is holy; and we are not to throw our pearls before pigs. The picture is fairly clear. A Jew would not dream of handing holy food – that is probably sacrificial food, that has been offered in sacrifice – to unclean, pariah dogs. Nor would he dream of throwing his pearls to his pigs: they might think they were nuts or peas, and first try to eat them; and finding them inedible, trample them in the mire.

What is the application to us? Well, it cannot possibly be taken as a prohibition to preach the Gospel to unbelievers, otherwise we should have to turn the whole New

Testament on its head. Besides, this very Gospel of Matthew ends with the great commission to 'go and make disciples of all nations.' What, then, is it? Well, if the holy thing, or the pearl, is the Gospel – a pearl of great price – then the dogs and the pigs with whom we are forbidden to share the Gospel are not just unbelievers, but those who have had an opportunity to hear and believe, and have decisively rejected the Gospel. Calvin puts it, 'They are those who by clear evidences have manifested a hardened contempt of God, so that their disease appears to be incurable.' So to go on beyond a certain point, offering the Gospel to such is both to cheapen the Gospel, inviting its rejection with contempt and blasphemy; and it is even to endanger ourselves, for, not content with rejecting our message, they may go on to attack and to assault us. Jesus spoke of this principle when He talked about 'shaking the dust off your feet' when they hardened their hearts against the Gospel: and Paul did it several times in the Acts, when he said, 'If the Jews decisively reject the Gospel, I shall no longer cheapen it by casting my pearls before swine. I turn to the Gentiles.'

Now perhaps I could pause a moment, and say how remarkable is the vivid contrast Jesus draws between a holy message and an unholy people; between the great pearl of infinite price, and the pigs who despise it. But notice what this contrast tells us both about the Gospel of God on the one hand, and about the nature of man on the other. I trust that each of us has discovered that the Gospel is a pearl of great price. Anybody knows that, whose eyes have been opened by the Holy Spirit to see the truth as it is in Jesus. But we also learn that human nature can become so depraved, so bestial, as to mistake God's pearl for a bit of stone, and actually trample it into the mud. This tells us something about human nature, as well as about the beauty of the Gospel of God.

Thirdly we come to our relation to:

Our Heavenly Father (vv7–11). Various explanations are given about the sequence of thought. It may be that Christ turns from our relation to each other, to our relation to our heavenly Father, to God; or it may be that our Christian duty to discrimination – of not judging on the one hand, and not casting pearls before swine on the other – is so difficult that it is natural at this point to turn to God in prayer for grace. But whatever the actual sequence of thought may be, Jesus here makes wonderful promises about prayer.

This passage is not the first instruction about prayer that He has given in the Sermon on the Mount. He has already warned His followers against Pharisaical hypocrisy, and against pagan formalism, in prayer; and He has given us the pattern prayer, the Lord's prayer. But now He goes further, and He actively encourages His disciples to pray by some wonderfully gracious promises. I wonder if you have ever observed how forcefully Jesus seeks to imprint His promises on our minds and on our memories. He does it by the hammer-blow of repetition.

First, *the promises are attached to direct commands.* 'Ask – and it will be given you. Seek – and you will find. Knock – and it will be opened to you.' Three commands to which the promises are attached. Second, *the promises are expressed in universal statements.* Every one who asks receives; and he who seeks, whoever he may be, finds; and to him who knocks, it will be opened (v8), Thirdly, *the promises are illustrated in a homely parable* (vv9–11). Jesus envisages a situation with which each of His hearers will have been very familiar: a child coming to his father with a simple request. Jesus says, 'If your son asks you for food, are you going to give him something that looks a bit like food, but is actually utterly and disastrously different? Are you going to give him a stone, instead of a loaf of bread – or a snake instead of a fish? If he asks you for something wholesome to eat, like bread and fish, are you going to give him something unwholesome, something that isn't edible, like a stone, or positively harmful, like a poisonous snake? Why,' Jesus says, 'it's ludicrous. Of course you wouldn't do any such thing. Parents love their children. Parents give their children good gifts. Yes,' Jesus goes on – and notice this: 'even though they are evil,' that is, selfish by nature.

Jesus asserts the inherent sinfulness of human nature. 'If you, being evil, know how to give good gifts . . .' But at the same time He does not deny that bad men are capable of doing good. On the contrary – and there is deep theology here: evil parents give good gifts to their children. But what Jesus is saying is that even when they are doing good – and bad men can do good – even when they are following the noble instincts of parenthood, even then they do not escape the designation 'evil,' for that's what human beings are.

So the great force of this little parable is more a contrast than a comparison. Jesus is not saying that as human parents give good gifts to their children, so your heavenly Parent gives good things to you: it's not a comparison, it is a contrast. He says, 'If you who are evil parents know how to give good things to your children, how much more will your heavenly Father give good gifts to His children; for your heavenly Father is not evil: He is infinitely good and kind.' I wish we could remember who God is when we come to Him in prayer. Sometimes we come to Him as if He were an ogre, as if He were a tyrant, an autocrat, a totalitarian despot; as if His will for our lives was paltry and mean, and He was going to cramp our style, and squash us. Our God is our heavenly Father, of infinite goodness and wisdom and kindness, and He never gives to His children anything but good.

'Ah, but,' somebody says, 'you don't know my problems. It's all very well for Jesus to make these promises, but they don't come true. It doesn't work.' 'I prayed,' says a student, 'to pass my exam: but I failed it.' 'I prayed to be healed of an illness: but it got worse.' 'I prayed for peace, and war broke out.' How do you explain the problem of unanswered prayer? Well, although this is an over-simplification, what I should want to say from this passage is this: the promises of Jesus in the Sermon on the Mount are not unconditional; and a moment's thought will convince us of this.

Surely it would be absurd to suppose that the promise, 'Ask, and you shall have,' is unconditional; and 'Knock, and you shall find' is an open sesame to every closed door; and by the recitation of a formula, or the waving of a prayer-wand, every prayer will be answered, every wish granted, and every dream come true. To imagine that is plain ridiculous. It would turn prayer into magic. It would turn man into a magician like Aladdin, and God into our servant like those affable genii, summoned to do our bidding whenever we rub our little prayer lamp. Do you think of God like that? It would place an intolerable strain on any sensitive Christian if he knew he was bound to get whatever he asked for. Alec Motyer has expressed it very well in his studies in James: he says, 'If it were the case that whatever we ask, God was pledged to give, then I for one would never pray again, because I would not have sufficient confidence in my own wisdom to ask God for anything.' And I think if you consider it, you will agree. It would impose an intolerable burden on frail human wisdom, if by His prayer-promises God was pledged to give whatever we ask, when we ask it, and exactly in the terms we ask. How could we bear the burden?

Let me put it like this. Being good, our heavenly Father gives only good gifts to His children. But being wise as well, He knows which gifts are good, and which gifts are not. We have already seen how human parents would never give a stone or a snake to children who ask for bread or a fish: but, think of this, what would a parent do if the children – whether through ignorance or folly – actually asked for a stone or a snake? Now irresponsible parents might grant their children's request; but wise parents would deny it. And certainly our heavenly Father would never do such a thing, because He only gives good gifts. So then, if we ask good things of God, He grants them; but if we ask things which are not good – either not good in themselves, or not good for us, or not good for others in some way – He denies them. And thank God that the granting of our needs is conditional, not only upon our asking and our seeking and our knocking, but also on whether what we are asking seeking or knocking, is in fact good. Thank God He answers prayer; thank God He also sometimes denies our requests. Dr. Lloyd-Jones puts it very well when he says, 'I thank God that God is not prepared to do anything I may chance to ask Him. I am profoundly grateful that He did not grant me certain things for which I asked, and that He shut certain doors in my face.'

So we leave that paragraph. We come to the fourth: Our relation to –

All Men, with 'the golden rule' (v12). Now the logic of the '*therefore* whatever you will that men should do to you . . .' is not very plain. It may refer to the previous verse, and imply that if God is good to all who seek Him, we must likewise be good to all. Or it may refer back to the 'judge not that you be not judged,' and take up the underlying argument against censoriousness and hypocrisy.

The golden rule was already in existence in a negative form, before Jesus spoke it. For example, in the book of Tobias in the Apocrypha, 'Do that to no man which you hate.' Rabbi Hillel said, 'What is hateful to you, do not do to your neighbour.' Jesus took it, turned it round, and made it positive. 'Whatever you want your neighbour to do to you, do to your neighbour.' Now the non-Christian way is to do to others as they do to us. The Christian way is to do to others as we wished they would do to us – which is a very different thing. It may seem a very low standard, like 'Love your neighbour as you love yourself.' 'Is self-love to be the standard of my love for my neighbour? What a low standard!' you may say. But actually it is a very high standard, because we love ourselves a great deal. It is also a very flexible principle, for self-advantage can guide us in all our behaviour to others. All we have to do is use our imagination, put ourselves into the other man's shoes, and ask ourselves, 'How should I like to be treated in his situation?' When you do that, you have your answer as to how to treat him in that situation. Treat him as you would like to be treated yourself. As Bishop Ryle says, 'It settles a hundred difficult points.' It prevents the necessity of laying down endless little rules for our conduct in specific cases. It is a universal principle of such wide application that Jesus could go on to say, 'this is the law and the prophets.' That is, whenever anybody directs his conduct toward others according to how he would like others to direct their conduct to him, he has fulfilled all the teaching of the law, and all the teaching of the prophets.

That brings us, five, to –

Our Fellow Pilgrims (vv13–14). Jesus turns from this universal principle governing our relation to all men, to the need to enter the narrow gate and join the pilgrim minority on the narrow way. We have to see how stark is the contrast between the alternatives, and how absolute is the choice. We saw yesterday in chapter 6 that there are two treasures, two masters, two ambitions, two preoccupations; and there is only one choice – we have to choose the one or the other. Now all of us are so made that we wish we had a lot of choices; or we wish we could fuse them all into one, and avoid having to make any choice at all. Jesus cuts across our syncretism. Look at what He says.

(a) There are *two ways* – easy and hard. The easy way is broad and open – that is what the Greek word means. There is plenty of room on it, diversity or opinions and laxity of morals. There are no boundaries on the broad road: you can think anything you like, you can do anything you like – no boundaries of thought or conduct. But the hard way is narrow: and its narrowness is due to something called revelation, the revelation of God which restricts pilgrims on the narrow way to what God has revealed to be true, and what God has revealed to be right.

(b) There are *two gates*. The gate leading to the easy way is wide: it is very easy to get on the easy road. There is no limit to the luggage that you can take with you; you need leave nothing behind. But the gate leading to the hard way is narrow: it is easy to miss, and it is narrow as a needle's eye. You have to leave everything behind – your sin and your selfishness; and it is like a turnpike gate, you have to enter one by one.

(c) There are *two destinations*. The easy way, entered by the wide gate, leads to 'destruction,' a terrible word; for whatever may be precisely the nature of hell – and I wish that we were a little more tentative in our teaching about it; for I myself would want to say that hell is as much beyond our full understanding as is heaven – whatever may be its precise nature, everything good in it is destroyed. Hell is destruction – the destruction of beauty, love, hope, peace; and that for ever. But the hard way, entered by the narrow gate, leads to life – the life that is life indeed; the life that is truly life, lived in communion with God, in which we see His face, behold His majesty, and share His glory.

(d) There are *two crowds*. Entering by the wide gate and travelling along the easy path to destruction, are many. It is a busy and a populous thoroughfare. But as for the narrow gate leading to the hard way that ends in life, those who find it are few. Jesus seems to have known that His followers would be a despised minority movement; just a small, but a very happy band of pilgrims, 'stepping fearless through the night.'

Have you got that stark contrast? There are only two ways, easy and hard. There is no middle way. There are only two gates, broad and narrow. There is no other gate. There are only two crowds, large and small. There is no neutral multitude. There are only two destinations, destruction and life. There is no third alternative. *And it is very unfashionable talk today.* For in our day, men are lovers of Aristotle and the golden mean. The most popular path today is the *via media*, the middle of the road, and people resent being faced by so stark a choice. But that is the choice that Jesus told us we have to make.

That brings us to the sixth group –

The False Prophets (vv16–20). It is very natural that Jesus immediately refers to them, after He has outlined the way of salvation – the narrow road that leads to life – because false prophets are adept at blurring the issues of salvation. What they love to do above all else is to keep people off the narrow way, and blind their eyes to the narrow gate. Their refrain is 'Peace, peace!' – when there is no peace. Sometimes they try to make out that the narrow way is in reality quite broad; and the hard way, you know, is really very easy: and they turn the teaching of Jesus topsy turvy. Sometimes they insist that the broad road in fact does not lead to destruction, but that all roads, even if they go off in opposite directions, ultimately lead you to God and to the same destination. These are false prophets. They make it hard for seekers to find the narrow gate and the hard road to life. Jesus says, 'Beware of false prophets.'

There is a great deal in that phrase. Jesus assumed and taught by that phrase that truth is not relative. There are false prophets; there is such a thing as falsehood, the opposite of truth; there are such things as lies.

Jesus did not teach that truth was relative. He did not teach that contradictory opinions are in reality complementary insights into the same truth. He said there is such a thing as truth, and there is such a thing as falsehood. There are true preachers, and there are false prophets: and you want to beware of the false prophets. There is such a thing as absolute truth, from which the falsehood of the false prophets is to be distinguished.

Jesus evidently assumed that there would be false teachers in the Christian church, as there had been false prophets in the Old Testament; and He says, 'Beware of them!' There is no sense in telling people to beware of what isn't there! You wouldn't put a notice on your garden gate, 'Beware of the dog,' if all you had at home was a couple of cats and a budgerigar. You say, 'Beware of the dog' because there is a dog, and a dangerous one, to beware of. Jesus says, 'Beware of false prophets' because they are there in the church, and they are dangerous. He says they are like wolves. They are wolves bent on dividing and destroying the flock; and they are ravenous wolves. But they won't be easy to recognise, as these wolves will come in the disguise of sheep. They are wolves in the clothing of sheep, and unwary people will mistake them for sheep, and will give them an unsuspecting welcome. So Jesus says, 'Be on your guard. Don't relax your vigilance.' Alas, the church has often been taken off its guard.

Now to this general teaching Jesus adds the specific test, changing His metaphor from sheep and wolves to trees and their fruit. Twice He says, for emphasis (verses 16 and 20): 'You'll know them by their fruits.' What is the fruit? The analogy is plain: you *can* tell a tree by its fruit. You tell a pear tree when it bears pears; figs grow on fig trees, and not on thorn trees; and you don't get thistles from a fig tree. I mean, it's obvious. Now, what of the fruit of the false prophet? To begin with, of course, their *character*. Since in the allegory of the vine and the branches in John 15 the fruit-bearing Christian is one who abides in Christ, and Christian fruitfulness is Christ likeness, then whenever we see the meekness and the gentleness of Christ, the purity of Christ, and His love and holiness, we may guess that the prophet is a true one, because of his fruit of Christ likeness. But whenever these qualities are missing, however specious his teaching may be, we recognise it is false.

Next, it is not only his character, it is his *teaching*. In Matthew 12:33–37 Jesus applies the same fruit-tree metaphor to our speech. He says, 'How can you speak good, when you are evil? For out of the abundance of the heart the mouth speaks.' So you've got to listen to what he is saying, as well as looking at his character.

Thirdly, there is their *influence*. We have to ask ourselves, what effect does their teaching have on their followers? Sometimes the falsity of false teaching does not at once emerge in a teacher's character, or in his doctrinal system, but it is seen in its disastrous effects. It upsets people's faith; it promotes godlessness and moral laxity; it causes division in the flock of Christ. By their fruits you shall know them – their character, their teaching, their influence. Now, brethren, this paragraph is not an invitation to take up as your hobby the sport called heresy-hunting. It is not an invitation to us to become suspicious of everybody. It is simply to recognise that there are false prophets in the church, and to be on our guard, because truth matters, and needs to be preserved in the church.

Now, seven, we come to the last relationship: our relation to –

Jesus Christ, our Teacher and our Lord (vv21–27); and Christ's call to obedience, to a radical commitment of our mind, our will, and our life, to His teaching. Here Jesus warns us of a few dangers – of a merely verbal profession, with our words (vv21–23); and of a merely intellectual knowledge (vv24–27). There is no substitute for obedience. Jesus emphasises with great solemnity that upon this moral obedience our eternal destiny hangs.

First, *the danger of a merely verbal profession*. 'Not every one who *says* to me, Lord, Lord, shall enter the kingdom' (vv21). 'On that day many will say to me . . .' (v22). Their words: a verbal profession. Our eternal destiny is determined, Jesus said, neither by what we *are* saying to Jesus Christ now, nor by what we *shall* say to Jesus Christ on the judgment day; but by whether we *do what we say*, whether our verbal profession leads to obedience. Now the Christian profession that Jesus describes appears to be admirable. It is *polite*. It addresses Jesus as Lord; and the most courteous way to refer to Jesus is still, 'our Lord.' It is polite; it is orthodox. To call Jesus Lord is an accurate style of address. It acknowledges Him to be what He is, the Lord. He is the Lord: it is the divine title. God has exalted Him, and given Him all authority; He is the Lord. The title corresponds to the reality. It is an orthodox confession of Jesus as Lord. It is polite; it is orthodox; it is fervent. It is not a cold 'Lord'; it is an enthusiastic, 'Lord, *Lord*!' repeated for emphasis, as if the speaker wishes to draw attention to the strength and zeal of his devotion.

Next, it is *public*. He does not just say, 'Lord, Lord,' to Christ personally and privately. Some claim that they have even prophesied in Christ's name – that is, spoken publicly in His name, and called Him Lord. Next, it is *spectacular*. To make His point, Jesus cites the most extreme example of a verbal profession: that is, those who claim to exercise a supernatural, spectacular ministry in the name of Jesus. And the name of Jesus is the emphasis: the name they profess. Three times they use it: 'In the name of Christ we prophesy; we cast out demons; we have done many mighty works in this name.'

Now, you might ask, 'What better Christian profession could you ask than this? Here are people who call Jesus Lord, with courtesy, with orthodoxy, with enthusiasm, in private devotion, in public ministry: what's wrong with this?' The answer is: Nothing, in itself; and yet everything. Because we have seen that what they say and will say to Christ, does not tally with what Christ says to them. It will be a solemn profession: 'I never knew you. You may claim to know me, and use my name. But I don't know you.' How is that? Well, because their confession was verbal, not moral; it was with the lips, and not the life. They said to Him, 'Lord, Lord,' but they had never submitted to His Lordship. He would have to say to them: 'Why do ye call me, Lord, Lord, and do not the things that I say?' (Luke 6:46). 'Not every one who *says* to me, Lord, Lord, shall enter the kingdom of heaven, but he who does the will of my Father.' Verbal profession is not enough, if it does not lead to obedience.

Secondly, *the danger of a merely intellectual knowledge* (vv24–27). In verses 21–23 the contrast is between saying and doing. The contrast in verses 24–27 is between hearing and doing. 'Every one who hears these sayings of mine and does them . . .' (v24); 'every one who hears these sayings of mine and does them not . . .' (v26). Jesus illustrates the contrast between obedient and disobedient hearers by His parable of the house-builders. Both are building houses, and the casual observer might well notice very little difference between them. But the fundamental difference between the house-builders is in the foundations on which they build: and, listen – the foundations of a house are hidden. You can't see them. Not until a storm broke were the foundations revealed. For the house on the rock stood firm; but the house on the sand gave way in irreparable ruin.

So, too, professing Christians, the genuine and the spurious, often look very much alike. You cannot immediately tell which is which. Both groups are building their lives apparently on the teaching of Christ: they appear to be. This teaching of Jesus here at the end of the Sermon on the Mount is not between Christians and pagans: it is between professing Christians and real Christians. For both lots hear the sayings of Christ; and what is common to both spiritual house-builders is the teaching of Jesus. Both of them in some sense are members of the visible church. They read their Bible; they go to church; they hear sermons; they come to Keswick. You cannot tell the difference between them at first sight, because the deep foundations of their lives are invisible.

The real question is not whether they hear the teaching of Jesus, but whether they do it. Jesus said that only a storm will reveal it; sometimes the storms of life – crisis, calamity – betray what manner of men and women we really are. When the storm breaks the foundations are revealed; and above all, the storm of the day of judgment.

So are we clear that what Jesus Christ stresses in these two paragraphs at the end of the sermon is plain and simple? That an intellectual knowledge of Christ, although essential, is not enough; a verbal profession of Christ, although essential, is not enough. The question is not whether we *say* nice, polite, orthodox, fervent things about Jesus; and it is not whether we *hear* His word, listening to Bible Readings, studying, memorising, till our minds are stuffed with the teaching of Jesus. The question is quite simply, Do we *do* what we say? Do we *do* what we know? The Lordship of Christ which we profess, must be the central reality of our lives.

Now I have left myself a few minutes for a conclusion, in which I want to look back over the whole sermon. There are many people who will say they are prepared to accept the Sermon on the Mount. You meet them. They know it contains sayings like, 'Blessed are the merciful, for they shall obtain mercy . . . Whatever you would that men should do to you, do to them.' 'Lovely teaching,' they say. 'Here is Jesus of Nazareth, a moral teacher at His simplest and best. Here,' they say, 'is the original Jesus; plain ethics and no dogmas, an unsophisticated prophet of righteousness and love.'

But, as I hope we have seen, they are wrong. For the Sermon on the Mount discloses above all else the uniqueness of the Teacher; and the major question the Sermon on the Mount forces upon us is not even, 'What do you think of His teaching?' but, 'Who on earth is this Teacher?' This was the reaction of those who heard it. 'When Jesus had finished these sayings, the crowds were astonished at His teaching, for He taught them as one who had authority, and not as their scribes' (7:29–29). Jesus had authority. He did not hum and haw and hesitate. He wasn't apologetic. He knew what He wanted to say, and He said it with quiet, dogmatic assurance.

So will you consider in these last minutes –

The Authority of Jesus Christ. First, His authority as *Teacher.* There have been many teachers in the world, but there is something exceptional about the teaching of Jesus. Commentators have described it variously in these words – James Denny: 'His sovereign, legislative authority.' Machen: 'He claimed the right to legislate for the kingdom of God, to lay down the law.' Spurgeon: 'He spoke royally.' Plummer writes of 'His royal assurance.' Calvin: 'A strange, indescribable and unwonted majesty drew to Him the minds of men.' He did not speak like the scribes, who never spoke without quoting their authorities. He did not speak like prophets, who hid behind the authority of Jehovah, and said, 'Thus saith the Lord . . .' He said, 'Verily, verily, *I* say unto you . . .' With this majestic 'I' He spoke in His own name and on His own authority. And the crowds were astonished and awed by His authority as a Teacher.

Secondly, His authority as *the* Christ. He said He had come as the Lord's Anointed, on the Lord's mission. We saw it on the first morning: 'I have come not to abolish . . . but to fulfil' (5:17). Jesus dared to claim that all the teaching of the law and the prophets found their fulfilment in Him. He was the Christ. The whole prophetic testimony of Old Testament Scripture converged upon His person. 'I have come to fulfil it all.' His authority as the Christ.

Thirdly, His authority as *the Lord.* He did not only teach: He expected to be obeyed. His complaint was not that they addressed Him as Lord: He accepted the title as an appropriate one – but that they did not submit to His Lordship. He expected His followers to build the whole of their lives upon the foundation of His teaching, and put it in practice. He said, 'If you do it, you are wise; if you don't, you're stupid, you're fools.' He measured men's wisdom and folly by their obedience, or lack of it, to His Lordship.

Next, His authority as *Judge*. He claimed to be the central figure on the judgment day. 'On the judgment day,' He said, '*I will say to you* . . . you will speak to *me*. I shall be the central figure on that day. And you will speak to *me*, and *I* will say to you, 'I never knew you. Depart from *me* . . .' 'This 'I, I,' 'me, me': He dares to cast Himself in the role of the judge.

And, five, His authority as *God*. Yes, I do not hesitate to say He claimed not only to be the Son of God, and to speak of God as 'My Father,' and 'the will of my Father': He puts Himself on equality with God. Let me put it to you like this. In the last Beatitude, 'Blessed are you when men . . . persecute you on my account, for so men persecuted the prophets who were before you' (5:11–12). Now think, please, carefully. He expects His followers to suffer for His sake, and likens them to the Old Testament prophets who suffered for God's sake. And the implication is inescapable. If He is likening His disciples to the prophets of God, He is likening Himself to God.

Here, then is your 'original Jesus'; here is your 'simple teacher of righteousness.' He teaches with the authority of God. He claims to have come to fulfil Old Testament Scripture. He is the Lord to be obeyed. He casts Himself in the role of Judge. He speaks of God as His Father, and He puts Himself on an equality with God. To this authority of Jesus we must submit. We must submit our minds to His teaching: we have no liberty to disagree with Jesus. We must submit our wills to His command: we have no liberty to disobey Jesus. There is only one place for us to occupy – in the dust, on our faces, with the words of Thomas on our lips: 'My Lord, and my God.'

The Spirit in the Believer

The Bishop of Norwich has been helping us to understand the teaching of Jesus about the Holy Spirit and His
varied ministries, and I want to invite you now to consider with me some of the teaching of the apostle Paul on
the same subject. The main text that I pray that God will
write in our hearts is, 'Blessed be the God and Father of
our Lord Jesus Christ, who has blessed us in Christ with
every spiritual blessing in the heavenly places' (Eph.
1:3). The repetition of the word 'bless' is very remarkable, is it not? We bless God for blessing us with every
conceivable blessing in Christ.

If we are Christian people, God has united us to Jesus
Christ. That is what it means to be 'in Christ.' It doesn't
mean to be inside Him spatially. It means to be in Him as
a limb is in the body, or a branch is in the vine. To be in
Christ is to be joined to Christ; vitally, organically united
to Christ. This is the great thing that God has done to all
of us, Jesus Christ for us is not 'above the bright blue
sky.' He is not living in the pages of the history books or
Gospels. Jesus Christ is alive and our contemporary; and
we are in Christ, united to Him in this organic way. Now,
by joining us to Jesus Christ, God has blessed us with
every spiritual blessing.

This is a major theme of the great epistles that Paul
wrote while he was in prison. For example, in the letter
to the Colossians he speaks of God's 'fulness' – and he
says this fulness dwells in Christ. And so we, if we are in

Christ, have come to fulness ourselves. The fulness, he says, devolves from God to Jesus Christ, and from Jesus Christ to us. First of all this fulness is in Christ; but if I am in Christ, then it is mine as well.

And what in the letter to the Colossians is called the fulness, here in the letter to the Ephesians it is called 'every spiritual blessing in Christ in the heavenly places.' The 'heavenly places' mean the unseen world of spiritual reality. The phrase emphasises that these blessings, with which God has blessed us in Christ, are spiritual blessings. Paul say so. And the reason why they are called spiritual blessings is that they are bestowed by the Holy Spirit.

So you see once again, as in the passages that the Bishop of Norwich was leading us to understand, so here there is a clear Trinitarian reference: 'Blessed be the God and Father of our Lord Jesus Christ, who has blessed us in Christ with every spiritual blessing' – every blessing of the Holy Spirit. The great blessings of a Christian originate with God the Father, who is the Father of our Lord Jesus Christ, and our Father if we are in Christ. They originate with God the Father; they are enjoyed by all who are in Christ; and they are bestowed by the Holy Spirit. God the Father is the source from whom the blessings come; Jesus Christ is the sphere in whom the blessings are enjoyed; and the Holy Spirit is the agent through whom the blessings are given. I just long, with my heart and mind, that every Christian could understand this truth, believe it, and act upon it. God has blessed us . . . If He is our Father, and made us His children, and we are in Christ, then every conceivable blessing is ours, at least in the bud, if not yet in the blossom. No spiritual blessing, no blessing of the Holy Spirit is not ours if we are Christ's. So the great blessing of God with which He blesses us is past, not future. It is ours already. He did it. He blessed us when He joined us to Jesus Christ. I would sum it up in these words: if we are in Christ, we have everything, because everything we need is in Christ.

Now the rest of this great letter to the Ephesians is really devoted to an exposition of this theme. It expounds every spiritual blessing with which God has blessed us, and the implications of the blessings we have received. And I thought it might help us if I make with you a brief survey, in order to understand what Paul is talking about, and then come at the end to see how we can enter into these blessings in greater enjoyment which are already ours in Christ.

So let us take a survey. Did you know the Holy Spirit is mentioned in every one of the six chapters of the letter to the Ephesians? What are these blessings? To help us remember them, I will give you the five major ones.

First –

The Seal of the Spirit. 'In Christ you also, who have heard the word of the truth, the gospel of your salvation, and have believed in Him, were sealed with the promised Holy Spirit, who is the guarantee of our inheritance . . .' (1:13–14). That is, all who have heard the Gospel and believed in Jesus, are said to have been sealed with the promised Spirit of God. The same verb is used in 4:30, which exhorts us not to grieve the Holy Spirit, by whom we were sealed unto the day of redemption. This indicates that the sealing took place when we believed. It is something past. It is something that has happened. It is something that God has given us, the seal of the Holy Spirit.

Now, a seal is *a mark of ownership*: whether it be the affixing of some personal seal to a legal document; or stamping your name upon some tool or instrument; or branding of sheep or cattle with a hot iron, the purpose of sealing is to mark something as belonging to us. And God's seal, by which He brands us as belonging for ever to Him, is the Holy Spirit Himself. The Holy Spirit is the identity tag of the Christian. If the Holy Spirit dwells within you, you are a Christian. If the Holy Spirit doesn't, you are not a Christian. For God has sealed us if we believed in Jesus, with the seal of the Holy Spirit Himself who dwells within us.

This seal is an *indelible* seal: it cannot and it will not be erased. We have been 'sealed unto the day of redemption' (4:30). That is, until the final day, when our bodies have been redeemed. God has branded us with His seal the Holy Spirit, and will never take Him from us; and this divine seal is God's guarantee that we shall enter into our heavenly inheritance one day.

That is the first spiritual blessing that Paul particularly mentions with regard to the Holy Spirit here. What a precious blessing it is! There is so much uncertainty and insecurity in the world. The very survival of our human civilisation is in jeopardy. There are many men and women whose hearts are failing them for fear, and there is deep insecurity. Brother, sister, God has sealed you for eternity with the Holy Spirit. He has blessed you with His spiritual blessing, the seal of the Spirit upon your heart.

Secondly, there is –

The Illumination of the Spirit. In 1:16–19 we have another Trinitarian statement, that God the Father gives us the Holy Spirit of wisdom and revelation that we should know Christ. I hope we are all clear that the Holy Spirit delights beyond all else to bear witness to Jesus. He is the author of Scripture, and the Holy Scripture is testimony to Jesus. Through the prophets of the Old Testament and the apostles of the New Testament, the Holy Spirit has bequeathed to the church His unique definitive witness to

Christ. The whole Bible is witness to Jesus Christ by the Holy Spirit. But that doesn't mean that His work was finished when the Canon of Scripture was completed, but only that His work has changed. For now His work is no longer one so much of revelation as of illumination; to illumine our minds and the eyes of our hearts to understand what He has revealed in Christ and in Scripture. And He longs to open our eyes in particular to the hope to which God has called us in heaven, the riches of His glorious inheritance, and the immeasurable greatness of His power that He can put forth to us who believe. That is the second spiritual blessing that is already ours in Christ. God has blessed us with the seal of the Spirit, the illumination of the Spirit, and He will go on opening our eyes wider to see these things throughout our Christian life.

Thirdly –

The Strength of the Spirit. Notice that the words 'strength' and 'might' and 'power' occur in Paul's second prayer in 3:14–19 as they occur in the first, in chapter 1. In the first prayer the Holy Spirit enlightens us that we may *know* these things; in chapter 3, that we may *experience* them. Notice that the strength of the Holy Spirit is not a shallow thing; it is not a superficial work. Do you believe this? He is able to penetrate into your inner man, into the innermost recesses of your human personality, right into your inmost being. You are able to be strengthened into your innermost being by the Holy Spirit, so that Christ may reside and reign in your heart by faith. He is able to deepen our love for righteousness, to intensify our appetite, to strengthen our resolve, to fortify our will. Oh that we might know the strength of the Holy Spirit right into our innermost being; the seal of the Spirit, the illumination of the Spirit, the strength of the Spirit, all given us already, because the Spirit dwells in our hearts.

Fourthly –

The Unity of the Spirit. It is a great mistake to think of the Holy Spirit exclusively in individual terms. He is the individual possession of the believer. He seals the individual. He enlightens our mind. He strengthens us into our innermost being. But He is also at work in the church, in the Christian community, in the fellowship. And this is the fellowship of the Holy Spirit. Look at 4:4–6, 'There is one body and one Spirit (the unity of the Spirit), just as you were called to the one hope that belongs to your call; one Lord, one faith, one baptism, one God and Father of us all . . .' (yet another Trinitarian reference). You see, there is only one God and Father of us all (v. 6); there is one Lord (v5), our Lord Jesus; and there is only one Spirit (v4). It is this unity of the Godhead that is reflected in the unity of the church. There is only one Christian family. We may try to break it up in our different denominations, but it remains for ever one Christian family, because there is only one heavenly Father. There is only one Christian faith, hope and baptism, because there is only one Lord Jesus, in whom we have believed, into whom we have been baptised, and for whose coming we are hoping, expecting. And there is only one Christian body because there is only one Holy Spirit animating the body. The unity that we have at Keswick is the unity of the Spirit dwelling within each of us and making us one. The fundamental spiritual unity of the church is as indestructible as the fundamental unity of the Godhead. You can no more divide the unity of the church than you can divide the unity of the Godhead. The one Father creates the one family; the one Lord Jesus creates the one faith, hope and baptism; and the one Holy Spirit creates the one body.

But Paul doesn't leave it there. He adds to the affirmation that there is one body, one Spirit (v4), an exhortation that we are to maintain the unity of the Spirit (v3). Now you may say that if there is only one body and one Spirit, how can we be exhorted to maintain that which can never be destroyed? I think the only answer is, we are to maintain it visibly. We are to seek to exhibit visibly the unity that is indestructible because there is only one Father, one Lord Jesus, one Holy Spirit.

So let me ask you about your local Christian assembly, or church, or community, or congregation. Is the unity of the Spirit there? Are you bound together in love? Can you truly sing, 'They will know that we are Christians by our love'? Is the unity of the Spirit maintained, visibly manifested? What is the good of saying, 'We are all one in Christ Jesus' if we go back to our bickerings and our squabblings and our cliques and factions and jealousies? God has blessed us with this spiritual blessing, the unity of the Spirit. It is a given thing. It is a blessing we have received. And we must maintain this unity, and enjoy this blessing more and more.

Fifthly –

The Sword of the Spirit (6:17). Now you know this is in the passage about the armour of God, describing vividly the Christian's warfare with the devil and principalities and powers, urging upon us the indispensable necessity of clothing ourselves from head to foot in the armour of God. Six pieces of armour are mentioned. There are the shoes and the girdle which are parts of every soldier's equipment. There is the breastplate, the shield and the helmet, which are essentially worn for protection. Only the sword of the Spirit could be called an offensive weapon, used in attack as well as in defence. And the sword of the Spirit is the Word of God; the Word that God has spoken, not only in the living Word, Jesus Christ, but in the Scriptural Word – in the Word that is written for our learning, that God in His gracious providence has caused to be preserved. This sword of the Spirit, the Word of God, is living and active and powerful; and it pierces the mind and the conscience. It exposes our motives. It divides soul from spirit, revealing the difference between what is natural and what is spiritual, and shows whether we are born again or not.

I hope all of us are learning to make the Spirit sword our sword. I hope we are learning to use God's Word in combat with the devil, as Jesus did. I hope you sometimes turn on the devil, as I find I have to every day, and say to Him, 'In the name of Jesus, I command you be gone, Satan, because it stands written in Scripture, you shall not do whatever you are tempting me to do.' That is using the sword of the Spirit, and I hope we are using it, wielding it with skill in our witness; and if you are a pastor or a missionary, and called to public speaking, I hope you are conscientious in speaking Biblically, wielding the sword of the Spirit that is sharp, and penetrates, and pricks the conscience.

Well, I hope this brief survey has shown us how comprehensive, how pervasive is the work of the Holy Spirit. At every point His work is indispensable. Let me sum it up. God has given the seal of the Spirit for our hearts, the illumination of the Spirit for our minds, the strength of the Spirit for our wills, the unity of the Spirit for our fellowship; and the sword of the Spirit, for our hands to wield it in Christian combat from day to day.

Now God says to us, as He said to His people in Old Testament days, 'What more could I have done, than I have done? I have given you everything that is necessary for the living of the Christian life. I have blessed you with every spiritual blessing, every blessing of the Holy Spirit: His seal and illumination and strength and unity and sword, and many others beside. I have blessed you

with every spiritual blessing in Christ. What more could
I have done for you than I have done?'

No, I think I know what is in your mind at this point.
You are saying, 'Well, I know that is true. God could say
that to me. Then why is it that my Christian life frequently falls so far short of what it ought to be? And why
does my attainment lag so far behind my potential, if
God has given me all these things, and blessed me in
Christ with all these spiritual blessings?' The answer is
quite simple, and I want us to try and unpack it and
unfold it, and then I hope we shall act upon it. It is this:
it is not because God has denied us any blessing. It is not
because God has withheld from us any spiritual blessing. It is because we have not exploited the blessings we
have already received. God has blessed us with every
spiritual blessing in Christ in the heavenly places. Then
why don't we enjoy them? Because we are not exploiting
them, not entering into them, not possessing our possessions; not walking through the promised land, north,
south, east and west, and taking possession of that
which God has given us. That is the reason.

You know the story of the old Indian – in the United
States, not in India – who died of starvation. When he was
dead they found round his neck a little bag containing an
old yellow parchment. He had kept it as a kind of charm.
He had no idea that it meant anything. But it turned out to
be a document granting a pension to the man's grandfa-
ther for his bravery in the American War of Independence,
and the terms of the deed made this pension available to
the first recipient and his son and his grandson – the man
who had died of starvation. The document had been
signed by George Washington himself. This man had been
blessed, but he had never exploited his blessing.

That is exactly the state of many Christians, many of
us here, indeed all of us to a certain extent. In particular

there are two failures that we have got to look at. Paul gives two commands in this letter to the Ephesians, to help them to understand how they can enter into these blessings that have already been bestowed upon them. One is in 4:30, 'Do not grieve the holy Spirit of God'; and the second is in 5:18, 'Be filled with the Spirit.'

Let us look at them briefly. *'Don't* grieve – don't hurt – *the Holy Spirit.'* Don't sadden the Holy Spirit. Don't cause Him grief and sorrow. The Holy Spirit is a sensitive Spirit. The Holy Spirit is a tender Spirit. We cannot even begin to understand the delicacy of His sensitivity. It is not an accident that He is called the *Holy* Spirit. The Holy Spirit cannot bear contamination with anything unholy. Do you know some sensitive or shy person, who in certain uncongenial company wants to run out of the room, or if he cannot run out of the room, simply withdraws into his own shell in embarrassment? The Holy Spirit is like that, so sensitive that He shrinks away from contamination by any evil, and all unholiness – the things that are mentioned in this chapter: lying, anger, dishonesty, hypocrisy, slander, bitterness, malice, immorality. All these things make the Holy Spirit withdraw, not I think from us, but within us; not out of the front door, but into the attic or into the cellar. Don't grieve . . . And if we have grieved the Holy Spirit we need to repent, to confess what we have done, to turn from it; because when the Holy Spirit is grieved, He is not able to give us in our experience these blessings which are already ours in potential, but cannot be ours in actuality when the Holy Spirit is grieved.

Second, *'Be filled with the Spirit.'* Don't be drunk with wine, for that is excess. Be filled with the Spirit. Notice that drunkenness and being filled with the Spirit are contrasted. Drunkenness is due to a lack of self-control, and it leads to a further loss of self-control. People who are drunk lose their humanity and behave like animals. The fulness of the Holy Spirit leads to the precise opposite; far from losing our self-control and indulging in excess like drunkenness, self-control is the ninth fruit of the Holy Spirit in Galatians 5. Those who are filled with the Holy Spirit never behave like irrational animals. On the contrary, whereas excessive alcohol robs us of our humanity, the Holy Spirit is the only person who can make you a real human being. The Holy Spirit is the only person who can lead you into a fully human existence, and make you the man and woman that God wants you to be.

So it is a great mistake to suppose that the fulness of the Holy Spirit is a kind of spiritual intoxication. The only reason why, on the day of Pentecost, Christians were thought to be drunk was not because they had lost their self-control, but because they were speaking in foreign languages that people couldn't understand, so they thought they must be drunk. They had not lost their self-control at all. Drunkenness is excess. Being filled with the Spirit leads to love, joy, peace, patience, kindness, goodness, faithfulness, gentleness, self-control.

But although the two states are different, intoxication leading to lack of self-control, and the fulness of the Spirit leading to self-control, the way in which both are reached is similar. How do people get drunk? Answer: by going on drinking. How do people get filled with the Spirit? Answer: by going on drinking. And my authority for saying that is Jesus Christ, who said, 'If anybody is thirsty, let him come to me and drink. And he who believes in me . . . out of his inner man shall flow rivers of living water' and He was speaking about the Holy Spirit, John adds. So that somebody filled with the Spirit is so full that the blessing overflows into the lives of others. How does that happen? Well, he has to come to

Christ, and keeps coming to Christ – the verb is present tense – and keeps drinking from Christ.

I was in several Asian countries the month before last when it was very hot, and whenever I got thirsty I had a drink. And as soon as I got thirsty again, I had another drink. And as soon as I got thirsty again, I had another drink. I kept getting thirsty, and I kept drinking. That is what Jesus says we have to do. It is what is meant by faith. Faith is coming to Jesus, keeping coming to Jesus, drinking from Jesus, keeping drinking, asking Him to fill us with the Holy Spirit.

So you see, the answer is very simple. It is repentance and faith. If you grieve the Holy Spirit you must repent and turn from this sin. If you know you are not filled with the Spirit because you are thirsty, you must come to Jesus in faith and drink. Repentance and faith. Keep repenting. Whenever anything is on your conscience, whenever you realise that you have grieved the Spirit, repent at that moment. You will never increase in blessing if you don't repent. If you are conscious of this, go back to the point where you disobeyed, and repent. Keep repenting every day, the moment you are conscious of grieving and hurting the Spirit. And whenever you are conscious of being thirsty, come to Jesus for another drink, and ask Him to fill you with the Spirit. Keep repenting, keep believing, keep repenting, keep drinking.

Repentance and faith, the great secrets; and if you do this you'll experience in a progressively fuller measure all the spiritual blessings with which God has already blessed you in Christ.

*   *   *   *

We are going to have a few moments of quiet. I want us to have an opportunity to repent. I need to repent. I have needed to repent many times already today. All of us do. We don't love the Lord our God with all our heart, mind, soul and strength. We need to keep repenting.

I want to help you to repent. And as I say some words of confession and then say, 'I have grieved your Holy Spirit,' I want you to reply with the words, 'I turn from my sin in repentance.' Don't say it if you can't; but if you can, and want to make it real.

Lord Jesus, I confess to you my pride, my hunger for the praise of men, my love of flattery, my self-conceit. I have grieved your Holy Spirit. *I turn from my sin in repentance.*

Lord Jesus, I confess to you my falsehoods, the lies that I have told, the shams that I have maintained, hypocrisies of which I have been guilty. I have grieved your Holy Spirit. *I turn from my sin in repentance.*

Lord Jesus, I confess to you my anger, malice, slander, jealousy, impatience, unkindness, immoral thinking or deeds. I have grieved your Holy Spirit. *I turn from my sin in repentance.*

O Jesus I confess to you every loss of self-control in thought, word or deed, every time I have been more like an animal than a human being. I have grieved your Holy Spirit. *I turn from my sin in repentance.*

Now Lord Jesus, we thank you that you are the only one who can give the living water to us to drink. Heavenly Father, we thank you that you have blessed us with every spiritual blessing in Christ. We are thirsty. Nothing in this world could ever satisfy us. We come to you now, Lord Jesus. We want to drink. We drink deeply of the wells of salvation, deeply of the Holy Spirit. We ask that He may fill us with Himself. Lord Jesus, fill us now with your Holy Spirit, as we have repented of all our sin, and as we come to you in simple trust to drink.

Now send us forth to keep repenting and to keep believing and to keep coming and to keep drinking and to keep enjoying all these blessings with which we have been blessed by our heavenly Father in Christ. Hear our prayer, for your name's sake.

1975

God's New Society

An Exposition of the Letter to the Ephesians

1. New Life (1 –2:10)

It may seem ludicrous that we should attempt in four hours to encompass the whole letter to the Ephesians. In some ways it is ludicrous. There are depths of divine truth in this letter which we shall not fathom in a lifetime, and which in four hours we can only begin to explore. Nevertheless I believe that our task will be worthwhile, because it is one of our characteristic Evangelical weaknesses to concentrate so much on microscopic and atomistic study, that we miss the overview, the grand sweep of the revelation of God. And when we do this, our Christian faith becomes a lot of disorganised bits and pieces; and we fail to see things whole.

This great letter to the Ephesians divides itself naturally into two parts. In chapters 1–3, Paul declares what God has done; in chapters 4–6 he tells us what we must do and be, in consequence.

What has God done? Through the death, resurrection and exaltation of Jesus, God has given us *a new life*, and He has created *a new society*. And God's new society is a single, new, reconciled humanity, in which all the old divisive barriers have been broken down. So now the people of God are to live a life that is worthy of what God has called them to be. We are a new society; so we must live like it. We must cultivate new standards of unity and purity in the church; and our Christian life will be one of war and peace – peace in the harmony of our home relationships, but warfare in combat with the powers of evil, a warfare which by God's strength alone can be turned into victory.

Here, then, are the four major topics of the letter, which we shall study on four successive mornings. First, the new *life* that God has given us in Christ (1:1–2:10). Second, the new *society* that God is creating through Christ (2:11–3:21). Third, the new *standards* that God expects of us as His people (4:1–5:21); and fourth, the new *relationships* into which God has brought us – harmony at home, and hostility to the devil (5:22–6:24). The whole letter is a magnificent combination of Christian doctrine and Christian duty; of Christian faith and Christian life; what God has done and what we must be and do as a result.

We come, then, to our first topic – *The New Life*; and we begin with the *preface* to the letter (vv1–2), which we can only consider very briefly. It is the usual conventional introduction, in which the author announces himself and his readers, and greets them. Yet it is safe to say that nothing in the Bible belongs to meaningless convention. There is Christian significance here, in Paul's definition of himself, and of his readers, and of his message.

The *author* is the apostle Paul: (v1). True, some scholars deny the Pauline authorship of Ephesians; but conservative scholars still affirm it. I think you will agree that this Convention is not an appropriate time to debate the arguments for and against the Pauline authorship. What is important is that we regard the author neither as a private individual, who is airing his own opinions; nor as a fallible human teacher; not even as the church's greatest missionary hero, but as an apostle of Jesus Christ by the will of God: Paul, commissioned and inspired by Jesus, and as such an infallible teacher, so that if we would bow to the authority of Christ, we must bow to the authority of his apostle Paul. So let us listen to Christ as He speaks to us through His apostle, Paul.

The *readers* are variously described at the end of verse 1. They are 'the saints,' who, of course, are not a spiritual elite, a minority of exceptionally holy Christians, but all God's people, set apart (like Israel in the Old Testament) to belong to Him. They are also 'believers,' as the word 'faithful' should perhaps be rendered, because God's people are a household of faith, whose confidence for their salvation rests in Christ alone. Then they are 'in Christ Jesus,' personally and organically united to Jesus Christ, for this is the New Testament understanding of what a Christian is. Then they are 'at Ephesus,' living in a secular city – although many of the best manuscripts omit those words, so that Archbishop Ussher in the seventeenth century plausibly suggested that this was originally a circular letter to several Asian churches, of which the Ephesian church was the principal, because Ephesus was the capital city of Asia.

And then the *message*, 'Grace and peace' (v2), the customary greeting in Paul's letters, and yet particularly appropriate in the Ephesian letter, because grace and peace are key-words in this letter – grace indicating God's free, saving initiative in Christ; and peace, what He's taken the initiative to do, namely to reconcile us to Himself, and to one another, 'so making peace.' It would be difficult to find a better summary of the whole letter, than those three words, 'peace through grace.'

Now let us notice that our text divides itself into

praise and prayer. Firstly *praise* (vv3–14), that God has blessed us in Christ, and given us a new life; and then *prayer* (1:15–2:10), that God will open our eyes to grasp the fullness of His blessing in Christ. Firstly, then –

Praise (vv3–14). The sentence is a doxology, that God has 'blessed us with every spiritual blessing.' There seems to be a deliberate reference to the Trinity, because the *origin* of the blessing is God the Father; the *sphere* of the blessing is God the Son – God has 'blessed us in Christ' by virtue of our union with Him; and the *nature* of the blessing is spiritual, not material like Old Testament blessings, but 'in heavenly places,' in the heavenly realm rather than on earth, and 'every spiritual blessing' may very well mean, 'and every blessing of the Holy Spirit.' So this teaching is most important. We are Trinitarian Christians; we believe in God the Father, in God the Son, and in God the Holy Spirit. And we affirm that God the Father has 'blessed us in Christ with every spiritual blessing'; every blessing of the Holy Spirit has been given us by the Father, if we are in Christ. No blessing has been withheld. Oh, of course, we must grow into maturity in Christ; we must enter ever more fully into our spiritual inheritance; and God may give us many deeper and richer experiences of Christ from the Word. But already, if we are in Christ, 'all spiritual blessings' are ours by right.

What are these blessings? In the rest of the paragraph Paul unfolds them, and he refers to the past, the present, and the future. The past: 'before the foundation of the world' (v4) The present: 'in Him we have' certain things now (v7). And the future: a plan for the fullness of the time (v10).

(a) *The past blessing is election* (vv4–6). Paul reaches back in his mind 'before the foundation of the world,' before creation, before time began, into eternity in which only God existed in the fullness of His divine Being. In that pre-creation eternity God did something. He formed a purpose in His mind: He made a decision. It concerned both Christ, His only-begotten Son, and us, who did not yet exist, but whom He proposed to make His adopted sons. '*He* chose us in *Him*' (v4). Notice the three pronouns: *He* chose *us* in *Him* – *in* Christ. He put us and Christ together in His Mind. And in verse 5 he teaches the same truth in different words: 'He destined us in love to be His sons through Jesus Christ, according to the purpose of His will, and to the praise of His glory' – we're coming back to those phrases later.

Now everybody finds the doctrine of election difficult. 'Didn't I choose God?' somebody asks indignantly. To which we reply, 'Yes, indeed you did choose God, and freely; but only because in eternity He has first chosen you.' Scripture nowhere unravels the mystery of election; but here are three straightforward truths about it in our text. One, the doctrine of election is a *divine revelation*, not a human speculation. It wasn't invented by Augustine, or by Calvin; it is a Biblical doctrine, and no Biblical Christian can escape it. In the Old Testament God chose Israel to be His special people; and in the New Testament He has chosen us. He has made us His own people. So let us not reject the doctrine of election as if it were some weird phantasy of men: let us humbly accept it, even if we do not fully understand it, as a truth that God has revealed. Secondly, the doctrine of election is *an incentive to holiness*, and not an excuse for sin. Some people say, 'I'm one of God's chosen ones, you know, so I am safe and secure. There is no need for me to bother about holiness. I can live as I please. On the contrary: according to verse 4, God has chosen us in Christ *in order that* we should be 'holy and blameless before Him.' So far from encouraging us in sin, the doctrine of election tells us that holiness is its very purpose. Ultimately the only proof of our election is our holiness. Thirdly, the doctrine of election is *a stimulus to humility*, and not a ground for boasting. Some people think that to believe that one is one of God's chosen people, is just about the most arrogant thing that anybody could believe. And so it would be if we imagined that God had chosen us because of some merit in ourselves. But there is no room for merit in the Biblical doctrine of election, because God chose us in Christ 'before the foundation of the world,' which is before we existed, let alone before we could lay claim to any merit. So the doctrine of election should lead us to holiness, not to sin; to humility, and not to boasting.

Now we turn from the past blessing of election to (b) *the present blessing of adoption* (vv5–8), for the key word here is 'sons.' Election is with a view to adoption. 'He chose us in Him before the foundation of the world' and 'destined us' that in time we might become His sons. Sonship of God brings both a privilege and a responsibility. The privilege first: it is those who are the sons and daughters of God who can say that in Christ we have 'redemption through His blood, even the forgiveness of sins,' (vv7–8). Because, you see, the sons and daughters of God have free access to their heavenly Father; and this confidence before God as His children is ours only because we have been redeemed, and our sins have been forgiven, through the blood-shedding of Jesus. So that redemption, and forgiveness, and adoption into the family of God, all go together. And redemption and forgiveness are the privileges which all God's children enjoy.

If that is our privilege, our responsibility is that we should be holy and blameless as His children, manifesting the family likeness, and glorifying our heavenly Father.

Then we turn from the past blessing of election and the present blessing of adoption, to (c) *the future blessing of unification* (vv9–10). For God has also made known to us His plan for the fullness of time, for the future. He has given us wisdom and insight into the mystery of His will. What is this will of God, this purpose of God, this plan of God, for the future? Well, God's plan for the fullness of the times – where time merges into eternity again – is to unite everything in and under Christ. The Greek verb in verse 10, to *'unite* all things,' contains within itself the word for 'headship.' It indicates that the summing-up of everything is going to take place, when God unites all things, under the Lordship, or the headship, of Jesus Christ.

Now that immediately prompts a question: Who and what will be included in this unity, and under this headship of Jesus? We need, I think, to begin by saying that we cannot use this text as a foundation on *which* to build universalistic dreams that everybody is going to be saved in the end, even the impenitent wicked, and even demons. No, no. We cannot say that, because other passages of Scripture teach with great plainness the awful reality and eternity of hell. What, then, are the 'all things,' the things in heaven and the things in earth that are going to be united under the headship of Christ? Well, certainly the Christian living and the Christian dead, the *church* on earth and the *church* in heaven, and probably angels as well. But Paul seems also to be referring again to that cosmic renewal, that regeneration of the universe, that liberation of this groaning creation, to which he has already referred in the middle of Romans 8, for the phrase 'all things' in the Greek usually means the universe. God's plan is that 'all things' that were created through Christ, and that cohere in Christ, are one day going to be united under Christ, by being totally subjected to His headship. So the New English Bible translates it, 'that the universe ... might be brought into a unity in Christ.'

What a wonderful prospect it is, that in the fullness of time God's whole church, and God's whole universe, are going to be united under the headship of Christ! Now let us pause a moment, and consider how much all of us need this eternal perspective of the apostle Paul. Let me remind you that when he was writing this letter he was a prisoner in Rome, under house arrest, handcuffed to a Roman soldier. But though his wrist was chained, and his body was confined, his mind and his heart inhabited eternity. He peered back to the foundation of the world; he peered on to the fullness of time; and he grasped what we have *now* as Christians, and what we ought to be *now* in the light of these two eternities. Brethren, how restricted is our vision in comparison with the apostle Paul's! How small is our mind! How narrow are our horizons! How easily we become engrossed in our own petty little affairs! We need to see time in the light of eternity; and then, if we shared Paul's perspective, we should share his praise. Our whole life would become a doxology. We should be blessing God constantly, that He has blessed us with 'every spiritual blessing in Christ.'

Now we move on to (d) *The scope of these blessings* (vv11–14). The purpose of this paragraph is to show that these blessings in Christ that we have been considering are given now to Jewish and Gentile believers alike. 'For in Him . . .' in Christ, 'we' – that is Jews: Paul is writing as a Jew – 'who first hoped in Christ, have been . . .' (v12); and 'you also, you Gentiles, have been sealed by the Holy Spirit, who is the guarantee of *our* inheritance' (v14). He moves, you see, from we – himself and his fellow Jews, Jewish Christians – to you Gentile readers, to *our* inheritance, which seems to embrace both Jews and Gentiles equally. It is thus a paragraph about all God's people, whatever our racial or religious origins may be. And what is stressed in particular is how it is that we became God's people, and why God has made us His people. Or if you like, where everything begins and ends.

First, *How did we become God's people*? The answer is, 'According to the will of God,' because that's where everything begins, in the will of God. Three times in the first half of this chapter Paul uses a similar expression: 'According to the purpose of His will' (v5); 'The mystery of His will according to His purpose which He set forth in Christ' (v9); 'According to the purpose of Him who accomplishes all things according to the counsel of His will' (v11). You can't read this passage without seeing that it is full of the will of God, and the pleasure of God, and the purpose of God, and of the plan and the programme of God in which His will is expressed. Paul could hardly have insisted more emphatically that our becoming the members of God's family is due neither to chance, nor to choice – if you mean by that our choice – but to God's choice, His sovereign will and pleasure.

Not that we are inactive; on the contrary. This context attributes our salvation to the will of God, and yet if you glance at verse 13 you will see that we heard the Word of truth, the Gospel, and that we believed in Christ, and as a result we were sealed by the promised Holy Spirit. The indwelling Spirit is the seal of God upon us, and also God's pledge, His guarantee that the full inheritance will be ours in the end. So let nobody say that the Biblical doctrine of election, by the sovereign will of God, makes either evangelism or faith unnecessary. For the very opposite is the truth; it is only because of the sovereign will that evangelism has any hope of success, and faith becomes possible. The preaching of the Gospel is the very means that God has ordained, by which He delivers those whom He has chosen from blindness and bondage, sets them free to believe in Jesus, and causes

His will to be done. Everything begins in the will of God.

Then secondly, *Why did God make us His people*? Answer: 'to the praise of His glory.' Because that's where everything ends. Here is another expression that comes three times in the first part of this chapter: 'To the praise of the glory of His grace' (v6); 'To live for the praise of His glory' (v12); 'To the praise of His glory' (v14). I shall always be grateful to one of my former colleagues in London, who when he left our staff team gave me a little paper knife for my desk on which he had had engraved the words, 'To the praise of His glory.' So that every time I sit at my desk, I am reminded and challenged that God's will for me, as one of His people, is to live to the praise of His glory.

Here, then, you see, is the how and the why of the people of God. Everything that we are in Christ comes from God, and returns to God. It begins in His will, and it ends in His glory. This is where everything begins and ends. Now, all this comes into violent collision with the man-centredness of the modern world. Fallen man, who is imprisoned in his own self-centredness, has an unbounded confidence in the power of his own will, and an insatiable appetite for the praise of his own glory. But God's people have been turned inside out, or at least have begun to be. We see ourselves quite differently now. Our calling is to live by the grace of God, and for the glory of God; not in order that we might get our own will, or see our own glory promoted, but in order that we may do God's will and promote God's glory. Now we turn to –

Prayer (1:15–2:10).

Notice that every Christian is both a believer and a lover. 'Because I have heard of your faith . . . and your love . . . I do not cease to give thanks for you . . . but I also remember you in my prayers.' We need to consider what Paul prayed for: not so much that they might receive a further blessing, a second blessing, as that they might know the greatness of the blessings they had already received.

It is very important to understand the construction of this first chapter of Ephesians. It is divided into two halves: the praise section, 'Blessed be the God and Father of our Lord Jesus Christ, who has blessed us . . .'; and then the prayer section, in which Paul prays that 'the God of our Lord Jesus Christ' would enable us to *know the fullness* of the blessings that are ours in Christ. To me it is extremely important for a healthy Christian life to keep Christian praise and Christian prayer together. Praise that all spiritual blessings are ours in Christ, and prayer that we may know them in our experience as well as in our understanding. Yet there are many Christians nowadays who do not succeed in preserving this balance. There are some who seem to do little or nothing but pray for new spiritual blessings, apparently oblivious of the fact that God has already blessed them with every spiritual blessing in Christ. Then there are others who make the opposite mistake; they emphasise so much that everything is ours if we are in Christ, that they become complacent, and they have no hunger to know or to experience these blessings more deeply. I suggest there is no need to polarise. Let us keep praising God that everything is ours, if we are in Christ; and let us keep praying that we may know the fullness of the blessing that He has already given us. And if we keep praise and prayer together, we are unlikely to lose our balance.

Now the prayer, then, is for knowledge in the full Biblical sense of understanding plus experience. He prays in verse 17 that God would give them 'a spirit of wisdom and revelation' to know Christ better. And in verse 18, that 'the eyes of their heart . . .' because our heart has eyes, as well as our body, '. . . may be enlightened.' By this enlightenment of our spiritual eyes by the Holy Spirit we may perceive spiritual reality – and in particular three things about God, concerning His call, and His inheritance, and His power. Paul prays that we may know the implications of these things: 'The *hope* of His calling . . . the *riches* of His inheritance . . . and the *greatness* of His power.'

(a), *The hope of God's calling*. Now the call of God takes us back to the very beginning of our Christian lives, because our Christian life began when God called us. But what is the *hope* of His calling; that is, what did He call us for? God's call is not a random thing, a purposeless thing. He called us for something, and that is the hope of our calling. And the rest of the New Testament tells us what it is. He called us to belong to Christ. He called us to have fellowship with Christ. He called us to be His saints, for our calling is a holy calling. He called us to freedom. He called us to peace. He called us to glory. He called us to suffering meanwhile. All these things are the hope of God's calling. And Paul wants us to know it.

(b), *The glory of His inheritance*. Some understand this inheritance as being the inheritance that God possesses in His people, for there is a sense in which the church is God's heritage, God's inheritance. But I take it the other way round, that it is the inheritance that God is going to give us; what in Colossians is called 'the inheritance of the saints in light.' If that is so, then God's call looks back to the beginning of the Christian life, and God's inheritance looks on to the end of the Christian life, when we inherit in heaven. For God's children are God's heirs, and the inheritance will one day be ours. And Scripture reveals a little bit of what it is going to be like. We are going to be like Christ in our bodies and in our characters. We are going to see God, and we are going to worship Him; and we are going to have perfect fellowship with Him and with one another, because God's inheritance is 'among the saints,' the great company that no man can number. And Paul prays that the eyes of our hearts may be opened to know this, and the glory of it: 'to know the riches of the glory of God's inheritance among the saints.'

Then, thirdly, he prays that we may know – (c) *The greatness of God's power*: and it is on this that he concentrates. If God's call looks back to the beginning of our Christian life, and God's inheritance looks on to the end, then God's power surely spans the interim between. It is only God's power that can fulfil the hope that belongs to our call; and it is only God's power that can bring us safe to the glory of our final inheritance. And Paul is deeply convinced, as we ought to be, that God's power is sufficient. He accumulates words in order to convince us. He writes not only of God's power, but of His might and of His energy, and of His strength. And Paul adds that he wants us to know the *greatness* of God's power, indeed the surpassing greatness of the power of God.

How are we going to come to know it? Partly because Paul prays that the eyes of our heart may be opened, may be enlightened. And we shall never know the greatness of God's power unless these inward and spiritual eyes are enlightened by the Holy Spirit. But we need more than this inward and subjective illumination. God has also given us an objective and external demonstration of His power, in the resurrection and exaltation of Jesus; and in the resurrection and exaltation of Christians who have been raised from the death of sin.

First, then, God's power (i) *in raising and exalting Christ* (vv19–23). Paul refers to two great historical events in verse 20. First, the resurrection, when God raised Jesus from the dead; and secondly, the ascension, when God exalted Him to heaven over all the forces of evil, and made Him sit at His right hand, and put everything under His feet. Now this double event, the resurrection and the exaltation, was a tremendous demonstration of divine power. Because if there are two powers that man cannot control, they are death and evil. Man is mortal: he cannot escape death. Man is fallen: he cannot overcome evil. Death and evil are two things we cannot overcome by our own power. But God in Jesus Christ has conquered both, and therefore He can rescue us from both.

(a) *He overcame death.* Now death is a bitter and relentless enemy. It comes to all of us some time. I remember not long ago visiting an elderly lady in hospital, who had been taken ill suddenly, and she told me when I got to the hospital that as soon as she had arrived the doctors and everybody gathered round her bed, as if, she said, they thought she was going to die. 'But I decided I wasn't going to die!' she said. Well, it was a spirited remark, but not an entirely accurate one. We cannot decide when we are going to die. We may succeed in postponing death, but we cannot escape it; and after death nothing can stop the process of decay and decomposition. Even Egyptian mummies crumble to dust in the end; even the most sophisticated embalming techniques of modern American morticians cannot prevent the body from ultimate decay. We are dust, and to dust we shall return. No human power can prevent it, let alone bring the dead back to life again. But God has done it. God raised Jesus from the dead; that is, first He arrested the natural process of decay: He did not allow His holy One to see corruption. And then He didn't just reverse the process, restoring Jesus to this life, He transcended it: He raised Jesus to an altogether new life that is immortal, free, and glorious, which nobody had ever experienced before, or has yet experienced since – until the resurrection day. In Jesus God overcame death.

(b) He *overcame evil*. God set Jesus at His right hand, the place of supreme honour and executive authority. 'Far above all rule and authority and power and dominion,' and every title of this age and the next. The context suggests that these are the powers of evil. The principalities and powers, the worldwide rulers of this present darkness, to which Paul is going to refer again in chapter 6, God has put them all under the feet of Jesus. He has made Christ the Head of the universe, and of the church, which is His body, the fullness of Him who fills everything, both the church and the universe (vv22–23).

So God in Christ is the supreme Conqueror of death and of evil, 'by His mighty power.' How can we doubt the power of God? Have we never looked at the resurrection and the exaltation of Jesus? Have we never seen this power of God raising Jesus from the dead, setting Him at His right hand, putting everything under His feet? This is the supreme historical demonstration of the power of God.

But the second is (ii) *God's power in raising and exalting us with Christ* (2:1–10). It is this great power of God, that raised Jesus from the dead, that is available for us. Just before we come to those verses, notice what Paul is saying in verses 19–20. He wants us to know the greatness of God's power, literally '*toward* us who believe' which 'He accomplished in Christ when He raised Him from the dead.' Have you ever seen that 'us' and 'Christ' together? This power of God toward us who believe, that He accomplished in *Christ*. He deliberately puts Christ and us in juxtaposition; the very same resurrection power of God displayed in Christ can be displayed in us, and in exactly the same two ways, over death and over evil (2:1–10).

Now, in order to emphasise the greatness of God's power in Christian experience, Paul first plumbs the depths of pessimism about man, and then rises to heights of optimism about God. It is, you know, this mixture of pessimism and optimism, or, if you like, of despair and faith, that constitutes the refreshing realism that we constantly find in the Bible. What Paul does here is to paint a vivid contrast between man by nature, and man by grace.

First, then (a) *Man by nature*, or the human condition (vv1–3). This is a description of man, every man. No, not of some particularly degraded segment of society, not some particularly decadent period of human history; but man, every man. 'You . . .' Paul begins, that is Gentiles, 'among whom we . . .' that is sophisticated Jews, 'also lived . . . like the rest of mankind' (v3). This is the universal human condition.

What is it? Well, first, men are *dead through the trespasses and sins in which they walked*. But he goes on to say in chapter 4, 'alienated from the life of God.' Eternal life is fellowship with God; so spiritual death is alienation from God. Now some human beings who are not Christians seem very much alive. You think at once of the vigorous body of an athlete, another who has the lively mind of a scholar, a third who has the vivacious personality of a film star – very much alive. Yet, in the sphere that really matters – which is neither the body nor the mind nor the personality, but the soul – they are dead, blind to the beauty of Jesus, deaf to the voice of the Holy Spirit, and as unresponsive to God as a corpse. Life without God is a living death, and those who live it are dead while they are living. And I believe, brethren, that we need to feel deep within us the terrible tragedy of the human condition, that men and women who were made by God, and for God, are now living without God. Men and women are dead.

Second, they are *enslaved by the world, the flesh, and the devil*. Paul mentions the three. He mentions 'the course of this world' – that is, contemporary fashion, or what we should call 'pop culture.' He mentions 'the prince of the power of the air, the spirit now at work in the children of disobedience' – that's the devil. And then he mentions 'the passions of the flesh' and the desires of body and mind, which we freely indulged, and to which we were enslaved – that's the flesh, our fallen human nature. So, you see, we were subject, as all men are outside Christ, to strong influences outside and inside. Outside is the world: secular, godless society, with all its pressures upon us. Inside us is the flesh, or fallen human nature. And beyond both, actively working through both, is an evil spirit called the devil, and he holds us in captivity. Oh, not that we can shift all the blame on to the world, the flesh and the devil, and accept no responsibility ourselves, for we are called in these verses 'the sons of disobedience,' and the NEB translates that as 'God's rebel subjects.' We've rebelled against the authority of God, and come under the dominion of Satan as a result. Men are dead; men are enslaved, by the world, the flesh and the devil.

Thirdly, men are *condemned*. We are by nature the objects of wrath – which is what 'the children of wrath' means (v3). This is a Hebraism; it means the objects of God's wrath. And God's wrath is not bad temper; it isn't spite, or animosity, or revenge. God's wrath is His perfect, righteous, settled hostility to evil; and we are under the wrath and the condemnation of God. Is this too pessimistic? Well, let us admit that this is not the whole truth. It is not the whole Biblical truth about man. Paul says nothing here about man being made in the image of God. He believes it; he refers to it later in the letter when he says that in Christ we are re-created in the image of God. He believes men are made in the image of God, and that vestiges of that image remain, even after the Fall.

But nevertheless his emphasis here is that men are dead and enslaved and condemned.

It is a failure to recognise the gravity of this human condition that is the major reason for people's naive faith in superficial remedies. Universal education is highly desirable; so is a just society, whose structures and laws guarantee justice and freedom for every man. Both these things are pleasing to God the Creator: education, and just legislation. But neither education nor legislation can rescue man from death or slavery or wrath. A radical disease requires a radical remedy; and moreover a superficial man-confident evangelism cannot reach men in this condition either. If human beings are dead, they have to be raised from the dead; if they are slaves, they have to be set free; and if they are under condemnation, they need to be pardoned. And only God can do those things.

So let us turn from man by nature to man by grace; from the human condition to *(b) The divine compassion* (vv4–10). 'But God . . .' (v4). Two monosyllables that are a strong, a mighty adversative, which set over against the desperate condition of man the mighty, gracious, sovereign activity of God. Let us *see what God has done*. Paul coins three verbs which take up what God did to Christ, and by the addition of a prefix, link us to Christ in every case. First, He made us alive – with Christ (v5). Second, He raised us up – with Christ (v6). Third, He made us sit – with Christ in heavenly places (v6). These relate to the three historical events we call the resurrection, the ascension, and the session. We declare our belief in them in the Creed: 'On the third day He rose again; He ascended into heaven; He sat down at the right hand of God.'

What is amazing is that in these verses Paul is not now writing about Christ; he is writing about us. He is affirming that we have had a resurrection and an ascension and a session. *We've* been raised with Christ, exalted to heaven with

Christ, seated with Christ in heavenly places, in the heavenly places where Christ is seated upon His throne. That's what God has done. He has raised us, exalted us, seated us with everything under our feet, if we are in Christ.

Why has God done it? Well, the major emphasis of the whole paragraph is that what prompted God was not something in us, some supposed merit of our own; but something in Him, His unmerited favour. Paul gathers four words to express this. He writes of God's mercy and love in verse 4: 'Rich in mercy, for His great love wherewith He loved us'; of His grace in verse 7, 'The unsearchable riches of His grace'; and 'His kindness toward us in Christ Jesus.' It is because of His mercy and love and kindness and grace, that He's done these things – and that highlights why He has *not* done it, in verses 8 and 9. We have been saved from slavery, and death, and wrath, not because of any works of ours, but by grace, His unmerited favour, through faith; and even that is not of ourselves – as it probably seems to mean – but it is a gift of God. There are no such things as meritorious works of ours on account of which God has saved us. Nor has our faith any merit: we must not interpret salvation by grace through faith, as if faith were a human work, and salvation was a kind of transaction in which God contributes grace, we contribute faith, and the mixture produces salvation. No, no, there is no merit in faith. Faith is a gift of God. Other passages of Scripture make that plain as well, that the only purpose of faith is to lay hold of Jesus Christ. As Martin Luther writes, 'Faith apprehendeth nothing else but that precious jewel, Jesus Christ.' Verse 10 repeats the truth, that we are His workmanship, His creation: the work is His, it's not ours. And He created us in Christ unto good works. Salvation is a creative work of God in Jesus Christ. He has not re-created us in Christ because of our good works, but unto the good works that we shall now perform because He has ordained them for us.

Well, now, let us look back, and conclude. Let us get this message in our own hearts and minds. Paul is praying that 'the eyes of our heart may be enlightened to see the greatness of God's power,' and he adds that twice God has already demonstrated His power objectively and historically: first, in raising and exalting Christ, and putting everything under the feet of Christ – death, and evil, and all things. Secondly, in raising and exalting us, if we are Christians. Already He has overcome death in us: He has raised us; He has exalted us; He has sat us at God's right hand, sharing the throne of Christ, with everything under our feet. This is the resurrection power of God, power over death, power over evil – and Paul prays that our eyes may be open to see it.

Now, my brothers and sisters, what is our weakness? We have been talking about God's power: what about our weakness? What is it that you and I cannot control? I know the things I can't control. What are the things you can't control by yourself? Is it your tongue, your temper, your thoughts, your lust, your ambition, your malice, your jealousy – what is it? These things are altogether beyond our power to control. But, do you think they are beyond the power of God – the power of God that raised Jesus Christ from the dead, gave Him this new and victorious life in heaven; the power that has already raised us from the dead, given us a new life, that became a victorious life, with everything under our feet? So let us pray to God for the blessings with which He has already blessed us in Christ, and let us pray that He will open our eyes to see the greatness of His power, that is well able to be made perfect in our weakness. Resurrection power in human weakness!

2. New Society (Ephesians 2:11–3:21)

Our subject yesterday was 'New Life,' and our title now is 'New Society,' as we turn from the new life that God has given us in Jesus Christ to the new society that He is building, His own family, the church. A fashionable word in contemporary society is 'alienation.' Many people, especially young people, disillusioned with what they call 'the system,' or 'the technocracy,' describe themselves as alienated. It was Karl Marx who popularised the word. I don't think a Keswick platform is the right place to expound Marxist philosophy, but nevertheless I think we need to understand what he meant by alienation. To him the real plight of the proletariat was economic alienation; that if the worker puts into his craftsmanship a part of himself, and then his employer sells his product, he is alienating the worker from himself. And this, according to Marx, was the basis of the class struggle between the proletariat and the bourgeoisie.

Nowadays the word is used more generally of the working man's alienation, not so much from his craftsmanship and from his due reward, as from the exercise of economic and political power. Those of you who come from Scotland very well know the name of Jimmy Reid, the leader of the Upper Clyde Shipyard workers, and formerly rector at Glasgow University. In his remarkable inaugural address to the university in 1972 he spoke about alienation; he said, 'Alienation is the cry of men who feel themselves to be the victims of blind economic forces beyond their control. Alienation is the frustration of ordinary people who are excluded from the processes of decision-making.' So you see nowadays alienation is a sense of powerlessness, and it has made many a man either an embittered revolutionary or a social drop-out.

Long before Karl Marx or Jimmy Reid had been thought of, the Bible spoke about alienation. And it speaks of two even worse alienations than economic and political, namely alienation from God our Creator, on the one hand, and alienation from one another, our fellow creatures, on the other. Many men and women feel themselves to be strangers in a world in which they ought to feel at home. The epistle to the Ephesians alludes to both these alienations, and indeed the apostle Paul uses the word 'alienation' of both conditions.

In the first part of chapter 2, men are portrayed as alienated from God – 'dead, through the trespasses and sins in which they walked' (v1). This condition Paul calls in 4:18, 'alienated from the life of God.' In the second half of the chapter, men are portrayed as alienated from one another (vv11–22), and in particular, Gentiles are described as 'alienated' – the same Greek word – 'from the commonwealth of Israel' (v12). Now, it is almost impossible for us to think ourselves back to those days before Christ, when humanity was deeply divided between the Jews and the Gentiles. But we need to try to understand that division, and that sense of alienation. Of this double Gentile alienation – from God and from the people of God – the so-called 'middle wall of partition,' to use the familiar expression of the Authorised Version, or 'the dividing wall of hostility,' to use the Revised Standard Version expression in verse 14, was the standing symbol.

Will you try to picture in your mind's eye what King Herod's temple was like? For the middle wall of partition was a notable feature of the temple built by Herod the Great. The temple building itself was constructed on an elevated platform. Round it, on the same platform, was the court of the priests, and to the east of that was the court of Israel, and to the east of that was the court of the women, these two being reserved respectively for the laymen and the laywomen of the Israel community. From these courts upon this elevated platform round the temple, one descended five steps, and then fourteen more steps to what was called the court of the Gentiles, the outer court. But between the court of the Gentiles and the steps leading to the elevated platform, there was a thick stone barricade, five foot high, and on it were displayed notices in Greek and Latin, threatening, not 'Trespassers will be prosecuted,' but 'Trespassers will be executed.' It is interesting that during the last hundred years a couple of these notices have been discovered, and this was the wording on them: 'No foreigner may enter within the barrier and enclosure round the temple. Anyone who is caught doing so will have himself to blame for his ensuing death.' This, then, is the background to the second part of Ephesians 2.

Although all men are alienated from God because of sin – and of that alienation the veil of the temple was the symbol – the Gentiles additionally were alienated from the people of God, and of that alienation the temple wall was the symbol. Worse even than this static alienation was the active enmity or hostility into which it erupted, enmity between man and God, and enmity between the Gentiles and the Jews. The glorious theme of the passage that we are considering is that the Lord Jesus has destroyed both enmities: 'He has broken down the dividing wall of enmity, hostility . . . that He might reconcile both unto God, thereby bringing the hostility, the enmity, between God and man, to an end' (vv14 and 16). So the enmity between man and man, or Gentile and Jew; and between God and man, has been ended by Jesus Christ – that is, in the new society that He has built, the Christian church. So as the result He has created a new humanity, a new society; what in verse 15 is called 'one new man,' that is, a single new humanity, in which alienation has given way to reconciliation, and hostility to peace. Firstly, then, let us look at –

Paul's Affirmation (2:11–22). You notice how he divides this passage into the portrait of an *alienated humanity*, or what we once were (vv11–12); and the portrait of the *peace-making* Christ, what Christ has done (vv13–18); and the portrait of the *new society*, the church, what we have now become as a result (vv19–22). First, then –

An Alienated Humanity: what we once were (v11). The reference is to the Gentile world, the heathen world, before Christ; those whom the Jews, that is the circumcision, called the uncircumcision, and dismissed as being beyond the pale. Notice then in verse 12 Paul lists their five disabilities: 'Separated in Christ.' Now remember that Paul has been describing in chapter 1 the benefits and the blessings of being *in* Christ. 'God has blessed us *in* Christ with every spiritual blessing.' Ah, but the Gentiles were not *in* Christ: they were separated from Christ. Next, they were 'alienated from the commonwealth of Israel, and strangers to the covenant of promise.' That is, they were not members of God's chosen people, to whom He bound Himself by a solemn covenant; they were excluded from this privilege; they were foreigners. Next, they were 'without hope and without God,' hopeless because although God had planned and promised one day to include the Gentiles, they didn't know it. They didn't have that hope; they were without hope. And they were godless, because although God has not left Himself without witness – for He reveals Himself even to the Gentiles in nature, in the glories of heaven and earth; they suppressed the knowledge of God that they had – and turned to idols. They did not know God as Israel knew Him.

There is the terrible five-fold deprivation of the Gentile world. In William Hendrikson's words, in his commentary: 'They were Christless, stateless, friendless, helpless, hopeless, and godless.' Or in Paul's single phrase in verse 13, they were 'far off,' alienated from God and from the people of God.

Now we ourselves in our pre-Christian days were in exactly this plight. We were alienated from God, and from the people of God. Worse than that, we were at enmity with God, rebelling against His authority, and we knew little or nothing of true human community. Still, you see, outside the fellowship of the Christian church men build walls of partition and division, like the Berlin wall; they erect invisible curtains of iron or bamboo; they construct barriers of race, and colour, and nation, and tribe, and caste, and class. And Paul says, 'Remember . . .' and he repeats it again in verse 12, 'Remember . . .' Remember this double alienation from God and from one another, out of which the Lord Jesus has rescued us.

So we turn from the portrait of an alienated humanity, to the portrait of – *A Peace-making Christ*: what Christ has done (vv13–18). Verse 13 sums up what has happened. It is a beautiful statement – 'But *now* in Christ Jesus you who once were far off, alienated from God and from the people of God, have been brought near in the blood of Christ.' Don't miss the two expressions, 'In Christ Jesus,' and 'By the blood of Christ.' 'The blood of Christ' refers to His sacrificial death, by which He achieved the reconciliation; and 'in Christ' refers to our personal union with Jesus Christ today, through whom the reconciliation becomes effectively ours, because He, Jesus 'is our peace' (v14): *He* has effected reconciliation between God and man, and between Jew and Gentile. And 'He has made both one, and broken down the middle wall of partition.'

Now, historically speaking, when Paul was writing the middle wall of partition had not been broken down. Literally and historically the middle wall of partition excluding the Gentiles still stood. It was not destroyed until AD 70; it was still standing. But Paul, you see, with this wonderful insight that God had given him into the work of Jesus Christ, states that although materially speaking the wall still stood, spiritually speaking it had already been destroyed somewhere round AD 30, when Jesus died on the cross. In His flesh He abolished (v15) the law that was symbolised in the wall.

Now how Jesus Christ broke down the middle wall of partition is described in verses 15–16, and they are packed tight with theology. I think it may help us to clarify a difficult sentence if I draw your attention to the three principle verbs – 'to abolish,' 'to create,' and 'to reconcile.' For what Christ has done is to abolish the law of commandments, in order to create a single new humanity, and to reconcile both parts of the divided humanity, Jew and Gentile, to God.

Let us look at those three. (i) *The abolition of the law of commandments*. Jesus broke down the middle wall of partition by abolishing the law. Now at first sight that is surprising, especially if we remember that in the Sermon on the Mount Jesus said, 'I have not come to abolish the law. I have come to fulfil it.' 'Well, there you are,' people say. 'I told you so. The Bible's full of contradictions. Jesus said He hadn't come to abolish it; Paul said He did abolish it. Who are you to believe?' Well, it's easy, isn't it, to use this kind of superficial discrepancy. There is no discrepancy at all if you look beneath the surface. In the Sermon on the Mount Jesus is referring to the moral law, primarily. He has not come to abolish the moral law. The moral law of God is still binding upon Christian people. We are to obey the moral commandments of God in His law; and we are not free to disobey the law, the moral law. It is primarily the ceremonial law that Jesus has abolished: circumcision, which was the main issue between Jew and Gentile; the material sacrifices that had been fulfilled in Christ; and the food regulations, what they were allowed to eat and not to eat. These erected a serious barrier between Jew and Gentile, and Jesus had swept the whole ceremonial aside.

Now probably there is another reference to the moral law, which is still in force as a standard of behaviour – but not as a ground of our salvation. The law has been abolished as a ground of salvation. We cannot win acceptance by obedience to the moral law. We have to obey it now we have been reconciled to God, but we can't win justification by obedience to the law. Jesus took to Himself on the cross the curse of the broken law, and has thus freed us from its condemnation. Acceptance with God is through faith in Jesus Christ; and this is a wonderfully reconciling and uniting thing. Whatever our cultural or racial background may be, we are one at the foot of the cross, by faith in Jesus Christ. So Jesus abolished the law of commandments, the regulations of the ceremonial law on the one hand, and the condemnation of the moral law on the other.

That was the abolition, in order that He might create (ii) *a new humanity* in place of two, 'so making peace.' Now it is impossible to miss Paul's move from the negative to the positive; from the abolition of the law of commandments and these regulations that were against us to the creation of a single new humanity in the Christian family. And He did it 'in Himself' (v15). It is by union with Jesus Christ, by relationship with Jesus Christ, that we experience this new unity, with the old divisions broken down.

The abolition of the law; the creation of the new humanity; and then (iii) *the reconciliation of Jew and*

Gentile to God: 'That He might reconcile us both to God in one body through the cross, thereby bringing the hostility to an end' (v16). This, then, was the achievement of the cross of Jesus: an abolition, a creation, and a reconciliation of this new humanity to God.

Now this does not mean, of course, that the whole human race is now united and reconciled. It rather means that all those – whether Jew or Gentile, or whatever their background may be – who are *in Christ* experience the reconciliation that He has achieved. You see how Paul goes on: Having *made* peace 'by the blood of the cross' (v15), He 'came and *preached* peace,' the good news of reconciliation (v17). But that good news has to be accepted, it has to be believed, in order that the peace may be enjoyed. First He achieved it, then He announced it. And since the announcement came after the achievement, it must be a reference, not to His preaching when He was on earth, but perhaps to His resurrection appearances, when, significantly, His first official word was 'Peace be unto you,' or 'Peace be with you,' in the Upper Room; and then the continuation of His proclamation of peace through the apostles and the apostolic church.

It's rather wonderful, isn't it, that when we proclaim 'Peace' to others today, it is Jesus who is proclaiming it through us. And the good news is addressed today to those who are 'far off' in the Gentile world, and those who are 'near.' For the good news is addressed to everybody, and as a result those who receive it, both Jew and Gentile, by receiving the Gospel have access together unto the Father, through Christ, and by the one Spirit who has regenerated us, and now indwells us (v18).

So, you see, in the Christian experience of access to God we have no difficulty with the doctrine of the Trinity, for there it is – what Paul Rees last night called 'a bright mystery' – that we experience access to the Father, through the reconciling work of Jesus, the Son, and by the indwelling of the Holy Spirit, who teaches us to pray, and who cries within us, 'Abba, Father.'

So we move now to the portrait of *God's New Society*, what we become as a result (vv19–21). 'So then . . .' (v19), as a result of the achievement of Jesus on the cross, and the announcement of the good news we have come to believe, you Gentiles are no longer what you used to be; you are no longer strangers, or aliens, alienated. You are not even sojourners, that is, visitors without legal rights. On the contrary, your status has dramatically changed.

First, you are *citizens of God's kingdom*, 'fellow-citizens . . .' You can't be a citizen without there being a kingdom of which you are a citizen! '. . . with the saints,' that is with the Jewish people. According to verse 12 they were alienated from the citizenship of Israel; but now they are 'fellow-citizens' with Israel. That is, God's people, whether Jews or Gentiles, are equally citizens of the kingdom of God, where God rules His people in His grace.

Secondly, we are *members of God's family*. The metaphor changes; it becomes more intimate. A kingdom is one thing; a household or family is another. In Christ Jesus we are not only citizens of the kingdom of God, we are children in the family of God.

Thirdly, we are *stones in God's temple* (vv20–22), 'built into a holy temple in the Lord.' Let us look at this temple. Its foundation is the apostles and prophets (v20); that is, the temple is built on the fundamental, authoritative teaching of those apostles and prophets whom Christ appointed to teach the church. The church is built on Biblical truth. There is a sense in which the Bible is the foundation of the church; and the church is built on this teaching of the prophets and the apostles, whose teaching is recorded in Scripture. Then the chief cornerstone of the church, holding it steady and in line, is Jesus Christ Himself. The stones, 'living stones' Peter calls them, are Christian people, Jews and Gentiles alike: 'In whom you also are being built' like stones in this massive building of God (v22). Its nature is a holy temple in the Lord (v21); and its purpose is to be 'a dwelling place of God in the Spirit' (v22, RSV), accommodating the living God Himself.

Now isn't it marvellous to look back and trace the secrets of the apostle's teaching. Once, maybe not long ago for some of us, 'you were alienated from Israel, and Israel's God' (vv11–12); but 'now in Christ Jesus . . . you have been brought near' (v13). Christ has abolished the law, created the new humanity, reconciled it to God: 'so then you are no longer aliens and strangers . . .' (v19); you are God's kingdom which He rules, God's family which He loves, and God's temple in which He dwells. More simply: You were alienated; you have been reconciled: and Christ has brought you home. That's the vision.

But pause a moment, as we turn from the ideal portrayed in Scripture, to the concrete reality experienced today. And it is a very different and a very tragic story, because even in the church there is often alienation and disunity and discord. Christians sometimes erect new barriers in place of the old that Christ has abolished: now a colour bar; now racism or nationalism or tribalism; now a divisive caste or class system; now a clericalism which sunders clergy from laity. These things are doubly offensive. First, they are an offence to Jesus Christ. How dare we build walls of partition in the one and only community in which they have been destroyed? Secondly, they are an offence to the world, because they prevent the world from believing in Jesus. God means His people to exhibit to the world outside what a human community looks like when it is under the righteous rule of God. In a word, God means His church to be a sign of the kingdom, a sign of what a community looks like when God is ruling it in His love, joy, and peace. The tragedy is that the church that is intended to be a stepping-stone to faith is so often a stumbling-block to faith.

Brethren, we need to get the failures of *the church* on our conscience. We need to feel the offence to Jesus Christ and to the world, which these failures are. We need to repent of our readiness to excuse our failures, or even condone them; and we need to determine to do something about it. I wonder if there is anything more urgent today than that the church of Jesus Christ should be, and should be seen to be, what in God's purpose and Christ's achievement it is – a family of brothers and sisters who love their Father, and love one another: a model of human community, and the evident dwelling-place of God by His Spirit. Only then will men believe in Jesus, the Peacemaker; and only then will God receive the glory due to His Name.

We turn now from Paul's great affirmation of what Christ has done on the cross, this creation of the new humanity, the new society, to –

Paul's Ministry; his personal contribution to this great work of God (3:1–13).

He introduces himself: 'I, Paul, a prisoner of Christ Jesus . . .' (v1), a notable phrase. Humanly speaking, he was a prisoner of Nero in Rome; but Paul never did think or speak in purely human terms. He believed in the sovereignty of God over the affairs of man; so he called himself the prisoner of Christ. He was convinced that his whole life, including his imprisonment, was under the Lordship of Christ. In particular, he was a prisoner of Christ 'on behalf of you Gentiles,' because what had led to his arrest, and his imprisonment, and his trials, and his appeal to Caesar, was the fanatical Jewish opposition to his mission to the Gentiles. So Paul himself was suffering for the theme that he was expounding.

Now twice in verses 1–13 he uses the same expression, 'the grace of God that was given to me' – 'Assuming that you have heard of the stewardship of God's grace that was given to me' (v2); and 'Of this Gospel I was made a minister according to the gift of God's grace which was given to me' (v7). What were these two gracious gifts that God had given to Paul? Well, the first, in verses 2–3, was a certain *revelation*, as a result of which he had come to know something; and the second, verses 7–8, was a certain *commission*, as a result of which he had a responsibility to make known to others what God had made known to him. The first had to do with a mystery that had been revealed to him; and the second a ministry that had been entrusted to him.

First, *the Divine Revelation* to Paul, or the mystery (vv2–6). Three times he uses the word 'mystery' (vv3, 4 and 9), but it is important to grasp that the English word 'mystery' and the Greek word, *musterion*, do not have precisely the same meaning. In the English a mystery is something secret, dark, obscure, puzzling; and what is mysterious is inexplicable and almost incomprehensible. But the Greek word *musterion*, although it is still a secret, is no longer a closely-guarded secret; it is an open secret. It is something that has been hitherto concealed, but is now disclosed by the revelation of God.

Well, what is this 'mystery' Paul keeps talking about, that God has revealed to him? In verse 4 he calls it 'the mystery of Christ,' so it's something about Christ. But he explains what it is in verse 6, namely, that in Christ, by union with Christ, Gentiles and Jews have become one people. He uses three parallel expressions in verse 6, and all have the same prefix, meaning 'together with' Israel.

So that in Christ, through the Gospel, the Gentiles have become fellow-heirs – that is with the Jews – of the same blessing; fellow-members of the same body; and fellow-sharers in the same promise. So to sum it up, the mystery of Christ that God had revealed to Paul is the complete union of Jews and Gentiles with each other, through the union of both with Christ.

Now the Old Testament did reveal that God had a purpose for the Gentiles. God told Abraham that through his posterity He was going to bless all the families of the earth; and God through Isaiah said that it was His purpose that Israel should be 'a light to lighten the nations.' The Old Testament does speak of a destiny for the Gentiles; but the Old Testament did not reveal the radical nature of God's purpose. It did not reveal that what we call the theocracy, that is the Jewish national kingdom under the rule of God, was going to be terminated, and replaced by an international community, the Christian church. The Old Testament did not reveal that this Christian church was going to be the body of Christ, organically related to Jesus Christ, as a body is related to the head; and it did not reveal that Jews and Gentiles would be incorporated into Christ in the church, on equal terms, without any distinction whatever. It is this complete union of Jew and Gentile with each other, through their common union with Christ, that was radically new. And it is this that God revealed to Paul, as the apostle to the Gentiles. So that is the divine revelation.

Now, second, *the Divine Commission to Paul* (vv7–13). This was to make known to others what God had made known to him. 'Of this Gospel I was made a minister according to the gift of the grace of God that was given me' (v7). You see, this was his commission, to preach the good news. And he regards it as an enormous privilege: he is 'less than the least of all saints' (v8). Paul here takes the superlative, 'least' in the Greek, and he turns it into a comparative, as if in English we should say, 'leaster,' that is, 'less than the least.' Now Paul is not grovelling in insincerity; he means this. He is deeply conscious of his own unworthiness, not least because he persecuted the church of God, which it is God's great purpose to build – as he is unfolding here.

Well, how does Paul go on to describe the privilege? It is in three stages, and it is really rather wonderful, in verses 8–10. It was – (a) *To preach Christ's riches among the Gentiles* (v8). The good news he shares with the Gentiles is about Jesus, and about the riches of Jesus. There isn't anybody here, is there, who thinks that if you come to Jesus Christ He will impoverish your life? Shame on you! When we come to Jesus Christ He immeasurably enriches us. He bestows His riches upon those who come to Him, and these riches are 'unsearchable.' Now commentators vie with one another in trying to find an English equivalent of the Greek word. They use the words 'inexplorable,' 'untraceable,' 'unfathomable,' 'illimitable,' 'unsearchable.' The word literally means, 'that cannot be tracked out': that is, it is like the earth, too vast to explore; and like the sea, too deep to fathom. The unsearchable riches of Christ: you'll never come to the end of them. And the first part of the commission was to proclaim *that* good news.

It was also – (b) *To make all men see the mystery* (v9). That is, his task was to share with Gentiles (all mankind) not just the riches of Christ, but the mystery of Christ; in a word, his Gospel was not just the Gospel of Christ, but of the church. Because the 'mystery' means the church: the mystery is the union of Jew and Gentile through union with Christ. The mystery is the new humanity that God is creating, and it is part of the Gospel. Paul wanted to make all men know this mystery that had been kept secret, but had now been revealed.

Thirdly, in order that – (c) *Through the church, the cosmic powers might learn God's manifold wisdom* (v10). You see, the result of the preaching of Christ and the church will be that, through this church that emerges, God's many-coloured wisdom (which the Greek word means: it is like a tapestry, a carpet, a beautiful piece of silk, many-coloured, the mosaic, the intercultural, international, interracial Christian community that God's manifold wisdom has created) – that through this many-coloured commun-ity, the many-coloured wisdom of God will be made known to the cosmic intelligences who are watching. So that these angelic beings who are watching the emergence of the church, as they see its international and inter-racial and intercultural nature, are discovering the many-coloured wisdom of God. Wonderful, isn't it!

Now before we pass on to Paul's prayer, I want us to learn two lessons. The first is that – *the church is central to history*. I wonder if you believe that. The church is central to history, and its unfolding development. Verse 11 refers to 'the eternal purpose of God,' that He is working out through Jesus Christ, and through the church, in the historical process on earth. This is the creating of a new, united humanity, God's new society; this mystery that is central to history. I wonder if that is our view of history. What's the point of history? Was Henry Ford right when he said in 1919, in that famous libel suit with the *Chicago Tribune*, 'History is bunk!' Is history just a random succession of events, the meaningless development of the human story? No. As is often said, history is 'His story,' God's story, God at work moving from a plan conceived in eternity, through a historical disclosure and outwork-ing, on to a climax in history, and a future eternity beyond that. At the centre of all this historical develop-ment is Jesus Christ and His church, His redeemed, reconciled community, the new humanity.

Now let us contrast the perspective of secular historians and the Bible, and where they concentrate. Secular
history concentrates on kings, queens, statesmen, gener-
als, and other VIPs. The Bible concentrates on the saints,
often little, unknown people, but the people of God.
Secular history concentrates on wars and battles and
peace treaties; but the Bible concentrates on the decisive
victory won by Jesus Christ over the powers of evil on
the Cross; the peace treaty that was ratified by His blood;
and the sovereign proclamation of an amnesty for all
rebels who repent and believe. Again, secular history
concentrates on changes in the map of the world, as one
nation conquers another nation and annexes its territory,
and empires rise and fall. The Bible concentrates on a
multi-national community, the Christian church, that has
no territorial frontiers; that claims nothing less than the
whole wide world for Christ; and whose empire will
never come to an end. The church is the centre of history
in the perspective of God.

The second point is that – *The Church is essential to the
Gospel*. The Gospel we proclaim is sometimes too indi-
vidualistic: it's just 'Jesus died for me.' Well, He did die
for me – and you. Thank God that's true. But it's not the
whole truth; and it's not the full Gospel. The full Gospel
concerns not only Christ, but the mystery of Christ: and
that is the creation of the community of Christ, which is
the new humanity of God. And we need to make sure,
then, that the church as the new community of Jesus is
an integral part of the Gospel. Now we come to –

Paul's Prayer (vv14–21).

One of the main ways to discover a Christian's deepest
concerns, is to eavesdrop when he's praying; because if you
can overhear a Christian at prayer, you know what concerns him most. Now that is certainly true of this prayer of
the apostle Paul, in which he pours out his soul to God.

In chapter 2 he has expounded what God has done in Christ; how He has ended the terrible alienation, and is creating this new society, this redeemed and reconciled community. Now he follows his exposition with a prayer that this wonderful plan of God will be completely fulfilled in their experience. Glance first at the *introduction* to the prayer: 'I bow my knees . . .' The normal posture for prayer among the Jews was standing. In Christ's parable of the Pharisee and the publican, both men stood to pray. So kneeling was unusual: it indicated an exceptional degree of earnestness, as when Jesus knelt in the garden of Gethsemane, and fell on His face to the ground, prostrating Himself before His Father. That's what Paul was doing now. He bowed his knees; he prostrated himself before God, so intense was his longing about what he was going to pray for. Scripture lays down no rule about the posture that we should adopt in prayer: it is possible to pray kneeling, or standing, or sitting, or walking, or lying. But I agree with Hendrickson that 'The slouching position of the body while one is supposed to be praying, is an abomination to the Lord.' Paul goes on to say, 'I bow my knees to *the Father*.' He has been talking about the family, the one family of brothers and sisters; and now he bows his knees to the Father, of whose family Jews and Gentiles are equal members. It is natural that he should do this. Now it may be that the next phrase means 'of whom *the whole family* in heaven and earth . . .' – the heavenly family, the earthly family, '. . . is named.' Or it may mean, as some translate, 'of whom, or from whom,' the very concept of fatherhood is derived. But whether it is the family or the *fatherhood*, it is to the Father that he prays. That is the introduction.

Now for the *substance* of the prayer (16b–19). I sometimes think this prayer is rather like a staircase, by which he ascends higher and higher in his aspiration for them.

His first staircase has four steps, whose key-words are *strength* – that they may be 'strengthened' by Christ's indwelling through the Spirit; secondly, *love* – that they may 'be rooted and grounded in love,' strengthened, if you like, to love; thirdly, *knowledge* – that they may know Christ's love in all its dimensions; and fourthly, *fullness* – that they may be filled right up to the fullness of God. We've time only to glance at these four petitions.

First, strengthened through 'the Spirit in the inner man, that Christ may dwell in your hearts by faith.' These two seem to belong together; they are parallel. Both belong to our innermost self, our inner being, or our heart. And although one refers to the strength of the Spirit, and the other to the indwelling of Christ, they surely refer to the same experience; because Paul never separates the second and the third Persons of the Trinity. To have Christ dwelling in the heart, to have the Spirit strengthening us in our innermost being, these are the same thing. It is Christ, through His Spirit, dwelling in the heart, deeply strengthening us in our innermost being.

Then, 'rooted and grounded in love.' Paul's desire for strength is surely that we may be strengthened to love; that this new humanity, this new society, may be loving; that it may be bound together in love. And for that, we need the strength of Christ through the Holy Spirit. So he prays we may be rooted in it, and grounded in it. Love is to be the soil in which our roots go down: love is to be the foundation upon which our life is built. Paul, you see, links together a botanical and an architectural metaphor. We are rooted in the soil of love; we are grounded, or founded, upon the foundation of love. Love is to be the very root and foundation of our Christian life, so important and central is it.

Then, thirdly, knowledge; power to comprehend the love of Christ – although it passes knowledge. Paul prays that we may comprehend it in its full dimensions, its breadth, length, height, and depth. Modern commentators warn us not to be literal in our interpretations of these dimensions, but it seems to me legitimate to say that Christ's life is broad enough to encompass Jews and Gentiles, indeed all mankind. It is long enough to last for eternity. It is deep enough to reach the most degraded sinner; and it is high enough to exalt him to heaven. And that certainly is in keeping with the teaching of this letter. An ancient commentator saw these dimensions in the cross of Christ. For the upright pole reached down into the earth, and pointed upwards to heaven; while its cross-bar carried the arms of Jesus stretched out as if to embrace the whole world. And Paul prays that we may know the full dimensions of the love of Christ. We can only comprehend it 'with all the saints,' with all the people of God to whom he is writing. Of course the individual Christian in his isolation can know something of the love of Christ; but our individual grasp of it is limited by our limited experience. It needs the whole people of God to grasp the whole love of God. And we shall be exploring its dimension throughout eternity. For it 'passes knowledge': if the riches of Christ are unsearchable, the love of Christ is unknowable.

Fourthly fullness; 'filled right up to the fullness of God.' This surely looks beyond time into eternity: that although we can be filled with the Spirit now, nevertheless this fullness right up to the very fullness of the Godhead must look on to our perfection in heaven, when we shall receive that fullness of the Godhead which is possible for us without our ceasing to be human beings. What a prospect lies before us!

Then the conclusion of the prayer (vv20–21): God's ability to answer prayer, forcefully stated in a composite expression of seven stages. God is described first as able to work, or able to do; because He is not idle or inactive or dead. And He is able to do what we ask. Secondly, because He answers prayer. Thirdly, He is able to do what we ask or think, for sometimes we imagine what we dare not pray for. Fourthly, He is able to do *all* that we ask or think. Fifthly, He is able to do more than all that we ask or think. Sixth, He is able to do much more than all that we ask or think. And seventh, He is able to do very much more than all that we ask or think. As J.B. Phillips puts it, 'infinitely more.' And this is according to 'the power that is at work within us,' within us individually, Christ dwelling in the heart by faith; and within us as a community: God dwelling in His people, making His people His temple. And it is the power of Christ's resurrection, the power that raised and exalted Jesus Christ. And to Him be glory. The power comes from Him; the glory goes to Him. 'In the church' and 'in Christ Jesus': in the body and in the Head; in the bride and in the Bridegroom. The church is the reconciled community, and Christ is the Agent of the reconciliation for ever and ever.

Paul's prayer concerns the fulfilment of the vision, and it is only this limitless power of God that can give us this limitless love that we need to bind us together in the redeemed community. Brethren, let's dream dreams, as Paul dreamed this dream of the new humanity, the new society, the family of God, without any distinctions, united and reconciled to God and to one another; and as we dream this dream and see this vision, let us remember that it is only by the power of God that the dream will come true.

3. New Standards (Ephesians 4:1–5:21)

For three chapters the apostle Paul has been describing the new life that God gives us in Christ, and the new society that He is creating through Christ. It is a most magnificent vision. Now he comes to – *the New Standards* that God expects of His people. He therefore turns from exposition to exhortation; from what God has done to what we must do and be; from doctrine to ethics; from Christian faith to Christian life. Or, if you like, from theology to its practical, concrete implications in the nitty-gritty of everyday living.

He begins, 'I therefore . . .' (4:1). Because of all this magnificent doctrine that he has been expounding, of the new life and the new society, 'I therefore . . . beg you to lead a life that is worthy of the calling to which you have been called.' Well, what is a life that is worthy of God's call? I want to illustrate the theme by reminding you that just over three years ago the Duke of Windsor, our uncrowned king of England, died in Paris. That night on television in this country there was a very interesting programme about his life, in which excerpts from films which had been shot earlier in his life were shown. We saw the Duke of Windsor speaking about himself, his boyhood, his upbringing, his brief reign, and his abdication, and so on. I shall never forget these words that we saw him speaking. He said, 'My father . . .' that was, of course, King George V, '. . . was a strict disciplinarian. And sometimes when I'd done something wrong, or misbehaved, he would admonish me, saying, "My dear boy, you must always remember who you are." ' In other words, if only he had remembered that he was the crown prince of England, that he was going to ascend the throne one day, he would behave in a princely fashion. And when he misbehaved, it was due to his forgetfulness as to who and what he was.

I believe that every day as we go out into the world, our heavenly Father says to us, 'My dear child, you must always remember who you are.' And then, you see, we should behave like it. So the question is, Who are we? Well, we are the people of God; we are the new society that God has called into being. And this new society has two major characteristics. First, it is *one* people: it is a reconciled people, consisting of Jew and Gentile, and every colour and culture: the one and only family of God. Secondly, it is *a holy* people: it is distinct from the world; it is a community that belongs to God. Therefore, because God's people are one people, they must manifest their unity. And because God's people are a holy people, they must manifest their purity. That is why unity and purity are two fundamental features of the life that is worthy of our calling. We *are* the people of God, one people. Show it! We *are* the people of God, a holy people. Live like it! That is the theme: the unity and purity of this new people of God. Firstly, then –

The Unity of the Church (4:1–16)

Now in the last half-century we have heard a great deal about the unity of the church, about the reunion of the churches and of Christendom; and I think it will be helpful to look again at this classic Biblical passage on the unity of the church. It will prove, I think, a healthy corrective to a number of misleading ideas. There are four particular truths about the Christian unity that God intends, that are unfolded here. It depends on the charity of our conduct; it arises from the unity of our God; it is enriched by the diversity of our gifts; and it necessitates the maturity of our growth. So charity, unity, diversity, and maturity, are the key words here.

First – *it Depends on the Charity of our Conduct* (vv1–2). Paul has prayed at the end of chapter 3 that we may be 'rooted and grounded in love.' Now he exhorts us to walk in love. Prayer and exhortation, you see, go together. The apostle begins with charity: that's where we, too, should begin. There are too many people who, when talking about the unity of the church, begin with structures. Now personally I believe that structures are essential; an unstructured church seems to me just impossible. There must be some structure, however minimal. But we must not begin with structures. Paul begins with moral qualities; and if we have to choose, the moral is more important than the structural.

What moral qualities? First, *lowliness*. Have you ever thought that pride lurks behind all discord – the conceit that despises other people, or the vanity that demands their respect? I know – if I may be personal for a moment – that the people I instinctively and immediately like are the people who seem to be giving me the respect I think I deserve; and the people I instinctively dislike are the people who treat me like mud! Is that true for you? It's vanity, you see. Behind all discord lies vanity. That's why the great secret of unity is humility – and the Greek word means 'lowliness of mind,' the humble recognition of the worth and the value and the importance of other people, the 'humble mind' that was in Christ Jesus. Then *meekness*: meekness that is the gentleness of the strong personality who is nevertheless master of himself, and the servant of others. *Patience*, which is long-suffering towards aggravating people, of whom the churches seem to be full! 'Forbearing one another' – which is *mutual tolerance*. And finally *love*, that embraces the preceding four, that is the crown of the sum of all Christian virtues, and that constructively seeks the welfare of other people. We may be quite certain that no unity is pleasing to God that is not the child of charity.

Second – *It Arises from the Unity of our God* (vv3–6). Now here in these verses the word 'one' occurs seven times: one body, one Spirit, one hope, one Lord, one faith, one baptism, one God and Father of us all. And as you look carefully at these seven unities you will see that three of them allude to the three Persons of the Trinity; and the other four allude to our experience in relation to the three Persons of the Trinity. So that in verse 4 the Holy Spirit is called 'one Spirit,' in verse 5 the Lord Jesus Christ is called 'one Lord,' and in verse 6, God the Father is called 'one God and Father of us all.' Now notice how the unity of our Christian experiences arises out of the unity of our God. It is clear from the remaining phrases; and I bring it to you in three affirmations:

First, *There is one body*, because there is one Spirit. Of course Paul says in verse 4, 'There is one body and one Spirit,' but surely what he means is, 'There is one body *because* there is one Spirit.' There is only one Holy Spirit, and if He dwells in you and you and you and you – and me – then of course we are one. The one Spirit animates the one body. And there is only one body because there is only one Spirit indwelling and animating the body.

Secondly, *There is one hope, one faith, and one baptism*, because there is only one Lord Jesus. What is the object of our faith? Jesus Christ. So there is only one faith, because there is only one Lord in whom we all believe. Again, what is the object of our baptism? Well, we are baptised into Jesus Christ. There is only one baptism because there is only one Christ into whom we are baptised. And what is the object of our hope? Jesus Christ, and His coming again in glory. So there is only one hope because there is only one Christ, for whom we are waiting. There is only one faith, hope, and baptism, because there is only one Lord Jesus, who is the object of all three.

Thirdly, *There is only one family*, embracing us all (v6), because there is only 'one God and Father of us all, who is above all, and through all, and in . . . all.' So, to put it the other way round, the one Father creates the one family; the one Lord Jesus creates the one faith, hope, and baptism; and the one Holy Spirit creates the one body. There *can* only be one Christian family; and there *can* only be one Christian faith, hope, and baptism; and there can only be one body – because there is only one God. You can no more multiply churches than you can multiply God. Is there only one God? Then there's only one church. Is the unity of the Godhead inviolable? Then the unity of the church is inviolable. The unity of the church is as indestructible as the unity of God Himself. It is no more possible to split the church than it is to split the Godhead.

Oh, I know what you're thinking! And as I affirm this with the dogmatism with which the apostle Paul affirms it, questions immediately arise in our minds. We ask, 'Well, then, is the quest for the visible unity of the church a false preoccupation? If the church is inviolably one, is there any need to bother about our apparent disunities? And what about our disunities? How can we reconcile the phenomenon of disunity that we see all around us, with the Biblical insistence upon the fact of unity?' Well, in answer to those questions, I think we need to draw a distinction between the church's unity as an invisible reality in the mind and the sight of God, on the one hand; and the church's disunity, as a visible appearance, on the other – contradicting the invisible reality. We are one; God says so: and we sense it when we come to

Keswick. And yet outwardly and visibly we belong to different churches, which even work sometimes in competition with one another.

Now the apostle Paul recognises this, and in the very passage in which the unity of the church is so emphatically asserted, the possibility of disunity is also acknowledged. Have you ever noticed verse 3, that I've so far skipped? 'Eager to maintain the unity of the Spirit in the bond of peace': that's a very strange affirmation. How can the apostle Paul urge *us* to maintain something that he says cannot be destroyed? If it can't be destroyed, then why urge us to maintain it? Besides, if it's a unity of the Spirit, created and maintained by the Spirit, what is the sense of urging us to maintain the unity of the Spirit? There's something odd in that exhortation, isn't there? Well, I suggest it's only got one possible explanation, and that is that to maintain this unity means to maintain it visibly. It means to maintain it 'by the bond of peace,' that is, by living in peace with one another. It means to preserve in actual, concrete realities of love that unity that God has created, and neither man nor demon can destroy. It means that we are to demonstrate to the world that the unity we *say* exists indestructibly is not the rather sick joke it sounds, but is a true and glorious reality.

Now, if I may say so, I sometimes wonder whether we, who rejoice that *at* Keswick we are 'All one in Christ Jesus,' feel sufficient pain that *after* Keswick we separate into our different, and sometimes competing, denominations. Now let us imagine, if I may illustrate this, a human family consisting of father, mother, and three boys: Mr and Mrs Smith, Tom, Dick, and Harry. There can be no doubt whatever that they are one family; but in the course of the years the family disintegrates. The father and the mother quarrel, and get a divorce. The boys also quarrel, first with their parents, and then with one another, and separate. And the boys dislike one another so much that they go and live in different countries. They never meet, they never correspond, they never telephone; they entirely lose contact with one another. More than that, so determined are they to repudiate one another, that they actually change their names by deed poll. Now it would be difficult to imagine a family that had disintegrated more completely than that.

Well, supposing we were cousins of the Smith family, how would we react? Would we shrug our shoulders, and say, 'Oh, well, never mind. They're still only one family, you know!' What a sick thing to say, that would be. It's true, mind you: they are one family, and nothing can ever destroy the unity of that family: father, mother, three boys – brothers. The facts of marriage and birth have constituted it a family that is indestructibly one. But would we acquiesce in this disintegration of that family? Of course not! We'd do our utmost to reconcile them; we'd urge them to maintain the unity 'by the bond of peace'; to demonstrate visibly the unity that the facts of birth have imposed upon them. Surely it would be the same in the Christian church.

Thirdly, the church is – *Enriched by the Diversity of our Gifts* (vv7–12). Now the contrast between verses 6 and 7 is very vivid. Verse 6 speaks of God as Father of us all, above all, through all, and in all. We've all got the same Father. But verse 7 begins, 'But grace was given to each . . .' So Paul turns from all of us to each of us, and so from the unity of the church to the diversity of the church; and he is deliberately qualifying what he has just written about unity. For this unity is not to be misinterpreted as a dull, lifeless, colourless uniformity. We are not to imagine that every Christian is an exact replica of every other, as if we'd all been mass-produced in some celestial factory. On the contrary, the unity of the church, far from being a boring monotony is in fact a very exciting diversity: not only because of our different cultures and different personalities, but also because of our different gifts which Christ distributes, and which enrich our common life.

So Paul speaks of these gifts, and this is a reference to the *charismata*, the gifts of God's grace. What can we learn here about the *charismata*? I know that *charismata* is a controversial subject today. We all know about the charismatic movement; and there can be no doubt that the charismatic movement has brought blessing to many individuals and churches. Nevertheless I must say, if you will allow me a personal word, I think it is a great pity that they have pinched the word charismatic! Because it is a great mistake to apply the word charismatic to a group within the church. The word charismatic belongs to the whole church; the whole church is a charismatic community, its life enriched by the charismata, the gifts of God's Spirit. The whole church is the body of Christ, and every member of the body is endowed with some faculty to exercise in the service of God and of man.

So what does this passage teach us about the *charismata*? Three things: one, *The Giver of spiritual gifts is the ascended Christ*. Now in verse 8, quoting from Psalm 68, the ascended Jesus is likened to a military hero who returns after a victorious campaign with booty and captives, rides in triumphal procession into the capital city, and distributes largesse or gifts to his subjects. He gives gifts to men, like a victorious conqueror. Verses 9 and 10 are a parenthesis, and argue that the word 'ascended' pre-supposes His previous descent to the lower parts of the earth: whether that is a reference to the earth, or Hades, doesn't matter. But now He has ascended in triumph, 'far above all heavens'; He fills 'all things' – that is, the universe; and from this position of supreme authority He distributes gifts to the church. It is, therefore, a mistake to think of spiritual gifts as exclusively the gifts of the Holy Spirit, and to associate them too closely with the Holy Spirit, or experiences of the Holy Spirit, because here they are the gifts of Jesus Christ, while in Romans 12 they are the gifts of God the Father. It is always a mistake to separate the three Persons of the Trinity, the Father, the Son, and the Holy Spirit. All three are together involved in every aspect of the well-being of the church.

Secondly, *The character of the gifts is of wide variety.* Already in verse 7 we have been told that grace was given 'according to the measure of' Christ's gifts. In other words, the same grace is given to all, but in different measure, expressing itself in different gifts. Some people write of 'the nine gifts of the Spirit'; and there are nine in one list in 1 Corinthians 12. Others seem obsessed with only three: tongues, prophecy, and healing. But, you know, there are four lists in the New Testament, and if you tot them up, there are at least twenty *charismata*, and there is no indication that these are exhaustive lists in the New Testament.

Here Paul gives only five, and all of them are teaching gifts, necessary for the building up of the church. First, 'apostles and prophets.' They come first here, as they come first in both lists in 1 Corinthians 12; and because they head the list in this prominent way, and are even enumerated in 1 Corinthians 12: 28 – First apostles, second prophets, and then, third, teachers, and so on. 'Apostles' here evidently refers to the twelve apostles, and the apostle Paul; probably James, the Lord's brother, who seems to be an apostle; and possibly one or two others. But a small, unique and authoritative group of inspired apostles of Christ. The word 'prophets' here evidently refers to direct organs of original revelation, through whom God spoke His word, and who were able to say, 'The Word of the Lord came to me, saying . . .' Now this is the sense in which Paul uses the words 'apostles and prophets' in this letter to the Ephesians. Yesterday morning, when we looked at 2:20, we saw that their teaching is the foundation on which the church is built. Now, an elementary knowledge of building and architecture will tell us that once you have laid a foundation of the building, and the superstructure is being raised upon it, you cannot lay the foundation again. Once a foundation is laid, it is laid – and it's finished: and that is the teaching of the apostles and prophets.

Now I can see that there may be subsidiary gifts today of apostleship, in terms of being a pioneer missionary, or a church-planter: what the New Testament calls 'the apostles of the churches.' Not the apostles of Christ – they were unique; but the apostles of the churches, sent out by the churches on a mission. And there may be a subsidiary gift of prophecy in terms of the exposition of Scripture, and a ministry of exhortation and encouragement and consolation. But in the primary sense in which the New Testament uses these words, there are no apostles or prophets in the church today. Certainly there are no apostles comparable to the apostle Paul, or the apostle Peter, or the apostle John; and there are no prophets comparable to the prophets in the Scripture, who can say, 'The Word of the Lord came to me, saying . . .' The Word of God doesn't come to people today; we come to it. It doesn't come to us in original revelations today; if it did, you see, we would need to add these to the canon of Scripture, and the whole church would need to submit to their authoritative teaching. But although there are no apostles and prophets in the church today in the primary sense in which the apostle is using the words, there are evangelists who proclaim the good news and win men and women to Christ; and there are pastors to care for the church; and teachers to expound God's Word – teaching gifts of great importance.

Now, thirdly, *The purpose of the spiritual gifts is service.* Verse 12 states why Christ gave these gifts to the church; and it is explained in two stages. Its immediate purpose was the equipment of the saints for the work of ministry. The NEB translates it 'to equip God's people for work in His service.' Christ gives ministers and pastors to His church, not just in order that they may exercise a ministry of their own; but in order that they may equip others to exercise *their* ministries. So the New Testament vision of a pastor is not of a man who jealously guards all the ministry in his own hands, and keeps his thumb well and truly on the laity; but rather of a man who helps and encourages all God's people to discover and to develop and to exercise their gifts. The pastor does it by his teaching and by his training; he is setting them free for their ministry, so that instead of monopolising all ministry, he multiplies it. That is the immediate purpose of pastors in the church: so to teach, so to train, that ministries are multiplied. But the ultimate purpose is the building up of the body of Christ.

So regarding the purpose of the gifts, all God's gifts are service gifts, to be used in the service of others. They are not given for selfish reasons, but for unselfish; and their overall purpose is the common good (1 Cor. 12:7). Therefore their comparative importance is to be assessed by the degree to which they edify; and the more they edify and build up the church, the more important they are. That's why the most important gifts in the church are the teaching gifts, because nothing builds up the church of Christ like the teaching of the Word of God and of the truth. I hope, then, we will try and remember those three truths about *charismata*. The giver of the gifts is the ascended Christ; the character of the gifts is of wide diversity; and the purpose of the gifts is service, equipping God's people for their ministry and building up the body of Christ.

Now the fourth thing is that – *It Necessitates the Maturity of our Growth*. The church is the body of Christ; and like the human body, Christ's body grows. Its growth is described in verse 13. It grows in size, as new members are added through the ministry of evangelists; and it grows in stature as old members develop and mature, through the ministry of pastors and teachers. So evangelists and pastors and teachers are building up the body of Christ. It's growing through their ministry. And this growth of the whole body depends upon the growth of individual members of it. We are to be 'no more children,' whose mark is instability (v14). Unstable Christians are like little children; and they are like little boats in a stormy sea, at the mercy of the wind and the waves; immature Christians tossed unsteadily about by the strange doctrines of crafty teachers. They don't know what they believe. They're so unstable in doctrine. But by contrast with them, we are to speak the truth in love (v15). If a sign of Christian immaturity is doctrinal instability, a sign of Christian maturity is conviction about God's revealed truth, and the ability to hold it and speak it in love.

Then (vv15–16): '. . . will grow up in every way into Christ, the head, from whom the whole body' derives its growth, when each part is functioning properly, and builds itself up in love. Now don't miss that wonderful truth contained in verse 16, 'maintaining itself in love.' There are some people so determined to 'fight for the truth' that they become unloving, and bitter, and acrimonious. There are others who are so determined at all cost to exhibit brotherly love, that they say, 'Let's drown our doctrinal differences in the ocean of brotherly love,' and they are not concerned about truth. Both these tendencies are unbalanced and un-Biblical. Truth becomes hard if it isn't softened by love; and love becomes soft if it isn't strengthened by truth. We are to hold the two together – which ought not to be difficult, because the Holy Spirit of *truth* brings forth the fruit of love.

Now I want to conclude this first section by saying that I believe that as we look at this passage and hear Paul's exhortation begging us to lead a life that is 'worthy of our calling,' we all need a greater discontent with the ecclesiastical *status quo*. Most of us are too complacent, too conservative, too content with the present situation; and we don't see with any clarity the vision of the kind of church that God wants, and the kind of new society that God is creating. Some are content with structures of unity, with little humility, meekness, longsuffering, or love. Others are content with the theology of unity: 'It's a fact,' they say; and they don't see the anomaly of a disunity that contradicts it. Others are content with a boring monotony; they don't see the variety that God intends in the church. And others are content with the progress of the church, its present size, its present stature, and have no desire to see it grow – either by missionary outreach or by the maturing of its members. All this complacency is unworthy of our calling. We want to live a life that is 'worthy of our calling,' and we need to keep this beautiful Biblical ideal before us.

We turn now from the unity of the church to –

The Purity of the Church (4:17–5:21)

The church is not only one people, manifesting its unity; it is a holy people, manifesting its purity. The gist of

Paul's message is at the end of verse 17, 'You must no longer live as the Gentiles do.' 'No longer.' Once you did, once you lived like pagans; now you must live like Christians. You are different; you must behave differently. Your new status as the people of God involves new standards.

First, then, he lays – *the Doctrinal Basis* (vv17–24), and it is essential to grasp the basic contrast he is drawing between what they had been previously, and what they had now become. What they had been is described in verses 17–19. They had empty minds: 'the futility of their minds.' Their 'understanding was darkened.' They were 'ignorant of God's truth,' so they were 'alienated from His life.' And all this was due to a wilful hardness of heart, which had led them to reject the knowledge they had. As a result they became callous, and gave themselves up to immorality. That is, having lost all sensitivity, they lost all self-control. Terribly downward path! Hardness, then darkness, and then uncleanness. That is what they were.

Now what they had become: 'But as for you, this is not how you learned Christ, if so be you have heard Him, and been taught as the truth is in Jesus' (vv20–21). Do you see? Over against the darkness and the ignorance of the heathen is the truth as it is in Jesus, which they had learned and which they had heard. What truth? Well, in a word, it is the truth of the new birth, of the new creation, and of the entirely new life that results from it (vv22–24). Now, I love the Revised Standard Version, but there are one or two places where one ventures to disagree with it; and this is one of them. I believe they made a serious mistake in translating these as commands – that is, 'Put off your old man! (v22) and 'Be renewed . . .' (v23), and 'Put on the new man!' (v24). I suggest that is very misleading: it cannot be right. In the parallel passage in Colossians – the two letters were written at the same time, and there are many parallels between them – these are not commands, but statements of *what the Colossians had done*. Surely it is so here. This is the truth as it is in Jesus, which they had learned; namely, that they should put off the old man and put on the new man. This is what they had learned, and this is what they had done. And Paul is reminding them of what they had learned, and what they had done. They had put off their former self, their fallen humanity, and their old life; they had been taught to be 'renewed in the spirit of their mind,' to seek a daily renewal of mind (notice again the importance of the mind), and they had been taught to put on the new man, their new self, a new humanity that God had created in the new birth.

Now not, of course, that they could bring it about. We can't bring about our new birth. It is God who creates the new humanity, and gives the new life, and renews our mind. But, when God re-creates us in Christ, we entirely concur with what He has done. We put off our old life, turning away from it in distaste; we put on this new life, this new humanity, that God has created. We embrace it, we welcome it; or in one word, regeneration that is God's work, and repentance that is our work (and we can only do it by grace), belong together. When God regenerates, we repent: the two belong together, and cannot be separated. And Paul reminds them of this. 'This is "the truth as it is in Jesus," that you learned when you were converted. You did put off the old man and put on the new. Have you forgotten it?' he is saying, in effect. So they must constantly remember what they had learned and done.

Now we turn from the doctrinal basis to – *the Practical Outworking* (4:24–5:21). 'Therefore, putting away falsehood . . .' (v25). Now that would have no meaning if he had just commanded them to put away the old man. No, it is because they had put away their old humanity that they are now commanded to put away everything that belongs to that old humanity – the conduct of their former life. This metaphor of putting on and putting off is, of course, drawn from the way we dress. The kind of clothing we wear depends on the kind of role we are fulfilling. When you go to a wedding, you wear one kind of dress; when you go to a funeral, you wear another. Our dress is determined by our job as well – soldiers, sailors, wear different uniforms; lawyers have a special dress; prisoners and convicts dress in a certain way. And when our role changes, our dress changes. When a prisoner is released from prison he puts off his old uniform, and he puts on ordinary clothing again. When a soldier becomes a civilian, and puts off one role and assumes another, he gets out of uniform into civvies. Since in the new birth we put off our old humanity and put on a new humanity that God has created, we must also put off the old standards and put on the new. Our new role means new clothing; our new life means a new life-style. So Paul now gives six concrete examples.

First, *Don't tell lies*, but rather tell the truth (v25). It's not enough for Christians to avoid telling lies; Christians ought to be known for their honesty, as trustworthy and dependable people. And the reason is given: it is because the other person is our neighbour. And if he's in the church he's our brother, and we are members one of another. If we belong to one another, as members one of another, how can we be dishonest to one another? Fellowship is built on trust, and trust is built on truth. So falsehood always undermines fellowship, while truth builds it.

Second, *Don't lose your temper*, but rather be sure that your anger is righteous (vv26–27). Verse 26 begins with a positive, 'Be angry . . .' The Bible distinguishes between two different kinds of anger, you see – righteous anger and sinful anger; and there is a great need in today's world for more Christian and righteous anger. We compromise with sin in a way that God never does, and in the face of blatant evil we should be indignant, not tolerant; we should be angry, and not indifferent. If God hates sin, His people should hate it too. At the same time we have to remember that we are fallen, and so we are always prone, in our anger, to intemperance and vanity. So Paul adds three qualifications, to be on our guard: 'Don't sin,' that is, be sure that your anger is free of spite and malice and animosity and pride and revenge. 'Don't let the sun go down on your wrath,' that is, never nurse your anger; and if you become aware of any sinful element in it, then apologise and put it away. And, 'Don't give any opportunity to the devil,' because he's always ready to exploit every situation of anger.

Third, *Don't steal, but rather work, and give* (v28). 'Don't steal' is the eighth commandment, but Paul goes beyond the prohibition, and draws out the positive counterpart. It is not enough for a thief to stop stealing: he has got to start working with his own hands, working hard, working honestly, working gainfully; then he will be able not only to support his own family as well as himself, but to give to people in need. Instead of sponging on the community, which is what thieves do, he begins to contribute to the community. And only Jesus Christ can turn a burglar into a benefactor.

Fourth, *Don't use your mouth for evil, but rather for good* (v29). Paul moves now from working with our hands, to our mouths. Speech is a wonderful gift of God. It is one of our human capacities which distinguishes us from the animals. Cows can moo, dogs can bark, donkeys bray, pigs grunt (so do Keswick speakers, actually, on the platform! But it is a delightful kind of grunting: it encourages the speaker!), and birds can sing: but only human beings can speak. It is part of the divine image we bear. God speaks; He's a speaking God. He made us speaking beings. So let us use our gift constructively, not for evil talk (whether it is dishonest or vulgar or unkind, it hurts the hearers); but for good, to benefit them, not to harm them. James reminds us, of course, of the fearful power of the tongue.

Don't grieve the Holy Spirit (v30), of which Dr. Paul Rees was speaking from Isaiah the other evening. Since the Holy Spirit can be grieved, as Dr. Rees reminded us, He is a Person; He can be wounded, He can feel pain. And since He is a *Holy* Spirit, what wounds Him is unholiness. Since He is the 'one Spirit' of 4:3–4 – you know, 'one body, one Spirit' – disunity gives Him pain as well. Notice a reference to the sealing for the day of redemption. We were sealed with the Spirit at the beginning of our Christian life: the indwelling of the Spirit is God's seal, or mark of ownership, by which He stamps us as belonging to Him. The day of redemption refers to the end of our Christian life, when our bodies will be redeemed and our redemption will be complete. So sealing and redemption are the beginning and the end of the Christian pilgrimage. And between the two termini, Don't grieve the Holy Spirit. Cultivate holiness, and don't grieve the Holy Spirit by unholiness. For the Spirit is a sensitive Spirit, and He shrinks away from sin. So don't let's give Him pain; let's seek to give Him pleasure.

Now, fifth, *don't be unkind*, or bitter, but rather kind and loving (4:31–5:2). Here is a whole series of unpleasant things we are to put away from us entirely. Bitterness – a sour spirit; wrath, anger, clamour – that's getting excited, and raising your voice, and shouting in a quarrel; slander – that's the whisper campaign, tittle-tattle behind people's backs; malice – ill-will, wishing people harm. All these evil things must be entirely put away from us. They don't belong in the new life that God is creating. Instead, we are to be kind – wishing people well; tender-hearted, or compassionate; forgiving one another – literally acting in grace towards others, as God has acted in grace towards us. 'Therefore' (5:1), 'be imitators of God.' He loves us; we imitate Him and love others. He is gracious; we imitate Him and are gracious too. And we are to 'walk in love as Christ loved us, and gave Himself up for us.' We are to love others; we are to give ourselves up in service for other people.

Then, sixth, *Don't joke about sex* (5:3–4), but give thanks for it. Paul turns, you see, from love to its perversion, in what we call lust. He mentions immorality (v3), impurity, or covetousness – because sexual lust is an especially degrading form of covetousness: the coveting of somebody else's body for our own personal gratification. 'Let it not even be named among you,' he says. Not only that we are to avoid the indulgence of these passions: we are to avoid even talking about them. And verse 4 goes beyond immorality to vulgarity, because filthiness is obscenity; and 'silly talk and levity' is coarse jesting. And all three refer to a dirty mind, that expresses itself in dirty conversation. Instead, let there be thanksgiving (v4b). Now in the context, surely it must be on the same subject; and the contrast is striking and beautiful. Why do Christians dislike vulgarity? Not because we have a warped view of sex, and are either ashamed of it or afraid of it, but because we have a high view of sex, as a gift of God; and therefore we do not want to see it degraded. All God's gifts, including sex, are subjects of thanksgiving, and not for joking. To joke about them is bound to degrade them; but to thank God for them preserves their nobility as the gifts of God, the Creator.

I want you to notice a word that occurs a couple of times in the Revised Standard Version: at the end of verse 3, the avoidance of immorality 'is fitting among saints.' And in the middle of verse 4, vulgarity and obscenity 'are not fitting.' They are different Greek words, but they have roughly the same meaning. The saints, you see, God's people, are a distinct people, and they have distinct moral standards. Certain things are fitting; certain things are appropriate to the people of God. Certain things are not fitting, or inappropriate to the people of God. And it's the same theme all through the chapter: what we are determines how we behave. Our conduct must fit our character as the people of God.

Now we move to – *More Arguments for Righteousness*. First, *The certainty of judgment*. Verses 5–7 introduce this solemn note of judgment, and they tell us that 'no immoral or impure . . . or covetous man (that is, an idolater), has any inheritance in the kingdom of God and of Christ,' because God's kingdom is a righteous kingdom. Now let us be clear, from the rest of Scripture, that this is not a reference to somebody who has fallen into immoral conduct in a moment of extreme temptation, and has then repented and been forgiven. This is a reference to those whose whole life is given up to immorality, and who do not repent. Such people are excluded from the kingdom of God, 'and let no one deceive you,' says the apostle Paul. There are some, you see, who teach that everybody is going to heaven, irrespective of their conduct and of their penitence. They are deceiving us. Universalism is a lie. The truth is that because of these things, the wrath of God is going to fall on the disobedient. Therefore, because God's kingdom is a righteous kingdom, and His wrath is going to fall on the disobedient, 'Don't associate . . .' or literally, 'Do not be partners with them' (New International Version). What is forbidden us, you see, is not any contact or association with such people, but any involvement in their practices. A warning of judgment.

Next, *The fruit of light* (vv8–14). The whole paragraph plays on the symbolism of darkness and light; and what Paul is saying is that 'you were darkness, but now you are light in the Lord; so you must live in the light, and walk as children of light, and take no part in the unfruitful works of darkness.'

Thirdly, *The nature of wisdom* (vv15–17). Paul assumes that Christians are wise men, and not fools. He says in verse 15, 'Look carefully, then, how you walk, not as fools, but like wise men,' that is, take trouble over your Christian life. We all take trouble over the things that seem to us to matter, so we must take trouble over our Christian life. 'Be most careful, then, how you conduct yourselves' (NEB). And there are two particular marks of a wise man who takes trouble over his Christian life. First, *he makes the most of his time* (v16). He knows that time is a precious commodity; time is passing, the days are evil: so he doesn't fritter away his time. He seizes every fleeting opportunity while it is there. The first mark of the wise man is his disciplined use of time. And the second is that *he discerns the will of God* (v17): 'understanding what the will of the Lord is,' because he knows that it is in God's will that there is wisdom. So he knows that there is nothing more important than to discover the general will of God for all His people in Scripture; and the particular will of God for each individual, partly from Scripture, partly in prayer, partly through discussing the issue with others, and partly through using the mind that God has given us. That's the wise man, discerning the will of God.

Then the fourth argument for holiness, is – *The fullness of the Spirit* (vv18–21). 'Filled with the Spirit.' I hope all of us know that there is a present imperative passive, and it

means 'go on being filled with the Spirit.' The fullness of
the Holy Spirit is not a once-for-all experience, that you
can never lose. It is something to be renewed every day.
I pray every day, and many times a day, that God will
graciously fill me with the Holy Spirit. We have been
sealed once and for all: we need to be filled continually.
As the New English Bible put it, 'Let the Holy Spirit fill
you' – and keep on filling you, too. Then Paul draws a
comparison between drunkenness and the fullness of the
Spirit, because a drunken man is under the influence of
alcohol, while a Spirit-filled Christian is under the influence of power of the Holy Spirit. But there the comparison ends. And it is a great mistake to suppose that to be
filled with the Spirit is a kind of spiritual intoxication, in
which a human being loses control of himself. On the
contrary, self-control is among the fruit of the Spirit: 'The
fruit of the Spirit is self-control . . .' On the day of
Pentecost the group who thought the apostles were
drunk was only a tiny minority, who didn't understand
the languages they were speaking. Most of them were
amazed, because they understood the languages; it was
only the others who thought they were drunk. The fullness of the Spirit and drunkenness are two quite different things; so after comparing the two states, Paul contrasts the results. The result of drunkenness, he said, is
debauchery. People who are drunk give way to wild,
dissolute, uncontrolled actions, and they behave like animals. But the results of the fullness of the Spirit are quite
different. Excessive alcohol dehumanises us, and turns a
human being into a beast. The fullness of the Spirit
humanises us, makes us more human, for it makes us
like Jesus Christ, who is the only truly human being who
has ever lived.

So Paul lists the fruits of the fullness of the Spirit. First,
fellowship: addressing one another in hymns and songs.

That does not mean when you are filled with the Spirit you stop talking to one another, and start singing to one another. The reference to hymns obviously shows that he is talking about public worship; and in our worship sometimes we don't just praise God, we talk to one another. In the Church of England, when we sing the *Benedicite*, we sing, 'O come, let us sing unto the Lord,' and we're not actually praising God at all – we ought to be turning to our neighbour, and saying, 'Come on, old boy, sing unto the Lord!' That is addressing one another in a spiritual song. It's fellowship.

Then *worship*: 'Singing in your heart'; 'Making music in your hearts for the ears of the Lord' (J.B. Phillips), an instruction from which unmusical people, unable to sing in tune, have always derived much comfort! For a Spirit-filled Christian has a song of joy in his heart. Then *thankfulness* (v20): 'Giving thanks . . .' A grumbling spirit is not compatible with the fullness of the Spirit. Grumbling was the besetting sin of Israel. A Spirit-filled believer is full of thanksgiving. Not that he can thank God for everything, including evil, as is being very strangely taught in circles of the church today. You can't thank God for evil; you can only thank God for those things that are compatible with His fatherly goodness, and in the name of Jesus Christ, in whom we give thanks. Things that are not compatible with God the Father and God the Son, we cannot give thanks for. Then, *submissiveness*, 'submitting to one another in the fear of Christ' – submitting to Christ, submitting to one another. Sometimes a person claiming to be filled with the Spirit is aggressive, self-assertive, and brash. But those truly filled with the Spirit show the meekness and the gentleness of Jesus. These are the wholesome results of the fullness of the Spirit.

Now throughout this long passage on the unity and the purity of the church, Paul's underlying argument has been consistently the same. Two words stand out in the whole passage – 'worthy,' and 'fitting.' 'I beg you to live a life that is *worthy* of the calling with which you have been called' (4:1); 'Avoid impurity as is *fitting* among saints' (5:3). You see, our Christian life must be worthy of what God has called us to be; and it must be fitting, or appropriate, to what we are. It is therefore essential to know what we are. Let no one say that doctrine doesn't matter. Doctrine is indispensable to holiness. All good conduct arises out of good doctrine. We have to remember who we are – the people of God, the one people, the holy people: then we'll live like it. And our Father says to us, as we said at the very beginning, 'My dear children, you must always remember who you are.'

4. New Relationships (Ephesians 5:22 – 6:24)

The apostle Paul has been unfolding, in this great letter to the Ephesians, the *new life* that God has given us in Christ; the *new society*, the single new humanity, reconciled and integrated humanity, that He is creating and building through Jesus Christ; and the *new standards* which God expects of His new society, particularly unity and purity in the church. We are to live a life that is both worthy of our Christian calling, and fitting to our Christian status, as the redeemed, reconciled people of God. Now we turn, fourthly, to –

The New Relationship into which we have been brought: for in the rest of the letter Paul adds two further dimensions to our Christian living. The first concerns the very practical, concrete, down-to-earth *relationships of our homes*. And the second concerns *the enemy we face*, and therefore the equipment or armour we need in unremitting spiritual warfare. These two responsibilities, home and work on the one hand, and spiritual warfare on the other, are obviously very different from one another: husband and wife, parents and children, employers and employees, are visible, tangible human beings. But the principalities and powers that are arrayed against us are invisible and intangible spiritual beings. Nevertheless, if our Christian faith is worth anything, it must be able to cope with both situations. It must be able to teach us how to behave Christianly in our homes and at our work every day; but it must also enable us to fight against the devil and the powers of evil, in such a way that we stand, and do not fall. So our two subjects this morning are – Harmony in the Home, and Stability in the Fight.

First – *Harmony in the Home*. Paul refers to three pairs of people – husbands and wives, parents and children, masters and servants – and to the reciprocal relationships that should exist in each pair. All three come under the heading of home life, because in those days slaves were part of the household: although the contemporary application of the third pair will be rather to our work than to our home. All three are examples of submission, and the RSV is surely right to begin the paragraph with 'Be subject to one another out of reverence for Christ,' and to see the three paragraphs that follow as examples of this general requirement of mutual submission. Thus wives are mentioned first, before their husbands, and are told, 'Be subject to your husbands' (5:22). Children are mentioned before their parents, and are told, 'Obey your parents' (6:1). Servants are mentioned before their masters, and are told, 'Be obedient' (6:5). All three, you see, are particular examples of the general Christian responsibility to be submissive.

I know that the concept of submission to authority is extremely unfashionable today. Ours is an age of liberation – for women, for children, for workers; and anything that savours of oppression is deeply resented in our society. So how are we Christians to react to this modern mood? It would be very interesting to know how you would answer my rhetorical question! I'll tell you my own answer: Our initial action to these liberation movements, I believe, should be one of welcome, because we all ought to agree that women in many cultures have, without doubt, been exploited; and they have been treated like servants in their own homes. We need to distinguish between what Scripture clearly teaches, and what culture may seem to dictate for a woman in a particular culture. You know, I am sure, the daily thanksgiving in a Jewish household: 'Thanks be to Thee, O Lord God, who has not made me a woman.'

But if women in many cultures have been exploited, children have often been suppressed and squashed, not least in Victorian England, in which they were supposed to be 'seen and not heard.' Similarly workers have often been unjustly treated, and have been given inadequate wages and living conditions, and an insufficient share in responsible decision-making. And we Christians should acknowledge with shame that we ourselves have often acquiesced in, and so helped to perpetuate, some forms of human oppression, instead of being in the vanguard of those who are seeking change, according to Scripture.

I want to emphasise that there is nothing in the paragraph that is incompatible with the true liberation of human beings from exploitation and oppression. On the contrary, to whom do women, children, and workers chiefly owe their liberation? Is it not to Jesus Christ? It is Jesus Christ who treated women with honour and courtesy in an age in which they were despised. It is Jesus Christ who said, 'Let the children come to me,' in an age in which unwanted babies were consigned to the local rubbish dump. It is Jesus Christ who taught the dignity of service, by saying, 'I am among you as a serving man,' and by getting on His hands and knees and washing His apostles' feet. We Christians must constantly affirm at least these three truths: First, the dignity of womanhood, of childhood, and of servanthood. Secondly, the equality of all human beings, irrespective of sex, age, class, race, or culture: because all human beings have been made in the image of God, and are God-like human beings. And thirdly, the even deeper unity of all believers as fellow-members of God's family, and of the body of Christ.

Now let me remind you that the apostle Paul has been describing, in the early chapters of this Ephesian letter, God's new humanity, God's new society: and he has been emphasising the complete oneness of Jew and Gentile in Christ. We may be quite certain, therefore, that he does not now contradict himself, and destroy his own thesis. He is not now erecting new barriers of sex, age, or rank, in the only society in which they have been abolished. Paul plainly affirms in Galatians 3:28, 'There is neither Jew nor Gentile, slave nor free, male nor female; for all are one in Jesus Christ.' The same truth underlies the whole letter to the Ephesians; and on the principle of interpreting Scripture by Scripture, we must not interpret these paragraphs in such a way as to overthrow the major message of the epistle, which is God's new society without any distinction or discrimination between us in this single new humanity.

Well now, in the light of that, how are we to interpret this difficult teaching about submission? Well, let me go on negatively for a moment, and say that the submission he enjoins on the wife, the child, and the servant, is not another word for inferiority. It has nothing to do with inferiority at all: it simply teaches the equality of human beings, as creatures made in the image of God, and our total oneness in Jesus Christ. Submission is not inferiority. I believe we need to grasp what Martin Luther very clearly grasped, and what his followers, Lutherans, also clearly understand today: that is, the difference between persons on the one hand, and their roles or offices on the other.

Let me give you an example. Let us imagine that there are two men in the law court. They are equal in the sight of God, and they have an equal dignity as creatures made in the image of God. But one happens to be the magistrate, and the other stands before him in the dock.

They are equal in the sight of God; they have an equal dignity as God-like beings. But because one is the magistrate, and the other appears before him in court, the magistrate's office or role gives him an authority to which the other must submit. And it is the same with husbands and wives, parents and children, and masters and servants. They have equal dignity as God-like beings, but different God-given roles. The husband, the parent, the employer, has a certain authority of office or of role to which the others must submit.

Now there are two questions about this authority – Where did it come from? and How is it to be used? First, Where does it come from? *It comes from God.* The God of the Bible is a God of order in nature, in society, and in the church. An ordered society is the will of God; and in His ordering of society in the state, and in the family, He has established certain authoritative roles, certain leadership roles. And since this authority, although exercised by human beings, is delegated to them by God, others are required conscientiously to submit to it. Now this is clearly in our text: 'Wives, be subject to your husbands, *as unto the Lord*' (5:22), because your husband's authority has been given to him by the Lord. 'Children, obey your parents *in the Lord*' (6:1), because parental authority has been given by the Lord. 'Slaves, be obedient to your earthly masters, *as unto Christ*' (6:5), because the authority of the earthly master has been delegated to him by Christ. So you see, behind the husband, and the master, and the parent, you must see the Lord Himself, who has given them their authority. So, if you mean to submit to Christ, you must submit to them, because it is His authority which they exercise.

Now in stating that, it is very important not to overstate it. It does not mean that the authority of husbands, parents, and employers is unlimited. It does not mean that wives, children and workers are required to give unconditional obedience. No, the submission commanded is to God's authority, delegated to men; therefore if men misuse their God-given authority, and if they command what God forbids, or forbid what God commands, then our duty is no longer conscientiously to submit, but conscientiously to refuse to submit. Because to submit in such circumstances would be to disobey God. The principle of Scripture is abundantly plain: it is that we must submit to this authority – right up to that of the state – up to the point where obedience to human authority would involve disobedience to God. At that point civil disobedience becomes our Christian duty, because in order to submit to God we have to refuse to submit to men who are misusing their God-given authority. Of this there are examples in Scripture: Daniel, Shadrach, Meshach, and Abednego in the Old Testament; the apostles Peter and John in the New Testament, refusing to obey human authority, in order to obey the authority of God. But that is the exception. The general rule is humble submission to God-given authority.

Secondly, How is it to be used? And the answer is, *For the benefit of others*. The most striking feature of these paragraphs is that in each relationship there are reciprocal duties. True, wives are to submit to husbands, children to parents, servants to masters: and this requirement of submission presupposes an authority in the husband, the parent, the master. But – this is very significant: when Paul comes to the duties of the husband or the parent or the master, in no case is it authority that he tells them to exercise. Isn't that striking? Instead, explicitly or implicitly, he warns them against the improper use of their authority; he forbids them to exploit their position, and he commands them to give to the other party the respect they deserve, and the rights which are their due.

So husbands are to love their wives, and care for them. Parents are not to provoke their children, but to bring them up tenderly, responsibly. And masters are not to threaten their servants, but to treat them with justice.

Let me sum up the introduction: Authority, in Biblical usage, is not a synonym for tyranny. God has indeed established certain authority or leadership roles in society; but every person with authority is responsible, both to the God who has delegated the authority to him, and to the human beings made in God's image, for whose benefit the authority has been given.

Now we come, first, to – *Wives and husbands* (5:22–33): 'Wives, be subject . . . Husbands, love . . .' Two reasons are given for the wife's submission to her husband. The first is drawn from creation, and the second from redemption. *Creation*: 'The husband is the head of the wife' (5:23): and the fact is only stated there, but it is elaborated by Paul elsewhere, both in 1 Timothy 2 and in 1 Corinthians 11. There Paul uses three arguments, all drawn from creation, namely, that the woman was made *after* the man, *out* of the man, and *for* the man. And since Paul argues from the facts of creation, the fundamental truth that he states is permanent and universal, and is not culturally limited. And I believe we should not be afraid to maintain this, however unpopular and however unfashionable it may be today. Our human sexuality is part and parcel of our creation. Masculinity and femininity represent not only a physiological, but a psychological distinction. And as the result of our creation, God has given to man – and especially to the husband in marriage – a certain headship, a certain leadership, a certain authority, a certain responsibility. And his wife will also find her true, God-given role, not in rebelling against that authority, but in joyfully submitting to it. And what God has established by creation, no culture will ever be able to destroy. It is an argument from creation. The husband is the head of the wife.

Then *redemption*. 'As Christ is the Head of the church . . .' (5:23). If creation explains the relation of husband and wife, redemption illustrates it. 'The husband is head of the wife, as Christ is the Head of the church,' His body, and is its Saviour (5:23). The wife is subject to the husband in everything, 'as the church is subject to Christ' (5:24). It is a beautiful truth, is it not? The husband and wife, in their reciprocal relations, are intended to reflect and exhibit the Gospel, the relations between Christ and His church. And the addition, '. . . and is Himself its Saviour,' indicates that headship is not rule without responsibility, for provision and protection are included in it. That is what the headship involved.

Then, 'Husbands, love your wives' (5:25–33). Here Paul uses two metaphors to emphasise the sacrifice and care which his love will involve. The first is Christ's love (5:25–27). Jesus showed His love to His bride, the church, by 'giving Himself up for her,' in order that He might 'sanctify her' now, having 'cleansed her by the washing of water with the Word' – probably a reference to baptism and the preaching of the Gospel; and in order that one day He might 'present her to Himself faultless.' And husbands are to love like Christ, with a love that seeks the wife's highest welfare, and is prepared for the utmost self-sacrifice in order to attain it. Husbands are to love with the love of Christ.

Then the second metaphor is *self-love* (vv28–33). Just as we are to love our neighbour as we love ourselves, the husbands are to love their wives 'as their own bodies.' For in a sense the wife is that, for the two become one flesh. 'He who loves his own wife, loves himself,' for nobody ever hated his own body (v29): on the contrary, he takes care of it and feeds it. So, too, Christ loves His body, the church. And the great Biblical statement, 'They shall become one flesh,' that applies, of course, to husband and wife in marriage, also contains a great mystery. 'It is a great truth that is hidden here' (5:32, NEB), for it applies to the union between Christ and His church.

Paul sums up, 'Each of you must love his wife as he loves himself, and the wife must respect her husband,' (v33). So the standards of a husband's love for his wife are Christ's love, and self-love. He is to love his wife as Christ loves the church, and as he loves himself. Now that second one may seem a low standard, but it isn't actually: it is an *ad hominem* argument, an argument from our own fallen humanity, because we love ourselves a very great deal, and such love inevitably leads to sacrificial caring.

Now I want to add a word to wives – or to girls who may not yet be married – in case you find this teaching difficult. I want to suggest four wonderful truths from this passage about the wife's submission. The first is that it is *a particular example of a general Christian duty*: in other words, 5:22 follows 5:21. If it is the wife's duty to submit to her husband, it is also the husband's duty to submit to his wife as a fellow-Christian, for we are all to submit to one another. Submissiveness is to be mutual, and the wife's submissiveness is a particular example of a general Christian grace. Secondly, *the person to whom the wife is to submit is not an ogre, or a tyrant, but a lover*. The instruction is not 'Wives, submit: husbands, boss!' It is, 'Wives, submit. Husbands, love.' And if a husband believes that this is permanent Biblical teaching and the will of God, then the husband must win the wife's submission by his love for her. Thirdly, she is to submit to *a lover who loves like Christ*. Does it sound hard, submission? I honestly believe if the wife thinks that she has the worst of the bargain in this Biblical teaching, it is actually the husband who has the more difficult role! He is to love his wife with Calvary love. He is to love his wife with the love that took Christ to the cross. Which is the higher standard? Then the fourth truth is that *submission is another aspect of love*. It is true that when you look at the reciprocal duties: 'Husbands, love; and Wives, submit,' love and submission are two different words; but what is the difference between them? When you begin to define these two words, it is very difficult to do so. What does it mean to submit? Well, it is to give yourself up to somebody. What does it mean to love? It means to give yourself up to somebody. Love and submission are two examples or expressions of that basic self-giving which is the secret of enduring happiness in married life.

We move now to – *Children and parents*: children who are to obey their parents in the Lord (6:1–4), because their parents' authority is the Lord's authority; and that's why obedience is right. But if natural law teaches it, Scripture enforces it, and the fifth commandment says we are to honour our parents. It is the last commandment of the first table of the law concerning our duty to God, because – at least during the years of our minority – our parents stand to us *in loco Dei*, in the place of God, and mediate to us the authority of God. So in submission to God, we submit to our parents during the years of our minority. 'Fathers' – and no doubt mothers are included as well – says Paul, 'Don't provoke your children to anger.' 'Don't goad your children to resentment' (6:4, NEB). 'Don't exasperate your children' (New International Version). In a word, don't misuse your parental authority, either by making irritating or unreasonable demands or by harshness, or cruelty, or favouritism, 'lest they become discouraged,' as Colossians 3:21 adds.

Now here is a clear recognition that although children are to obey their parents, children have a life and a personality of their own. They are to be respected. Don't exasperate them; don't crush them; don't exploit them. They are little people on their own, made in the image of God, with rights of their own. So instead, nourish them: Calvin puts it, 'Let them be fondly cherished'; Hendrickson, 'Rear them tenderly' – in the discipline and instruction of the Lord. So the upbringing of children will include both the mental instruction, and the moral discipline. I've always liked a phrase of somebody known as 'Daddy Hall,' an Episcopal clergyman in America, who died in 1950 – known as 'the Bishop of Wall Street': he said, 'I was brought up at the knee of a godly father, and across the knee of a determined mother.' And because he was an American, he added, 'She gave me the stripes, and I saw the stars!'

Now we come to – *Slaves and masters.* Slaves are to obey their earthly masters, because behind them they could see their heavenly Master, Jesus Christ. That is repeated in almost every verse: 'Be obedient to . . . your earthly masters . . . as to Christ' (6:5); 'Don't be menpleasers,' but the slaves of Christ (6:6); Render service willingly 'as unto the Lord,' not men (6:7); If you do good, you will receive good 'from the Lord' (6:8). You see, once a slave was clear about this, that his primary responsibility was to serve the Lord Christ, then his service to his earthly master would be exemplary. It would be respectful, 'with fear and trembling' (6:5); it would be whole-hearted, 'in singleness of heart' (6:5); it would be consistent 'not with eye-service,' only when being watched (6:6); it would be conscientious, 'doing the will of God from the heart' (6:6); and it would be willing, 'rendering service with a good will' (6:7). All because behind the human employer, he saw the divine Lord.

Masters were to do the same to them (6:9), that is, treat them with the same respect. Give your slaves the respect that you expect them to give to you; and don't threaten them, don't misuse your authority by threats of punishment; remember that you and they have the same heavenly Master, 'and there is no partiality with Him.'

Now just a word about the problem of slavery. Many people ask, Why didn't the New Testament condemn slavery outright? Slavery is a horrible thing, not because of service: service is an honourable thing. But slavery is a horrible thing because it implies the ownership of one human being by another. Now the reason why the New Testament did not condemn it outright is probably that in those days, in the Graeco-Roman world, slavery was so much part of the fabric of society that to have abolished it at a single stroke would have caused the disintegration of society altogether. But although the New Testament does not condemn it, it does not condone it either. And of the three pairs of relationships treated here, it is of the utmost importance to realise that husbands and wives, parents and children, are permanent, rooted in creation. But slavery is not derived from creation; it was a part of the culture of those days, and the New Testament never implies its permanence. On the contrary, Paul urges slaves to take their freedom if they can (1 Cor. 7:21). But what the Gospel does is to plant seeds of liberation, especially here, by something that was entirely new in the first century, and that is the reciprocal duties of slave and master. You see, in Roman law, masters who bought or inherited their slaves *owned* them; they possessed them, just as they possessed their animals or their furniture. And because they owned them, they had absolute rights over their slaves; they could do anything they liked with them. On the whole they treated them kindly, for the same reason that they treated their animals kindly; namely, that they were valuable property, part of their capital, and it was to their own advantage to look after their own property. But if they ill-treated their slaves; if they thrashed them, or tortured them, or killed them, there was nothing in Roman law to stop them. There was no legal redress for cruelty. The slave had no possible appeal to justice, because slaves had no rights in Roman law. And where there are no rights, there is no justice.

Now this is the wonderful thing, the beautiful thing: it is the Gospel that insisted that slaves had rights – it is clear here from the reciprocal duties. It isn't only slaves who have duties to masters; it's masters who have duties to their slaves. And the master's duty becomes the slave's right, just as the slave's duty becomes the master's right. That is why in Colossians 4:1, in the parallel passage, the master is to treat his slaves 'justly and equally,' or fairly. 'Justice and equality?' people would have said in the first century. 'What on earth are you talking about? There's no such thing for slaves as justice.' 'Ah, but there is,' Paul says. 'You must treat them with justice.' And that was a revolutionary idea, centuries in advance of its time.

Now in labour relations today, I suggest, the same principle holds good. Employers and employees alike have duties; the employee to give good work, the employer to pay a just wage. Moreover, each man's duty becomes the other man's right. If it is the employee's duty to give good work, it's the employer's right to expect it. But if it is the employer's duty to pay a fair wage, it is the employee's right to expect it. And although this is a ridiculous over-simplification, surely the problem today in management-labour disputes is that each side concentrates on its own rights. But Paul says you are to concentrate on your own duties, and on securing the other man's rights. And if we concentrated on our duty, and on securing the other man's rights, labour relations would be sweetened in a moment.

We turn now from harmony in the home to –

Stability in the Fight

'Finally . . .' says Paul (6:8), as he comes to the end of his letter. So far, you see, it has all sounded a beautiful ideal: harmony in the home; unity, purity in the church. Very desirable goals, very lovely, not so difficult to attain. Now Paul brings us down to earth with a bump. He reminds us of the opposition; that beneath surface appearances an unseen spiritual battle is raging. He introduces us to the devil, and to certain 'principalities and powers' which are at the devil's command. He gives us no biography of the devil, no account of the origin of the powers of darkness; but he assumes their existence. His purpose is not to satisfy our curiosity, but to warn us of their hostility.

Is God's plan to create a new society? Then the principalities and powers will do their best to destroy it. Does God intend His people to live together in harmony and purity? Then the devil will seek to sow seeds of discord and sin. And it is with these principalities and powers that we are called to wrestle, and only when we see clearly how formidable are the enemies arrayed against us, shall we recognise our need of 'the whole armour of God.'

So let us look first at – *The enemy*. Thorough knowledge of the enemy, and a healthy respect for him, are indispensable preliminaries to victory in war. If we underestimate our spiritual enemies, we shall see no need for the armour of God. We shall go out to the conflict every day unarmed, with no weapons but our own puny strength; and we shall be quickly and ignominiously defeated. 'We are not fighting against flesh and blood' (that is, human beings), 'but against principalities and powers' (that is, cosmic intelligences). Our enemies are not human; they are demonic. They are evil spirits mustered under the leadership of the devil, who is the god and prince of this world.

They have at least three characteristics. First, they are *powerful*. They are principalities and powers, which indicates something of the authority that they wield. They are world rulers, *cosmocratoras*. That shows the extent of their rule. They are spiritual powers, or hosts, in heavenly places: that doesn't mean, of course, in heaven, but in the unseen world in which they operate. They are powerful. Secondly, they are *wicked*. Power itself is neutral; it can be used well, or misused. But our spiritual enemies use their power destructively, and not constructively; for evil, and not for good. They are 'the worldwide rulers of this present darkness,' and they are 'spiritual hosts of wickedness.' Make no mistake about it, our spiritual enemies have no moral principles, no code of honour, no higher feelings, no sensitivity. They are utterly unscrupulous and ruthless in the pursuit of their malicious designs. They are wicked. And thirdly, they are *cunning*. Paul writes in verse 11 of 'the wiles of the devil,' as in 2 Corinthians 2:11, 'We are not ignorant of his designs.' The devil seldom attacks openly. He prefers darkness to light. It is his natural habitat. And so we are all the more unsuspecting and unprepared when he transforms himself into an angel of light. He is a wolf, but he enters the flock in the disguise of a sheep. And he is as subtle as a serpent.

We must not therefore imagine that open temptation to sin is his only weapon. He also deceives into error; and in many other ways he works subtly behind the scenes, and in the darkness. It is significant that in 4:14 the same word translated 'the wiles of the devil' here, is

used of the cunning of false teachers and their crafty
scheming. Our enemy is powerful; our enemy is wicked;
and our enemy is cunning. So how can we possibly stand
against the assaults of such an enemy? We are far too
weak, far too ingenuous. Yet many, if not most, of our
failures and defeats are due to a foolish self-confidence
when we forget the power and the wickedness and the
cunning of our enemy. Only the power of God can
defend and deliver us from the might, the evil, and the
craft of the devil. True, the principalities and powers are
strong; but the power of God is stronger. It is the power
that 'raised Jesus Christ from the dead, and set Him at
His own right hand . . . far above principalities and powers, and every name that is named.' And He has 'put all
thing under the feet of Jesus.' And not only did He raise
Christ, he has raised us from the dead, set us at His right
hand, put everything under our feet. And the principalities and the powers are under our feet *if we are in Christ*.
That is the glorious truth of this letter. It is in these same
heavenly places, you see, that the principalities and
powers are waging their warfare, that Jesus Christ
reigns, and that we reign in Christ. So, 'Be strong in the
Lord and in the power of His might,' and 'Put on the
whole armour of God, that you may be able to stand'
against the power and the cunning of the devil
(vv10–11). These two commands are conspicuous examples of the balance of the Bible. Some Christians are so
self-confident that they think they can manage on their
own; and some other Christians are so self-distrustful
that they think there is nothing they can do in spiritual
warfare. Both are mistaken. For here in verses 10 and 11
is a combination of divine enabling and human co-operation. The power is God's; but we've got to strengthen
ourselves in it. It's either a passive or a middle. 'Be
strong in the Lord' is, 'Strengthen yourselves in the Lord,

and in the power of His might.' Again, the armour is God's armour; but we've got to put it on. Divine enabling and human co-operation – together – in the fight.

So we move from the enemy, to, secondly – *The armour*. We are to 'take the whole armour of God.' It translates a single Greek word, *panoplia*; we often use the word in English, 'the panoply of God.' It is all the equipment that an infantryman would use on the battlefield. And Paul details the six main pieces of a soldier's equipment: the girdle, or belt; the breastplate; the shoes or boots; the shield; the helmet; and the sword. Paul was very familiar with the Roman soldier; he was actually chained to one by the wrist, as he was dictating his letter. And although it was unlikely that such a bodyguard would be wearing the full armour, yet the sight of him may well have kindled the apostle's imagination.

A Puritan minister, William Gurnall, pastor of the church at Lavenham, in Suffolk, published in 1655 his treatise, called *The Christian in Complete Armour*. Its rather delightful Puritan sub-title is – 'The Saint's War against the Devil, wherein a Discovery is Made of that Grand Enemy of God and His People, in his Policies, Powers, Seat of his Empire, Wickedness and Chief Design he hath against The Saints. A Magazine Opened from whence the Christian is Furnished with Spiritual Arms for the Battle, Helped on with his Armour, and Taught the Use of his Weapon, together with the Happy Issue of the whole War.' In his dedication of the book to his parishioners, he writes of his 'much weakness,' and he refers to himself as 'that poor and unworthy minister,' and his treatise as 'but a mite, and a little present' to them. But it runs to three volumes, 261 chapters, and – in my 1821 eighth edition – 1472 pages! And yet is an exposition of only eleven   verses; and I've only got nine minutes in which to expound them!

The girdle of truth. Now the soldier's girdle was really part of his underwear, but it enabled him to be unimpeded in the march; it gave him a hidden strength; it gave him confidence when he was well-girt invisibly. And the Christian soldier's girdle is truth. Now that may be 'the truth,' the revelation of God: it is 'the truth that sets us free,' Jesus said; and only God's truth can conquer the devil's lies. But in the Greek there is no definite article. It is not 'the truth,' but 'truth' and I think it means that: sincerity or integrity, that we should be delivered from unreality and make-believe and playing games; that we should be men and women of sincerity and transparency and truth. You see, to be deceitful ourselves, and to lapse into hypocrisy, is to resort to the wiles of the devil, and play the devil's game. The devil loves lies; Christians love truth. We can't beat the devil at his own game. The only way to stand before him is in transparent truth. He loves the darkness; Christians walk in the light.

Then we move from the girdle of truth to the *breastplate of righteousness*. The soldier's breastplate covered his back as well as his front, and it was the major piece of armour. Now *dikaiosune*, righteousness, in Paul's letters usually means justification. And it may mean that here: to have been justified by grace through faith; to have a righteousness that is not our own, but Christ's; to stand before God not condemned, but accepted, is an essential defence against the accusing conscience, and the slanderous attacks of the devil. The devil is a slanderer; he attacks the conscience. But if I'm justified, if I have the breast-plate of righteousness, I stand against him. But it may mean moral righteousness against the devil's temptations to evil.

Then, thirdly, the *Gospel shoes*. No soldier can march without good strong boots. And the Christian needs boots; and they are 'the Gospel of peace.' There is some doubt whether the genitive there is objective or subjective; but I would take it as an objective genitive, and therefore it refers to our readiness to share the good news of peace with others. We should always be ready to speak of Jesus, and give an answer of the hope that is in us. Such readiness to speak for Christ can put the devil to flight.

Fourthly, the *shield of faith*: not, I think, 'Above all . . .' but 'In addition to all this, take the shield of faith' (New International Version). This wasn't a little round shield, that left most of the body unprotected, but the long, oblong shield of the Roman soldier, measuring about four foot by two foot six, that covered his whole person. But what is the Christian's shield that guards him and can quench 'the fiery darts' of the devil? Paul says it is faith. It might be *the* faith – the Christian faith. It might be faithfulness, our own reliability. But I believe still it is faith, or trust in God. According to Hebrews 11 it is by faith that the saints, the heroes, conquered kingdoms, and enforced justice, and received promises, and stopped the mouths of lions, and quenched raging fire, etc. It is by faith that we lay hold of the power of God. And against this shield the devil's fiery darts have no chance.

Then the *helmet of salvation*. Now the Roman soldier's helmet was decorative as well as protective. It had a lovely plume, you know. And according to 1 Thessalonians 5:8, the Christian soldier's helmet was 'the hope of salvation.' So whether the salvation, or the helmet, is salvation that has already been received and is being enjoyed today, or whether it is our confident expectation of full and final salvation on the Last Day, there is no doubt that God's saving power is a mighty defence for us against the enemy of souls. Charles

Hodge, in his great commentary on this letter, wrote: 'That which adorns and protects the Christian, which enables him to hold up his head with confidence and joy, is the fact that he is saved.' The helmet of salvation: I have been saved, and I shall be saved. That confidence is power against the enemy.

Then sixth, the *sword of the Spirit*, the only one of the six pieces of armour that can be used for offence as well as defence. It is the Word of God, by which God acts; for God's Word is not like the words of men. It has power, and it accomplishes that which He purposes, and prospers in the purpose to which He sends it. Jesus used this sword against the devil when tempted in the wilderness of Judaea. And it is the sword of the Spirit. The Holy Spirit uses it, both in moments of temptation and in evangelism. When we go out into the world to conquer for Jesus Christ, and to win people for Christ, we need the sword of the Spirit, which is the Word of God.

So here are the six pieces that together make up the whole armour of God. And we've got to put it on. And with this provision we have no excuse for failure. Then Paul adds, in verses 18–20, a reference to prayer – probably not because it is an extra, though unnamed weapon; but because prayer is needed in using all the weapons. 'Each piece put on with prayer,' prayer in the Spirit, because it is the Spirit who prompts us and teaches us to pray, just as the Word is the sword of the Spirit, which He Himself employs. Prayer and Scripture go together as spiritual weapons. And Paul is not too grand to ask them to pray for himself, that he might be given both utterance and boldness, both clarity and courage, obscuring nothing by muddled speech, and hiding nothing because he is afraid to speak it. Although the ambassador of the Gospel, he is an ambassador in chains; though his wrist is chained, he longs that his mouth may be opened, and his tongue unloosed to make the good news known. Then comes the –

Final Greeting

Tychicus is perhaps the scribe to whom Paul is dictating the letter, now to be the messenger to take the letter to Asia; and he will bring them information and encouragement. Then in verses 23 and 24 Paul wishes them peace and love with faith; and says, 'Grace to you all.' Paul began his letter by wishing his readers 'grace and peace from God the Father, and the Lord Jesus Christ,' and he ends as he began, wishing peace to the brothers (v23), and grace (v24) 'to all those who love our Lord Jesus with love undying.' And as I said at the beginning I say at the end, no two words can summarise the message of the letter better than these two words, peace and grace. Certainly both keep recurring. *Peace*, the great achievement of Jesus Christ, reconciling us to God and to one another in the new society that God is creating. And *grace*, the reason why, and the means by which, He has achieved the reconciliation. So 'peace to the brethren' is the appropriate final greeting: a wish, a prayer, that God's new society, God's own family, may live together as brothers and sisters at peace with Him and with one another; and it is only by grace that such a dream can come true.

So as we conclude our study of this magnificent letter of the apostle Paul, I would venture to take upon my lips the very words with which Paul concluded his letter, and I say to you: 'Peace be to the brethren, and grace be with you all.'

1978

Gospel and Church

Lessons from First Thessalonians

1. Christian Evangelism; How the Gospel Spreads (1 Thessalonians 1)

In chapter 1, Paul refers to both the church (verses 1–4) and the Gospel (verses 5–10): the church of God, which the Gospel has created, and then the Gospel of God and how the church spreads it. First, then,

The church of God (verses 1–4)

It is really amazing to read Paul's beautiful and comprehensive description of the Thessalonian church. I remind you, it was only a few months old. Its members were new-born Christians, with the fresh bloom of conversion upon them. Both their convictions and standards were being tested by persecution. Now you'd think, wouldn't you, that it would be a very wobbly church? But no. Paul is confident about this church. He knows it's God's church in three ways.

1. It is a community in God the Father and the Lord Jesus Christ. Verse 1, 'Paul, Silas and Timothy to the church of the Thessalonians in God the Father and the Lord Jesus Christ.' (Notice in passing the unselfconscious way in which Paul brackets God the Father and Jesus Christ together as the one source of the church's power. Already, within twenty years of the death and resurrection of Jesus! It's universally accepted. He doesn't need to argue it.) In his later letters Paul tended to describe the church the other way round, for example 'the church of God in Corinth'. And he could have put it like that here: the church of God in Thessalonica. But he reverses it. 'The church of the Thessalonians "in God".' Both were true. Every church has two homes, two habitats. It lives in God and it lives on earth, in the world. Why, do you think, did Paul decide to describe the church in Thessalonica in this particular way? Well, we can guess that he did it because he knew the insecurity they felt. He wanted to remind them that even if they were oppressed by men their security was in God. It is from him that every church derives its life and power; and so Paul wishes them grace and peace. We today can derive no greater blessings and desire no greater blessings for the church than God's peace, his *shalom*, through reconciliation with God and one another; and God's grace, his free and unmerited favour to bring about and sustain this peace.

So the church is a community in God the Father and in the Lord Jesus Christ, rooted in God, deriving its life and power from him.

2. It is a community characterised by faith, hope and love. Verses 2, 3: 'We give thanks . . . mention you . . . remember you.' Memory, thanksgiving and prayer belong together in a Christian's devotional life. Perhaps some of us who are getting middle-aged or elderly need to pray for the stimulation of our rotten memories! It's when we remember people, their names, faces and situations, that we're stimulated to want to thank God for them and pray for them.

Now what Paul specially remembers about the Thessalonian church is what we usually call the three cardinal Christian graces or virtues; their faith, love and hope. They're indispensable characteristics of an authentically Christian life (we all know 1 Corinthians 13 where Paul elaborates them further). So let's test ourselves. Are we authentic Christians? It depends if we're characterised by faith and love and hope. A trustful commitment to God through Jesus Christ. Love for others both in the church and beyond it. And hope for the future, as we look for the coming, in great magnificence, of our Lord Jesus. Every Christian without exception is a believer, a lover, a hoper (not an optimist; optimism is hoping for the best without any grounds. Hope is quite different. It looks for the Lord's return and rests upon sure promises). So faith, love and hope are sure evidences of our regeneration by the Holy Spirit. Together they seem to turn us inside out, as they reorientate our whole life, so that we find ourselves drawn upwards to God in faith, outwards to other people in love, and onwards to the second coming of Christ in hope.

Paul lays emphasis on one more point about faith and hope and love. Each is productive. They sound very abstract, but they have concrete, practical results. Our *faith in God* leads to good works, without which faith is spurious. The Christian is no Little Johnny-Head-in-Air. Who says there is a dichotomy between Paul and James? They both say that faith leads to works. Our *love for people* leads to labour, the labour of love. If it doesn't, our love isn't real. It's sentimentality. And our *hope in Christ* leads to endurance as we wait for his coming in the face of persecution, otherwise we can't really be expectantly awaiting our Lord's return. The New International Version puts it very succinctly, following the Greek: 'Your work produced by faith, your labour prompted by love and your endurance inspired by hope in our Lord

Jesus Christ.' Faith, hope and love, if they are authentic, are very productive in Christian living.

3. *The church is also a community loved and chosen by God*. Verse 4: '. . . we know, brethren, beloved by God, that he has chosen you.' Here is the teaching of the New Testament and the Old, that God has set his love on his people in eternity and chosen them. Thus the love of God and the election of God are joined invariably to one another in Scripture. We find it in Deuteronomy 7:7,8 where Moses says to Israel

> It was not because you were more in number than any other nation that the Lord set his love upon you and chose you. No, the reason why he set his love upon you and chose you is that he loves you.

He loves you because he loves you. There is no explanation of the love of God except that love of God. And there is no explanation of the election of God except the love of God. 'And we know, brethren, beloved by God' – your election by God. He loved you. He chose you. Beyond that mystery we cannot penetrate.

However what is striking in verse 4 is not so much that Paul describes them as loved and chosen by God as that he says he knows their election. How could he possibly be so sure that these Thessalonian Christians belong to the elect people of God? Well, the context tells us. When the Gospel came to them it came to them not in word only but in power, so they received it. And it bore fruit in their lives, in a work of faith, and a labour of love, and an endurance of hope. It's because of that that he knew their election. It worked in their lives. When he preached the Gospel to them they responded to it and were transformed by it.

The doctrine of election, you see, can never be made an excuse either for giving up evangelism or for giving up the pursuit of holiness. On the contrary; it is precisely by evangelism that God's elect are discovered. It's precisely *by* holiness that they give evidence of their election, and it is only when people respond to the Gospel and grow in holiness that their secret election by God becomes apparent and visible to men.

Now what's the main thing we learn from all this? Well, I want to emphasis this. The main element in the church's identity is that it is the church of God. We need so badly to develop Paul's perspective. To him the church isn't a kind of religious club, united by a common interest. Still less is it a group of Paul's followers, united in their allegiance to him. It is *God's church*. A people chosen and loved by God in all eternity, rooted in God the Father and in the Lord Jesus Christ, drawing its life and power from him, and exhibiting this divine life in a faith that works, a love that labours and a hope that endures. And you and I, in our man-centred age, especially, I think, if we're pastors and leaders in the church, need to check ourselves by Paul's God-centredness. We need to learn to think of the church as a people whose primary relationship is neither to us, not to each other as fellow-members, not to the world that they are called to serve; but to God, on whose love they depend and from whom they derive their life and power. Only so can we be confident of the church's stability. And thank God for the church.

The Gospel of God (verses 5–10)

From the church of God we turn to the Gospel of God. Paul, as we've seen, cannot think of one without the other. In these verses he sets out the progress of the Gospel in three clear stages.

1. *It 'came to you' (verse 5)*. It didn't come by itself. It came because it was brought, by Paul and Silas and

Timothy. Before they arrived in Thessalonica there wasn't a Christian church there. When they left, the church had been planted and taken root. The planting of the church is the direct result of the preaching of the Gospel. Paul describes how he proclaimed it.

He proclaimed it *in word*. The Gospel itself is a word. Paul calls it that in verse 6. It's the word of God, the word of the Lord. The Gospel has a specific content. And that content is to be found in Scripture. The Gospel can come to people only in words. Ah, but not in words only!

It came *in power*. By themselves, human words are weak and ineffective. People don't always hear them. If they hear them they don't always grasp them. If they grasp them, they don't always feel their impact. Words need to be confirmed by divine power. Otherwise they don't reach the minds and the consciences and the wills of the hearers. The Gospel came in words, and it came in power.

The Gospel came with *full conviction*. Power refers to the objective result of the preaching. Conviction refers to the subjective state of the preacher. He is sure of his message, sure of its truth and relevance, and so he is bold in its proclamation. And this assurance and this courage are precisely what so many modern preachers lack.

The Gospel was proclaimed *in the Holy Spirit*. I take this expression last because it seems to me that it belongs to all the other three. Truth, conviction and power all come from the Holy Spirit. It's he who illumines our minds, so that we formulate our message with clarity. It's he whose inward witness assures us of its truth, so that we proclaim it with conviction. It's he who carries it home with power so that the hearers respond in penitence and faith. Three characteristics of all true preaching, all springing from the Holy Spirit.

Oh, that we had preachers of that calibre in our pulpits today! Men with a message, men with conviction, men of power and men of the Holy Spirit. 'Our Gospel came to you' – like that!

2. *'You received' it (verses 6, 7).* That is, their hearts were opened by the Holy Spirit to understand and believe and obey the message. Again, four points.

You received it *in much affliction.* In Thessalonica there had been considerable opposition to the preaching of the word, to those who preached it and those who listened to it. But the Thessalonian Christians welcomed the Gospel, in the midst of opposition and in spite of it.

You received it *with joy, inspired by the Holy Spirit.* Don't miss this second reference to the Holy Spirit. The same Spirit worked at both ends – in the preacher and in the hearer. He always brings the two together. And there was joy, because joy is the fruit of the Spirit. Wherever the Gospel goes and people respond, there is joy. There's joy in heaven among the angels, and there's joy on earth among the people of God. So there was affliction and there was joy.

You became *imitators of us and of the Lord.* That is, in your experience of affliction and joy, and indeed in every other aspect of your Christian life, you followed the example of us, Paul says, that is the apostles, and so of Christ whose apostles they were. To receive the word included that. It's not just to give an intellectual acquiescence in its truth. It is a complete transformation of life.

Lastly, you became *an example to all the believers.* For those who take Christ as their model become themselves models for others. Marvellous, isn't it? To see the beneficial effects of the Gospel in those who receive it. Oh, it may mean opposition – it often has done. But it also involves inward joy through the Holy Spirit, the imitation of Christ and his apostles, in transformed and obedient lives, and the setting of an example to other believers.

3. *The word of the Lord sounded forth from you (verses 8–10).* The Greek word means to sound, to ring, to peal, to boom. It's used in the Greek version of the Old Testament of bells, zithers, trumpets and other loud noises. In the New Testament it's used of a 'noisy gong and clanging cymbal', and, in some manuscripts of Luke 21, of the roaring of the sea. So in either case, you see, whether Paul is likening Gospel preaching to a peal of bells or to the sound of a trumpet, it's a loud noise that the Gospel made. It reverberated throughout Greece, through Northern Greece (Macedonia and Southern Greece [Achaia]). And all over the country the noise echoed on and reverberated among the hills and the valleys of Greece. The Thessalonians simply hadn't been able to keep the good news to themselves! Besides, Thessalonica was a seaport and a capital city as well, so it was strategically placed. From that city the message of the Gospel spread far and fast, as the messengers carried it out of the city.

But there was something more than that, and it's very important to see this. Verse 8: 'Not only has the voice of the Lord sounded forth from you' – that is, not only have you preached it and sent out messengers to preach it, but, your faith in God has gone forth everywhere – 'so that we need not say anything'!

I think it's a very, very important lesson to learn here about Christian evangelism. We live in a media-conscious generation. We know the power of the mass media. Consequently we want to use the media for evangelism, by print, by film, by radio, by television. And rightly so: we Christians should use every modern medium of communication available to us. But don't let us forget that there is another medium of communication even more effective. It's very simple indeed. It's spontaneous. It costs nothing. What is it? It's *holy gossip*. It's the excited transmission of the impact that the good news makes upon people. 'Do you know that so-and-so's a completely changed person?' 'Why, something's going on in Thessalonica – a new society is coming into being. Have you heard about it?' You see, the Gospel is spreading!

Now the result of all that gratuitous publicity was tremendous. 'We need not say anything.' Not only were the media redundant. The missionaries were redundant! The message was spreading without them and everybody seemed to know it already. Now mind you, I don't think Paul quite literally meant that he was no longer necessary. At least, he didn't apply for an indefinite furlough! He carried on preaching the Gospel, especially where Christ wasn't known. Nevertheless, we take his point. The good news was spreading spontaneously.

What exactly was the good news that was spreading from Thessalonica? Well, at the end of verse 8 Paul says it was 'your faith in God'. That's what people were hearing about. But in the last two verses, 9 and 10, Paul gives a three part analysis of what he meant by their faith in God. And it's one of the fullest and most succinct descriptions anywhere in the New Testament of what is meant by conversion. Conversion, according to Paul, involves at least these three things: one, you turn to God from idols, two, you turn from idols in order to serve the living and true God, and three, you wait for his Son from heaven. In those three verbs – turning, serving, waiting – you have an analysis of what the New Testament means by conversion.

Firstly *a decisive break with idols*. I think it would be difficult to exaggerate how radical is the change of allegiance that is implied. Idols are creatures, the work of men's hands, dead, false, many and visible; God is the Creator of the universe and of all mankind, and he is living, true, one and invisible. A tribe's traditional idols have a tremendous hold upon the people's minds and their whole lives. For centuries the tribe has lived in superstitious dread and obsequious submission to them. The very thought of breaking away from the idols or from the spirits fills them with alarm because they're afraid that the idols or spirits will take revenge upon them. And the same is true in the West. Our more sophisticated idols, or God-substitutes, are equally powerful in men's lives. Think of a man or woman simply eaten up with ambition for power or fame or money. Or another obsessed with work, or another addicted to sex or alcohol. In each case it is an idolatry, because it demands a total allegiance. And idolater is a prisoner, an addict of his idol.

And then suddenly, completely, this person turns, from the idols that have controlled his life so far into a liberating experience of the living God. It is an encounter with Jesus Christ in which the spell of the idol is broken and the superior power of the living and true God is demonstrated, and people are amazed, and they are filled with awe, and they spread the news 'the idol's power is broken'.

Secondly, *an active service of God*. The claim to have turned from idols is manifestly bogus if it doesn't result in serving the God to whom we turn. We mustn't think of conversion in purely negative terms: we must think of it also in positive terms as the beginning of a new life of service. You turn from idols to the living and true God – to serve him. We could say that it is an exchange of one slavery for another, so long as we add immediately that the new slavery is a real liberation. Indeed, so total is true conversion that it involves a double liberation: firstly *from* the power of the idols to whom we previously bowed down, and then *into* the service of the true and living God, whom to serve is authentic, human freedom.

Thirdly, *a patient waiting for Christ*. To me it's very striking indeed that waiting and serving go together in the Christian life. Serving is active: waiting is passive. Serving is getting busy for Christ on earth. Waiting is looking for Christ to come from heaven. So this coupling, you see, of waiting and serving, expresses a very important recognition. On the one hand, however hard we work and serve, there are limits to what we can achieve. We have to wait for Christ to come from heaven, and only then will he secure the final triumph of God's reign of justice and of peace. But on the other hand, although we must wait patiently for Christ to come, we have to work while we are waiting. So working, serving the true and living God, and waiting, belong together. And this combination will deliver us on the one hand from the presumption that we imagine that we can do everything, and from the pessimism that imagines that we can do nothing. And of the coming of God's own Son from heaven, for which we wait, we can be absolutely sure, because (verse 10) God has raised him from the dead.

Now I think we're in a position to summarise the report about the Thessalonians which was being disseminated throughout Greece and beyond. And so we can understand the essentials of Christian conversion; the turning from idols, the serving of the living God, and the waiting for Christ. We're given a model of Christian conversion. It's not only comprehensive, it's actually invariable. It's always the same. Of course there will be different forms which one's service of the living God will take. But always the break with the past will be decisive, the experience of service will be liberating, and the look for the future will be expectant. And without this turning, this serving and this waiting, one can scarcely claim to have been converted.

I want us to try to grasp the indispensible relationship between the church and the Gospel. We must not, indeed we cannot, separate the two. Every true church is a Gospel church and we need more Gospel churches in the world today. So I finish with these two points.

1. The church that receives the Gospel must pass it on. Don't you agree with me? Nothing really is more impressive in chapter one than the sequence: it came to you, you received it, it sounded forth from you. Every local church is to be a sounding board for the Gospel. God's simple plan for the spread of the Gospel is absolutely plain. The church that receives it, sounds it forth. And if the church had been faithful to God's purpose, the world would long since have been evangelised.

2. The church that passes it on must embody it. Because we saw, didn't we, that the Thessalonians passed it on not only by the word of the Lord sounding forth verbally, but by news of their conversion. This holy gossip about what had happened to them was spreading abroad. It was exciting. People came to Thessalonica to have a look for themselves, and were convinced not by what they'd heard but by what they saw for themselves. Let me quote from Canon Douglas Webster:

The communication of the Gospel is by seeing as well as hearing. This double strand runs through all the Bible: image and word; vision and voice; opening the eyes of the blind, unstopping the ears of the deaf. Jesus is the word of God. Jesus is the image of God. The word became visible, the image became audible. Now the verbal element in evangelism is clear. Where is the visual?

And the answer is: in Gospel churches, communities that are changed by the power of the Gospel.

So I end on that note. No church can spread the Gospel if it doesn't embody the Gospel. If a church is contradicting by its life what it is professing with its lips, then the credibility gap between what it says and what it is is so wide that it cannot be bridged by even the most energetic leap of faith. The church must seem like what it is talking about. It has to embody the Gospel of liberation. So may God enable us in our churches to receive the Gospel deeply, to sound it forth loud and clear, and to embody it in our common life of faith, love, hope, joy, peace, and all the rest.

2. Christian Ministry: How Pastors Serve Both Word and People (1 Thessalonians 2 and 3)

Radical questions are being asked today about the nature of the Christian ministry. People are asking, what does it mean to be (in Paul's phrase) a good minister of Jesus Christ? Is there a place for pastors at all? If so, what are their qualifications and responsibilities? These questions are not new, but I think that today they are more urgent than ever before.

In chapters 2 and 3, the apostle Paul supplies a wonderful model of Christian ministry in his own attitudes and behaviour. Although in some ways we shall be thinking here particularly of pastors, I hope we shall be applying this to all forms of oversight in the local church. It's quite true that Paul was an apostle and Silas and Timothy were missionaries, and not all aspects of their ministry are intended as a model for pastors. Yet I think the principles apply.

A word about the historical context. The enemies of the Gospel in Thessalonica were criticising Paul, accusing him of running away from Thessalonica. 'He's not sincere,' they were saying. 'He's in it for what he can get. And when the situation got too hot, he took to his heels. He doesn't care about the church in Thessalonica.' Now there were the criticisms, and it may be that some of the Thessalonian Christians had begun, under this smear campaign, to have doubts about the sincerity of the apostle Paul. So here Paul describes and defends his ministry against his critics, both during his visit (2:1–16) and subsequently (2:17–3:13).

Two preliminary points come out very clearly in the first two verses of chapter 2. Two characteristics emerge of Paul's ministry, and, I hope, of every form of Christian ministry. They are, firstly, *Paul's openness.* Already, he has told the Thessalonian church: you know what kind of people we were (1:5). And in the present passage he emphasises this even more strongly. He says his ministry in Thessalonica was public; he had had nothing to hide. Glance at 2:1, 9–11. 'You know . . . you remember . . . you are witness . . . you know.' Happy are those Christians who, like the apostle Paul, exercise their ministry in the open, before God and men; who are well known by the public for what they are, who have nothing to conceal, nothing of which to be ashamed, and can publicly appeal to God and human beings as their witnesses. God is our witness. You are our witness. It's all in the open. And I tell you, brethren, we need more fearless openness in our Christian ministry today.

And then see *Paul's sufferings (verse 2).* Before reaching Thessalonica, he says, he's suffered insult and injury at Phillipi. He was imprisoned, beaten, his feet put in the stocks. And then in Thessalonica he met opposition and a riot broke out and so on. Yet none of these things deterred him. On the contrary: 'We had courage in our God, to declare to you the Gospel of God . . .' It's true, isn't it: people are willing only to suffer for what they believe in. So Paul appeals to his openness and his sufferings as witnesses to his sincerity.

Four metaphors of ministry

After these two preliminary points about his ministry, Paul goes on to portray it by using four vivid metaphors for himself. He describes himself as follows.

1. A Steward (verses 3, 4). Stewards are entrusted with precious treasure, to guard it, and the particular treasure with which Paul has been entrusted is the Gospel. In verse 1, he reminds the Thessalonians 'Our visit to you was not in vain'. It had purpose, it was to bring them the Gospel of God. And the developing of this picture, that he came not empty-handed but with the Gospel, is his use of the image of stewardship. His sense of trusteeship and responsibility to God for the treasure has been put in his care very strongly affects his ministry. Negatively, (verse 3): his appeal did not spring from error, he had no false motives, and he made it without guile. What a tremendous three-fold claim that is! His message was true, his motives pure, his methods above-board. He was entirely free of anything devious.

But positively (verse 4), he recognised, on the contrary, his solemn responsibility to God. See how this shines out of the statement. Again, you can't miss his God-centredness. God has *approved* him, and having approved him has entrusted the Gospel to him. The Greek verb means 'examine for genuineness' – it's used of coins as well. Ordination candidates make much of their final examinations, the passing of which is the gateway to ordination. But Paul concentrates not on a human examination but a divine one that is never final. It is continuous. And at any time we may fail the examination, and be put on the shelf and be no longer usable to Almighty God.

God continues to test our hearts; so God was the person Paul was concerned to please. 'We speak, not to please men, but to please God . . .' Do you get that? We are seeking to please God, who tests our hearts. No secret of Christian ministry is greater than this fundamental God-centredness. We Christian pastors are primarily responsible neither to the church nor to our superiors. We are ultimately responsible to God. It's God himself, no church or bishop, who examined and called and appointed us, who has given us our message, made us stewards of it, told us to guard it faithfully, who goes on examining us, and to whom we are responsible. Now in one sense this is very discomforting, because God's standards are very high. And in another sense it's marvellously liberating, to be responsible to God and not to men. Because God is a more merciful judge than any human being or ecclesiastical court. He is compassionate and kind. And to be responsible to him delivers us from the tyranny of human criticism and enables us to ride the fiercest storms of human opposition.

2. *A Nursing Mother (verses 5–8)*. He comes to it in verse 7: 'We were gentle among you like a nurse.' The Greek word may, and I think probably does, mean a nursing mother. Once again Paul begins negatively; he's about to declare his great love for them as the motivating power of his ministry, but first he declares that he is entirely free of unworthy motives. Verse 5: '. . . we never used either words of flattery, as you know, or a cloak for greed, as God is witness, nor did we seek glory from men.' Now there, you see, are two of the major false motives in the ministry; material gain, and prestige. The two commonest selfish motives, and Paul claims that he's free of them both. They didn't motivate him in his ministry. Instead (verse 7) '. . . we were gentle with you, like a nursing mother with her own children.' Isn't it a beautiful truth that a man as tough and masculine as Paul could use such a delicate feminine metaphor to describe an aspect of his ministry?

And it was very appropriate. What are the characteristics of a mother with her babies? He mentions gentleness first. And it's all too easy for pastors, especially when opposed, to assert authority, and to throw their weight about. Not Paul. He was opposed, but he was gentle. A servant of the Lord must not be quarrelsome or autocratic (2 Tim. 2:24). But then not only was he gentle like a mother, he was affectionate and sacrificial. Look at verse 8: so far from the ministry being a means of gain, he simply gave himself for and to the people. There wasn't anything perfunctory about it. He loved them: he longed to serve them like a mother. A mother's whole life is determined by the needs of the baby. The household revolves around it. That was how Paul felt towards the new-born Christians in Thessalonica. And I venture to say that in the ministry and in all pastoral work – I know it's true of myself and I guess it's true of others – we need more gentleness, more self-sacrificing love, towards the people we're called to serve.

3. *A Father (verses 9–12)*. The reference to a father comes in verse 11. It's striking to see Paul combining the metaphors of mother and father. For the third time he begins with a negative statement. He's very anxious (verse 9) not to be a financial burden to them. So even while preaching the Gospel to them he also made time to earn his own living, presumably to pay his board and lodging with Jason (we happen to know the name of his landlord in Thessalonica). He worked at his tent making trade, presumably, and he did it night and day. I think he preached in the day and did his tent making work at night. And they remembered his labour and toil (verse 9) – both words indicate strong physical exertion. And moreover they and God were witnesses that in all points his behaviour was blameless.

If you look carefully, at the metaphor in verse 11 it seems clear that Paul is thinking of the educative responsibility of fathers. His fatherly ministry included personal example, exhortation and encouragement and witness (this is what the Greek means). All these were directed towards urging them to live a life worthy of God who was calling them into his kingdom and glory.

There is a father educating, teaching, bringing up his children to understand who they were and what they were going to be. I don't think there's any need to deduce from these two metaphors that Paul is laying down a stereotype of sexual roles. Scripture, as I understand it, discourages this, and it's striking as we've seen how Paul combines both roles in his own ministry. What is important is that Paul saw his ministry in parental terms. His responsibility was to love the people committed to his care as if they were his own children, to give himself to them, to serve, feed, educate them, gently but firmly, in the discipline and instruction of the Lord. What an ideal for the Christian pastor!

4. A Herald (verses 13–16). The commonest New Testament word for the preacher is the herald, and the commonest word for preaching is 'to herald'. It's the verb Paul has just used in verse 9, '. . . that we might not burden any of you while we preached'. In other words, while we proclaimed it like a herald or town crier.

Here he concentrates his attention on the message which he taught the Thessalonians. And (verse 13) he thanks God constantly that when he brought them the word of God, they welcomed it. How? Not as the word of men, but '. . . what it really is, the word of God which is at work in you believers.'

Now that's a beautiful verse. It's a really important word for our understanding of the authority of the Bible and especially of the New Testament. For here in verse 13 is Paul's unambiguous claim that the message of the apostles was and is the word of God. Though he did not begin his letter with an assertion of apostolic authority as he did in most of his letters, and though he had (verse 7) renounced his right as an apostle to financial support, he now reminds the Thessalonians that he has an apostle's teaching authority. His word was God's word, and they had recognised it as such.

We're all very accustomed to the claim of the Old Testament prophets, that they were bearers of the word of God. They claimed it constantly. But here you see in verse 13 is a comparable claim, by a New Testament apostle, that his teaching is equally the word of God. Paul doesn't rebuke the Thessalonians for regarding his message too highly. On the contrary he thanks God constantly that they recognised and received it for what it truly was. It is a clear indication of Paul's conscious apostolic authority. He knew he was an apostle, and he knew his word was God's word.

Then he adds, at the end of verse 13, that this work of God is 'at work in you believers'. God's word is not only true, it's powerful. It's efficacious in believers. Notice the careful balance. The word of God has no magical properties. It is on the contrary ineffective, unless it is received by faith. Its effectiveness is in arousing faith and then transforming those who believe. So let's rejoice together that the word that is now enshrined in the New Testament, the word of the apostles, is the word of God; and it effectively works in those who believe it and receive it with faith.

Now we come to verse 14, and we see that that's exactly what happened in Thessalonica. In response to the word of God, they became imitators of the first Christian churches, the churches in Judea. They imitated them both in receiving the word and in suffering for it. The Thessalonian Christians were mostly Gentiles and had suffered from their own countrymen what the Judeans had suffered from theirs, the Jews. Paul gives an account in verses 15, 16 of contemporary Jewish opposition to the Gospel. They hindered the spread of the Gospel of salvation, and so they were hindering Gentiles from being saved. Paul sees this as the terrible thing it is. To stop others being saved, to stop other people hearing the Gospel is one of the most terrible things we can ever do, and as a result, he says, they are filling up the measure of their sins. 'God's wrath has come upon them at last.'

Now reading these verses, we need to be cautious. Paul himself was a very patriotic Jew. He gloried in his ancestry. He longed for the salvation of his people. He said later in his letter to the Romans that he would be willing to forfeit his own salvation if they could be saved. And he also taught in those chapters (Rom. 9–11) that God had not cast off his people but that he intends later to include them. In other words, we have to balance verses 15 and 16 of this chapter with what Paul was to write in Romans 9–11. It's a good example of the importance of interpreting Scripture by Scripture. So there's no reason to suppose Paul changed his mind when he wrote Romans, or that there is anything here vengeful or incompatible with the spirit of Christ. Nor of course is there any justification for anti-semitism. Paul is simply stating bald facts, that the majority of his Jewish contemporaries were rejecting Christ, opposing the Gospel and hindering the salvation of the Gentiles. And this was an extremely serious thing, and God's judgement was going to fall upon them as Jesus himself had plainly foretold.

The pastor's responsibilities

Now we have got these four metaphors clear we can, as it were, narrow the theme down and consider the chief functions of Christian pastoral ministry. There are two primary responsibilities to God. The first is to the word of God, the second is to the people of God. The stewarding and heralding metaphors belong to our responsibility to the word of God; the mother-father metaphors, to our responsibility to the people of God. So let's enlarge on these responsibilities.

1. *Our responsibility to God's word.* In chapter 1, we saw the word of God spreading, coming to the church and being received by it and being sounded forth. Now in chapter 2 he goes further and defines the message. Three times (verses 2,8,9) he calls it the Gospel of God, and twice (verse 15) he calls it the word of God. In other words, it was Paul's unshakeable conviction that his message came from God. His Gospel (he calls it that in 1:5) is God's Gospel. Paul had not invented his message. So we cannot disagree with Paul on the grounds that he was ventilating his own opinions. He wasn't. He was an apostle, a steward entrusted with the Gospel of God, a herald commissioned to proclaim it. Every truly Christian ministry begins here, with the conviction that we have been entrusted by God with a message to share with mankind. To share, not our doubts, but our faith. Not what Peter Berger calls 'rumours of God', but the Gospel of God, including its ethical implications. Yet it's this conviction that is so disastrously rare in the church today. It has become almost tedious to read of church leaders today denying the faith which they have solemnly undertaken in their ordination vows to guard and to teach. Prominent theologians contradict fundamentals of Christianity without any apparent sense of shame. A few years ago it was the fashion to deny the personality of the living God. Now it is the fashion to deny the Deity of Jesus of Nazareth, and patronisingly to describe him as perhaps the most wonderful man who has ever lived. There are clergy today who preach God's word with diffidence and their own word with confidence. And it is a disgrace to the church and a stumbling block to the world.

The very first qualification for any authentically Christian ministry is a firm conviction that God has spoken in Christ and in the biblical witness to Christ, that Scripture is God's word written down for the instruction of all subsequent ages, and that it works powerfully in those who believe it. Our task is to guard it, study it, expound it and apply it, to the people to whom we minister.

2. *Our responsibility to the people of God.* Christian ministers are ministers of the word and ministers of the church. And Paul, having expressed his deep love for the Thessalonians by the parental metaphors, maybe quite unconsciously and unselfconsciously gives in the rest of the passage (2:17–3:13) a marvellous illustration of his parental love. Let me remind you of the historical situation: the serious criticism of Paul that was being expressed both for his hasty departure and failure to return, and for his supposed lack of concern. Paul makes a fourfold rebuttal of the accusations.

One, *he longed to visit them* (2:17–20). He flatly denies both major criticisms. He left them reluctantly. The Greek word means 'we were orphaned from you'. He'd never been separated from them in spirit. And he had tried repeatedly to return (verse 17). We don't know whether it was his preoccupation with the Corinthian ministry, illness, or other circumstances, but Satan used something to stop Paul from doing what he desired to do, which was to return to them. 'You are our glory and joy', he says. He longs to return.

Two, *he sent Timothy in his place* (3:1–15). Now this had been a real sacrifice on Paul's part. He needed Timothy's friendship, he wanted his support, yet he was willing to be left alone in Athens in order to send Timothy to Thessalonica. He could bear the loneliness better than the suspense of waiting for news from Thessalonica, and

fearing that the church there had been overcome by persecution. I want us to try to feel this suspense of Paul in
our hearts. It's to relieve it, and to encourage the
Thessalonians, that he sends Timothy (verses 3, 4).

Three, *he had been overjoyed by Timothy's good news*
(3:6–10). It seems to have been a recent event. Timothy
had come back, found Paul had left Athens, rejoined him
in Corinth, and Paul was simply overjoyed with the
news that Timothy brought. The Greek phrase in verse 6
means: 'Timothy has come to us from you and evangelised to us your faith and love'. It's really about the only
place in the New Testament where the verb is used in a
secular sense, of good news other than the Gospel. 'Now
we live' (verse 8) 'if you stand fast in the Lord.' What an
amazing expression that is! So much is my life bound up
with yours, says Paul, that my life is your life, and I live
when you stand fast in the Lord. And then, in verses 9
and 10 he says that he cannot adequately express his
thanksgiving to God for them and the joy before God
which they have brought him.

Four, *he was praying for them meanwhile* (3:11–13). In
verse 10 he asserted that he prayed for them night and
day that he might visit and see them. Now in verse 11, he
actually does the praying. He tells them what he's praying for, that 'God the Father and our Lord Jesus Christ'
(note the bracketing again, more striking still in the
Greek where the plural subject has a singular verb)
'direct our way to you.' A prayer that was answered in
the affirmative, because during the third missionary
journey, on his way back to Jerusalem, he did visit
Macedonia again. And he prays that the Lord 'make you
increase and abound in love to one another and to all
men . . .' and so on through to verse 13.

In all these things, these four things we've just been
looking at, a true pastor's heart is laid bare before us.

Paul just loved those Thessalonian Christians. They were only a few out of the thousands he must have got to know in his journeys. But he loved them and he longed to see them. Absence of news filled him with anxiety, good news filled him with joy. His heart went out to them. In a word, his life was bound up with their lives. 'Now we live if you stand firm in the Lord.' Now I ask myself: what are these expressions? What is this loving and this longing, this intolerable suspense, these fervent prayers? I think we can answer those questions. This is the language of parents, when they're thinking and talking about their kids, and when they're missing them dreadfully, when they're separated from them. So we see this parental side of Paul.

Here are two indispensable qualities of Christian pastoral ministry: faith in God's word, and a love for God's people. A commitment to the Gospel and a commitment to the church. A commitment to truth and a commitment to love. What we need to do is to pray for those who are training for the pastoral ministry of the church. We need to pray for those who are responsible for training the future pastors of the church. We need to pray for all pastors and those who share in the pastoral oversight of a congregation, that God will give pastors to his church who, like the apostle Paul, are both faithful, as stewards and heralds, and loving, as fathers and mothers. And who are prepared, in the words of 2:8 to share with those who serve, on the one hand, the Gospel of God, and on the other, their very selves, so great is their commitment to the Gospel and the people. God give us pastors like that in the church today.

3. Christian Standards: How To Please God More and More (1 Thessalonians 4)

It seems to me that one of the great weaknesses of contemporary evangelical Christianity is our neglect of Christian ethics, that is to say, practical instruction in Christian moral standards. Christians have become known rather as those who preach the Gospel than as those who live it. We are not always conspicuous in the community as we should be, for strict honesty, simplicity of lifestyle, happy contentment and stable Christian homes. Now the main reason for this, I believe, is that our churches don't teach ethics as they should. We're too busy preaching the Gospel, we're scared of being branded legalists: 'Oh, we're not under the Law,' we say piously, as if that meant we're free to ignore it.

To this neglect of Christian ethics Paul presents a striking contrast. It's not only that all his letters contain detailed ethical instruction. It's also that he gave Christian moral instruction to very young converts. Look at 1 Thessalonians 4:1, 2, 6, 11. Four times in one passage he refers to moral instruction he gave them when he was with them.

We don't know how long he stayed in Thessalonica. Luke says that he argued three Sabbaths running in the synagogue with the Jews. He may have stayed a few weeks or months longer on the Gentile mission field, but not much longer. So within a few weeks of their conversion Paul taught them not only the essence of the good news, but also the essence of the good life. He taught them not only the necessity of faith in Jesus but also the necessity of good works, without which the authenticity of our faith in Jesus is inevitably called into question.

There is an urgent need today, especially in Europe as the culture diverges more and more from its Christian origins, to take seriously the example of Jesus and his apostles and give plain, practical, down-to-earth ethical instruction. We live in a permissive, relativistic, immoral situation, today; it is urgent that we teach Christian morality, and it isn't any harder today than it was in corrupt, immoral Graeco-Roman society, in which Paul himself was teaching and writing. And we must teach with authority. We saw in our previous study that Paul claimed that his Gospel was the word of God. (2:13). Now look at the first two verses of chapter 4. Paul is teaching that if moral instruction is given with the authority of the Lord Jesus, then moral teaching has as much authority as the Gospel. 'Therefore', he says in verse 8, 'whoever disregards this, disregards not man but God, who gives his Holy Spirit to you.'

As we look at chapter 4, we see distinct paragraphs, each clearly addressed to a different group in the Thessalonian church. The topics are sexual self-control (3–8), brotherly love (9–12), and bereavement (13–18). We don't know for sure why Paul chose these three subjects. It has been suggested that they refer to the three groups mentioned in chapter 5.14: the idle, the fainthearted, and the weak. We'll go on to consider each of those groups in turn.

1. The Weak (verses 3–8). Now Christians in general, and evangelical Christians in particular, have had a reputation (sometimes a deserved one) for being preoccupied with sex; so that whenever they hear the word morality they think sexual morality is what's meant. In self-defence against that criticism, we biblical Christians want to remind one another that we try to be realists.

Our sexuality, we know, is part of our created humanity, and we need to assert it as a good gift of God. But we also know that sex has become twisted and distorted by the Fall, and it is surely as a result of the Fall that this God-given instinct has become the most imperious of human urges. So it is destructive, when uncontrolled, of human dignity, human community, personality and maturity. Uncontrolled sexual passion is a very destructive thing.

Paul recognises sex as a good gift of God tarnished by the Fall. He teaches two fundamental principles here.

Firstly, *sex has a God-given context: marriage*. Look at verses 3, 4. Now there is some disagreement among translators and commentators on how verse 4 should be translated, and there are certainly some problems. But most commentators take the same reading as the Revised Standard Version: '. . . that each one of you know how to *take a wife* for himself . . .' That's the way I'm going to understand it.

So Scripture, being the realistic book it is, recognizes the strength of human sexual desires. It teaches that marriage was from the beginning, long before the Fall, God's gracious provision for his creatures. And Scripture insists that heterosexual marriage is the only context in which God intends sexual love to be experienced and enjoyed. Of course, 'enjoyed' is the right word, as you know if you've read the Song of Solomon. Outside marriage sexual experience is forbidden.

Now at this point I think I need in all integrity to add an appendix, for those of us who are single and have therefore been denied the only God-given context for sexual love. What about them?

Well, to begin with, we must accept this teaching of God, however hard it may seem, as God's good purpose for us and society. The only God-given context for sexual love is marriage. And we will not become a bundle of frustrations and inhibitions and neuroses if we gladly accept this standard; we will only become so if we rebel against it. We need to say to one another that it is perfectly possible for our sexual energy to be redirected both into affectionate relationships with many people and into loving service for others. There are a multitude of Christian single men and women who have been able to testify that alongside a natural human loneliness and sometimes acute pain, there can be immense and joyful fulfillment in the loving joyful service of God and our fellow human beings. You see, God has given sex this one and only context: marriage. That's the first thing Paul teaches, quite uninhibitedly.

The second point Paul makes is that *sex has a God-given style: honour.* Marriage is not legalised lust. The fact that it is the God-given context for sex doesn't mean that 'anything goes', within marriage. We've all heard about the sexual demands that are sometimes selfishly made by one married partner of the other, in terms of aggression, violence, or cruelty. And we need to consider what Paul teaches in verses 4–6. Note, 'Let each take for himself a wife in consecration and *honour*, not in the passion of lust like heathen who do not know God, and that no man transgress or wrong his brother in this matter, because the Lord is an avenger . . .' Again, there are various interpretations of 'in this matter' – some have thought it referred to 'in business'. But I think the Revised Standard Version is right, that the kind of behaviour Paul is forbidding is the opposite of honour. It's any kind of selfish exploitation of the marriage partner. We all know there's a world of difference between love and lust, between the selfish desire to possess the other person and the unselfish desire to express love and respect. As the old *Book of Common Prayer* Marriage

Service has it, 'With my body, I thee worship' (or, 'I thee honour').

Indeed at the end of verse 6 we read, 'The Lord is an avenger in all these things.' For the Lord sees even the intimacies of the bedroom. He hates every form of human exploitation, and that includes sexual exploitation. And though there may be no redress in law, there is at the bar of God.

And finally Paul says that God has called us to holiness, not for uncleanness; and to disregard that is not to disregard man but God who has given to us his Holy Spirit.

Well, there are sex ethics for the weak. The God-given context for sex is marriage, the God-given style for sex is honour. Oh, it's elementary instruction, no doubt; but it's plain, it's frank, it's authoritative, it's uninhibited, it's straight from the shoulder, it's just what new converts need.

What impresses me about the whole passage is that it's what the experts call 'theological ethics'. It's ethics arising out of our doctrine of God. Why do the heathen behave as they do (verse 5), with total lack of sexual self-control? Because they don't know God. But Christians behave differently. Why? Because we do know God, and we know that he's a holy God. It's fundamental to the passage.

In our previous reading we saw the God-centredness of Christian ministry. Now I want to draw out the God-centredness of Christian morality. Look at verses 1, 3, 6, 7 and 8. You see, in one short passage, Paul brings together the will of God, the judgement of God, the call of God, and the Spirit of God; and he makes these truths the basis of his appeal to please God more and more. Now, brethren, we know these truths. We're not ignorant of them. They are the foundation stones of Christian faith and life. The call, the will, the Spirit, the judgement of God. We know them all. And every one of them is related to holiness. Well then, this will show us how to live so as to please God. We've got to live in such a way that we remember his call is a holy calling, his will is our holiness, that the Holy Spirit is a holy spirit and that he judges unholiness. And when we get hold of these things, and when we think Christianly about these things – why then of course we shall want to please God more and more, in holiness.

2. *The Idle (verses 9–12).* It seems clear that there was a group in the Thessalonian church needing a very different kind of exhortation. In 5:18 they are called, in the Greek, *ataktoi.* In classical Greek this word was used for undisciplined soldiers. So the King James version translated it 'disorderly', and for centuries it's been supposed that there was in Thessalonica an undisciplined or bolshy group. But recently it has been discovered that the word had acquired another meaning by the first century AD, in non-literary or common Greek. It was used for playing truant. So it appears that the group in Thessalonica were playing truant from work – that was how the word was used – hence they were not 'disorderly' as in the King James Version, but 'idle' as in the Revised Standard Version. Paul doesn't use the word in the present paragraph, but he does elsewhere in the Thessalonian epistles and it seems certain that this is what he means.

It's possible – commentators have suggested – that they had misunderstood Paul's teaching about Christ's second coming, and had given up their jobs, thinking it was imminent. So to them Paul's teaching is very plain. They are to aspire to live quietly, not to get excited, and to mind their own business and get on with their jobs as Paul charged them when he was with them. Then (verse

12) they'll command the respect of outsiders and enjoy economic independence. Now Paul frames his appeal in terms of *Philadelphia*, or brotherly love, the special love that binds families together. He uses the word because we are brothers and sisters in Christ. It's natural that those who know God as their Father should love one another as brothers and sisters. He doesn't need to write to them about it, he says; they themselves (verse 9) have been 'taught by God to love one another', and indeed they do love all the brethren throughout Macedonia. It's interesting how these churches of Northern Greece seemed to know one another. They loved each other. Nevertheless, although they didn't need any instruction, he gave them some all the same. Verse 10: he exhorted them to love each other 'more and more', and in particular to express that love by working for their living and not depending on one another.

Now we need to be careful how we apply this today. I don't think we're free to apply this teaching about work in an insensitive way to everybody who is out of work and drawing unemployment benefit. Unemployment today is a complex social problem, a symptom of economic recession. What Paul is here attacking is not unemployment as such, when people can't find work, but idleness, when people don't want it. Paul says that we should want to work. It's an aspect of our love for one another that we don't become spongers.

3. *The Fainthearted (verses 13–18).* We have the phrase in 5:14 'encourage the faint-hearted', and it's possible that Paul is using this word to describe the sorrowing bereaved.

Now bereavement is a very poignant human experience. Most of us have had the experience, and however firm our Christian faith may be, the loss of a close relative or friend causes a profound psychological and emotional shock. It needs a very painful and radical readjustment that sometimes takes months or years to overcome. It also raises anguished questions: 'What has happened to the loved one? Is he or she all right?' Such questions arise partly out of curiosity, partly out of concern for the lost person, partly because we perceive death as a threat to our own security, and so on. It's understandable. In addition to all that, the Thessalonians had some theological questions. Paul had taught that the Lord Jesus was coming back to claim his people and take them to himself. I don't believe he dogmatised about the timing of this, but it seems at all events that some of the Thessalonians were expecting Jesus to come very soon indeed – we've seen that some of them gave up their jobs. And then others were deeply distressed when their friends died. They had thought Jesus was coming back before anybody died. How would the dead fare when Jesus came for his own? Would they be at a disadvantage? Evidently they had raised these questions already with Paul, and in verse 13 Paul begins to answer them.

'Those who are asleep' is a beautiful phrase for Christian death. It probably refers to the body living in the grave as if sleeping. And Jesus himself used the metaphor to indicate that death is temporary – one wakes after sleep. We are not forbidden to grieve altogether. Don't misinterpret verse 13. Mourning is natural and necessary. If Jesus wept over the tomb of Lazarus, then most certainly we are at liberty to do the same. What is forbidden is grieving like those who have no hope. There's a difference between Christian and non-Christian grieving. The philosophers, the Stoics and the Epicureans denied existence after death. But we have a hope. It concerns the coming again of Jesus. This is referred to in the middle of verse 14, the *parousia* or coming again. It was the official term for the visit of a dignitary. So Paul may be hinting that the coming of Jesus will be the visit of the 'Emperor', the personal visit of the King of Kings. We know from Luke in Acts that in Thessalonica Paul proclaimed the kingship of Jesus, for his detractors said of him, 'He preaches another emperor, one Jesus.' And here Paul is saying, the King is coming again, and we must be ready for the King's coming.

But the Christian hope is not just the coming of the King. It is that when he comes his subjects will be with him. Look at verses 14, 16. He's going to bring the Christian dead, the redeemed dead, the angels as well. And (verse 14) God is going to preserve total impartiality between the Christian dead and the Christian living – neither will have an advantage. God is going to bring with Jesus those who have died. What a glorious truth that is! And having stated it, Paul elaborates the Christian hope in four affirmations.

The Lord himself will descend from heaven (verse 16). That we call the return. The Lord is going to descend in glory.

The dead in Christ will rise first (verse 16). That's the resurrection. Having raised the Christian dead, God is going to bring them with Christ, as we saw in verse 14.

We who are left will be caught up (verse 17). That, we call the rapture, because we're going to be seized or snatched away to Christ; the Latin word *raptus* means to seize, and that's what the Greek means.

And so we shall always be with the Lord (verse 17). I call that the reunion. We are going to be caught up in the clouds to meet the Lord with them and we shall be with him and with one another for ever. 'Therefore, comfort one another with these words' (verse 18).

What glorious doctrines these are. No doubt there is a great deal more in Scripture about these events, but let's rejoice in these things which are plain.

What I want to ask you to notice as we conclude is that Paul doesn't only help these three groups with doctrine. He helps them by reminding them of the two major means by which Christians are sustained in the Christian life and led into maturity and security in Jesus Christ. And I want to enlarge upon those two things as we close.

1. We are to please God more and more. We're not to think of this obligation primarily as law, but of love. Our heavenly Father, who made us, redeemed us, adopted us into his family, put the Holy Spirit within us, loves us, and we love him. Of course we want to please him if we stand in that relationship with him. And the more we come to know him, the more we develop a certain spiritual sensitivity, so that in every moral dilemma it is a safe and practical principle to ask, 'Would it please my Father?'

2. Comfort one another with these words. We all get discouraged. We lose heart, we lose faith. Now in that, Paul says, comfort one another. 'Encourage one another', he says in 5:11, 'and build one another up.' Of course God comforts us secretly by the Holy Spirit within. He comforts us by the public pulpit ministry. But he intends his church to be a community of mutual comfort. If only the church were a caring community! Comfort one another, encourage one another, build one another up, hold on to one another. This one-another-ness of the Christian community is very important, for by pleasing God and encouraging one another, we shall grow into Christian maturity.

4. Christian Community: How To Care for Each Other in the Church Family (1 Thessalonians 5)

We are all concerned for the church of Jesus Christ. All of us are concerned for its renewal. And this naturally prompts the question, 'What does a renewed church look like?' What do we, God's people, look like when we're living by the word of God and filled by the Spirit of God? In this final chapter of 1 Thessalonians, Paul develops two beautiful pictures of Christian people which should profoundly affect how we behave. First (verses 1–11) we're children of light. And secondly (verses 12–28) we're brothers and sisters in the family of God.

We are children of the light (verses 1–11)

This paragraph, like the foregoing paragraph, relates to the second coming, but some readers I think are too ready to lump the two paragraphs together as though they concerned the same issues. It should help us to see that two quite distinct problems are being faced in these chapters, problems that have always fascinated human minds, and not least Christian minds. The first is the problem of bereavement, it concerns those who have died: what happens after death? Where are our loved ones? Are they all right, shall we see them again? The second is the problem of judgement, and concerns us as well: what will happen at the end of the world? Is there going to be a judgement? If so, can we prepare for it?

Now it's evident that the Thessalonian Christians were anxious on both counts. And I think you'll agree with me that these are modern apprehensions as well. And Paul, realistic pastor that he was, applied himself to both these fears. We saw in 4:13–18 that he has dealt with bereavement and the Christian dead. Now in 5:1–11 he deals with judgement and the Christian living; how we can be ready for Christ the Judge, when he comes.

Verses 1–3 state the problem. The Thessalonians were asking about time and season. Not, it seems, out of idle curiosity; they wanted to make preparation for the coming of Jesus. They knew that the day of the Lord would be a day of judgement, and they thought they could most easily prepare if they might know when he was coming. And Paul here indicates that the solution did not lie in discovering the date of the Lord's return. No, the day of the Lord will come like a burglar in the night (Jesus had used the same expression), like labour to a pregnant woman. Both pictures tell us that Christ's coming will be sudden, yet there is a significant difference between the two. The burglar's coming is unexpected; labour is expected. What Paul is emphasising is that there'll be no escape. Once pregnancy has begun, labour is not only expected, but, all being well, unavoidable. So putting these two pictures together we may say that Christ's coming to judge will be sudden and unexpected (like the thief) and sudden and unavoidable (like labour). In the first case, no warning; in the second, no escape. Now that's the problem. If we can't know the date, and he is going to come suddenly and unexpectedly and unavoidably, how can we get ready?

Well, Paul explains that there's no need for Christians to be alarmed at the prospect or be taken unawares. Why not? Well, we're getting to the heart now of the argument in verses 4, 5. I am so anxious that we will really grasp the apostolic argument here that I want to enlarge upon it.

The main reason that the burglar takes people by surprise is that he comes by night. It's dark; most people are asleep, or if awake they're probably out at a party and the chances are they might even be drunk. So (and see verse 7), darkness, sleep and drunkenness are three reasons why people are not ready for the burglar when he comes. Just so with the coming of Christ. Will he come in the darkness or will he come in the light? The answer is, both. He's going to come in the dark and the light. For unbelievers he's going to come in the dark, but (verse 4) 'As for you, brethren, you are not in the darkness . . .' You are in the light.

Let me elaborate. The Bible divides human history into two ages. From the Old Testament perspective they are called the present age, which is evil, and the age to come, the age of the Messiah. They are sometimes presented in terms of night and day. It comes clearly, for example, in the *Benedictus* sung by John's father Zechariah: 'The day shall dawn upon us from on high . . .' (Luke 1:67 ff.). Now the Bible also teaches that the new age dawned when Jesus Christ, the long awaited Messiah, came. He is the dawn of the new era. At the same time, the old age has not yet come to an end. 1 John 1.8: '. . . the darkness is passing away and the true light is already shining.' This is the key thing. The two ages are now overlapping. Unbelievers belong to the old age, and they're in the darkness still. But those who belong to Jesus Christ are transferred into the new age and are children of the light. Already we have tasted the powers of the age to come. And when Christ comes again in glory, the overlap between the two ages will finish.

So then, here is the point. Whether we are ready for Christ's coming or not depends on which age we're in. To which age do you belong? Are you still in the darkness, or are you in the light?

Now verses 4–8 become quite clear, once we have grasped the biblical teaching about the two ages. The imagery of day and night is continued right through these verses. Notice it's a day that is coming. We are not children of the night. So don't let us sleep as the rest of the world does; let us keep awake and be sober. 'Since we belong to the day,' (that's a crucial phrase, the day that dawned when Christ came), 'let us be sober and put on the breastplate of faith and love, our armour, and for a helmet the hope of salvation.' Now I hope it's clear. If we are Christians and belong to Christ, we've entered the new age of light. Therefore let our behaviour be daytime behaviour. Let's not sleep, let's not live in our pyjamas. Let's stay awake, let's get up, be sober, alert, let's put on the armour of light, because we belong to the day. And then we shall be ready when the day of the Lord comes. It will be sudden and unexpected, but it won't take us by surprise, because we're ready.

The section ends, like the previous paragraph, with an exhortation to mutual encouragement. Glance on to verse 11, which is so similar to verse 18 of the previous chapter. As we saw in the previous study, the Christian church is a community of mutual comfort, edification and encouragement. It's with these words, this doctrine, that they are to comfort one another.

Now in saying this I have not forgotten one of the lessons of the book of Job and his so-called comforters. We have to give them credit that at first, for seven days and nights, they sat in silent sympathy where he sat. And one rather wishes they'd kept their mouths shut when the week ended. Instead they drowned him in a torrent of cold, traditional words, until in the last chapter God appears and contradicts the cold comfort these men gave. Their mistake, however, was not that they talked.

It was that they talked nonsense. Generally speaking, words do encourage. Words do comfort. And we can derive great comfort from Christian doctrine as we stay our minds on these truths.

So what Paul gave the Thessalonians and urged them to give to one another in their anxieties about bereavement and judgement was not soothing, contentless words, but the foundation truths of the Christian Gospel. He says, I don't want you to be ignorant. I want you to know these truths, and stay your minds on them. What truths were they? The truth of the second coming of Christ is only part of the answer. That's what he refers to in these two paragraphs. But the major truth from which they were to derive comfort wasn't just that Jesus is coming again – that strikes some people with terror. It is rather that he who is coming again is the very same person who died and rose again. It is this truth that is at the heart of both sections. Glance back to 4:14. When Jesus comes he will bring with him those who've died. But the one who's coming is the one who died and rose again. Look at 5:9, 10. The one who is coming to complete our salvation is the one who died for us, that whether we wake or sleep we might live with him. So when he died he overcame the two great enemies of mankind, sin and death. And if we are united to Jesus Christ, neither sin nor death can ever separate us from him. Nothing can come between us. This is the emphasis. Read 4:14, and then 5:10. 'With him . . . With him.' Did you notice the repetition? The supreme achievement of the death and resurrection of Jesus is to bring us into a personal union with him. A union with him which nothing, neither death, nor bereavement, nor judgement, could ever destroy. 'Therefore comfort one another with these words.'

We are brothers and sisters in the family of God (verses 12–28)

The key word of this paragraph is: brethren, brothers and sisters. It's the commonest word in the New Testament for Christians. It occurs seventeen times in this whole letter and five times in this paragraph, verses 12, 14, 25, 26, 27. The word bears witness to our common membership of the family of God, our belonging to one another. We don't only belong to the day, but we belong to the family, and it profoundly affects our relationships with one another and our life and behaviour in the church. So what Paul does in these verses is to take up three aspects of the life of the local church; all items of contemporary debate and discussion, and gives important instruction about each of them.

1. The Pastorate (verses 12, 13). Historically speaking, the church of Jesus Christ has lurched unsteadily from one unbiblical extreme to the other in this area. Sometimes we have veered towards the extreme of *clericalism*, in which the clergy have dominated the scene, monopolised the leadership of the ministry, and received from the laity, the congregation, an exaggerated and quite improper deference; while the laity have been well and truly sat on, the only contribution desired from them being their presence on Sunday to fill otherwise empty pews, and of course their cash as well. That's clericalism; suppressing the people of God by clergy.

At other times we veer towards the opposite extreme of *anti-clericalism*. And nowadays we thank God that we are recovering the doctrine of the church as the body of Christ and the concept of an 'every member' ministry, every member of the body of Christ exercising his or her gift to the common good. But sometimes when recovering this glorious concept of the 'every-member' ministry, people go too far in that direction and say 'Well, the clergy are obviously redundant. We're all ministers now, so let's fire the lot, we can do better without them.' That too is an unbiblical extreme. There is a place at least for some sort of pastoral oversight in every congregation. Now I want you to observe how Paul, with this wonderful balance that the Holy Spirit has given him, will not allow either extreme in the church. So we notice how he describes the pastors and then how he describes what attitude of the congregation to them should be.

Describing pastors, he uses three expressions, with only one pronoun covering the three. Firstly, those *who labour among you*. A significant expression, because some regard the pastorate as a sinecure. On the contrary, says Paul, they labour – the Greek word means hard work, it's the word Paul uses for his tentmaking – among you. The picture this word conjures up is one of rippling muscles and pouring sweat.

Secondly, *those who are over you in the Lord, your spiritual leaders*. The Greek verb is interesting. It means to preside, or direct and rule, and it is used of a variety of officials and superintendents and managers and chiefs and so on. But it also came to mean to protect, to care for, and to help. Consequently it was used for parents, who not only managed the home but also cared for the children. I suspect we need to combine in our understanding of this Greek word the concepts of managing and caring. We can't altogether eliminate the concept of authority from the verb, but we have to add that the form this authority takes (as we saw in chapters 2 and 3) is one of parental or pastoral care. And this is in keeping with the startling originality of Jesus, who taught that the first must be last, the leader the servant, and the master the slave.

Thirdly, *those who admonish you*. The pastor's teaching ministry includes the responsibility to warn, and even rebuke.

So these three expressions leave us in no doubt that Paul envisaged a distinct group of leaders in the congregation. What attitude was the congregation to adopt towards its leaders? Well, it was neither to despise them nor to fawn upon them, but to respect them (verse 12), to appreciate them and esteem them highly in love, because of their work. In other words, to have for them, because of their pastoral labours, an affectionate Christian regard.

Brethren, you know, don't you, that there are many churches where the pastor and congregation are at loggerheads with one another. And it is a very sad situation. By contrast, happy is that church family in which clergy and laity, or pastors and people, live at peace with one another, recognising that God calls different people to different ministries. Happy is the church family in which the pastors exercise their authority not in autocracy but in loving care. Happy is the church family in which the congregation gives to its leaders the respect and love which their God-given work demands. And then they will live at peace with one another.

2. The Fellowship (verse 14, 15). Notice that although in verses 12, 13 some sort of pastorate is envisaged, in verses 14, 15 Paul addresses his exhortations to all church members to accept responsibility for one another. This seems to me very important. The existence of a pastorate is not to exempt us from this brotherly, sisterly responsibility for each other. He's addressing his exhortation to the whole congregation. He begins with the three categories we thought about in our previous study: the idle, the fainthearted (maybe the bereaved) and the weak (maybe the sexually uncontrolled). Admonish, encourage, support, and then be patient with them all, says Paul (verse 14). For they are in a way the problem children of the family of God. They have problems of doctrine, character, and conduct.

Of course we're all problem children in a way. And we're not to grow impatient with problem children because they're difficult and demanding. On the contrary we are to be long-suffering towards them. To me it is a very beautiful thing to see Paul's vision of the local church, not only as a community of mutual comfort but of mutual support; a genuine family.

From these particulars, Paul goes on to the general behaviour in the fellowship. Look at verse 15. All retaliation is forbidden to the followers of Jesus. Instead we're to be kind to everybody. Now what an extraordinary exhortation that is! An exhortation to the whole church. All of you see to it. Paul lays upon the congregation the responsibility for ensuring that all its members are following the teaching of Jesus. It's a responsibility that is not to be left to the pastors alone. It is not an exhortation to pastors but to all the brethren in the fellowship. A one-anotherness of mutual responsibility in the family of God.

3. The Worship (verses 16–28). On first reading this you might not think it has much to do with public worship. But I want to suggest to you that it is a public situation that Paul has in mind. For one thing, all the verbs are plural. For another, the prophesying of verse 20 is obviously public. The holy kiss of verse 26 can't be given to yourself. And in verse 27, the public reading of the letter is required. So Paul has in mind public worship, when the people come together. Public worship is an extremely important part of the local congregation's life – some of us evangelical Christians are far too slovenly in our attitudes to it – and Paul issues four instructions that relate to it.

Firstly, *rejoice always* (verse 16). Now of course you could take that as a command to every Christian to rejoice. But you know the full New Testament exhortation as in Phillipians 4:4 is to rejoice in the Lord always, and the main time we rejoice in the Lord is when we sing his praises and come together to worship. It's reminiscent of many Old Testament commands, for example in the Psalms. So I'm suggesting this is not just a command to be happy. It's an invitation to worship, and to joyful worship at that. Some of our evangelical worship is positively lugubrious! But every worship service should be a celebration, a joyful rehearsal of what God has done for us through Jesus Christ. So let there be organs and trumpets and guitars and singing, and let's make a joyful noise! Rejoice in the Lord, Paul says, always.

Secondly, *pray constantly* (verse 17). To this he adds in verse 25, 'Brethren, pray for us.' So if praise is one indispensable part of worship, prayer is another. The time of intercession in the service needs, in my opinion, to be much more carefully prepared than it usually is, and sometimes led by lay people rather than the pastor. They can often intercede better because they see what goes on in the world better than the pastor, who tends to be cloistered.

Thirdly, *give thanks in all circumstances* (verse 18). So in public worship there's not only praise and prayer, there's thanksgiving. There's a place of what we in the Church of England call 'general thanksgiving' when we thank God for our creation and preservation and all the blessings of this life, and above all for his priceless love in redeeming the world through Jesus Christ. The Lord's Supper, too, is nothing if not a thanksgiving, and in one way it is the heart of our Christian worship and our Christian thanksgiving. But there is need also for more specific thanksgiving, for specific blessings of which each congregation is aware. We're to give thanks, not *for* all circumstances, but *in* all circumstances. We may not feel like praising and praying and thanking, but we shall do it whether we feel like it or not. Why? Because (at the end of verse 18) '. . . this is the will of God in Christ Jesus for you.' These are three indispensable aspects of our public worship.

Fourthly, *we are to listen to the word of God* (verses 20–22). Verse 20: 'Do not despise prophesying.' There seem to have been many prophets in the New Testament church, and all of us know that Pentecostal and Charismatic Christians are claiming that God is again in these days giving prophets to his church. This is a controversial question, and I don't want to be drawn into controversy; all I can do is, I hope with humility, to share with you my own personal conviction on this matter on which I've tried to think and pray carefully.

It's of course very understandable that God should have sent prophets to the church before the New Testament was available. At that time the word of God came to the church through apostles and through prophets, who were the living and infallible teachers of the church. Today, all of us have to admit, whatever our viewpoint, the situation is entirely different. We have the written word of God. So certainly there can be no apostles comparable to Paul or Peter or John, and equally certainly no prophets comparable to the biblical proph-ets. Otherwise we should have to add their words to Scripture and the whole church would have to obey. No, in the primary sense in which these words are used in the New Testament, there are no more such. Paul calls them the 'foundation of the church' (Eph. 2:20). The foundation is their teaching, and that is finished. That really isn't controversial.

The question is whether there are today some kinds of lesser gifts. Certainly God does give to some of his people a remarkable degree of insight, into Scripture, or the contemporary world, or into his will for particular people in particular situations. And perhaps it would be right to describe this insight as prophetic insight, or a prophetic gift.

Anyway, what Paul says is 'Don't despise prophesying.' We are never to treat with contempt any message that claims to come from God. Instead (verse 21) we are to listen and evaluate it by the clear light of Scripture, by the known character of the speaker and by the degree it will edify the church. And when you've evaluated it, 'hold fast to what is good' (verse 21) and 'abstain from every form of evil' (verse 22).

Now we come to verse 27, an exhortation, couched in extremely strong terms, that the letter be read publicly. It's a quite extraordinary instruction. Already the Old Testament Scriptures were read in the public assembly, a custom taken over from the synagogue by the early Christian assemblies. But now the apostle says his letters are to be read in the public assembly as well! The clear implication is that he regarded the letter as on a par with the Old Testament Scriptures. Furthermore – have you ever noticed this? – he gives them no command to weigh or sift his teaching. There is no need to sift the wheat from the chaff, as in the case of those claiming to be prophets. No, they were to listen to everything the apostle wrote, and they were to believe and obey it all. So clearly Paul puts his authority as an apostle above that of the prophets. So today, even if there is some kind of subsidiary prophetic gift of insight, of far greater importance for the church is the teaching of the apostles, as it has been bequeathed to us in the New Testament, and the public reading and exposition of the Scriptures. It's that which edifies the church.

So in public worship there are always these two complementary elements: on the one hand, there is praising and praying and giving thanks to the Lord; and on the other hand, there is listening to his word. Thus God speaks to his people through his word, and they respond to him with praise, prayer and thanksgiving. Throughout the service the pendulum swings rhythmically as God speaks and the people respond. Moreover, in both aspects of public worship, we are to recognise the sovereign freedom of the Holy Spirit.

'Don't quench the Spirit.' The command comes right in the middle of all the other commands. The word for quench is used for extinguishing either a light or a fire in the Greek, and the Holy Spirit is both. We are never to put him out. Let him shine into our minds. Let him warm and burn in our hearts. We must allow him his full freedom to speak and move in the congregation. Much of our Christian worship in these days, especially in the traditional denominations, is much too formal, liturgical, and stuffy. The Holy Spirit is bound hand and foot, and gagged as well. But there is place for freedom as well as fixity and spontaneity as well as liturgy. And in my own conviction, it is a combination of the two that is more enriching than anything else.

So the conclusion. Paul has given us at the end of his letter an idyllic picture of the local church, referring to the pastorate, the fellowship, and the worship. And he touches on church members' three relationships: to their pastors, respect and love; to each other, mutual care and support; and to God, listening to him and responding to him. To me, the key word of the whole section is 'brethren'. The pastorate is transformed if the pastoral oversight humble themselves and recognise the congregation as their brothers and sisters. The fellowship is transformed when we greet one another with a holy kiss, that is to say, when we recognise that we belong to one another. And the worship is transformed as well when we say 'Brethren pray for us', and 'let the letter be read to all the *brethren*.'

Yet this living-out of brotherly love and family life in the local church is possible only by the word of God. So I ask you simply to notice, in verse 23, that he is called the God of peace, of harmony, who desires the wholeness of his people and his church – that he will 'sanctify you wholly, and that your whole spirit and soul and body be preserved blameless.' The God of peace and wholeness. In verse 24, the God of faithfulness; and in verse 28, the God of grace.

So if our local church is ever to be a truly Gospel church, receiving the Gospel, proclaiming it, embodying it, and if it is to be a true church family, whose members worship God and love one another, then only the peace, the faithfulness and the grace of God can make it so. And therefore it is into his loving hands that we commend ourselves, one another, and our churches.

The Lordship of Jesus Christ

If I were to ask you what is the really master-key doctrine, I wonder what you would answer. It would be very interesting if we could sit down and compare notes with one another. Some of you no doubt would say the Sovereignty of God: others, the Cross of our Lord Jesus Christ. Others would say, the Fullness of the Holy Spirit. And I would agree that they are all vital, central doctrines. But I want to argue that the master-key is somewhere else. It is in the Lordship of Christ.

I believe that the key Christian doctrine is in the affirmation 'Jesus Christ is Lord', and if that isn't central in our Christian belief, behaviour and experience then I think something is out of gear. But if we do see and acknowledge Jesus as Lord, then all our Christian doctrine and behaviour and experience mesh in with one another and we have found the integrating secret of the Christian life. I honestly believe that; I hope I may demonstrate it biblically, that the Lordship of Jesus is a wonderfully liberating doctrine. It is when Jesus is Lord that we are made whole and free.

1. Our relationship to the Lord (Romans 14: 7–9). Let me suggest in the first place, when we acknowledge Jesus as Lord, our relationship to him is right. The alternatives are clearly set before us in verses 7, 8: 'None of us lives to himself, none of us dies to himself', and 'If we live we live to the Lord, if we die we die to the Lord.' That's the alternative. We're all either living to ourselves or living to the Lord. Of course the 'us' and the 'we' there mean Christians, because non-Christians are doing exactly what verse 7 says 'none of us' does, that is, they are living and dying to themselves. That is what it means to be a non-Christian. It is to be self-centred, self-absorbed, self-obsessed. That's what we are till Jesus liberates us. But it's inconceivable that a Christian should live like that. You see the whole of our human experience centres on Jesus Christ. Nothing, if we're Christians, is outside the sphere of his dominion. How is that? Verse 9: 'To this end Christ died and lived again in order that he might be . . .' What? Supposing you didn't know that verse, and I'd said, now, fill in the blank. Ninety-nine out of a hundred would say 'Saviour'. Isn't that why he died, and rose again, to be our Saviour? But it's not what Paul said. He said, '. . . that he might be Lord.'

The idea still lingers in some circles that it is possible to accept Jesus as your Saviour and postpone indefinitely the question of his Lordship. That is a preposterous idea. The New Testament knows nothing of such bogus Christianity. There is only one Jesus Christ, he is our Lord and Saviour Jesus Christ; and response to Jesus is response to the totality of Jesus our Saviour and Lord. It's inconceivable that we should cut him up and respond to only part of him. You can't. He can only *be* our Saviour because he is Lord. It's from that position at the Father's right hand that he justifies the believing sinner and bestows the Holy Spirit upon us, because he has the authority to do so. Let's not separate what God has joined or contradict the purpose for which Jesus has died and risen again. He's died and risen again in order that he might be Lord of both the dead and the living.

He's certainly the Lord of the Christian dead. In heaven, you know, the Christian dead give no grudging acquiescence to the Lordship of Jesus. There's only a joyful wondering adoration that Jesus Christ is Lord, the Lamb upon his throne. But he died and rose again not only to be Lord of the dead but of the living. He means our Christian life on earth to approximate as far as possible the glorified life of the believer in heaven. And that means a totality of surrender, to the Lordship of Jesus: joyful, ungrudging, wondering, total allegiance to Jesus. That includes everything, my friends; everything, you name it, it's under the Lordship of Jesus. When we acknowledge Jesus as Lord then our relationship to him is right.

2. Our relationship to one another (Romans 14). Secondly, when we acknowledge Jesus as Lord our relationship to one another is right. Do you know Romans 14? It's mostly about the 'weaker brother'. The weaker brother is the Christian with a weak under-developed and over-sensitive conscience. In the church or churches in Rome there were Christians with a weak conscience and those with a strong conscience. One of the issues was whether Christians were allowed to eat meat. Those with a strong conscience felt perfectly at liberty to eat it, but those with a weak one felt they shouldn't and became vegetarians. Again, some regard some days as better and more important than others, and other people regarded all days as alike. So you see in the church at Rome there was difference of opinion about certain foods and days.

Well, there's nothing wrong in differences of opinion about these minor matters. Of course we must be agreed about the major doctrines and all the fundamentals of the faith. But there's no reason why we shouldn't differ about minor matters; nothing wrong in that. Let's face reality: we're not going to agree with one another totally until we get to heaven, and Christians have got to learn to be tolerant of one another in the Christian family. After all, in the human family we learn to tolerate one another's idiosyncracies, don't we?

What disturbed the apostle Paul was not the existence of minor differences but the attitudes the Christians had to one another on account of their differences. They despised one another, they sat in judgement on one another (verses 2, 3). Let's understand this. What is Paul saying? How does he deal with the situation in the church at Rome? He deals with it theologically. He doesn't just appeal to those Roman Christians to be nice and kind and tolerant. No, he reminds them of a doctrine which they had forgotten or weren't applying to their situation.

We have no business to despise one another, no business to stand in judgement on the servants of Christ (verse 4). Again, don't let's misunderstand this. Paul considered some opinions to be false. For example, he was not a vegetarian and he didn't see any reason why he shouldn't eat meat that had been offered in sacrifice to idols. He knew that idols were nothing, they didn't exist. He could eat such meat with thanksgiving without any scruples at all. But, you remember, he would refrain, he would voluntarily curb his own liberty of conscience in the presence of a weak brother or sister, because it might cause them to do something against their conscience. If you do that you're sinning, and Paul didn't want them to do that, even if their conscience was mistaken. Scripture has a very high view of the human conscience. And when a conscience is weak and uneducated, it must still be respected.

Now the secret then of our relations with one another in the Christian church, especially when we have differences, is 'Jesus Christ is Lord'. To despise or stand in judgement on a fellow-Christian isn't just a breach of fellowship. It is a denial of the Lord Jesus. It is a presumptuous attempt to usurp Christ's prerogative as Lord. I need to say to myself, who am I, that I should cast myself in the role of another Christian's lord and judge? I must be willing for Jesus Christ to be not only my, but also my fellow-Christians', Lord and Judge. They are responsible to him and I must not interfere with Christ's lordship over other Christians. Do you know, our fellowship in the local church would be immediately sweetened and tension lightened if we were prepared to 'let other Christians go' – they're not responsible to us. I'm not their lord and judge; you're not my lord and judge. It's before him that we stand or fall. And if we acknowledge Jesus as Lord then immediately our relations with other people, with one another in the fellowship of the church, are put right.

3. *Our relationship to the outside world.* If we acknowledge Jesus as Lord then our relationship with the world outside is right as well, that is, the secular, the unbelieving, the Christ-rejecting world. Look on to verse 11. It's a favourite from Isaiah that Paul quotes on several occasions. The context here (verses 10, 12) is judgement. Each of us is going to give an account of himself to Christ the Lord and Christ the Judge, and we mustn't therefore be lords and judges of each other. Nevertheless these words have a wider implication, justified because Paul uses the verse in other senses elsewhere. It is a quotation from Isaiah 45:22, 23. It's a wonderful missionary verse in the Old Testament, an astonishing flash of conviction that one day all the nations – not just Israel – are going to be included in the purpose of God, and in his best known use of this verse Paul applies it to Jesus.

In Philippians 2:9, 10 Paul says that God has exalted Jesus so that at his name 'every knee shall bow and every tongue confess that Jesus Christ is Lord'. So what then is the supreme missionary motivation? It's not obedience to the Great Commission, or even love for a lost and lonely world, important as these are. It's the universal

Lordship of Jesus. God has exalted Jesus and enthroned him at his right hand. God has given him universal authority over all nations, hence the affirmation of the risen Lord in Matthew 28:18. Exactly! And God's purpose in doing this is that every knee should bow to Jesus and every tongue confess him Lord. We should be full of indignation and jealousy for the honour and glory of Jesus Christ, and we should be full of restless energy to go and make him known. When we acknowledge Jesus as Lord, our relationship to the outside world is right.

So let me summarise. God has made Jesus Lord of all by creation, and also by his death and resurrection and ascension and enthronement at the right hand of God. Universal authority has been given to Jesus, he is Lord as a divine fact, and he is the undisputed Lord of the Christian dead for they ceaselessly worship him in heaven. So it's only on earth (if we leave aside the demons) that there are millions still withholding from Jesus the honour that is due to his name. And yet he died and rose again to this end, that he might be the Lord 'both of the dead and the living'. So I want to ask, did Jesus die and rise in vain, as far as we are concerned?

I began by suggesting that this is the key doctrine, the Lordship of Jesus. It's like the last piece of the jigsaw, the keystone in the arch, the final digit in the combination lock. If we acknowledge Jesus as Lord, everything else fits into place. Our relationships to him, to one another, and to the world, are put right.

So I end with some personal questions. Is Jesus Christ your Lord? Or are you denying his lordship in some way? To reject his teaching, to disobey his moral commandments, to rebel against his providential will, are all to deny the lordship of Jesus. To boss other Christians around and try to control them, to despise or stand in judgement on fellow-Christians – these are to deny the

Lordship of Jesus. To care, and do, nothing about the Christian mission in areas of the world where he is not acknowledged is to deny his lordship. And to deny the lordship of Jesus in any respect is to set ourselves against the purpose for which he died and rose again, for to this end he died and rose again: that he might be Lord both of the living and the dead.

Will you surrender to him that thing you have been withholding for years, whatever it be? For Jesus said, 'If you come after me you must take up your cross every day and follow me.' To deny his lordship is to skulk around in the darkness of fantasy. To acknowledge that Jesus is Lord is to come out into the sunshine of reality and then to go out and be the embodiment of my text tonight.

2000

Studies in 1 Corinthians 1–4

Calling Christian Leaders

1. The Ambiguity of the Church (1 Corinthians 1:1–17)

Introduction

I have entitled this series, 'Calling Christian Leaders!' and I think all of us, to some degree, are in leadership roles, whether as parents or teachers, pastors or leaders in our local church, hence the subtitle, 'Corinthian studies in Gospel, Church and Ministry'. Let me introduce the topic. I reckon that one of the great things that unites us in Keswick is that we are all committed to the church. Of course we are all committed to Christ – all one in Christ Jesus, but we are also committed to the body of Christ. We come from different races, countries, nations, cultures and denominations, but we are all members of that amazing phenomenon called the worldwide Christian community – at least I hope we are. I hope there is nobody present who is that bizarre anomaly, 'an un-churched Christian', because the New Testament knows nothing of such a monster. If we are committed to Christ, we must be committed to the body of Christ. The reason we are committed to the church is because God is committed to the church. His purpose, we are told in the New Testament, is not just to save isolated individuals and so perpetuate our loneliness, God's purpose is to 'build the church'. Christ died for us, we are told in Titus 2, not only that we might be redeemed from all iniquity, but that He might purify for Himself a people who are enthusiastic for good works.

The image of the church, which these chapters present, is extremely ambiguous. There is a paradox at the very heart of the church: the painful tension between what the church *claims* to be and what the church *seems* to be; between the divine ideal and the human reality; between romantic talk about the bride of Christ and the very unromantic, ugly, unholy and quarrelsome people we know ourselves to be. It is a tension between our final glorious destiny in heaven and our present very inglorious performance. This is the ambiguity of the church.

The apostle describes himself as the author of the letter, and the Corinthians as the recipients of the letter. Paul, the 'apostle of Christ by the will of the God', writes to the Corinthian Christians, 'the church of God in Corinth'. So an apostle of Christ addresses a church of God and both of them are exalted, noble titles.

a) Paul's self-description (v. 1)

In nine out of the thirteen letters attributed to the apostle Paul, he identifies himself as an apostle of Christ by the will of God, by the command of God or by the commission of God. How are we to understand this word 'apostle'? It is used in three different senses in the New Testament.

Firstly, it is used once only in the New Testament of all disciples of Jesus, 'the messenger is not above the one who sent him' (Jn. 13:16). The word 'messenger' is in the

Greek, *apostalos*. The messenger is not above the one who sent him. All of us have been sent into the world to share in the apostolic mission of the church and to share the good news of Jesus Christ with others.

Secondly, it is used three or four times in the New Testament of the so-called 'apostles of the churches'. Not the apostles of Christ, but the apostles of the churches – people sent out by a particular church on a particular mission. We would call them missionaries or maybe mission partners, but Paul called Epaphroditus the *apostalos* of the church of Philippi (Phil. 2:25). He refers to him as your apostle, the man sent by you in order to minister in this case to me. In 2 Corinthians 8:23 there are people called the representatives of the churches, literally the apostles of the churches.

Thirdly, the overwhelming number of times in the New Testament, the word is applied to the twelve, to Paul who was added to their number, to James who was also added and probably that's all. They were not apostles of the churches, they were apostles of Jesus Christ and they were a unique group with the following characteristics:

a) They had been chosen, called and appointed directly by Jesus Christ, not by any human being or by any church.

b) They were eye witnesses of the historic Jesus, either of His public ministry, like the twelve for three years, or of His resurrection, like Paul. Paul could be an apostle because he had seen the risen Lord (1 Cor. 9:1). 'Am I not an apostle?' he says. 'Have I not seen Jesus our Lord?' He could not have been an apostle if he had not seen the historic Jesus.

c) They were promised a special inspiration of the Holy Spirit as we read in John 14 and 16, to remind them of what Jesus had taught them whilst on earth, and to supplement that teaching, adding to it that 'He will guide you into all truth' (Jn. 6:13). Those great promises were fulfilled in the writing of the New Testament.

It is extremely important, in these days, to hold fast to the uniqueness of the apostles of Christ and to hold their unique authority as the apostles of Christ and so the unique authority of the New Testament. The New Testament is precisely the teaching of the apostles. It is in the New Testament that their teaching has come down to us in its definitive form.

Theological liberals are sometimes brash and foolish enough to say, 'Well that was Paul's opinion, but this is my opinion. Paul was a first-century witness to Christ, but I am a twenty-first-century witness to Christ.' And they claim an authority equal to that of the apostles. Recently, an American episcopal bishop said, 'We wrote the Bible, so we can rewrite it.' Excuse me, bishop, we did not write the Bible! Biblical authors did not write in the name of the church. On the contrary, they wrote to the church in the name of God, in the case of the Old Testament prophets and in the name of Christ, in the case of the New Testament apostles. That is why we receive their teaching as the Word of God, not as the word of men but as the Word of God.

As we start in the first four chapters of 1 Corinthians, let us not wander through the text like a gardener in a herbaceous border, picking a flower here and discarding a flower there. Let us not imagine that the New Testament is a collection of the fallible opinions of fallible human beings. Let us, rather, acknowledge and receive these chapters as part of the Word of God. Let us be ready to humble ourselves under the authority of the Word of God, determined that we will listen attentively to what He has spoken, with a view to believing and obeying it. For the New Testament is the teaching of the apostles and the apostles teach the Word of God.

So much then for Paul's self-description. He had been called to be an apostle of Christ. True, he also mentioned Sosthenes, but he only calls him 'our brother'. Sosthenes was not an apostle like Paul. Indeed, I weigh my words carefully, but we need to have the courage to insist today that there are no longer any apostles in the church. There are people who could be described as having 'apostolic ministries': bishops, superintendents, pioneer missionaries, and church planters. But there are no apostles comparable to the apostle Paul, or the apostle John, or the apostle Peter and if there were, we would have to add their teaching to the New Testament. There is nobody from the Pope downwards or the Pope upwards (whichever way you would like to put it), with that authority in the church today. These are the apostles of Christ and we submit to their authority in the New Testament.

b) Paul's Description of the Corinthian Church (v. 2)

The words 'to the church of God in Corinth' sound innocent enough, at first hearing, until we reflect upon them. Is it not extraordinary that such a community should exist in such a city? The church of God in Corinth. Let's think about Corinth. Its distinction is due mainly to its strategic location on the Corinthian Isthmus, where it commanded the trade routes north-south by land and east-west by sea. It was a manufacturing city and a trading centre which hosted the famous Isthmian Games every two years. It was also a religious city. Its temple to Aphrodite dominated the Acrocorinth behind the city and its temple of Apollo stood in the very centre of the town. It was also an immoral city. To 'corinthianize', the

Greek verb, meant to live an immoral life. It had political significance because it was the capital city of the Roman province of Asia. Thus Corinth was a busy, thriving, affluent and permissive city. Merchants and sailors, pilgrims and athletes, tourists and prostitutes jostled with one another in its narrow streets.

Yet, in this heathen city there lived a small group of people whom the apostle calls 'the church of God' – the divine community in the midst of the human community. Those were its two habitats simultaneously: it lived in Christ and in Corinth. It's a marvellous thought – it was like a fragrant flower growing in and out of rather smelly mud. It had two habitats – in Christ and in Corinth; two sanctities – actual and potential; and two callings – objective and subjective. God calls us to be holy and we call on God to make us holy. God calls us to be the holy people we are and we call on God to be the unique person He is according to His name. Indeed, it is only by calling upon God to be Himself, that we have any hope of becoming more truly ourselves as God intends us to be.

Fundamental, then, to New Testament Christianity is this ambiguity of the church and of salvation. We are living in between times. We are living in between the First and the Second Comings of Christ; between what He did when He first came and what He is going to do when He comes back. We are living between Kingdom come and Kingdom coming, between the 'now already' of the Kingdom inaugurated and the 'not yet' of the Kingdom yet to be consummated. And this living in between times is a key to our understanding of 1 Corinthians. The great John Newton, author of 'Amazing Grace', once said, 'I am not yet what I ought to be and I am not what I want to be. I am not what I hope to be in another world, but still I am not what I used to be. And I am, by the grace of God, I am what I am.'

Having looked at the apostle Paul, an apostle of Jesus Christ by the will of God, and at Corinth, we are now going to put the two together and see that Paul had a close, longstanding, affectionate, personal and pastoral relationship with the Corinthian church. It began in the year AD 50, when he first visited Corinth on his second missionary journey and founded the church there. If we use the three metaphors which he himself developed a little later in chapter 3, we may say that Paul planted the church; Apollos and others watered it. Paul laid the foundation of the church; others erected the superstructure on the foundation. He fathered the church; others were its guardians and its tutors. Over the years Paul visited Corinth at least three times and wrote to the church at least four times, although only two of his letters have survived.

That may have seemed a lengthy introduction, but I think we need to understand the background before we plunge into the text. Now you will notice, firstly, Paul *greets* the church (1:1–3), secondly, Paul *gives thanks* for the church (1:4–9) and thirdly, he *appeals* to the church (1:10–17). In each section, the greeting, the thanksgiving and the appeal, he singles out one essential characteristic of the Christian community. In relation to the first – *holiness*; in relation to the second – *giftedness*; and in relation to the third – *unity*. So let's look at these three.

1) Paul greets the church (1:1–3)

In his greeting he emphasizes the holiness of the church. What he has called the church of God in Corinth, he now also designates those who have been; it's a perfect tense, those who have been sanctified in Christ Jesus. And then he goes on to call them those who are called to be saints or called to be holy. The ambiguity is obvious: the church is already sanctified and it's not yet holy. Moreover, this is true of all those who, everywhere, call on the name of the Lord Jesus Christ, both their Lord and ours. So, on the one hand, the Christian community of the church of God, like Israel before it, was the holy people of God. Its members have been set apart to belong to God. He had chosen them to be His special people: that is their status, set apart and sanctified, to belong to God alone. On the other hand, as the coming chapters make clear, much unholiness lingered in the Christian community: quarrelling, pride, complacency, immorality, taking one another to court, disorders in public worship, boastfulness of spiritual gifts. This holy church of Corinth was very unholy. There is the first example of ambiguity.

2) *Paul gives thanks for the church (1:4–9)*

In his thanksgiving he emphasizes the giftedness of the church. In spite of its many failures he begins with this positive evaluation. Beginning at verse 4 he says, 'I always thank God for you,' and we can always thank God for one another. But what did he thank God for? First because God's grace was given to you in Christ Jesus. And that is surely a reference to their salvation, the grace of God had come to them and saved them. Next, verse 5, he gives thanks to God because in Christ you have been enriched in every way and by what he goes on to say, he is evidently thinking of their spiritual gifts, their knowledge and their ability to communicate the knowledge which they have been given. And finally, verse 6, because Paul's apostolic testimony to Christ had been confirmed in them. Christ had proved, in their own experience, to be everything which the apostle Paul said that He was. And for those things, the grace, the enrichment, the confirmation of the apostle's testimony, Paul gives thanks. In consequence, verse 7, you don't lack any spiritual gift.

It's an amazing thanksgiving to God. It sounds as if the Corinthian church was perfect, in every way enriched, in no way deficient, in other words – complete. Not, of course, that every individual Christian has all the spiritual gifts. We know that from chapter 12 in particular. A wide diversity or variety of gifts are given to different people and if you bring together all the lists of the charismata in the New Testament, there are at least twenty-one mentioned. So it isn't each individual that has all the gifts, but each local church may expect to have, collectively, all the gifts it needs. And yet, this is not the end of the story.

Even though the Corinthian church had been graced and gifted and enriched in Christ, so that they lacked nothing, they were not yet blameless. That's why they were still eagerly waiting for the revelation of our Lord Jesus Christ. In spite of everything He had given them, as a result of His First Coming, they were longing for His Second Coming, when they would become blameless. He would keep them strong until the end, and on the last day they would be blameless in His sight. How do we know that? Well, not because of our faith but because of God's faithfulness: 'Faithful is the God who called you into the fellowship of His Son Jesus Christ' (v. 9). So, one day He will perfect the fellowship into which He has already brought us. 'God called us' is a past reality; 'into the fellowship of Christ' is a present experience; 'God is faithful' is the ground of our confidence for the future. That beautiful verse 9 speaks of the past, the present and the future. So here is the second ambiguity of the church. First the church is holy, but is called to be holy. Second, the church is complete and yet it is incomplete, which is why we are eagerly waiting for the revelation of Jesus Christ.

3) *Paul appeals to the Corinthian church (1:10–17)*

In his appeal he emphasizes the unity of the church.
Herein lies the ambiguity: this united church is also
divided. The very same tension between the reality and
the ideal. Let's look back to verse 2 about the unity of the
church. Paul describes Corinth as *the* church of God, not
the churches of God. There may have been several house
churches, or house fellowships in Corinth, we don't
know for certain, but he still calls it *the* church of God,
one and undivided. I've no doubt God says to Himself
from time to time, 'I have only one church – it is the body
of Christ, it is the temple of the Holy Spirit, there is only
one church, *My* church.' Or again, we might say as Paul
does in Ephesians 4, there is only one family because
there is only one Father. And there is only one body
because there is only one Holy Spirit who indwells the
one body. There is only one faith, one hope, one baptism
because there is only one Jesus Christ in whom we have
believed, for whom we are waiting in hope and into
whom we have been baptized. The one Father creates the
one family, the one Christ creates the one faith, hope and
baptism and the one Holy Spirit creates the one body.
And there is only one church to which we bear witness
at Keswick. So a little later, in chapter 3, he will say, 'You
are God's field, you are God's temple, you are the body
of Christ.' Collective nouns which all declare the unity of
the church.

But we Christians, who are one, have nevertheless
succeeded in dividing from one another. We have divided the indivisible. We have made God's one and only
church into many churches and we ought to be ashamed
of ourselves. Like the Corinthian Christians, as Chloe's
household had told Paul in verse 11, although there was
one church it was torn apart by factions. Paul has given

thanks for them, but now he appeals to them. He has been affirming them, but now he rebukes them. And we need to look at that.

What can we learn from his appeal? Notice first, he addresses them as brothers (vv10,11), reminding them of the family of God in which all Christian people are sisters and brothers. But unfortunately, although they are all members of the family of God, they are contradicting that by their behaviour. Notice the basis of his appeal. It is in the one and only name of our Lord Jesus Christ – the name that is above every name, on which all Christian believers call (v2), 'the name into which we have all been baptized' (vv13,15). They named human names, I belong to Paul, I belong to Peter, I belong to Apollos. But as the great Chrysostom in the fourth to fifth century, one of the fathers of the church, says in his commentary, 'Paul keeps nailing them to the Name of Christ,' diverting their attention from Paul, Apollos and Peter, to Christ – the one and only Jesus Christ.

Paul repeats his appeal in verse 10, 'that all of you agree with one another so that there be no divisions with each other'. Already there are quarrels, but he says, 'Let there be no divisions among you . . . that you may be perfectly united in mind and in thought.' In verse 11 he goes into more detail about being informed about their quarrels by some members of Chloe's household, concluding in verse 12, 'What I mean is this: One of you says, "I follow Paul"; another, "I follow Apollos"; another, "I follow Cephas"; still another, "I follow Christ."'

Now there is much debate and discussion about the identity of these different groups in the church of Corinth. Some try to find different theologies here in contradiction with one another. The most famous is the theory of the nineteenth-century German theologian F.C. Baur, who was a New Testament professor at Tübingen in Germany.

He argued that in the early church there was a fundamental opposition between the Gentile party, headed by the apostle Paul, and the Jewish party, headed by the apostle Peter. He interpreted the whole of the New Testament in the light of this quarrel and antagonism between Paul and Peter, between Gentiles and Jews in the Christian community. He found support for his opinion here in this passage that we are looking at. But honestly, as we look at the text here, there is no evidence that these groups were divided by theology or by doctrine. No, they were divided by personalities not by principles. The groups are separated from one another by the cult of celebrities, by pride, by jealousy, by boastfulness, of their different church leaders, and all this deeply disturbed the apostle. He was their brother, he calls them my sisters and brothers, he is not their master, that they should think they belong to him. If anybody belongs to anybody in the church, he belongs to them, they don't belong to him.

So what about the fourth slogan, 'I belong to Christ'? How could one faction, in Corinth, possibly claim an exclusive monopoly of the Lord Jesus? All Christians belong to Christ, not one clique or faction within the church, and for that reason some suggest, and I myself believe this is correct, that although the first three were watchwords in the Corinthian church – I belong to Paul, to Apollos, to Peter, the fourth was not a fourth faction, but Paul's own indignant retort: You may say that you belong to Paul and Peter and Apollos, but as for me, I belong to Christ and not to any human leader.

This was serious. Although the divisions were not doctrinal in origin, they had profound doctrinal implications, especially in relation to Christ, to the gospel and to baptism. To show this, the apostle asks three leading questions in verse 13, all of which demand an emphatic 'No!' as the answer.

1) Is Christ divided? J.B. Phillips translates it, 'Is there more than one Christ? Are there lots of different Christs?' C.K. Barrett translates it, 'Has Christ been shared out? Fragments of Him being distributed to different groups in the church?' No! No! No! There is only one Christ.

2) 'Was Paul crucified for you?' Are you trusting for your salvation in Paul and him crucified? Answer: No! No! No! The idea is preposterous. Jesus Christ is our crucified Saviour in whom alone we have put our trust.

3) 'Were you baptized into the name of Paul?' No! No! No! Of course not! Baptism is into allegiance to Christ. We are baptized into Christ, as Romans 6 makes clear, into union with Christ in His death and resurrection. Thus you see the effect of their divisions was to undermine these essentials of the gospel. It was to deny there was only one Christ, who is the only one who died to be our Saviour, and into whose name alone we have been baptized. So clearly, the person of Christ, the cross of Christ, the name of Christ into which we have been baptized, are all at stake when the church divides. The Corinthians were insulting Christ, they were dislodging Him from His supremacy, they were replacing Him with human leaders.

Now, we move on to verses 14–17. Paul lingers on the topic of baptism. Because they were putting their emphasis in the wrong place, they were exalting the human baptizer, the person who actually did the dipping or the sprinkling, at the expense of the divine Christ into whom they had been baptized. Consequently Paul expressed his thankfulness for what he saw as the providence of God. Gordon Fee calls it, 'a simple uncalculated, historical reality: namely, that he had not baptized any of them'. Oh, wait a minute (having had a little lapse of memory), I did baptize Crispus the ruler of the synagogue and Gaius who became the host of the church, verse 15, so no one can say you were baptized into my name, Paul, and I did baptize 'the household of Stephanas; and beyond that I can't remember if I baptized anyone else' (v16), so comparatively unimportant is it, as to who does the baptizing. What matters in baptism is not the person by whom we were baptized but the Person *into* whom we were baptized – Jesus Christ Himself. Besides, Paul adds, verse 17, Christ had sent him, literally, Christ had apostled him, not to baptize but to evangelize.

Now Paul is not being derogatory to baptism; he knew that Jesus had instituted baptism, he knew it was an integral part of the great commission, he had not forgotten that. He had a very high view of baptism himself, as you can tell if you read Romans 6. But Paul's specialty, as an apostle of Christ, was evangelism and not baptism. He was a pioneer preacher, not a local church pastor and his speciality was the gospel not the sacraments which make the gospel visible.

Moreover, the second part of verse 17, the evangelism Paul was commissioned to do was not with words of human wisdom. Literally not in 'wisdom of word' lest the cross of Christ be emptied of its power. This phrase expresses a double renunciation which the apostle Paul had made. On the one hand, he renounced the world's wisdom in favour of the cross of Christ. That's what he preached. On the other hand, he renounced the skills of Greek rhetoric, which were so popular in the ancient Graeco-Roman world. Instead of human rhetoric, he trusted in the power of God the Holy Spirit. And that double renunciation of human philosophy, for content and human rhetoric, for form, is elaborated later. Charles Hodge, in his fine Reformed commentary from the middle of the nineteenth century, said, 'Paul was neither a philosopher nor a rhetorician after the Grecian school.'

Conclusion

The ambiguity of the church is the thing I am anxious we should take away and maybe you are thinking of your own church back home. We need to come to terms with it in this way. On the one hand biblical Christians are not perfectionists. We don't dream of developing a perfect church on earth. Billy Graham wisely says, 'By all means look for the perfect church and when you find it, join it, but remember when you join it, it ceases to be perfect.' On the other hand biblical Christians are not defeatists, or pessimists. We don't tolerate sin and error in the community as if it didn't matter.

To perfectionists we say, 'You're right to seek the doctrinal and ethical purity of the church, but you're wrong to imagine that you will ever attain perfection in this life. Not until Christ comes will He present His Bride, the church, to Himself – a radiant church without stain, wrinkle or blemish, holy and blameless.' To pessimists and defeatists we say, 'You're right to acknowledge the reality of sin and error in the church. You're right not to close your eyes to it and pretend that it is perfect when it isn't. But you're wrong to tolerate it.' There is a place for discipline in the church and even, in extreme cases, for excommunication. To deny that Jesus is the Son of God made flesh, to deny the incarnation, is anti-Christ. We cannot have fellowship with antichrists. And to deny or contradict the gospel of the grace of God, Paul says, is anathema. He called down the judgement of God on those who deny the gospel. In these central matters, about the person and the work of Christ, we cannot tolerate error or sin.

So this is the ambiguity of the church. The church *has been* sanctified, but it is still sinful and called to be holy. The church *has been* enriched, but it is still defective, eagerly waiting for the Second Coming of Christ. The church *has been* united, there is only one church of God in Christ, but it is still unnecessarily divided. So, we are living in between times: between Kingdom come and Kingdom coming; between the divine ideal and the human reality; between the already and the not yet. Not until Christ comes will the ideal become a reality and all ambiguity will cease. Hallelujah!

2. Power Through Weakness (1 Corinthians 1:18–2:5)

Introduction

Let us consider the five references to power in this passage:

1:17 'lest the cross of Christ be emptied of its power'.
1:18 'the message of the cross to us who are being saved is the power of God'.
1:24 'to those whom God has called Christ is the power of God'.
2:4 'my message and preaching were with a demonstration of the Spirit's power'.
2:5 'so that your faith might rest on God's power'.

And for the sake of completeness we could add:

2 Cor. 4:7 'to show that the all surpassing power is from God'.
2 Cor. 12:9 'so that Christ's power may rest upon me'.

Here you see seven references to power: the power of God, the power of Christ, the power of the cross and the power of the Holy Spirit.

This concentration on power makes an immediate appeal to us at the beginning of the twenty-first century because we live in a society which positively worships power. Indeed, the three major human ambitions, the pursuit of money, fame and influence, are all a concealed drive for power. We see this thirst for power everywhere: in politics and public life; in big business and in industry; in the professions; in primitive societies in which the shaman or witch doctor trades secret power for money.

Unfortunately, we also see it in the church – in top-level ecclesiastical power struggles, in denominational disputes, in some local churches in which the clergy hold the reins of power in their own hands and refuse to share it either with lay people or, still less, with young people. We see it in para-church organizations, which dream of expanding into world empires. And we also see it here in the pulpit, which is a very dangerous place for any child of Adam to occupy. Power is more intoxicating than alcohol and more addictive than drugs. As Lord Acton said, 'Power tends to corrupt and absolute power corrupts absolutely.'

Lord Acton was a nineteenth-century politician, a friend and adviser of Prime Minister Gladstone, and he was very disturbed, in his day, to see democracy being undermined by this lust for power. He was also a Roman Catholic and in 1870, which was the first Vatican council, he opposed the decision of the council to attribute infallibility to the Pope. He saw it as power corrupting the church.

Now, moving from the Roman Catholic scene to the evangelical scene, I want to tell you frankly that I am scared of the contemporary evangelical hunger for power. Even the quest for the power of the Holy Spirit. Be honest, why do we want to receive power? Is it honestly power for witness? Power for holiness? Power for humble service? Or is it really a mask for personal ambition so that we may boost our own ego? Minister to our own self-importance? Extend our influence, to impress, to dominate, to manipulate? The lust for power is a very dangerous thing and even some evangelism can be a disguised form of imperialism. It can build human empires instead of building the Kingdom of God. There is only one imperialism that is Christian and that is a concern for the imperial majesty of our Saviour, the Lord Jesus Christ. All other imperialisms are sinful.

The Bible contains clear warnings about the use and abuse of power. In the Old Testament, Uzziah, king of Judah, 'was greatly helped until he became powerful'. Then his pride led to his downfall. In contrast, in the New Testament, our Lord Jesus Christ is the perfect symbol of the weakness of humility. He said:

> You know that those who are regarded as rulers of the Gentiles lord it over them, and their high officials exercise authority over them. Not so among you. Instead, whoever wants to become great among you must be your servant, and whoever wants to be first must be the slave of all. For even the Son of Man did not come to be served, but to serve, and to give his life as a ransom for many (Mk. 10:42–5).

In other words, Jesus came not to wield power, but to renounce it. Not to be served, but to serve and to give.

At no point does the Christian mind come into more violent collision with the secular mind than in its insistence on the weakness of humility. The wisdom of the world does not greatly value humility. We've drunk in more than we realize of the power of Nietzsche's philosophy. He worshipped power, dreaming of the rise of a ruling Aryan race, that would be tough, masculine, brash and oppressive. He despised Jesus for His weakness. The ideal of Nietzsche was the *Übermensch*, the super man. The ideal of Jesus was the little child. There was no possibility of a compromise between those two images. We have to choose between them. It is necessary to see what we are going to study in the light of the contemporary lust for power. The central theme of the Corinthian correspondence is not power, as I may have seemed to indicate so far, but power through weakness, divine power through human weakness.

The apostle Paul brings together three striking illustrations of this very same principle

1) Power through weakness in the gospel itself (1:17–25). Because the weakness of the cross is the power of God.
2) Power through weakness in the converts (1:26–31). God has chosen the weak people to shame the strong.
3) Power through weakness in Paul the evangelist (2:1, 5). He says he came in weakness, looking to the demonstration of the Spirit's Power (vv. 3, 4).

Thus the gospel, the converts, and the preachers, or if you prefer it, the Evangel, the evangelized and the evangelist, all exhibit the same fundamental principle: God's divine power operates best in the arena of human weakness. That's the theme. God help us to absorb it and to live it out in our lives.

Power through weakness in the gospel itself (1:17–25)

Every communicator has to answer two questions: What have I got to say? and How am I going to say it? The first is the message and the second the method. In the first century AD of Graeco-Roman culture these two questions were readily answered. The 'what' of communication was philosophy, the 'how' of communication was rhetoric – an elaborate ornamentation of language and style. But Paul immediately renounced both. He refused to preach the gospel, as we saw previously in verse 17, in the 'wisdom of world'. In the place of human philosophy he put the cross; in the place of human rhetoric, the power of the Holy Spirit. And the cross was both the wisdom of God and the power of God. Paul enlarges on this position in verses 18–21 and in verses 22 and 25, with the hammer blows of repetition that are so important in all our communication, even today.

I am going to take verse 21 only, in the first example, because it's a beautifully chiselled sentence. In summary it says that, whereas the non-Christian world failed, through its own wisdom, to come to know God, it pleased God through the folly of the gospel, or the *kerygma*, to save those who believe. In verses 22–25 Paul elaborates the same thesis, namely, wisdom through the folly of the cross and power through the weakness of the cross. To do so he divides the human race into three sections: Jews, Gentiles or Greeks and Christians and he pinpoints the essential difference between them.

Firstly, verse 22, Jews demand miraculous signs. They were expecting a political Messiah who would drive the Roman legions into the Mediterranean Sea and re-establish Israel's lost national sovereignty. So the Jews demanded appropriate evidence from every revolutionary, every messianic pretender. Give us a sign of power to indicate to us that you are able to do what is expected of the Messiah and drive the Roman legions out of the country. That's why the Jews kept asking Jesus, 'What signs do you do that we may believe in you?'

Secondly, the Greeks search for wisdom. Greece had a very long tradition of brilliant philosophy. The Greeks believed in the autonomy of the human mind and they listened eagerly to every new idea, every speculation, as long as it seemed, to them, to be reasonable. So the Jews demanded power and the Greeks were in search of wisdom.

Thirdly, Christian believers, whether Jews or Gentiles, preach Christ crucified (v23). Notice the contrasting verbs. The Jews make demands, the Greeks are seeking and searching, but we proclaim Somebody: the Messiah crucified for us on the cross. But a crucified Messiah was a contradiction in terms. If He was going to drive the Roman legions out of the country, how could He be crucified on a cross? The very word Messiah meant power, splendour, majesty, triumph, and victory. The word crucifixion meant weakness, humiliation and defeat and this was the very opposite.

So the message of Christ crucified provoked different reactions. To the Jews He was a stumbling block. They were expecting this military Messiah riding on a warhorse, at the head of an army. Instead they were offered a pathetic, crucified weakling. It was an insult to their national pride. How could God's Messiah end His life under the condemnation of His own people? How could He end His life under the curse of God on the cross? It was impossible. A crucified Messiah was inconceivable. You can't put the two words together, they make nonsense. The cross was an absolute stumbling block to those who worshipped power.

To the Gentiles, Christ crucified was foolishness. Crucifixion, in the ancient Roman world, was not only a painful execution, it was also a public humiliation, reserved for the dregs of society – slaves and criminals. No free man or citizen was ever crucified. It was inconceivable to them that the Son of God should end His life on a cross. Cicero, the great Roman orator, said on one occasion, 'The very name of the cross, the very word of the cross is absent, not only from the bodies of Roman citizens, because they were never crucified, but also from their minds. They would not even think about it, or imagine it. From their eyes they would never watch a crucifixion and from their ears they would never listen to talk about it.' So horrific was the concept of crucifixion to them.

However, to those who are called God's own people (v24), irrespective as to whether they were Jews or Gentiles ethnically, Christ crucified is not weakness, but the power of God. It is not foolishness, it is the wisdom of God. 'For the foolishness of God is wiser than human wisdom and the weakness of God is stronger than human strength' (v25).

This whole text is embarrassingly relevant to us today. There are no first-century Jews or Greeks who have survived but there are many modern equivalents. The cross is still a stumbling block to all those who, like Nietzsche, worship power, who are confident in their own ability to get to heaven under their own steam, confident of themselves. Or at least if they cannot earn their salvation, they are convinced they can contribute to it. William Temple, Archbishop of Canterbury until he died in the forties, said this, 'The only thing of my very own which I contribute to my redemption, is the sin from which I need to be redeemed.' It is a non-contributory gift of God and we have to humble ourselves to receive it as a free gift.

I remember trying to explain this to a fellow undergraduate in Cambridge. He was very smooth and aristocratic and I was trying to humble him and tell him that he could not do anything to earn his own salvation. Suddenly, without warning, he shouted at the top of his voice, 'Horrible, horrible, horrible!' I was quite surprised. I didn't know I had said anything horrible, but I have often thanked God for that experience. It gave me a glimpse into the arrogance of the human heart. Because we worship power, we want to get there ourselves, make our own contribution. But the cross tells us it is impossible. Christ came and died to save us because we cannot save ourselves. So the cross is a stumbling block to the morally proud.

The cross is also foolishness to the intellectually proud. It makes no sense to them. Sir Alfred Ayer, the Oxford philosopher, hated Christianity and lost no opportunity to be rude about the gospel. As one of the pioneers of so-called logical positivism, he wrote *Language, Truth and Logic* and he said, 'Of all the historic religions there are good reasons for regarding Christianity as the worst. Why? Because it rests on the allied doctrines of original sin and vicarious atonement which are intellectually contemptible and morally outrageous.' That is our precious gospel: intellectually contemptible, morally outrageous. That's the wisdom of the world.

To God's people the cross is not weakness but power, it's not folly but wisdom. It's the power of God because through it God saves those who cannot save themselves and it's the wisdom of God because through the cross God has solved not only our problem of sin and guilt, but also His own problem. And it is not wrong to speak of a divine problem or a divine dilemma. We cannot avoid doing so: it arises from God's character of Holy Love. God's dilemma: how could He express His holiness in judging and punishing sin without comprising His love for sinners? Or, how could God express His love in forgiving sinners without comprising His justice in the judgement of sin? How could God be at one and the same time a just God and a Saviour? And God's answer was and still is the cross. Because on the cross He took our place, bore our sin, died our death and so paid our debt. On the cross, God demonstrated his justice (Rom. 3:25), and his love (Rom. 5:8). And in that double demonstration of love and justice the wisdom of God is displayed: His wisdom in the foolishness of the cross and His power in its weakness.

Power through weakness in the converts (1:26–31)

Paul had been inviting the Corinthians to reflect on the gospel and its weakness and now he invites them to reflect on themselves and their weakness. Consider the situation in Corinth. 'Not many of you were wise by human standards [of education]; not many were influential [in the community]; not many were of noble birth' (vv26–28). In other words, wisdom and power were not conspicuous among the Corinthians. Indeed the opposite had been the case. 'God chose the foolish things of the world to shame the wise; God chose the weak things of the world to shame the strong. He chose the lowly things of this world and the despised things – and the things that are not – to nullify the things that are' (v27). It's the same theme: wisdom through folly and power through weakness.

What was the purpose of God in this action? Why did God choose the weak and the foolish and the non-entities? He did it so that nobody might boast in His presence. So that it might be clear beyond any doubt that the credit for their salvation belonged to God and to God alone (vv29–32). They couldn't strut round heaven like peacocks displaying their plumage to show they had got there under their own steam. No! God chose the weak and the foolish to demonstrate that no human being may boast in His presence. So, verse 30, 'It is because of him', God, that they, the Corinthians, were 'in Christ Jesus'. They hadn't put themselves in Christ Jesus, God had put them in Christ Jesus. In consequence, Christ Jesus has become for us, on the one hand, the wisdom of God, on the other, the power of God – our righteousness which is justification, our holiness which is sanctification and our redemption which is the redemption of our bodies or our glorification. So all three tenses of salvation past, present and future, justification, sanctification and glorification are due to God's sheer grace, to His wisdom and power, displayed in and through the cross. Wonderful! Therefore, verse 31, quoting Jeremiah 9, he says, 'Let him who boasts boast in the Lord.' For all other boasting is excluded.

It's evident, from this paragraph, that most of the Corinthian converts were drawn from the lower ranks of society. Mostly, they belonged neither to the intelligentsia nor to the city's influential leaders, nor to its aristocracy. On the whole, they were uneducated, powerless, socially despised and probably most of them were slaves. The fact that the gospel reached, saved and changed them was a dramatic illustration of this principle of power through weakness. Is Paul saying that God never calls and saves those who are clever or wealthy, influential or socially prominent? It can't mean that. Saul of Tarsus himself was a notable exception. He had a powerful intellect and personality and yet he had been saved. And even in Corinth, Luke tells us, in Acts 18, Crispus was converted and he was the ruler of the synagogue and in Romans 16, we read, 'Greetings from Gaius,' who was wealthy enough to accommodate and give hospitality to the whole church in his house. And then there was Erastus who was the city's director of public works. Both letters imply that some Corinthian Christians were wealthy because Paul appeals to them to give generously to the impoverished church in Judea. We cannot say that God never calls and saves these people The key to the interpretation of these verses is that in verse 26 Paul writes not 'that not *any* of you' but 'that not *many* of you'. Selina the Countess of Huntingdon, the eighteenth-century evangelical aristocrat, a personal friend of John Wesley and George Whitefield, used to say, as she tried to introduce the British upper classes to the gospel, 'I thank God for the letter m in the word many.'

What do we conclude from this? Is it wrong to take the gospel to such elitist groups as students and professional people? No. Paul's emphasis is that God's power operates only in the salvation of the weak. And therefore, if the strong hope to be saved, they've got to become weak first. They have got to acknowledge their inability to save themselves. They may be influential in the community, they may have wealth, they may be very clever, but they have got to humble themselves and admit their weakness in this area: they cannot, by anything they do or contribute, save themselves. Otherwise, God's grace will never reach them. As Jesus said, 'The Kingdom of God belongs to children. Therefore if you adults want to get into it you have got to become like a little child, because the only citizens of the Kingdom of God are children and the childlike' (cf. Mt. 17:3–4). Luther understood the same message, 'Only the prisoner shall be free, only the poor shall be rich, only the weak shall be strong, only the humble shall be exalted, only the empty shall be filled and only nothing shall become something.'

Power through weakness in the evangelist (2:1–5)

Not only were the Corinthian converts weak and feeble but the apostle himself was also weak and feeble. As the great Hudson Taylor sometimes said, 'All God's giants have been weak people.' This was in contrast to the false teachers who liked to think of themselves as super apostles. They were nothing of the kind! They were proud, arrogant, conceited and self-confident, boasting of their wisdom, authority and power.

Notice the cultural background to this situation. Rhetoric, which I have already mentioned, was a systematic, academic discipline, taught and practised throughout the Graeco-Roman world. In the first century AD it had become the primary discipline in Roman higher education. In public debates, in the law courts, and at funerals the rhetoric of display and ornamentation was tremendously popular as a form of public entertainment. Dr Donald Carson has written, 'It is difficult for us, at the beginning of the twenty-first century, to appreciate how influential was this allegiance to rhetoric.' Gradually, it became an end in itself – mere ornamentation with a desire to please the crowd, but without any serious content, and without any serious intent. A sophist was an orator who emphasized style over substance and form over content.

That was the situation in Corinth, where the Christians had assimilated the rhetorical culture of their day and were evaluating Paul's speech according to the commonly accepted criteria. But Paul was resolved not to use ornamental rhetoric lest the audience focus on form rather than on content. And in this situation Paul made this double renunciation that I have already mentioned. He said 'not with words of human wisdom' (cf. 2:1), 'not with eloquence of superior wisdom'. In both texts he uses the same vocabulary – *sophia*, wisdom, is human philosophy, *logos*, utterance, is human rhetoric and he renounced the philosophy and the rhetoric of the Greeks. While the Corinthians loved both, Paul rejected both. In place of philosophy: nothing but the cross; in place of rhetoric: 'I came to you in weakness', as J.B. Phillips puts it, 'nervous and rather shaky.' So he relied on the demonstration, the *apodeixis*, which the Holy Spirit gives to words spoken in human weakness.

These words would not be a very accurate description to many of us contemporary evangelists. Weakness is not an obvious characteristic of ours. In theological colleges, homiletics classes classes in the topic of preaching), aim to inculcate self-confidence in nervous students. If Paul had enrolled in one of our Bible or theological colleges today, he would have been regarded as very unpromising material! And since he was supposed to be a mature Christian, we might even have rebuked him and said, 'Paul, you have no business to feel nervous. Don't you know what it is to be filled with the Holy Spirit? You ought to be strong and confident and bold.' But Paul was of a different opinion. He was not afraid to admit that he was afraid. He came to them in weakness and fear and trembling. True, he had this massive intellect and strong personality, but he was physically frail, we have not forgotten his 'thorn in the flesh', and he was emotionally vulnerable. Second-century tradition says that he was unattractive, small and even ugly with a bald head, beetle brows, bandy legs and a hooked nose. His critics said that his bodily presence was weak and his speech contemptible (10:10).

He was nothing much to look at and he was nothing much to listen to and these disabilities would have disqualified him from succeeding in rhetoric, so consequently in his human weakness he relied on the power of God. He called it a demonstration of the Spirit and the power. Commentators seem to think that really means a demonstration of the power, or by the power of the Holy Spirit, because every Christian conversion demands a power encounter between Christ and the devil, in which the superior power of Jesus Christ is demonstrated. The Holy Spirit takes our words, spoken in human weakness, and carries them home with power to the heart, the mind, the conscience and the will of the hearers, in such a way that they see and believe. This is the *apodeixis* – the demonstration by the Holy Spirit and His power.

Now don't misunderstand, this is not an invitation to suppress our personality or to pretend we feel weak when we don't. It's not an invitation to cultivate a fake frailty or to renounce arguments. Luke tells us, in Acts 18, that the apostle continued to argue in Corinth and in the following cities that he visited. The Holy Spirit brings people to faith in Jesus, not *in spite* of the evidence, but *because* of the evidence when He opens their eyes to attend to it. Argumentation and the work of the Holy Spirit are not mutually incompatible. The Holy Spirit uses the truth of our argumentation to bring people to Christ. And we must not give up that thoughtful kind of proclamation of the gospel, knowing that human beings cannot save souls, whether by their own personality or their rhetoric or any other power beside. Only the power of God can give sight to the blind and life to the dead and He does it through the gospel of Christ crucified, proclaimed in the power of the Spirit.

So the power in every power encounter is in the cross, for content, and in the Holy Spirit, for communication. I don't like speaking about myself, but let me illustrate with an example from my own experience what Paul writes here in his letter. Many years ago, in about 1958, I was leading a mission in the University of Sydney in Australia and on the final Sunday afternoon I lost my voice entirely. I didn't know what to do, but it was decided that I would do my best. Student leaders laid their hands on me and prayed for me along the lines of 2 Corinthians 12. 'Most gladly will I rejoice in my infirmities that the power of Christ may rest upon me.' They prayed that that Scripture might come true and in my weakness the power of Christ might come upon me. I croaked the gospel like a raven and when it came to give the invitation, people immediately rose from the hall of over a thousand, to come forward. I have been back to

Australia about ten times since then and every time somebody has said to me, 'Do you remember that meeting in the Great Hall of the University? I was converted that night.' I have learnt too that it is in our human weakness that the power of God is demonstrated.

Summary

The central theme of the Corinthian correspondence is power through weakness. We have a weak message – the cross, proclaimed by weak preachers, full of fear and trembling and received by weak hearers – the socially despised. But through that triple weakness the power of God was and still is displayed.

Conclusion

Remember in the Judaean desert the devil offered Jesus power and He declined the offer? Instead, He gave Himself voluntarily to that ultimate weakness and humiliation of the cross. In Revelation 4–7, when the door is opened in heaven, the first thing John's eye lit upon was a throne, symbol of power. Sharing the throne with God the Father was a Lamb, as He had been slain: the symbol of weakness on a throne of power. In other words, power through weakness dramatized in God on the cross or in the Lamb on the throne lies at the very heart of ultimate reality and even at the being of God Himself. We pray for one another that this mind might be in us which is and was in Christ Jesus. The Christian leaders, who are needed in the church today, are those who have seen the Lamb on the throne, and who follow the Lamb wherever He goes, knowing that power is best displayed in weakness.

3. The Holy Spirit and Holy Scripture (1 Corinthians 2:6–16)

Introduction

You will notice that there is a heavy emphasis in this passage on the ministry of the Holy Spirit where He is mentioned by name, either directly or indirectly, nine or ten times. In particular, the emphasis is on His teaching role as the Spirit of Truth. This is one of the most important New Testament passages in regard to the relation between the Spirit and the Word. We all know that Holy Scripture and Holy Spirit are supposed to have something to do with one another, because the Holy Scripture is the creative product of the Holy Spirit. We say, if we recite the Nicene Creed, that He spoke through the prophets. And we read that 'holy men spoke from God as they were moved [or carried along] by the Holy Spirit' (1 Pet. 1:21). We are going to investigate the precise relationship between the Spirit and the Word in this passage and the part played by the Holy Spirit in the composition of Scripture. Because we evangelical people acknowledge as one of our main distinctives our submission to the supreme authority of Scripture, this is a very important topic.

Before we come to the details, we need first to see the text in its context – a wise hermeneutic principle whenever we are studying Scripture. Everybody agrees that in chapter 2 verse 6 the apostle Paul's argument changes course. Up to this point, he has been emphasizing the foolishness of the gospel. But now, he says, 'We do, however, speak a message of wisdom among the mature.' Paul is not contradicting himself. To quote Professor F.F. Bruce in his commentary on 1 Corinthians, 'The wisdom Paul now says he proclaims is not something additional to the saving message of Christ crucified, it is in Christ crucified that the wisdom of God is embodied. It consists rather, in the more detailed unfolding of the divine purpose summed up in Christ crucified.' But although he says 'we do speak wisdom', he immediately adds three qualifications to be sure that he is not misunderstood:

a) It is wisdom for the mature.

The *teleiis* is the Greek word. It's not for the unregenerate, it's not even for babes in Christ. Since it is solid food and not milk, it cannot easily be digested. It is for mature Christians who are anxious to penetrate into the fullness of the saving purpose of God.

b) It is wisdom from God.

It's not the wisdom of this age, it's not human philosophy, it's not the wisdom of the rulers of this age, it's not the wisdom of the world. Beginning in verse 7, it is wisdom from God.

c) It is wisdom designed for our glory.

Doxa is the word used and it is essentially an eschatological word referring to our glorification at the end of time and in eternity, when Christ comes in sheer magnificence and we share in His glory and even our bodies are glorified. So the wisdom of God, for the mature, is not just good news of our justification, it is good news of glorification; it alludes to our final perfection as we share in the glory of God.

All this seems to mean that there is a legitimate difference between our evangelistic message on the one hand and Christian nurture on the other. In evangelism we proclaim the folly of the cross which is the wisdom and the power of God. We resolve to know nothing but Jesus Christ and Him crucified. And through this folly of the preached message, the *kerygma* or the gospel, God saves those who believe – that's evangelism and Christ crucified is at the very forefront of our evangelistic message. In Christian nurture, however, as we build people up into maturity, we want them to understand God's total purpose and especially our forthcoming glorification.

This, verse 7, is God's secret wisdom and it can be known only by revelation. Paul insists in verse 9, a rather loose quotation from Isaiah 64:4, God's wisdom is something which no human eye has seen – it's invisible; no human ear has heard – it's inaudible; and no human mind has ever imagined – it's inconceivable. It's altogether beyond the reach of our eyes, our ears and our minds. It cannot be grasped either by scientific investigation or by poetic imagination. It is absolutely unobtainable by our little finite, fallen and fallible minds. Therefore, if it is ever to be known, only God can reveal it, which is exactly what He has done, verse 10. Many people stop at verse 9, but you must always go on to verse 10. These things that cannot be known by the eye, the ear or the mind, God has revealed by His Spirit.

Let's think, for a moment, about the necessity of revelation. When the apostle says that not even human minds have understood it, he is not denigrating the human mind; he is simply saying that the human mind, capable as it is of remarkable achievement in the realm of the empirical sciences, when it is seeking God, it flounders helplessly out of its depth. And the Old Testament equivalent of verses 9 and 10 is surely Isaiah 55:8–9, where it says, ' "For my thoughts are not your thoughts, neither are your ways my ways," declares the Lord. "As the heavens are higher than the earth, so are my ways higher than your ways and my thoughts than your thoughts." ' Heaven being higher than the earth means infinity. And there is no ladder by which we can climb up into the infinite mind of God. If this little mind cannot fathom the infinite mind of God, how can we know His mind? Answer: we cannot if He remains silent. We could never even begin to know the thoughts of God and the mind of God unless He had spoken. Why, we cannot even read each other's minds, if we are silent, so how much less can we read the mind of God. But God has spoken. You know what is going on in my mind at this moment because I am speaking to you, I am communicating the thoughts of my mind by the words of my mouth. That is exactly what God has done: communicated the secret thoughts in His mind by the words of His mouth. He has spoken. That's how we know what He is thinking.

'God has revealed His thoughts to us by His Spirit' (v10). 'Us' is emphatic in the Greek sentence and it must surely refer not to all of us. We are not all direct recipients of a revelation of God. It must refer to the apostles who were the recipients of divine revelation, not only Paul himself, but by extension, his fellow apostles as well. I am reminded of Ephesians 3:5 where we read that the mystery of Christ, the truth about Christ, into which Jews and Gentiles can enter on the same terms, has now been revealed by the Spirit to God's holy apostles and prophets who are the foundation on which the church has been built (cf. Eph. 3:5; 2:20). So this is the context and now in what follows, Paul gives a comprehensive statement of the Holy

Spirit's work as the agent of divine revelation which he presents to us in four stages.

1) The searching Spirit (2:10, 11)

Notice that this verb, *searching*, shows quite clearly that the Holy Spirit is personal. You can't search and research unless you have got a mind, and if you have got a mind, you must be a person. Every research worker knows that it's part of their personality that they are searching for the truth. Computers analyse the data fed into them, but true research work requires original investigation and reflection. Because the Holy Spirit is a person, searching the deep things of God, we must never refer to Him as 'it'. He is a *He*, as Jesus made clear in His own teaching. Because He is a person He has a mind of His own with which He is able to think.

Now Paul develops two fascinating pictures to indicate the Holy Spirit's unique qualifications in the work of divine revelation.

a) He searches the depths of God (v. 10)

The verb used there, which means 'to investigate', is the very same word that Jesus has used, or the Greek translation of Jesus' Aramaic, when He applied it to the Jews who *searched* the Scriptures (cf. Jn. 5:39). It refers to diligent study and investigation. Moulton and Milligan, in their famous lexicon, *The Vocabulary of the Greek New Testament*, quoted third-century AD papyrus in which the searchers, using the same word, are customs officials who rummage about in our baggage whether we want them to or not. Further, the 'deep things', the Greek word there, became in the second century AD a favourite term used by the Gnostic heretics, who claimed to have been initiated into the deep things of God. It is just possible that in the middle of the first century, Paul deliberately borrowed from the Gnostic vocabulary, insisting here that the deep things of God were known and investigated, not by the Gnostics who claimed to have been initiated into the deep things of God, but by the Holy Spirit alone. Only the Holy Spirit can investigate the deep things of God. So the Holy Spirit is depicted as a restlessly inquisitive research worker, even a deep-sea diver who is seeking to fathom the deepest depths of the infinite being of Almighty God. The Holy Spirit is God exploring the infinity of God.

b) He knows the thoughts of God (v11)

'Who among men knows the thoughts of a man except the man's spirit within him?' In the same way nobody knows the thoughts of God except the Spirit of God Himself. Now the thoughts there are literally the *things* of a man or the *things* of God. Maybe the things of a man mean what we would call humanness – what it means to be a human being. So nobody understands what humanness means except human beings. An ant cannot possibly understand what it means to be a human being, nor a rabbit, a frog, or even a chimpanzee, for all the richness of the DNA that it apparently possesses. Nor even can one human being fully understand another human being. How often, especially as an adolescent, we complained, 'Nobody understands me!' It's true nobody does, in fullness – we don't even fully understand ourselves. Yet to some degree we human beings are self-conscious and self-aware and have some understanding of what humanness means. This is the concept of human self-awareness and self-consciousness that Paul applies to the Holy Spirit. 'In the same way nobody knows the things of God except the Spirit of God' (v11b). So the Holy Spirit seems to be likened to the divine self-consciousness or the divine self-understanding. Just as nobody can understand a human being, except that human being himself, so nobody can understand God, except God Himself. Only God knows God. It's reasonable because of His infinity.

To sum up this first truth about the Holy Spirit: the Holy Spirit searches the depths of God, and the Holy Spirit knows the things of God. Both statements indicate that the Holy Spirit has a unique understanding of God because He is Himself God. The question then is what has the Holy Spirit done with what He has searched out and come to know? Answer: He has done what only He is competent to do, He has revealed it. Only He knows God, so only He can make Him known. It's logical. The *searching* Spirit became:

2) The revealing Spirit (2:12)

What the Holy Spirit had searched out and come to know He went on to make known. This has already been stated in verse 10: God has revealed it to us, the apostles, by His Spirit. Let's look carefully at verse 12 where the apostle Paul enlarges on this. 'We', the same emphatic plural of apostolic authority, 'We have not received the spirit of the world, but the Spirit who is from God' – the searching Spirit, the knowing Spirit. And we have received the Holy Spirit in order 'that we might understand what God has freely given to us'. That indicates clearly that God had given the apostles not one, but two separate, related gifts.

Firstly, they received God's salvation, what God has freely given to us. What has He freely given to us? Eternal life – salvation. And secondly, He's given us

God's Spirit to enable the apostles to understand that salvation. The apostle Paul himself is the best example of having received this double gift of God. First the gift of salvation, then the gift of the Spirit to understand the gift of salvation.

Paul's letters give us a superb exposition of the gospel of grace. How God set His love upon the very people who didn't deserve it. How He sent His Son to die for sinners like us who didn't deserve it. How God raised Him from the dead to demonstrate that He had not died in vain. And how we, by faith inwardly, by baptism outwardly, may become united to Christ in His death and resurrection. It's a moving exposition, which stretches the mind and sets the heart on fire. Where on earth did the apostle Paul get all this wonderful doctrine from? How did he understand all this? How could he make such a comprehensive statement of salvation? Answer: because he had himself received salvation, and because he received the Holy Spirit to interpret his experience to him. Thus the searching Spirit became the revealing Spirit, making God known to the biblical authors, which became:

3) *The inspiring Spirit (2:13a)*

'This is what we speak . . .' (NIV), or 'we impart this . . .' (RSV). This understanding of salvation, which the Holy Spirit had given to the apostles, is now imparted. The searching Spirit, who had revealed God's plan of salvation *to* the apostles, went on to communicate *through* the apostles what they had received. Just as the Spirit did not keep His researches to Himself but revealed them to the apostles, so the apostles, in their turn, did not keep His revelation to themselves but communicated it to others in the New Testament. They knew that they were trustees of the revelation of God. They couldn't claim a monopoly on this divine revelation and keep it to themselves. Truth is for sharing. So they delivered to others what they had themselves received.

Next question: How did they impart the truth that had been revealed to them? Answer: verse 13, 'Not in words taught us by human wisdom but in words taught by the Spirit'. The same Holy Spirit, who searched the depths of God and who revealed God's secrets to the apostles, now gave the apostles the words with which to communicate them to others. Verse 13 is an unambiguous claim, on the part of the apostle Paul, to what we call 'verbal inspiration' – the inspiration of God extended to the very words which the apostles used in their communication. Those words had been given to them by the Holy Spirit. Now verbal inspiration is a very unpopular doctrine in the church today. And I strongly suspect that is because it is misunderstood and that what people reject is not the true meaning of verbal inspiration but something of their own creation.

Because this is so important I take the liberty of allowing myself a little digression, in order to try to explain what verbal inspiration means. I want to use three negatives about what it does *not* mean and one positive about what it *does* mean.

a) Verbal inspiration does *not* mean that every word of the Bible is *literally* (I emphasize that adverb) true. That's a dictionary definition of verbal inspiration. The true understanding of verbal inspiration does not mean that. No. The biblical authors used a number of different types of literature: history, poetry, proverbs, letters, an apocalypse and so on. There are about twenty different kinds of literature and not all of them are to be interpreted literally. Each is to be interpreted according to its own literary style. We interpret history as history, prophecy as prophecy, poetry as poetry and so on. So what is inspired is the natural sense of the word, according to the intention of each biblical author, whether it is literal or figurative. Some of the Bible is deliberately figurative. For example, 'The heavens declare the glory of God, the firmament shows his handiwork and in them [in the heavens] God has set a tabernacle [a tent], for the sun to live in. And it emerges like a bridegroom out of his chamber and runs like an athlete across the track of the heavens' (cf. Ps. 19). Within three verses the sun is likened to a tent dweller, an athlete, and a bridegroom. You are not going to interpret those literally, are you? Beware of biblical literalism when the biblical authors themselves are not intending you to interpret it literally.

Remember, Jesus Himself was an opponent of biblical literalism when He was speaking symbolically. He said to Nicodemus, 'You have got to be born again.' 'What?' said Nicodemus. 'Re-enter my mother's womb and be born?' 'Don't be such a biblical literalist,' Jesus said. (I am allowing myself a little freedom!) 'I am not talking about a second physical birth.' And then to the woman of Samaria He said, 'If you knew who it is that asks you for a drink, you would have asked of him and he would have given you living water.' 'But you haven't got a bucket,' she replied. He said to her, 'Don't be a biblical literalist. I am speaking of eternal life – symbolically, figuratively.' So we need to understand what type of literature it is. Verbal inspiration does not mean that every word is literally true.

b) Verbal inspiration does *not* mean verbal *dictation*. The Christian understanding of the Bible is very different from the Muslim's understanding of the Koran. Muslims believe that Allah, through the angel Gabriel, dictated the Koran to Mohammed, in Arabic, and that Mohammed had nothing to do but take down the dictation. Christians do *not* believe that about the biblical authors. On the contrary, we believe the biblical authors were persons in full possession of their human faculties. They were not dictating machines, even during the process of inspiration, taking down divine dictation. Thus every biblical author has his own literary style, his own theological emphasis, and these distinctives of each author are not ironed out or destroyed by the process of inspiration. Moreover, many biblical authors were historians. Have you thought how much of the Bible is history? Genesis, Exodus, Leviticus, Numbers, Deuteronomy, Joshua, Judges, Ruth, two books of Samuel, two books of Kings, two books of Chronicles: it's all history. Matthew, Mark, Luke, John, Acts: it's all history. We don't imagine that that history was all supernaturally revealed. No, they did their own historical researches. Luke tells us so. In Luke 1:1–4 he says he had diligently investigated the things that had taken part from the beginning. So divine inspiration and historical research were not incompatible with one another. It's important to remember that. Verbal inspiration does not mean verbal dictation.

c) Verbal inspiration does *not* mean that every text of Scripture is true even in isolation from its *context*. As the Lausanne Covenant said, 'The Bible is without error in all that it affirms.' But not everything included in Scripture is affirmed by Scripture and the best example is seen in the long and tedious speeches of the so-called comforters of Job. You cannot take anything out of the speeches of Job's comforters and declare it to be the Word of God, because they said that Job was being punished for his sins. But Job chapters 1 and 2 affirm that he was not a sinner, he was a righteous man. He feared God and avoided evil and when you come to chapter 42, the last chapter, God says that Job's comforters 'have not said about Me what is right'. God Himself contradicts Job's comforters. So some of what the comforters said is included, not in order to be endorsed, but in order to be repudiated. Now don't misunderstand me, the book of Job is the infallible Word of God *if* you take it as a whole, if you allow it to interpret itself, but each text is not the Word of God apart from its context.

d) To be positive, verbal inspiration means that what the Holy Spirit spoke through the biblical authors, understood according to its literary genre, understood according to the plain, natural meaning of the words used, understood according to its particular context and the intention of its authors – that is true and without error. There is no need to be ashamed or afraid of verbal inspiration if it is properly understood. It is eminently reasonable because words matter. They are the building blocks of sentences and it is impossible to convey a precise message if you do not choose precise words. I have prepared my lecture because I don't want to confuse you. I have a precise message to convey so I have chosen precise words in which to convey it. Words matter and if they matter to God they matter to us, and vice versa. In the nineteenth century Charles Kingsley wrote this, 'These glorious things, words, are man's right alone; without words we shouldn't know any more of each other's hearts and thoughts than the dog knows of its fellow dog.' We always think in words and without words all our thoughts would be mere blind longings, feelings which we could not understand ourselves.

So this is the apostolic claim: the same Holy Spirit who searches the depths of God and knows the things of God, who revealed His findings to the apostles, went on to communicate them to others through the apostles in words which He gave them. Thank God for that! He spoke His Word through their words in such a way that their words were simultaneously His words. This is the double authorship of Scripture: God spoke, as the author, through human authors; His words were their words at the same time. This is the meaning of inspiration.

4) The enlightening Spirit (2:13–16)

How are we now to think of those who received this and other letters from the apostle Paul and read them? Were they left to understand by themselves what had been written? Indeed not. The same Holy Spirit who was active in the apostles, who wrote the letters, is active in those who receive and read them. The Holy Spirit was working at both ends of the communicating process, inspiring the apostles and not inspiring us. We are not inspired when we preach and teach, but He illuminates our minds to understand the inspired Word of God. This is implied at the end of verse 13 which the NIV translates, 'expressing spiritual truths in spiritual words'. It's a complicated and rather enigmatic phrase and different English versions explain it in different ways. But I am assuming that the verb *sugkrino*, which can mean 'to combine', means here, as it usually does in the Septuagint (the Greek version of the Old Testament), 'to explain'. I think the RSV is right to translate it, 'interpreting spiritual truths to those who possess the Spirit'. In other words, the possession of the Holy Spirit is not limited to the biblical authors, He is shared by the Bible readers. Certainly I say again, the Holy Spirit's work of inspiration was unique to the prophets and apostles who were the biblical authors and we preachers must not claim to be inspired, as they were inspired. But to this inspiration of the biblical authors, the Holy Spirit added His work of illumination or interpretation.

Let's distinguish between these words. *Revelation* and *inspiration* are objective. They describe an objective process by which the Holy Spirit drew aside the veil, to reveal Christ and the biblical witness to Christ. *Illumination* is a subjective process by which the Holy Spirit enlightens our minds to understand the revelation that He has given us in Christ and in Scripture. Let me illustrate. Supposing you brought a friend, who is blindfolded, to the unveiling ceremony of a portrait. You have a veiled picture and blindfold eyes. Two processes are necessary before you can read what is written on the inscription under the portrait. First the portrait has to be unveiled. But your friend still can't read it because of the blindfold over his eyes. So the second process is to remove the blindfold so that he can read. For us, there has been an unveiling, which is revelation and inspiration, and an enlightenment, which is the work of the Holy Spirit today.

But what difference does it make? Verses 14 and 15 elaborate this truth and are in stark contrast to one another. Verse 14 begins with a reference to the *psuchikos*, the person without the Holy Spirit, the unregenerate, the natural man (AV). Verse 15 is about the *pneumatikos*, the Christian with the Spirit, the born-again believer. This person with the Spirit discerns or evaluates all things. He has not become omniscient, or infallible, but the things to which he was before spiritually blind, now begin to make sense to him. He understands what he did not understand before, even though he himself is not understood and is discerned by nobody. These details are a little bit difficult, but we understand this: the Christian remains something of an enigma to other people because of the inner secret of his spiritual life which they have not experienced or understood.

I want to ask again, what difference does it make whether you are born again or unregenerate? The answer is that it makes all the difference in the world. It is the indwelling of the Spirit who enlightens our minds to grow in our understanding of the Word of God. And this illumination of our minds, by the Spirit, is a common Christian experience. I can bear witness to it. I used to read the Bible, as a teenager, because my mother had taught my sisters and me to do so. And I continued to do so out of respect for her, but it was all double Dutch to me, I had no idea what it meant. When I came to Christ and was born again, I am not saying that everything was clear, it isn't today, but immediately it began to make sense in a way that it had never done before. William Grimshaw, the eighteenth-century evangelical leader, said after his conversion, 'If God had drawn up His Bible to heaven and sent me down another one it could not have been newer to me than it was.' The Bible becomes a new book, a light unto our path.

Let me digress, because I think there will be in your minds this question: 'If the Holy Spirit is the enlightening Spirit, if He is the illumining Spirit, why don't we agree with one another more than we do? Why do we still disagree? If He enlightens you and He enlightens me, ought we not to agree more than we do?' Well, my general answer is this: we *do* agree with one another a great deal more than we disagree, otherwise we wouldn't be at Keswick. We are all 'one in Christ Jesus' and I would suspect that if we compared notes we would probably agree in 90 to 95 per cent of what we believe. I think we would agree even more with one another if we fulfilled the following conditions:

1) We must accept the supreme authority of Scripture. The big and painful divisions in the church are between the Reformed and the un-Reformed churches, between those determined to submit to Scripture and those who are unwilling to do so.

2) We must remember that the chief purpose of Scripture is to bear witness to Christ as Saviour. So that in the central truths of the Bible about Christ and salvation by grace alone through faith alone, Scripture is perspicuous – it's plain, it's transparent, you can see through it. It's in secondary matters that we allow ourselves some liberty for the interpretation.

3) We must develop sound principles of biblical interpretation. It is often said, 'You can make Scripture teach anything you like,' and I agree. You can make Scripture mean anything if you are unscrupulous enough. But if you are scrupulous in the proper use of interpretation, far from you manipulating Scripture, you'll find that Scripture controls you.

4) We have to study Scripture together and not only by ourselves. The church is the hermeneutical community, within which God means His Word to be interpreted. And it's very good not only to read Scripture on our own but to read it in a Bible study group, so that we can help each other, especially if our group is multicultural, to see through each other's eyes things to which we ourselves have been blind. And that's what Paul meant in Ephesians 3:18, 'that we may . . . together with all the saints . . . [not by ourselves in isolation] grasp. . .' the full dimensions of His love. We need each other.

5) We must come to the biblical text with a humble, open and receptive spirit, ready for God to break through our cultural defences and to challenge and change us. If we come with a closed mind, then we shall never hear the thunderclap of the Word of God, all we shall hear is the soothing echoes of our own cultural prejudice. We shall see what we want to see, unless we cry to God to open our eyes, not just to behold wonderful things in His law. He might say, 'What makes you think I have wonderful things to say to you? I actually have

some rather disturbing things. Are you prepared to listen?' 'Oh no!' we say. 'I come to the Bible to be comforted, I don't come to the Bible to be disturbed.' And so we go on in our prejudices because we are not willing to learn. But if we come to Scripture with an open, unprejudiced, humble, receptive mind there is no knowing what God may show us. He continues His work of illumination today.

Conclusion

I end with a little illustration from Charles Simeon, for 54 years the vicar of Holy Trinity in Cambridge at the beginning of the last century, who said, 'If you go out into the garden on a cloudy day when the sun is not shining, and you look at the sundial, all you see is figures but no message. But if the sun breaks through the clouds and shines on the sundial, immediately the finger points.' If I come to Scripture on a cloudy day, with sin between me and God, I will not receive any message from the Word of God; it is just ink and paper. But if the sunlight of the Holy Spirit breaks through on the printed page of my darkened mind and God says, 'Let there be light,' then the finger points and I receive a message that I would never have received otherwise. So the Word and the Spirit belong together. No word without the Spirit, and the Spirit's sword is the Word of God. Let's never separate what God has united in Spirit and Word.

4. The Trinity and the Church (1 Corinthians 3)

Introduction

At the beginning of this chapter the apostle refers to the divisions, *schismata*, of the Corinthian Christian community and as he does so, he attributes these divisions not only to sins like jealousy and quarrelling but also to their fundamentally defective understanding of the church. His thesis can be simply stated: if they had a true view of the church, they would have a true view of church leaders. Indeed, if they had a higher view of the church, they would have a lower, more modest view of the leadership and there would be no boasting about men.

Corinthians 3 is one of the greatest New Testament chapters on the church. We evangelicals are often justly criticized for being rugged individualists and for having a poor doctrine of the church. In so far as we do have a poor doctrine of the church, we have departed from the New Testament which has a high view of the Christian community as a community unlike any other community throughout the world and history. So may God give us a balanced, modest and biblical view and understanding of the church.

The connecting link between chapter 2 and chapter 3 is obvious. In chapter 2:14 Paul had insisted that spiritual truths can be discerned only by spiritual people and now he tells the Corinthians, quite bluntly, that they do not qualify as spiritual people – they are unspiritual. 'Brothers, I could not address you as spiritual people,' *pneumatikoi*, 'but as worldly' (v1). That's the NIV interpretation, which I think it is an unfortunate translation because Paul's reference is not to the world, *cosmos*, but to the flesh, *sarx*, and the flesh is of course our fallen, self-centred, self-indulgent nature. And in calling them fleshly, *sarkinoi*, or *sarkikoi* (both words are used in different texts), he is not suggesting that they are unconverted. He doesn't call them natural, *psuchikoi*, the word he used in chapter 2:14 for those who don't possess the Holy Spirit. No, they have the Spirit, he addresses them as sisters and brothers, but on the other hand, they are not truly spiritual Christians, governed and controlled by the Holy Spirit. So the apostle uses this term, *sarkinoi*, or *sarkikoi*, developing the same antithesis with which we are familiar from Romans 8 and Galatians 5, between those who live according to the Spirit and those who live according to the flesh – their self-centred, self-indulgent fallen human nature.

Paul has a second way of saying the same thing at the end of verse 1. He describes the Christians not only as carnal or fleshly but as mere babies in Christ. They have been regenerated by the Spirit but they are still infants, *nepios* in Christ. They had not yet become *teleios*, mature, the word he used in chapter 2:6. Don Carson says that they were 'wretchedly, unacceptably, spiritually immature'. That is their position and I fear that Paul would say the same thing to many Christian congregations throughout the world today. We rejoice in the statistics of church growth evident in many parts of the world. But we don't always remember that it is often growth without depth. There is superficiality and immaturity everywhere in the Christian community today. By what criteria did the apostle conclude the Corinthians were carnal not spiritual, that they were babies and not mature? You can tell a child's age in two main ways: diet and behaviour.

a) Diet

'I gave you milk, not solid food, for you were not yet ready for it. Indeed you are still not ready' (v2). Just as babies begin with milk that is easily digestible and only gradually go on to solid food, so Paul had been obliged to feed the Corinthians with spiritual milk – the rudiments of the faith, because they were not yet ready for the meat of the Word of God. In spite of their knowledge (you remember from chapter 1 they had been endowed with knowledge) and the fact that they had been enriched with many spiritual gifts, they were still at an elementary stage in their Christian life. As C.K. Barrett writes in his commentary, 'That was a hard saying for the Corinthians.' They were very pleased with themselves, very complacent. 'But,' the apostle says, 'you are babies. You haven't yet grown up.' What is the difference between meat and milk? Paul is certainly not saying that the cross is rudimentary teaching which Christians later grow out of; we never graduate from the school called Calvary. C.H. Hodge writes, 'The difference between milk and strong meat is simply the difference between the more or less perfect development of the things that are taught.' Gordon Fee says, 'The argument implies that for Paul the gospel of the crucified One is both milk and solid food. As milk it is the elementary good news of salvation. As solid food it is understanding that the entire Christian life is predicated on the same reality of the cross.' I think it is important for us to understand that. We don't grow out of the cross. We grow deeper into the cross and the fullness of its implications. So the continuing need for milk is the first evidence that the Corinthians were babies in Christ, were carnal rather than spiritual. The second criterion by which Christian maturity can be evaluated is:

b) Behaviour (v3)

'Since there is jealousy and quarrelling among you, are you not worldly?' or literally, are you not fleshly, carnal? The answer is, of course, yes, because both jealousy and quarrelling are found among the works of the flesh in Galatians 5 – the works of our lower, fallen, self-centred, self-indulgent nature. Then Paul adds, 'If you are quarrelling and are jealous of one another, are you not mere men?' That is to say you are behaving *kata anthropon*, according to a human being, following human instead of divine standards. 'For when one says, "I follow Paul," and another, "I follow Apollos," are you not mere men?' Are you not human rather than godly in your outlook? Now I wonder if you've ever noticed Paul's threefold indictment of the Corinthian Christians.

1) Their behaviour was carnal and not spiritual. They were controlled by their selfish nature instead of the Holy Spirit.
2) It was babyish and not mature. They were suffering from what Freud would have called 'infantile regression' – going back to their babyhood having never grown up.
3) They were human and not divine. Their mindset was not godly but ungodly.

Those are three very serious allegations of the Corinthian community and the evidence for their carnality, immaturity and ungodliness was partly their doctrinal diet – still learning the A B C, and partly their moral failures – their jealousy and their quarrelling.

I hope that all of us are really concerned that the church, our church, will grow into maturity. Because I think there are many church leaders here, I venture to digress a moment and ask if you are very familiar with Colossians 1:28–29? I believe that those two verses are a great motto for any minister or church leader to have. This is what the apostle writes: 'We proclaim Christ, warning everybody and teaching everybody in all wisdom in order that we may present everybody mature in Christ.' That was Paul's ambition. Now we think of him as a missionary, a church planter and an evangelist. However, he is not just concerned with the planting of the church, but that it will grow into maturity in Christ. And his desire is that everybody should do so. This is not out of anybody's reach. We proclaim Christ, warning *everybody*, teaching *everybody*, in all wisdom that we may present *everybody* mature in Christ. What a motto to have! What an ambition and a goal to have for the congregation that God has called us to serve.

Now the apostle delves deeper. He argues that the Corinthians have a defective understanding of the church, or they would not behave as they were doing, and he develops three pictures of the church, all of which have important implications.

1) You are God's field (5–9a)

Paul uses an agricultural metaphor. He begins by asking two indignant questions, 'What, after all, is Apollos? And what is Paul?' (v5). He doesn't politely ask, '*Who* do you think we are?' He deliberately uses the neuter, '*What* do you think we are that you should pay us such an exaggerated deference?' As Bishop J.B. Lightfoot comments, 'The neuter is much more emphatic than the masculine, it expresses greater disdain.' He is debunking himself and Apollos. We are not masters to whom the Corinthians owed their allegiance, we're only servants, *through* whom you came to believe, not servants *in*

whom you came to believe. We are not the objects of
your faith; we are not the authors of your faith; we are
only instruments through whom God has been at work
in order to elicit your faith. And further, this came about
as the Lord Jesus has assigned to each his task (v5a). So
neither the Corinthians nor their leaders had anything to
boast about.

In verses 6–8 the apostle identifies the different tasks in
the church, illustrating them from his agricultural
metaphor – you are God's field – and applying them to
himself and Apollos. There are three main tasks to be done
if a field is ever to produce a harvest: first, planting the
seed, second, watering the seed and third, causing the seed
to sprout – sowing, irrigation and growth. So how does
Paul apply this to the Corinthian experience? Answer: he
applies it chronologically, verse 6, 'I planted the seed,' he
said, 'I was the first to come to Corinth.' He came during
his second missionary journey about AD 50. He planted the
seed, he planted the church. After him came Apollos who
watered the seed that the apostle Paul had planted and
then he moved on. These two men did their pioneer tasks
in relation to the seed, but God made it grow.

The tenses of the verb, in the Greek sentence, enforce
this. In verse 6, 'I planted' is an aorist. Paul came to
Corinth, did his job, moved on. Then came Apollos who
watered the seed and that verb, 'watered', is another
aorist. He did what he had to do and then he too moved
on, but God made it grow. And that is an imperfect tense,
so that all the time when Paul was sowing, and Apollos
was watering, God was giving the growth, causing the
seed to sprout. So Paul's and Apollos' ministries would
not have been of any great value if God had not given
growth to the seed.

Now Paul compares the three actors involved, Paul,
Apollos and God, with each other. In the evangelization

of Corinth and the establishment of the church there, verse 7, neither the planter nor the waterer is anything because both the planting and the watering are unskilled and somewhat mechanical jobs. Anybody can do them, it doesn't require any professional expertise to drop seeds into the soil and water them. What really matters is neither the planting nor the watering, but rather the causing of the seed to sprout and to bear fruit. No human being can do it. Paul couldn't do it with all his apostolic authority; Apollos couldn't do it with all his knowledge of the Scriptures and his famous eloquence. Only God makes things grow.

Now Paul adds a further point, which demonstrates the stupidity of the Corinthians' behaviour. So far he has insisted that the planters and the waterers count for nothing in themselves, so it is silly to exalt their ministries. They have one purpose (8a), and their different tasks of planting and watering serve the same goal, namely, to secure a good harvest, so it's silly to put them in competition with one another. Further, each will be rewarded according to his labour (8b). God will do this on Judgement Day, so it's silly of the Corinthians to anticipate the Day of Judgement by promoting different personalities now. And the conclusion, verse 9, is, 'We are God's fellow workers; you are God's field.' Since the aim of the whole passage is to downplay the role exercised by human leaders, it seems very unlikely that it means we are the privileged workers with God. That is, He is working there and we are working there and we are doing it together. It is much more likely that it means we are fellow workers, that is Paul and Apollos, in the service of God. He is not speaking here of the privilege of working with God, as the Revised English Bible translates it, 'We are fellow workers in God's service.'

What can we learn from this first, agricultural metaphor? The metaphor of the field, the planting, the watering, the giving of the increase does not teach everything about Christian ministry. It's always dangerous to push an analogy beyond the point at which the metaphor is being made or the analogy is being drawn. It's very dangerous to argue from an analogy, that because the church is a field, therefore everything about fields has a parallel in the church. No, we have to ask, at what point is the analogy being made? This says nothing about spiritual gifts or gifts in distinction to roles and offices, or the honour that is attached to being an evangelist or a missionary or a pastor; other passages of the New Testament teach those things – this one doesn't. There is one main point that this is intended to teach: we human workers have very little importance in comparison with God who gives the growth. God allocates the tasks, God gives the growth, God rewards the labourers, so we must not give glory to ourselves, as leaders, or to our fellow workers, but to God alone. The church would be a much happier place and a much more harmonious community if we remembered this elementary principle. We don't matter in comparison to Him.

2) You are God's building (9b–16)

Paul moves on to an architectural metaphor. Whether we are cultivating a field or whether we are erecting a building, we are a team – a team of farmers, a team of builders. We are not labouring on our own. We are serving a common enterprise and we are pursuing a common goal. Just as in God's field one plants and another waters, so in God's building one lays the foundation, another erects the superstructure upon it. However, the two metaphors don't make precisely the same point. The emphasis in God's field is that only God gives the growth and the emphasis in God's building is that only Christ is the foundation. Indeed, Christ crucified.

So once again the apostle Paul applies the metaphor to himself, to Apollos, to other church leaders in Corinth, 'By the grace that God has given to me' (v10), a phrase that comes five times in his letters, and always refers to his commissioning as an apostle of Jesus Christ. 'By the grace that God has given to me, I laid a foundation as an expert builder.' The word expert is *sophos*, meaning wise. I am a wise builder. Perhaps he is again saying that the true wisdom is Christ even though he seems to be folly to some people. Certainly Paul has been given the pioneering task of preaching Christ crucified. And he goes on, 'but somebody else is building on the foundation that I laid.' There is no mention of Apollos by name here, because several teachers have followed Paul, both good and bad, both true and false.

His main point is to sound a warning that all of us who are Christian teachers need to heed. It's a warning both about the foundation we lay and about the superstructure we erect upon it. Each one should be careful how he builds. And what carefulness does the apostle have in mind? Well, think first about the foundation. Builders, having laid the foundation, should not tamper with it. They should not try to dig it up or relay it. Because (v11) there is only one foundation and nobody can lay any other foundation except the one that is already lying there, which is Jesus Christ. This is the foundation that Paul lays (v10). 'The church's one foundation is Jesus Christ her Lord' – the only authentic Jesus Christ there is, not some false Christ, but the Christ of the apostolic witness, Christ crucified and also, of course, risen and reigning. C.K. Barrett writes, 'Paul doesn't mean that it would be impossible to construct a community on a different foundation, but only that such a community would not be the church. The church only exists when it is built upon the one foundation of Jesus Christ.'

We move on to the superstructure. Builders must be very careful about the materials they use in the erection of the superstructure and, broadly speaking, there are only two possibilities. Either gold, silver and costly stones, probably meaning not jewels, but a stone like marble. These are valuable and durable and they represent the true teaching which will stand the test of time and of the Judgement Day. Or, the alternative is cheap, perishable materials like wood, hay and straw, representing false teaching, the wisdom of the world. In both cases (v13), the quality of the material used by the builders, that is by the teachers, will be shown for what it is because the Day of Judgement will bring it to light. It will be revealed by fire which will test the quality of every teacher's instruction.

What will be the result of this trial by fire? Answer: just as there are two possible materials, so there are two possible consequences. Either (v14) the builder's work will survive because it has been made of durable material – gold, silver, marble – and the builder will receive his reward. Or (v15), his work will be consumed because it is made of combustible materials – wood, hay and straw, in this case he will suffer loss. His teaching will not survive, it will be seen to be valueless, and he will lose his reward. But he himself, in the mercy of God, will be saved, although only as one escaping through the flames – or as we might say, 'by the skin of his teeth'. He will not lose his own salvation even if what he has taught will all be burnt up as valueless. There is no allusion here to purgatory; the fire is not a purgatorial fire. The reference in this passage is to teachers, in particular, and not to all believers, who Roman Catholics believe will have to pass through purgatory. The purpose of the fire is not to purify here, as in purgatory, but to test teaching and pass judgement on it.

There is a solemn warning here to all Christian teachers. The Christian teaching ministry is very important. It is designed to build up the church into maturity and we must be sure that our teaching is authentically Christian. If what we teach is true, biblical, balanced, we will be adding gold, silver and marble to the foundation and it will last. But if what we teach is unbiblical, the wisdom of the world, then we are adding a ramshackle superstructure of wood and hay and stubble which will not survive. Thus what we teach may either bless the church or harm it. It may last only for a time or it may last for eternity. So let us be careful if we are Christian teachers. May God enable us to be all the more conscientious in what we teach.

3) *You are God's Temple (16–17)*

This is an extension of the architectural metaphor because a temple is a building, but it is a special kind of building. And the apostle develops it differently because he is thinking of the Holy of Holies. It is, then, an ecclesiastical or religious metaphor. He begins (v16) with, 'Don't you know that you are the temple of God?' Paul asks that question, 'Don't you know?' ten times in 1 Corinthians. He obviously thinks that Christian knowledge is very important. 'Don't you know that your body is the temple of the Holy Spirit?' 'Don't you know that you belong to Christ?' 'Don't you know that the local church is God's sanctuary?' 'Don't you know this?' His implication is this: if you did know it, you would behave differently. Knowledge is in many ways the secret of sanctification. We need to know these things, to take them in and to understand them, to act upon them, and then our behaviour will be different. So Paul attributes the Corinthians' failures to their ignorance or their forgetfulness of some truth.

In the Old Testament the essence of the temple and of the Holy of Holies in Jerusalem, as in the tabernacle before it, was that it was the dwelling place of God. 'I will dwell among them' (Ex. 25:8). And God promised that the shekinah glory, the symbol of His presence, would inhabit and illumine the Holy of Holies. Notice the major promise about the rebuilt temple, ' 'And the name of the city will be: The LORD is There,' (Ezek. 48:35). It's very clear in the Old Testament.

In the New Testament God's temple or dwelling place is not a building but a people. Now it is the individual Christian's body. 'Don't you know that your body is the temple of the Holy Spirit?' Now it is the local church as here in verse 16 and indirectly in Ephesians 2:22, 'In Christ you are being built together to become a dwelling in which God lives by His Spirit.' So the individual Christian, the local community, the universal community are all said to be the temple in which God dwells. And in His sanctuary today, the church, there is neither an image as there was in pagan temples, nor a symbol, like the *shekinah* glory, but the Holy Spirit of God Himself, in person. So the sacred wonder of the church is that it is the dwelling place of God by His Spirit.

Of course, as I have said, the church means people and not buildings. God's presence is not tied to buildings. God's presence is tied to His covenant people, His redeemed people whom He has promised never, never, to forsake. So wherever *they* are *He* is also, as in this tent. When we leave the tent we do not leave Him and He does not leave us. He is with His people always, especially in our worship when thousands gather together, there He is through Christ by the Holy Spirit in the very midst of His people. Wonderful!

Because of the sacred nature of the Christian community, as the dwelling place of God, it must not in any way be dishonoured, either divided by jealousy and quarrelling or deceived by false teaching, or defiled by immoral conduct. These are acts of sacrilege which effectively destroy the Christian community as the temple of God and that's why Paul goes on to say, 'If anybody destroys God's temple, God will destroy him' (v17), perhaps the most severe saying in the whole of this letter. And surely, the one who destroys the temple cannot be a true believer. He must be, probably, a nominal Christian. He will be destroyed, and I fear that must mean hell, because hell is often referred to as destruction in the New Testament.

We need to keep reminding ourselves that the church is the temple of God. Our local church may be full of unpleasant people we don't like, but when we see these people we need to whisper under our breath, 'You are the temple of the living God. God, through Christ, by His Spirit dwells within you.' And how we should love those who are the temple of God.

You will have noticed Paul's Trinitarian portrait of the church which highlights the role of God, Father, Son and Holy Spirit, in relation to the church. And because it exalts God, Father, Son and Holy Spirit, it downplays the role of human beings. What matters most about the church, as God's field, is that God Himself causes the growth. What matters most about the church, as God's building, is that Jesus Christ is its only foundation. And what matters most about the church, as God's temple, is that it is the dwelling place of the Spirit. This is the apostle's vision of the church: it owes its existence and its growth to God the Father, it's built on the foundation of

God the Son and it's indwelt by God the Holy Spirit. It is a unique Trinitarian community. And there is no other community in the world which even remotely resembles it.

In verses 18–23 the apostle wraps up his godly perspective on the church with further reference to wisdom and folly. The wisdom of God includes this new community that he has been writing about, so if the Corinthians belittle God's church by exalting human beings, they are showing their folly and not their wisdom. 'Do not deceive yourselves. If any one of you thinks he is wise by the standards of this age [according to the prevailing wisdom of this age], he should become a fool [in the eyes of the world] so that he may become wise [truly wise that is]. For the wisdom of this world is foolishness in God's sight' (18,19). And Paul goes on to quote two verses from the wisdom literature of the Old Testament, one from the Psalms, the other from Job, both of which express God's rejection of worldly wisdom.

So what is needed? The Corinthians need to repent of their boastful, self-centred human wisdom. They need to develop a new humility, summed up at the beginning of verse 21, 'no more boasting about men'. That is the climax to the chapter and the verse I want you to take away with you. Paul goes on to finalize his argument. Instead of taking pride in their leaders, and claiming to belong to their leaders, the exact opposite was the case: 'All things are yours, Paul is yours, Apollos is yours, Peter is yours' (v21b). In other words, far from belonging to their leaders, saying 'I belong to Paul,' their leaders belong to them. Don't say, 'I belong to Paul, I belong to Apollos,' because Paul and Apollos and Peter are yours – you are not theirs. More than that, not only are their leaders theirs, but all things are theirs, including the world, life, death, the present, the future – 'it's all yours' – an incredible statement.

And the reason it is ours is that we belong to Christ and it belongs to Christ. He is the heir of all things and we are in Him, so we are fellow-heirs with Christ, and everything that He will inherit, we will inherit.

This question of who belongs to whom in the Christian community is still vital today. When I was ordained as a deacon in the Church of England, more that fifty years ago, you were taught, when writing to your bishop, to begin, 'My lord', or 'My lord Bishop', and to end, 'I am your lordship's obedient servant'. I gave it up after the first few letters, because I reckoned if anybody was anybody's obedient servant, he was mine!

Along the same lines, I doubt if pastors are wise if they ever use the possessive adjective in relation to the church, referring to 'my church', 'my congregation', 'my people', because they don't belong to us. We have no proprietary rights over them. It would be entirely biblical for them to refer to us as 'their minister', 'their pastor', but we should not refer to them as 'our people'. When we speak of them it would be much more modest to say, 'They are the people whom God has called me to serve and I am their servant, they are not mine.'

Conclusion

We earnestly need to develop a healthy biblical understanding of the church, for only then will we have a healthy understanding of the leadership of the church. We must not define the church in terms of its leaders. We must, rather, define the leaders in relation to the church. We must renounce secular views of the church as if it were a merely human institution, like any other corporate body with human leaders, wielding human authority as 'lionized' celebrities. All that must go. In its place we need to develop a godly view of the church as a unique community unlike any other community, the covenant people of God, the redeemed people of God, in which ministers give humble service and there is no boasting about human beings. For all boasting is directed to God the Holy Trinity, to God the Father who alone gives growth to the seed, to God the Son who alone is the foundation of the church, and to God the Holy Spirit who alone indwells and sanctifies the community. 'No more boasting in men' (v21). 'Let him who boasts boast in the Lord' (1:31).

5. Models of Ministry (1 Corinthians 4)

Introduction

There is much contemporary confusion today about the nature of the pastoral ministry. What are clergy? (If I may use that word). Are they primarily priests, presbyters, pastors, prophets, preachers or psychotherapists? Are they administrators, facilitators, managers, social workers, liturgists or evangelists? There are many options to choose from and this uncertainty is by no means new. Throughout its long history the church has oscillated between two opposite extremes: clericalism and anticlericalism. Clericalism puts clergy on a pedestal and almost worships them; anti-clericalism knocks them off their pedestal and declares them to be redundant. Now that many churches, throughout the world, have recovered the Pauline doctrine of the 'every member' ministry of the body of Christ, radical questions are being asked. Are clergy necessary any longer? Are they not superfluous? Wouldn't the church be healthier without them, so that we all had a ministry? And should we perhaps found a society for the abolition of the clergy? In Mark Twain's *The Adventures of Huckleberry Finn* there is a passage where Huck got into conversation with Joanna, the daughter of Peter Wilks, who had just died. And he said that in the church of the Reverend Harvey Wilks, her uncle in Sheffield, there were no less than seventeen clergy, though he added, 'They don't all of 'em preach the same day, only one of 'em.' 'Well,' says Joanna, 'what does the rest of 'em do?' 'Well nothing much,' says Huck. 'They loll around and pass the plate and one thing or another, but mainly they don't do nothing.' 'Well then,' says Joanna with wide-eyed astonishment, 'what are they for?' 'Why,' he says, 'they are for style, don't you know nothing?'

This confusion goes right back to the very beginning. Think again of this first-century Corinthian church in which different factions claimed the patronage of particular leaders. Paul was absolutely horrified by this personality cult – 'I belong to Paul, I belong to Apollos' – asking, 'What on earth do you think we are?' Now, in chapter 4, he answers his own question, saying, 'This is how one should regard us' (v1 RSV). And he proceeds to give four essentials of authentic pastoral leadership. They describe Paul's own, unique apostolic leadership but they also apply to Christian pastoral leadership today. Pastors are:

1) Servants of Christ (1a, 3)

Before they are ministers of the Word, and before they are ministers of the church, they are ministers of Christ. They must have a personal relationship to the Lord Jesus Christ. The word he uses here for ministers is a lowly word. It is well translated by one commentator as, 'We are Christ's underlings.' There are, of course, other New Testament texts that emphasize the nobility of the pastorate. For example, 'If anybody desires to be an overseer, a pastor, he desires a noble task.' It is a noble thing to be a pastor. And Paul calls the church to hold its pastors in high esteem and to love them on account of their own ministry or work. Nevertheless, Paul begins his account of his ministry, not with a title of honour or glory, but with a title of lowliness. The Revised English

Bible says, 'We are Christ's subordinates.' Fundamental to all Christian ministry and leadership is a humble, personal relationship with the Lord Jesus Christ Himself: a devotion to Him, expressed in daily prayer, and a love for Him, expressed in daily obedience.

In addition to being Christ's underlings, we are accountable to Him for our ministry, for He is our Lord and He is our Judge. This is both *comforting* and *challenging*. Comforting because it enables us to say, 'I care very little if I am judged by you or by any human court; indeed I do not even judge myself' (v3). Verses 4–7 enlarge on this. 'My conscience is clear' (v4), literally 'I know nothing against myself.' But even a clear conscience doesn't prove me innocent. It is the Lord Jesus who judges me. 'Therefore judge nothing before the appointed time [premature judgements are always unwise]; wait till the Lord comes' (v5). For He is the Judge and we are not judges of one another. As Jesus said in the Sermon on the Mount, 'Judge not that you be not judged' (Mt. 7:1 RSV).

That does not mean that we suspend our critical faculties, but it does mean that we don't stand in judgement on people as if we were their judges, for we are not. When He comes, Jesus will bring to light what is at present hidden in darkness and He will expose even the secret motives of human hearts; nothing is concealed from Him. So there will be no possibility of any miscarriage of justice, even the secrets of our lives are known. And it is then that each of us will receive either praise or maybe censure from Christ.

Now, verse 6, I am applying this principle, he says, to myself and to Apollos for your benefit, so that you may learn from us the meaning of the saying, 'Don't go beyond what is written,' or, as I think it should be better translated, 'Don't go beyond Scripture.' Scripture is what is written and when you are boasting of one leader against another, you are going against Scripture, against what is written. And don't make comparisons either, taking pride in one leader over against another. Comparisons, as we often say, are odious. So, verse 7, he asks a series of questions, 'Who makes you different from anybody else? [All distinctions come from God.] What do you have that you did not receive? And if you did receive it, why do you boast as though you did not?' Boasting is absurd. So the whole passage emphasizes that as ministers of Christ we are accountable to Him for our ministry.

Don't misunderstand this. We must, of course, listen to human criticism, we mustn't just sweep it under the carpet and refuse to listen. It may be painful, particularly if it's untrue, unfair or unkind. But ultimately, even though we listen to human criticism, we never forget that we are accountable to Christ. And the Lord Jesus is a much more merciful judge than any human being, committee, council or synod. So that tells us what to do with anonymous letters. I have received a number in my day. We shouldn't take them too seriously. If somebody doesn't have the courage to announce their identity, we should treat their criticism with a fair degree of cynicism. Do you know the story of Joseph Parker, who was minister of the City Temple at the end of the last century? One day he was climbing up to his pulpit, when a lady in the gallery threw a piece of paper at him. He bent down, picked it up and read it. It had one word on it, 'Fool.' So Joseph Parker began his sermon that day by saying, 'I have received many anonymous letters in my life and previously they have been a text without a signature, but today, for the first time, I have received a signature without a text!' We take human criticism seriously, but anonymous letters not so seriously. It's a very comforting thing to be accountable to God, to Christ and not to any human being or court.

But if, on the one hand, it is a *comforting* thing to be accountable to Him, on the other hand, it is a *challenging* thing – His standards are high and holy. Although much of a pastor's, and a leader's work is unseen and unsupervised by human beings, nevertheless, we are always in His presence. If we remembered this we would never grow slack or careless. If we remember that Jesus Christ is watching us and that one day we will be accountable to Him, then we will, I think, live at the highest possible level in His presence. We are Christ's underlings responsible to Him.

Pastors are not only servants of Christ, they are also:

2) *Stewards of revelation (1b, 2)*

Paul moves from our general responsibility as servants to our more particular responsibility as stewards. Now it is quite true that the Greek word for stewards, *oikonomoi*, is not used in the Greek text, but the idea is plainly there. The NIV says, 'We are those entrusted with the secret things of God.' The RSV translates it, 'We are stewards of the mysteries of God.' Stewards were dispensers. A steward in a household received food and clothing from the householder and dispensed it to the household. God has given us His revelation and we dispense the revelation, we teach it to others in the church. So God's mysteries, of which we are stewards, are of course His revealed secrets, previously concealed, but now revealed – truths that are known only by revelation, truths about Christ and His salvation and the fact that we are members of the universal Body of Christ, whether we are Jews or Gentiles, on the same terms. This incorporation of Jews and Gentiles in the church is one of the great mysteries that Paul said had been revealed to him. So of these revealed truths, contained in the New Testament now and in the gospel, the apostles were the original stewards: 'God has revealed these things to us apostles, by His Spirit' (2:10). Although this refers, in the first instance, to the apostles, it also applies to Christian pastors and teachers today. God has committed the Scriptures to us in order that we may expound and teach them to others in the church. This reminds us of three things:

1) Pastors are primarily teachers. That is very clear in the New Testament. One of the chief evidences is in 1 Timothy 3, where Paul gives ten or eleven qualifications for the pastorate and nine or ten of them are what you might call moral qualities: not drunk, gentle, not hungry for money, etc. Then he includes what you might call a 'professional quality' – *didaktikos*, having a gift for teaching. A candidate for the pastorate would not need to have a gift for teaching unless the pastorate was a teaching ministry: it is a teaching ministry. And it is plain that nobody should enter it without having some gift for teaching. Pastors are essentially teachers.
2) What we teach has been entrusted to us. We haven't invented it, it's not our own, it has been given to us by God.
3) We are called, above all else, to be faithful to the Scripture that has been entrusted to us. So the Revised English Bible translates verse 2, 'Now stewards are required to show themselves trustworthy.' It's all a play on words about trust and trustworthiness. We might say that having received a trust and been appointed trustees of the New Testament, we are expected to be trustworthy. But it is very easy to be unfaithful stewards and I am afraid that we have to admit there are many such in the Christian communi-

ty throughout the world today: rejecting the authority of the Word of God; preferring their own teaching; neglecting to study it; failing to relate it to the real contemporary world; manipulating it to mean what they want it to mean; selecting from it what they like and discarding what they don't like; even contradicting its plain teaching and substituting their own threadbare speculations; flagrantly disobeying its ethical teaching. No wonder the church is languishing in many parts of the world because of these unfaithful stewards who, in different ways, fail in their trusteeship.

Donald Coggan, a preacher himself, was a great believer in the teaching of the Word of God. He wrote three different books on preaching and in one, *Stewards of Grace*, he writes

The Christian preacher has a boundary set for him. When he enters the pulpit, he is not an entirely free person. There is a very real sense in which it may be said of him that the Almighty has set him his bounds that he shall not pass. He is not at liberty to invent or choose his message, it has been committed to him and it is for him to declare, expound and commend it to his hearers. It is a great thing to come under the magnificent tyranny of the gospel.

So our boundaries are set for us. We expound Scripture and nothing else. We are servants of Christ and we are stewards of revelation.

And now, prepare yourself for a shock. Pastors are

3) *The scum of the earth (8–13)*

The apostle uses three very vivid pictures from the Graeco-Roman world of his day, to illustrate what he is talking about. He takes us into a) the public amphitheatre in which criminals fight with gladiators or wild animals, even to the death; b) a kitchen in which the floor is swept and the cooking vessels are scraped; and c) a plague-ridden city in which scapegoats are sacrificed to the pagan gods. They are three very vivid metaphors and I think we need to spend a little time on each of them.

a) Paul takes us into an amphitheatre on a public holiday (v9). Imagine the arena packed with excited crowds. Event follows event throughout the day and at the grand finale, criminals are thrown to the lions or forced to fight with gladiators. One commentator says, 'God has put us apostles last on the programme of the day's sport like criminals condemned to die in the arena.' We have become a spectacle to the whole universe; to angels and humans we are like a bit of cosmic theatre (v9b).

Paul is deliberately contrasting himself with the smug security and self-satisfaction of the Corinthian Christians. 'Already,' he says, not without a touch of sarcasm, 'you have all you want! Already you have become rich.' 'Already,' he might have added for the third time, 'you have become kings – and that without us' (v8). So twice he uses the 'already' of a realized eschatology. And the third phrase means the same thing, although he does not use the word 'already'. They are enjoying a private little millennium of their own: eating, drinking, feasting, reigning and celebrating. 'Well,' Paul says, 'we wish we could get there with you, and be kings with you, but we know,' he implies, 'the only path to glory is the path of suffering.' It was for Jesus and it is for the followers of Jesus. We are like exhibits in the amphitheatre – condemned to die for Christ. 'You are kings, but we are criminals' is the striking contrast that he makes.

b) When Paul takes us into a kitchen, he uses two very unusual Greek words: *perichotharmita* means sweepings or rinsings, while *peripseema* means scrapings from a dirty saucepan or other kind of pot and both of them, if I may quote another commentator, are 'the filth that one gets rid of through the sink or the gutter'. Not very polite to us as leaders, is it!

Now he takes us out of the amphitheatre, out of the kitchen, and . . .

c) Into a plague-ridden Greek city stricken by some calamity. In order to appease the supposed anger of the pagan gods, some wretches are taken from the community and are thrown into the sea and drowned. These scapegoats were called the scum of the earth. And that is what we are, says the apostle Paul.

You will agree these are extraordinary statements. And in verses 10–13 he explains what he is talking about. He is referring to his sufferings in contrast to Corinthian complacency. He is being ridiculed for Christ. 'We are fools for Christ' (v10), 'but you, you are wise.' Notice the reference to weakness and strength, wisdom and folly, with which we began our Bible studies. 'We are weak,' he goes on, 'you are honoured but we are dishonoured, despised and rejected like our Master. We are hungry, thirsty, in rags, brutally treated, homeless, persecuted, slandered. We work with our own hands, etc. etc. Indeed, we are the scum or the refuse of the world' (cf. vv10–13). As we enjoy the safety and comfort of the Keswick tent and the grandeur of the lakes and mountains, it all sounds extremely remote from us. In fact, the difficulty we have in applying words like these to ourselves may indicate how far we have drifted from the New Testament. Today, even in our non-Christian society, even in a pluralistic, secular culture, it is still a tolerably respectable thing to be a pastor. However, it is not always so and it should definitely not be taken for granted.

I speak very personally now, but I believe that we need urgently to hear again the words of Jesus: 'Woe unto you when all men speak well of you.' Beware of the temptation to be a popular preacher. I doubt very much if it is possible to be popular and faithful at the same time. We either go for popularity at the expense of faithfulness, or we are determined to be faithful at the expense of popularity. We have to choose between them; it is not possible to be both simultaneously. For the cross is still foolishness to some and a stumbling block to others. What is it about the gospel that is so unpopular? Why is it that if we are loyal and faithful in our preaching and teaching we will suffer for it? Why will we be ridiculed? What is it about the gospel that is so offensive? Let me give three answers that may, or may not, be helpful.

1) The gospel offers eternal life as a free gift. 'The wages of sin is death, but the gift of God is eternal life through Jesus Christ' (Rom. 6:23). But we are such proud creatures that we don't want to be given a free gift. We looked at this earlier. We'd do anything to be able to earn our salvation, to achieve it or, at least, contribute to it. We need to remember that eternal life, salvation, is an absolutely free, utterly undeserved and totally non-contributory gift of God. The only thing we contribute is our sin and we find that unbearably humiliating.

2) `The gospel not only offers eternal life as a free gift, but it proclaims salvation in Jesus Christ alone and declares that He is the only Saviour. He is unique in His incarnation, in His atonement and in His resurrection. There is no other leader who is the God-Man. There is no other leader, all through history, who has died for the sins of the world. And there is no other

leader who has risen from the dead and conquered death. So we are not content to say that Jesus is 'the great'. We can say that Alexander was the great, we can speak of Napoleon the great, Charles the great, but not Jesus the great. He isn't the great, He is the Only, there is nobody like Him. He has no peers, no competitors and no rivals. He is unique. In this pluralistic world, that is anathema. Pluralism and postmodernism means we all have our own truth, but we mustn't try to persuade anybody to accept our truth. There is no such thing as a universal truth, or a truth that is objective and true for everybody. But Christianity says, on the contrary, God has revealed the truth in Jesus Christ who said, 'I am the way, the Truth and the life.' Now if we are loyal to the uniqueness and finality of Jesus Christ, however gracious and gentle we may be, I tell you, friends, we will suffer for it. We will suffer more and more as pluralism and post-modernity grow in many cultures in the world.

3) The gospel demands holiness. Not as the grounds of salvation, but as the evidence of our salvation. It calls us to surrender to the supreme Lordship of Jesus Christ. It compels us to accept His moral standards. We want Jesus to oblige us by lowering His moral standards for our benefit. We want to set our own standards and resent having to submit to His.

So here are three gospel stumbling blocks: the freeness of the gospel, the exclusiveness of the gospel and the high moral demands of the gospel. Each is an offence to human pride and arouses people's opposition. I quote from the great Bonhoeffer in his book *The Cost of Discipleship*. He was a Lutheran pastor during the Second World War, imprisoned because of his complicity in the attempt on Hitler's life and later executed in April 1945. He knew what suffering meant and he wrote, 'Suffering is the badge of the true Christian.' It's an amazing statement. You know what a badge is. We all wear a badge to indicate what society we belong to. If you want to indicate that you belong to the Society of Jesus, what is the badge? Answer: suffering. The disciple is not above his Master.

Luther reckoned suffering among the marks of a true church. One of the memoranda drawn up in preparation for the Augsburg Confession similarly defines the church – 'a community of those who are persecuted and martyred for the sake of the gospel'. Discipleship means allegiance to the suffering Christ and it is therefore not at all surprising that Christians should be called upon to suffer. Another Lutheran pastor, Niemöller, said, 'If a church is not a persecuted church it ought to ask itself whether it is a church at all.' We need to ask ourselves if we are ready to accept and experience these amazing things in our own lives.

Finally, pastors are

4) The fathers of the church family (14–21)

In the chapter's final paragraph the apostle calls the Corinthians 'his dear children' (v. 14), in which case he must be their father. He says he is writing to warn them but not to shame them. In verse 15 he adds that although they may have ten thousand guardians or disciplinarians or tutors who will discipline them, they don't have many fathers to love them. Whereas, he has become their spiritual father in Christ and through the gospel and he urges them to imitate him, telling them in verse 17 that he is sending Timothy to them and they are to listen to Timothy and imitate him.

Now this claim of Paul, to be the spiritual father of the Corinthian church, troubles and perplexes many Bible students, because Jesus told us, in Matthew 23:9, not to call anybody our father. Of course we all have, or have had, a father in our home. But he is saying we are not to call anybody our father in the church. Paul does call himself a father. So is Paul contradicting Jesus? No, indeed he isn't. He is not doing what Jesus told us not to do. Jesus was telling us not to adopt towards anybody in the church, and not to require anybody to adopt towards us in the church, the dependent attitude in the relationship of a little child to a father. Christians are to grow up and become interdependent. There are to be no gurus in the Christian community, no teachers in the Confucian mould whose authority is unchallengeable; no tribal chiefs as in Africa. Jesus was forbidding us to assume the authority of a father. But Paul is referring to a father's affection for his children, so he is not contradicting Jesus. Indeed, in 1 Thessalonians 2:5, he likens himself to a mother with her babies, as well as a father. It's a beautiful picture of the love, gentleness and self-sacrifice of a pastor in loving the flock like a father or a mother.

Now of course there is still a place for discipline in the church, which needs to be exercised collectively, as in 1 Corinthians 5. But what is the authentic characteristic of the Christian pastor or leader? Not severity, but gentleness. We are to be fathers and mothers towards those we are called to serve, we are not to be stern disciplinarians whom they fear. And Paul asks the Corinthians, 'What do you prefer? Shall I come to you with a whip [symbol of authority and discipline], or in love and with a gentle spirit?' (v21). He leaves this question unanswered because it is up to the Corinthians to reply and to choose.

As I travel in different parts of the world and observe the church and church leaders, I have become convinced that there is too much autocracy and not enough gentleness. There are too many gurus; too many autocrats who lay down the law in the local church in defiance of the teaching of Jesus; too many who behave as if they believe not in the priesthood of all believers, but in the papacy of all pastors! The great need among Christian leaders is for less autocracy and more affection and gentleness. In his book, *The Preacher and His Models* (1891), James Stalker wrote

> When I was first settled in a church I discovered a thing which nobody had told me and which I had not anticipated. I fell in love with my congregation. I do not know how otherwise to express it. It was as genuine a blossom of the heart as any which I had ever experienced and it made it easy for me to do anything for my people.

Conclusion

From the four pictures the apostle paints, this is how you should regard church leaders of any kind: we are the underlings of Christ; we are the stewards of revelation; we are the scum of the earth; we are the fathers and mothers of the church family. And the common denominator of all four is humility: humility before Christ whose subordinates we are; humility before Scripture of which we are the stewards; humility before the world whose opposition we are bound to encounter; humility before the congregation whose members we are to love and serve.

My prayer for you (and I hope your prayer for me), is that God will richly bless whatever ministry it is that He has called us to exercise. And that our ministry may be characterized above all else by what the apostle in 2 Corinthians 10:1 calls 'the humility and the gentleness of Christ'.

Keswick Ministries

Keswick Ministries is committed to the deepening of the spiritual life in individuals and church communities through the careful exposition and application of Scripture, seeking to encourage the following:

The Lordship of Christ – To encourage submission to the Lordship of Christ in personal and corporate living.
Life Transformation – To encourage a dependency upon the indwelling and fullness of the Holy Spirit for life transformation and effective living.
Evangelism and Mission – To provoke a strong commitment to the breadth of evangelism and mission in the British Isles and worldwide.
Discipleship – To stimulate the discipling and training of people of all ages in godliness, service and sacrificial living.
Unity – To provide a practical demonstration of evangelical unity.

Keswick Ministries is committed to achieving its aims by:

- providing Bible-based training courses for youth workers and young people (via Root 66) and Bible weeks for Christians of all backgrounds who want to develop their skills and learn more.

- promoting the use of books, DVDs and CDs so that Keswick's teaching ministry is brought to a wider audience at home and abroad.
- producing TV and radio programmes so that superb Bible talks can be broadcast to people at home.
- publishing up-to-date details of Keswick's exciting news and events on the website so that people can access material and purchase Keswick products on-line.
- publicising Bible teaching events in the UK and overseas so that Christians of all ages are encouraged to attend 'Keswick' meetings closer to home and grow in their faith.
- putting the residential accommodation of the Convention Centre at the disposal of churches, youth groups, Christian organisations and many others, at very reasonable rates, for holidays and outdoor activities in a stunning location.

If you'd like more details, please look at the website (www.keswickministries.org) or contact the Keswick Ministries office by post, email or telephone, as given below

Keswick Ministries, Convention Centre, Skiddaw Street, Keswick, Cumbria, CA12 4BY

Tel: 017687 80075; Fax 017687 75276; email: info@keswickministries.org